RIVER OF OCEAN

OF NIGHT

PAPHOS CYPRUS
SIDON
PHOENICIA

EGYPT

THEBES

OF DAY

THE WORLD
* according to *
HOMER
B·C·1000

THE OXFORD CHILDREN'S CLASSICS

# THE
# ILIAD & ODYSSEY
# OF HOMER

THE OXFORD CHILDREN'S CLASSICS

# THE
# ILIAD & ODYSSEY
# OF HOMER

RETOLD FOR CHILDREN BY
BARBARA LEONIE PICARD

ILLUSTRATED BY
JOAN KIDDELL-MONROE

CHANCELLOR
PRESS

This edition of THE ODYSSEY OF HOMER was first published in
Great Britain in 1952 by Oxford University Press

Copyright Oxford University Press 1952

This edition of THE ILIAD OF HOMER was first published in
Great Britain in 1960 by Oxford University Press

© Oxford University Press 1960

This one-volume edition first published in
Great Britain in 1986 by
Chancellor Press
59 Grosvenor Street
London W1

ISBN 1 85152 024 4

Printed in Czechoslovakia
50616

# THE
# ILIAD

# PREFACE

HOMER's two great epic poems, *The Iliad* and *The Odyssey*, both tell of happenings connected with the long war between the Greeks and the Trojans; but whereas *The Odyssey* is concerned with the adventures of one of the Greek heroes after the war was over, *The Iliad* relates incidents which took place in the ninth year of the siege of Troy: Achilles' quarrel with Agamemnon, his love for Patroclus, his friend, and how he avenged him.

Homer made his poems about three thousand years ago —at least four hundred years after Troy had fallen—and those for whom he made them would already have been familiar with the story and its characters. It was one of the great tales of their past, telling of the deeds of the heroes of the Greek people and of gods and goddesses they worshipped. Therefore, Homer wastes no time in giving the background to his story, but starts immediately with the quarrel between Achilles and Agamemnon, certain that his hearers will know both who they were and why they were besieging Troy.

It is different for us, three thousand years later, and so, in a prologue, I have set down the events which led up to the war of the Greeks with Troy; and, after Homer's tale of pride and love and vengeance is done, I have told briefly, in an epilogue, of the ending of the war and the fate of some of those who took part in it.

*Barbara Leonie Picard*

# CONTENTS

## PROLOGUE

## *How the War with Troy Began*

IN a small kingdom in the north of Greece ruled Peleus, king of Phthia, who was much favoured by the gods. When he was no longer young, he fell in love with the sea-goddess Thetis, daughter of blue-haired and blue-bearded Nereus, who dwelt in the depths of the Aegean Sea, together with his consort, Doris, and their fifty daughters.

Lovely Thetis, though a lesser goddess, scorned the wooing of a mortal and fled from him, changing her shape in turn to that of fire, water, a serpent, and a fierce lioness. But Peleus was undaunted, and at last, with the help of Proteus, the Old Man of the Sea, he forced her to yield to his wooing, and she consented to be his bride: the only goddess ever to wed with a mortal man.

To the marriage feast of Peleus and Thetis, on Mount Pelion in Thessaly, came all the gods and goddesses, bringing gifts: two immortal horses, a spear, and golden armour. Eris, goddess of discord, alone was not bidden, for discord has no place amid the joys of a wedding.

But when the feasting was at its highest, Eris came among the feasters, and in her anger at the slight that had been put on her, she flung before them a golden apple inscribed with the words, *'For the fairest'*. Immediately, the goddesses began to vie, one with the other, for possession of the apple, and their strife continued in Olympus for a long time to come.

To Peleus and his immortal wife, a son was born, whom they named Achilles, and he early showed promise of courage and great beauty.

At a distance from Phthia, in the city of Opus, ruled Menoetius, who had a son named Patroclus, a little older than Achilles. While only a boy, by misfortune he killed another lad who quarrelled with him over a game of dice. On the advice of his father, Patroclus fled to Phthia, where King Peleus received him kindly and gave him to Achilles for a companion. From that moment a great love grew between them, and they were never willingly parted for even a single day. A few years later, when he was a youth, Patroclus, like all the young lords of Greece, became a suitor for the hand of Helen, daughter of Tyndareus, king of Sparta, who was famed for her beauty throughout all the land.

To the house of Tyndareus came, amongst many others, Menelaus, the brother of Agamemnon of Mycenae, the high king of Greece; Odysseus, king of Ithaca; Antilochus, the son of Nestor, king of Pylos; Diomedes of Tiryns and Sthenelus, his friend; Ajax, son of the king of Locris; Podaleirius and Machaon, the physicians; Idomeneus from Crete; Ajax and his half-brother Teucer, the sons of King Telamon of Salamis; and Patroclus.

King Tyndareus was greatly perturbed by the presence in his house of all these wooers, and he feared to choose a husband for his daughter from amongst them, lest he should anger all those others whom he rejected, bringing trouble on himself and on the man whom he had favoured; so he delayed his choice from day to day.

Odysseus, king of Ithaca, whose sharp eyes missed little, guessed his plight, and knowing that, as the king of only a small island, he himself stood slight chance of being chosen as Helen's husband, he spoke secretly with Tyndareus, bidding him let Helen make her own choice, after first asking from all the suitors an oath that they would abide by her choice and, furthermore, pledge themselves to give their help to her chosen husband, if ever at any time he should have need of help. To this plan Tyndareus thankfully agreed, and as a reward for his counsel, Odysseus asked for the hand of Penelope, the daughter of his brother, a maiden far less beautiful than her cousin Helen, but fair enough.

When all the suitors had sworn the oath, Helen made her choice; and she chose tawny-haired Menelaus, brother of great King Agamemnon. After the marriage feasting, the unsuccessful wooers returned to their own homes, Odysseus taking with him to Ithaca his bride Penelope. Soon after, Tyndareus died, and Menelaus succeeded him as king of Sparta.

Meanwhile, on Mount Olympus, where the gods dwelt, the quarrel still raged for possession of the golden apple, there being yet three rival goddesses who claimed it: Hera, wife of Zeus and queen of all the gods, Athene, goddess of wisdom and all crafts, and Aphrodite, goddess of love and beauty.

The gods could not decide between these three, so it was determined that a mortal man should be chosen to award the apple to that one whom he considered the most beautiful. Accordingly, the apple was entrusted to Paris, son of King Priam of Troy, and to him was left the judgement. He gave the apple to Aphrodite, who promised him, in return, that he should have for his wife the most beautiful woman in all the world.

The most beautiful woman in the world was Helen, and later, when Paris came to Sparta, she had been the wife of Menelaus for some three years. Menelaus received Paris kindly and made him welcome in his house, but while he was the guest of Menelaus, Paris won the love of Helen; and when he left Sparta to return once more to Troy, she went with him.

Menelaus appealed to his brother Agamemnon, and the high king at once sent word to Helen's former wooers, bidding them keep the oath that they had sworn. And they, with many other kings and lords of Greece, gathered together a great army and a fleet of ships, that they might sail to Troy and win back Helen for Menelaus and be revenged on Paris, who had so shamefully broken the sacred laws of hospitality by stealing the wife of his host.

Patroclus, as one of Helen's suitors, was amongst those called to go to war, and Peleus was willing that Achilles, though he was no more than a boy, should go with him and lead the Myrmidons, the men of Phthia, to battle, since Peleus himself was too old to fight.

But Thetis, as one of the immortals, knew that her son was doomed to the choice of a long and uneventful life, with no one to remember him when he was dead and gone, or a short life full of glory, and everlasting fame; and in an attempt to keep the choice from him, she clothed him like a girl and sent him secretly to King Lycomedes, on the island of Scyros, bidding the king hide him amongst his daughters. There, for a time, on Scyros, Achilles remained hidden, and there Deïdameia, one of the young daughters of Lycomedes, fell in love with him, and a son was born to them, who was later called Neoptolemus.

But the support of the brave Myrmidons, who were warriors of renown, was needed by the Greeks, and Odysseus went all about Greece seeking Achilles. Disguised as a merchant, he came to Scyros to the house of Lycomedes, suspecting Achilles to be there. He asked that he might show his wares to the king's daughters and their friends and handmaidens, and it was granted him. He spread out jewels and embroidered robes, girdles, and costly ornaments, whilst they crowded about him with cries of pleasure at the sight. He looked closely at them, yet he could not guess which amongst them might be a youth. But amid the jewels and trinkets, cunning Odysseus had laid a sword.

After a while, he made a sign to one of his followers, who went outside the king's house and there blew a war blast on a horn. With screams the maidens fled, or clasped their arms about each other, sobbing and trembling in their fear. But one tall maiden with golden hair, and beautiful above most, ran forward swiftly and snatched up the sword, and holding it and handling it as a sword should be held and handled, waited for the approach of danger. Odysseus smiled and called Achilles by his name, and Achilles did not deny the truth, for he wanted to go to Troy with Patroclus.

Achilles returned to Phthia, and his father was glad to see him once again, but Thetis grieved, for she saw that she could no longer keep his choice of doom from him. She told him what was ordained for him, and unhesitatingly he chose a short life and everlasting glory, and she warned him that he would never return from Troy. And so the Myrmidons, led by young Achilles and Patroclus, who left Phthia with Nestor of Pylos and Odysseus, set sail for Troy with the other kings and warriors of the Greeks, under the leadership of the high king, Agamemnon.

The great army of the Greeks encamped upon the shores of Troy, besieging King Priam's city. But if they were a mighty army, the Trojans, too, had many allies, and for a long time there was skirmishing, and fighting on the plain before the city; and sometimes the Greeks were successful, and sometimes the Trojans, but no decisive victory was won. And every now and then the Greeks would send off a certain number of their ships to sail along the coast from Troy, to sack one town or another in the neighbouring lands, both for cattle and plunder—for so great an army needed much food—and to discourage any further allies from sending help to the Trojans.

And so the war with Troy went on until it was in its ninth year.

# The Quarrel

IN the ninth year of the war against Troy a great disaster came upon the Greeks.

A little time before, they had sacked a town, Lyrnessus, south-east along the coast from Troy. To young Achilles, son of King Peleus of Phthia, as the finest warrior amongst the Greeks, and to the Myrmidons, King Peleus' men, had fallen the greater part of the fighting, and they had taken much booty and many prisoners.

Amongst the captives was a young woman named Briseïs, and, when the fighting was done and the plunder gathered together, Achilles, as his share of the spoils, chose out Briseïs to be his slave.

Soon after this, Thebe, another town, close by Lyrnessus, was taken by the Greeks, and to the portion of Agamemnon, lord of Mycenae and high king of Greece, brother of

Menelaus for whose sake the war was being fought, and leader of the great army which had sailed to Troy, fell, as was customary, by far the largest portion of the spoils; and no one disputed his right. Amongst the captives whom he chose for himself was a fair maiden, Chryseïs, who was taken in his ship to the Greek camp on the Trojan coast.

Now, Chryseïs was the daughter of Chryses, high priest of the temple of Apollo, god of art and learning, and a man of riches and importance. Overcome with grief at the loss of his daughter, Chryses set sail from the ruins of Thebe with a great store of gold and silver, that he might ransom her from the Greeks.

On the coast of Troy, the Greeks had beached their ships in three lines along the low shore between two headlands; with the fifty ships of the Myrmidons farthest to the west, and those of tall Ajax, son of King Telamon, who had brought his father's men from the island of Salamis, at the extreme eastern point. Between the ships of Achilles and the ships of Ajax, the other ships were drawn up in three rows, for the stretch of level coastline between the high ground on either side was not long enough for a single line of ships.

The earliest to land had beached their ships in the first row, nearest to the fertile Trojan plain which stretched between the shore and the city of Troy, with the River Scamander winding through it.

Amongst the ships in this first row, and close to the middle of the line, were the forty ships which King Protesilaus had brought from Phylace. They were commanded by his brother, for Protesilaus was dead, in fulfilment of a prophecy which had declared that the first Greek to land

on Trojan soil should be the first to die. Protesilaus, boldly
leaping to shore while all the other Greeks held back, had
been slain by Aeneas, a Trojan lord.

In the second row lay, amongst many others, the forty
ships which had sailed from Locris under their leader Ajax,
namesake and frequent battle-comrade of the son of
Telamon, but, unlike him, short of stature, though valiant
and hardy and skilled with a spear. His men, however,
fought only with bows and slings, and carried neither spear
nor shield.

In the third row, and nearest to the sea, lay the ships of
the high king, Agamemnon, one hundred in all, by far the
largest number to have sailed under any one leader; with,
close beside them, the sixty ships which King Menelaus,
his brother, Helen's husband, had brought from Sparta.
In that row, also, were the ships of rich old Nestor, king
of Pylos; and those eighty vessels with which brave young
King Diomedes had sailed from his own land of Tiryns
with his good friend Sthenelus. At the midmost point of
this row were the twelve ships of Odysseus, king of the
rocky little island of Ithaca to the west of Greece. Odysseus
ruled over only a small kingdom, yet he was resourceful
and skilled in using words to suit his ends, and he was
much respected for his shrewd counsel.

In between the high hulls of the beached ships, raised up
on stone supports to prevent their keels from rotting, ran
narrow lanes, intersecting the two broad ways between the
rows; and behind his own ships, each leader of the Greeks
had built for himself and for his men, huts of wood and
earth, well thatched with rushes cut from the banks of the
Scamander, and shelters for their cattle and their slaves and

stabling for their mules and horses, all with a palisade of stakes around.

In the very midst of the camp, before the ships of Odysseus, and stretching well into the second row of ships, lay the assembly place, where the kings and princes of the Greeks, together with their lords, would meet in council for judgement or discussion, and to offer sacrifice to the gods on the altar which stood at the centre of the open space. It was the right of any of the kings or princes to call an assembly to which all should come, and it was to this assembly place that Chryses was brought, to stand before the leaders of the Greeks, where they sat upon the benches, each in his wonted place, summoned by Agamemnon's heralds to receive the suppliant.

The old man stood before them, holding in his hands the sacred garlands from the temple and the sceptre of the god, and he pleaded with the Greeks that they would accept the ransom he had brought and give him back his daughter.

'Kings and lords of Greece,' he said, 'hear the entreaties of a father and restore my child to me, and so may divine Apollo look with favour on you, and all the other immortal gods who dwell on high Olympus, and grant that you may be victorious in your fight against the Trojans.'

All the kings and princes of the Greeks pitied him and cried out that it was fitting that a priest's words should be respected, that the ransom should be accepted and Chryseïs restored to him.

But Agamemnon, who had chosen Chryseïs for himself from amongst the other captives from the town of Thebe, said, 'The girl is mine, won by my spear, and it is my right to keep her if I wish. I say she shall not go. She shall stay here with me until Troy has fallen, and then she shall sail with me for Mycenae, and there in my palace, amongst my other slaves, she shall pass her days in spinning and weaving. Now go, old man, and do not come here again, lest another time you find the sacred garlands and the sceptre scant protection.'

The old priest was afraid, and he fled away along the shore while Agamemnon laughed; and because Agamemnon was the greatest king amongst them, and the leader of them all, no one disputed his decree.

But with tears old Chryses prayed to shining, immortal Apollo, 'O Bright One, I have served you well for many years. If ever I have pleased you, hear me now. Deliver my daughter from the hands of the Greeks, and avenge their slighting words.'

From far-off Mount Olympus, home of the immortal gods, Apollo heard him and, filled with divine wrath, he snatched up his quiver and his silver bow and came swiftly across sky and sea, and the sun was clouded by his mighty rage. He sat himself down at a distance from the camp of the Greeks and let fly amongst them his sharp arrows, winged with pestilence. At first he struck down mules and horses and hounds, and then he struck down men, until throughout the camp there was lamenting, and all along the shore the funeral pyres of the dead burnt ceaselessly.

For nine days did the plague rage, and on the tenth day, Achilles from Phthia, who was the youngest of all the kings and princes of the Greeks, called the other leaders to an assembly. When they were all gathered together, he stood up and spoke. 'My friends, without a doubt one of the gods is angry with us, else would this plague not have come upon us. Let us with no more delay ask a priest, or one who is skilled in such matters, to tell us which of the gods we have displeased by our neglect, that we may speedily offer sacrifices to appease his wrath. For otherwise, or so it seems to me, we shall never live to take Troy. We shall all of us die here, on the shore, and the theft of Helen will go unavenged.'

Achilles sat down, and immediately Calchas the prophet arose. 'Lord Achilles, son of King Peleus, I can tell you which of the gods is angered with us, and why. But first, swear to me that you will protect me, whatever I may say, for I fear that my words will displease one amongst us, who is the best of all the Greeks. Promise me your protection, and I will speak.'

'Have no fear, Calchas,' replied Achilles, 'but speak the truth to us, for while I live no man of all the Greeks shall harm you.' He paused a moment and glanced across to where Agamemnon sat, before adding, 'Not even great King Agamemnon himself, whom I have often heard declare himself to be the best of all the Greeks, shall do you ill, I promise it.'

'Then,' said Calchas, reassured, 'I will tell you why this plague has come upon us. It comes from immortal Apollo, and not because we have forgotten to sacrifice to him, but because King Agamemnon would not heed the pleas of old Chryses, who is Apollo's priest. Until the maiden Chryseïs is given back to her father, freely and unransomed, the god will not lift his wrath from us.'

Agamemnon frowned at his words, and, when Calchas had done, the great king sat silent, glowering, knowing that the eyes of everyone were upon him. Then he rose.

'Your words always make ill hearing, Calchas. Never have
I heard you prophesy good fortune or the favour of the
gods, but warnings and bad omens come always easily to
your tongue. Now you choose to blame me for Apollo's
wrath and this plague, and say that in my hands alone lies
the remedy.' He paused, remembering how all the other
kings and princes had been for accepting the ransom and
restoring Chryseïs to her father. He flung out his arm in an
angry gesture. 'Very well, the priest shall have his daughter
back. I do not want to let her go, but I would rather lose
her than be the death of all the Greeks. Odysseus shall make
ready a ship and take the girl to Thebe.'

There was a murmur of approval from the assembled
Greeks, but Agamemnon looked about him sullenly. He
had been at fault and he had been set down before them all,
and he was not minded to be the only one to suffer. He
caught sight of Achilles, with his friend Patroclus sitting
at his side. They were smiling at each other, now that it
seemed likely that Apollo's wrath would soon be ended.
Agamemnon thought how it was young Achilles who had
called the assembly, and so caused his discomfiture. Suddenly he shouted out, 'I am the leader of you all, and the
greatest king amongst you. It is not fitting that I alone
should be without my chosen spoils. I shall send away
Chryseïs because I must, but I will have instead a share of
the booty of some other man—yours, perhaps, Achilles.'

Achilles sprang to his feet, his eyes blazing. 'You are our
leader, King Agamemnon, but in this you presume too
much. I have no quarrel with the Trojans. They have
never stolen my father's cattle or his horses, nor have they
harvested our fields of grain in Phthia. The mountains are

too high and the sea too wide that lie between Troy and my father's land. No, I have led the Myrmidons to battle against the Trojans for the sake of your brother's quarrel, that he might win back his wife; though, since I was never a suitor for Helen's hand—being too young by far—I was bound by no oath to do so. Remember that, before you talk shamelessly of sharing my booty.' He paused for a moment, and then went on hotly, 'And what is my share of the booty compared with all that you have taken from the towns that we have sacked? Because I am accounted a good warrior, and because my father's men are brave, to me falls more than my fair share of the fighting, so long as the battle lasts. But when the fighting is over, do I get a like share of the spoils? No. After you, King Agamemnon, have taken your pick, I get some small thing of little worth from whatever is left over, and I have to be content with that. What have I gained from this war with Troy? A little gold and silver and a few slaves—not many, since, unlike you, I am always ready to take a ransom for my captives.' He paused again, and then said, 'By all the gods, it would be better if I were to set sail with my father's men and return to Phthia, rather than stay here, slighted, to win more wealth for you to carry home to Mycenae.'

Agamemnon laughed. 'Go if you will,' he sneered. 'We shall do well enough without you. You may be brave, and a fine warrior, but of all the kings and princes of the Greeks, you, with your arrogance and your hot temper that you have not yet learnt to curb, you are the one whom I could best do without. Go home. Take your ships and your Myrmidons. Lord it over your own men, show your temper to your friends and rail at them and not at me. Go home; but part, at least, of your booty you shall leave behind. When we sacked the city of Lyrnessus, you chose as your share of the spoils the girl Briseïs, to be your slave. I must give up Chryseïs to her father, since it is the will of Apollo; but you shall give up Briseïs to me, since that is my will.' He laughed again, shortly. 'And when she is gone from your hut and dwells in mine, perhaps you will have learnt at last that I am indeed the leader of all the Greeks, and a greater king than your father Peleus.'

For a moment Achilles was too angry to speak or even move, and then he laid his hand upon the silver hilt of his sword, for in his rage he would have leapt upon Agamemnon and killed him there, in sight of all the other Greeks; but before even Patroclus could restrain him, prudent Athene, goddess of wisdom, who had been watching from high Olympus, came swiftly down amongst them, unseen of any, and standing behind Achilles, she took hold of his long yellow hair. He looked round and knew at once that it was one of the immortal gods who held him back, and he thrust his sword again into its scabbard, and immediately Athene left him.

Achilles, furious, but obedient to the divine injunction, said, 'Your wits must be befuddled with wine, Agamemnon, that you speak so to one who is braver than yourself. One day you will regret those words which have cost you my help and the help of my father's men, for neither I nor they, nor the friends who came with me to Troy, will fight any longer against the Trojans for your sake.' He sat down, flushed and still angry, beside Patroclus.

Agamemnon would have scoffed further at him, but old Nestor rose. He was the king of Pylos, and had come with

ninety ships to fight against the Trojans with Antilochus
his son, who had been one of Helen's suitors. He was the
oldest of all the kings and princes of the Greeks, and his
counsel was valued amongst them and his words were
always heard with respect.

'Shame upon you both!' he exclaimed. 'How King
Priam and his sons would rejoice to hear you now. I can
chide you both, since I am older by far than either of you.
In my time I have known greater warriors than any here
today, and called them my comrades in battle. I fought
beside Peirithoüs and great Theseus himself, against the
Centaurs who dwelt in the mountain caves. No such grim
fighting as that shall we see before the walls of Troy, yet
we destroyed the Centaurs utterly. Even Theseus did not
scorn my counsel, so why should you? Cease your quarrelling, my friends. Let Achilles keep the girl he won, King
Agamemnon, she is his by right. And, as you have said
yourself, he is a fine warrior, and the Trojans fear him.
As for you, Achilles, you are yet very young; you should
show more respect to a great king whose lands are far
wider than any you will ever rule.'

'What you say is true, good Nestor,' said Agamemnon,
'but I am weary of Achilles' arrogance, his flouting of my
authority, and his quick temper, which we see far too
often.'

Before he could speak further, Achilles broke in, 'Your
authority, King Agamemnon, do I no longer acknowledge.
If you will, come and take the girl from me. I shall not
prevent you. For I chose her by your favour: and what a
man has given, that may he take away. Yet I warn you,
lay but a finger on any of the goods I brought with me

from Phthia, and it will not be Trojan blood which will be red upon my sword.' He rose abruptly, flung his cloak about him, and gestured to his friend. 'Come, Patroclus.' And without another glance at Agamemnon, he left the assembly, and Patroclus went with him.

As Agamemnon had commanded, a ship was made ready and, escorted by Odysseus, Chryseïs was sent to Thebe, to her father; and the Greeks offered sacrifice to Apollo, and he was appeased.

But Agamemnon called to him his heralds, Talthybius and Eurybates, and said, 'Go to the hut of Achilles, son of King Peleus, and take from him his captive, Briseïs. If he resists you, come back and tell me, and I shall go myself to fetch her and my warriors will go with me, and Achilles shall soon regret his insolence and pride.'

Talthybius and Eurybates went unwillingly along the shore towards the ships of the Myrmidons, for they had no liking for the task they had been given. When they reached the farthest westward point of the Greek camp, where Achilles had his ships, they found Achilles sitting in the porch before his hut, and at the sight of his angry frowns they glanced at one another and stood silent, neither wishing to be the first to tell him of Agamemnon's commands.

But Achilles looked at them and said, 'Greetings, heralds. My anger is not against you, but against Agamemnon, who has sent you. Yet, now that you have come, you can be witnesses to my oath that never again will I fight in this war against the Trojans for Agamemnon's sake.' He turned away from the heralds. 'Fetch the girl, Patroclus, and give her to them.'

Patroclus led out Briseïs from the hut and gave her to the

heralds, but she clung to him, weeping, for he had been
kind to her on the day when she was taken captive, bidding her dry her tears and seeking to comfort her, saying,
'Achilles is young, and he has as yet no wife. You are nobly
born, perhaps he may marry you and take you back to
Phthia with him, where his father is a king, and you will
have a fine marriage feast among the Myrmidons.' In tears
again, now, she held on to his hand; yet there was no help
for it, and at last she had to go with the heralds, walking
with them along the shore towards Agamemnon's ships,
looking back often through her tears.

But Achilles went alone down to the sea's edge, where
the waves lapped upon the sandy shore and the rocks
threw purple shadows on the water. And there, with tears
of anger, he prayed to his mother Thetis that she might
come to comfort him.

From where she sat, in the depths of the sea, in the halls
of her father, blue-haired Nereus, Thetis, the immortal
goddess, heard her son. She rose up from the water like a
grey mist, and standing beside him, laid her hand upon his
head.

'Mother,' he said, 'when I was called to Troy to lead my
father's men you told me that the choice was ordained to
me of a long and peaceful life, after which I should be forgotten of all men; or a short and glorious life, and after it,
undying fame. As you know well, I chose a short life and
a name that would live for ever in the hearts of brave men
and in the songs of the minstrels. But of what avail was my
choice, if in that short life I have to suffer the slights of such
unworthy men as Agamemnon, son of Atreus? Oh,
mother, you have told me that I have but a little while to

live; soon, perhaps, may this brief life end before the walls of Troy. Where is the glory that was promised me?'

She stroked his hair and answered gently, 'My child, I would that you had never sailed to Troy. Yet here shall you win your undying fame and a place in brave men's hearts for ever. I will go myself to Father Zeus, and ask it of him.' And like a grey mist she faded from his sight, and he was alone again upon the shore.

Swiftly Thetis rose to the snow-crowned heights of Mount Olympus, to where Zeus, father of gods and men, sat upon his lofty throne, and there before him she fell down and clasped his knees in supplication.

'Father Zeus, there was once a time when all the gods rebelled against your rule, and I alone upheld you. If you are grateful for my loyalty, give me now the boon I ask of you for the sake of my son Achilles. So long as he holds himself from the war with Troy, by reason of his quarrel with Agamemnon, give the victory to the Trojans, that all the kings and princes of the Greeks may rue their leader's folly.'

For a time Zeus sat silent, deep in thought, seeing the things which were to come, and then he spoke gravely. 'I like it not, this thing that you have asked of me, for it will send many a good warrior, both Greek and Trojan, down to the land of my brother Hades, who rules the dead; and it will set all Olympus at strife, god warring with god and goddess against goddess, and all for the sake of your son. Yet since you have served me well, I will give you your boon, come of it what shall.' And he bent his head in token of assent.

## II

# *The Combat*

SOME twelve nights after, in fulfilment of his pledge, Zeus sent a lying dream to Agamemnon, which seemed to promise a great victory to the Greeks, and soon. In the morning after the dream, Agamemnon told the kings and princes of the Greeks how he believed that victory was certain and the end of the long war in sight at last, and he bade the whole army make ready for a mighty assault on Troy.

Up from their camp came the army of the Greeks, men and chariots—arms and armour flashing in the sunlight and the horses neighing shrilly—like a great wave from the shore, spilling on to the plain, leaving the camp empty save for the slaves and the captives, and the few sick or wounded; and—at the most western point—all those who had come with Achilles from Phthia.

Each leader of the Greeks, in his light battle chariot, its strong frame made of wood and bronze with sides of wicker work and, beneath, a platform of plaited strips of hide to lessen the jolting, went at the head of his men, his charioteer standing at his side to guide the horses, and his chosen warriors running beside the chariot; and after him, in the first rank, came his lords and nobles in their chariots, with their own followers; and after them, the men who fought on foot. And so the mighty army of the Greeks moved forward over the plain, and only Achilles and Patroclus and the Myrmidons were not with them, for, since the quarrel, Achilles had not left his hut to fight, though such inaction irked him; and his men, too, at his command, remained about his ships, mending and sharpening their weapons and gear, dicing and playing games, practising their fighting skill or training their hounds, drinking, fetching fodder for their horses from the banks of the Scamander, and finding time go slowly for them.

The Trojans, wary and ever watchful, saw the Greeks approaching, and instantly made ready; and soon, out through the wide Scaean Gate, poured men and chariots to meet this new attack, far greater than any they had had to face before. Along the broad, paved way which led from the city, past the wild fig-tree that stood before the walls, past the burial mound of Ilus, one of the ancient kings of Troy, and on to the level plain, came the Trojans and their allies, led by Hector, the eldest son of King Priam and Hecuba his queen, and the greatest warrior in all Troy.

Close by the River Scamander, a good bowshot from each other, the two armies drew up in the midst of the plain, thick-starred with little red and yellow flowers; and there they waited, ready to attack, each leader turning to shout encouragement to his own men; while here and there a Greek or Trojan warrior would pick up one of the stones which lay upon the plain, and fling it, with a shouted taunt, in the direction of the enemy, a foretaste of what was yet to come.

But in that moment, whilst each army waited for the signal to attack, out from the Trojan ranks into the open space between the armies drove a single chariot, and from it there leapt down a young Trojan lord, handsome above most, with shining, richly ornamented armour and the spotted skin of a panther swinging from his shoulders: Paris, son of Priam and Hecuba, and the most hated of the Trojan princes, who had stolen Helen from her husband Menelaus.

Now, Paris, light-minded and careless, was not wont to court danger on the battlefield, and his favourite weapon was the bow, with which one might, if one were skilled enough, kill a man from a safe and sheltered place, well out of the reach of sword or spear. But on this day, being in a braggart mood, and not yet considering the consequences, he was rashly seeking that danger which he usually shunned. Brandishing two spears, he cried out a challenge to the bravest of the Greeks to meet with him in single combat.

Menelaus, seeing him, thought with satisfaction that at last he might be avenged on the man who had taken his wife from him, and instantly he leapt down from his chariot and came forward in acceptance of the challenge. Menelaus, king of Sparta, Agamemnon's brother, was by no means their greatest warrior, but he was brave and a good comrade in the fighting, ever ready to help others; and he was well liked amongst the Greeks.

But when Paris saw him there, sturdy and menacing, with his thick, reddish brows drawn together in a frown and his sandy beard glinting in the sun, he regretted his own rashness, and immediately stepped back into the Trojan ranks as though he would avoid a meeting with the husband of Queen Helen.

For all he was the son of their king, the Trojans murmured against him for faint-heartedness, and his brother Hector strode to him in anger. 'Most wretched Paris, would you shame us further? Have you not brought dishonour and grief enough on Troy already? Coward, and stealer of other men's wives, I wish that you had died before you went to Sparta. Would you have the Greeks make mock of us and say that we choose our champions for their good looks and not for courage? That I should have been cursed with such a brother! Of what use on a battlefield are your good looks, your winning ways, your curled hair, your skill at playing on the lyre? Fool that you are, you have made a challenge, and Menelaus has accepted it. Go out now, and meet the man whom you have wronged.'

Paris, white-faced, answered him, 'I will fight with Menelaus, if I must. But let it be for possession of Helen and the ending of the war. Let this meeting decide the outcome of the quarrel between our two peoples. Let him who wins take Helen, and let the loser renounce all claim to her.'

Hector, both surprised and pleased by his brother's answer, bade the Trojans hold from fighting whilst he spoke with the Greeks. He went alone between the armies and called to the Greeks for a hearing, and Agamemnon ordered them to be silent and listen to what Hector had to say.

Hector, speaking both to Greeks and Trojans, said, 'Hear the words of Lord Paris, son of King Priam, whose deeds brought this war upon our two peoples. He will fight alone with King Menelaus, son of Atreus, for possession of Queen Helen, if every man here will swear to respect the outcome of the battle, and let the winning of Helen end the war.'

When he had finished, no one spoke for a time, then Menelaus glanced at Agamemnon, who gave his brother a nod of agreement, and Menelaus stepped forward and said, 'I agree to the conditions, but let King Priam himself come from the city and swear to them in the name of all the Trojans and their allies.'

Both Greeks and Trojans were glad when they saw the ending of the long war so close. They laid aside their weapons and took off helmets and breastplates and sat on the ground to wait, while Hector sent two heralds running to the city to summon Priam.

In Troy, Helen, in the house of Paris, sat embroidering on linen the tale of the enmity between the Trojans and the Greeks. When she heard of the challenge of Paris and how Menelaus had accepted it, she threw a veil over her lovely hair, and calling two of her handmaidens to go with her, she went out from the house, which stood close by the palace of King Priam and the house of Hector, on the high citadel called the Pergamus, in the very midst of the city. Down the wide street she went, which led to the Scaean Gate, beside which rose a tower from where one might watch what went on upon the plain.

She found King Priam and his counsellors sitting in the watch-tower, old men all of them, too old to fight, but respected for their wisdom and good advice. They looked up and saw her coming. 'It is Helen,' they said, and in low voices they spoke amongst themselves. 'It is small wonder that the Trojans and the Greeks fight over her, for she is as fair to look upon as one of the immortal goddesses. Yet for all that, I wish she were gone from Troy, for she has brought much grief to us, young and old alike.'

But when Priam saw her, he smiled and made room for her close by him on the stone bench where he sat, for he had always shown her courtesy since the day when Paris had first brought her home to Troy. 'Come, my dear child,' he said, 'and sit with us and point out to us the kings and princes of the Greeks, for they will all be known to you by sight.'

So Helen pointed them out: Agamemnon, his breast-plate ornamented with blue enamelling, Odysseus with the dark-red hair, tall Ajax, son of Telamon, carrying the huge shield, young Diomedes with Sthenelus, grey-bearded old Nestor, whose shield was solid gold, little, quick Ajax of Locris, and handsome Idomeneus, the king of Crete; and King Priam and his counsellors praised them for goodly seeming men. Yet the youngest and most beautiful of all the kings and princes of the Greeks was not amongst them. Achilles, on the shore, had climbed upon a ship, and standing at the high stern, narrowing his eyes against the morning sun, while the wind blew through his golden hair, he was looking out across the plain, to see what he could of all that was taking place.

While Priam and Helen and the old men sat talking in the watch-tower, old Idaeus, Priam's herald, came to tell the king of how two messengers were come from the battlefield with word of the single combat between Paris and Menelaus which was to decide the outcome of the war, and of how Priam himself was called upon to take an oath in the name of all his people.

Bidding wise old Lord Antenor, his chief counsellor, to go with him, Priam went down from the watch-tower to his chariot, awaiting him before the Scaean Gate. Followed by the heralds bearing wine and offerings for a sacrifice, he drove swiftly to where the two armies waited, and there, in the open space between them, he came down from the chariot and walked towards the Greeks, with Antenor at his side.

Immediately, Agamemnon rose, beckoning to Odysseus, and they went forward to meet the Trojan king, while the heralds brought the offerings. Then, when the two kings, Priam and Agamemnon, had cleansed their hands in water, they poured out the libation and sacrificed three sheep, and took an oath to end the war and abide by the outcome of the single combat.

Then Greeks and Trojans alike made ready eagerly to watch the combat, but old Priam said, 'I will go back to the city, for I have no heart to stay and watch my own son fight. Immortal Zeus will give the victory as he sees fittest.' And, with Antenor, he mounted into the chariot and returned to Troy, sad at heart for his son, guilty and worthless though he might be.

Hector and Odysseus measured out a space between the armies and cast lots from a helmet to see which of the two, Paris or Menelaus, should be the first to hurl his spear at the other; and the lot fell to Paris to throw first.

Menelaus and Paris armed themselves, Paris putting on the breastplate of his half-brother Lycaon, for it was stronger than his own, though far less richly ornamented. He had taken it for himself at the time when Lycaon had fallen captive to Achilles, who had sold him into slavery across the sea.

Then the two of them stepped forward and stood opposite each other in the space which had been measured out, and, since the lot had fallen to him, Paris was the first to cast his spear, and it struck the shield of Menelaus. The shield was made of layers of stout hide, with an outer layer of bronze, and the bronze held, and turned the point of the spear.

With a prayer to Zeus, 'Immortal Zeus, father of gods and men, protector of guest and host, grant I may now be avenged on Paris, who did me such great wrong; so that, in years to come, my vengeance may be remembered and men shrink from doing evil deeds in the house of a kindly host,' Menelaus hurled his spear, and with such a mighty effort, that it passed right through the shield of Paris and on through the edge of Lycaon's breastplate, even tearing the linen tunic which Paris wore beneath, but leaving him unharmed: yet by no more than a hair's-breadth had Paris escaped from death.

Menelaus drew his sword, and raising it, ran forward and struck him a mighty blow upon the helmet; but the

hard bronze ridge of the helmet, to which the crest was
fixed, broke the sword into four pieces, which fell upon
the ground. 'Zeus, Zeus,' cried Menelaus, 'do you deny me
my revenge?' But he was not daunted, and, weaponless,
he flung himself on Paris and, seizing him by the crest of
horsehair on his helmet, threw him down and would have
dragged him towards the Greek lines. Paris, almost choked
by the leather strap which fastened the helmet beneath his
chin, could do nothing to help himself; but the strap broke
and the helmet came away in Menelaus' hand. He flung
it from him and leapt again upon Paris, meaning to catch
him by the hair and hold him fast until he could take up
his spear from the ground.

But golden, laughing Aphrodite, goddess of love and
beauty, whom Paris had adjudged the loveliest of all the
immortal goddesses, would not permit him to be slain,
and in a cloud she gathered him up, carrying him in an
instant to his own house. There she set him down, astonished, but thankful indeed that he had come alive from his
battle with Menelaus.

Menelaus, baffled, saw Paris vanish from before his very
eyes, and catching up his spear, he sought him furiously
up and down amongst the Trojan lines, thinking that perchance some comrade was protecting him. But indeed, few
Trojans would have hidden him from Menelaus, for he
was too well hated for all the grief that he had brought to
Troy.

When Helen, who had watched the battle from the
watch-tower beside the Scaean Gate, learnt from Aphrodite
that Paris awaited her in his house, she could not at first

believe it, for she had seen him, only a little while before, being worsted in his fight with Menelaus.

But she knew that if Paris were indeed safe in his own house, it could only be through the protection of the immortal gods, and she made haste to go to him up the street that led to the high Pergamus. Yet she went silently and thoughtfully, for she had that day looked once again on Menelaus, her generous, trusting husband, whom she had loved and chosen from amongst all her many wooers; and seeing him once again, bold and sturdy, a man worthy of regard, she had bitterly regretted ever leaving him.

She found Paris in his own chamber, smiling and well pleased, looking more like one who had just come from a dancing ground than from a battlefield.

She sat down, but would not look at him. 'So,' she said, 'today you have fled from a better man than yourself. How often you have boasted to me in the past of all that you would do if you met with Menelaus in the fighting! Having slipped safely through his hands today, will you dare challenge him again? If you do, you will be a fool, for he is by far the better man.'

He went to her, gaily, tossing back his dark curls. 'Come, Helen, do not reproach me for it, that the gods were with Menelaus today. Another time, who knows, they may give me the victory.' He took her hand, coaxingly, with fond looks at her lovely, frowning face. 'Be kind, Helen, and smile at me again, for I still love you. Indeed, I think that I now love you even more than on that first day when you came so willingly with me from the house of Menelaus.'

## III

# *The Broken Truce*

So Paris spoke with Helen, and smiled; but Menelaus, having searched the plain and found no trace of him, returned to his brother Agamemnon, who said, 'Whether false Paris has hidden himself or has been hidden by one of the immortal gods—or, indeed, whether he is alive or dead—is of no consequence. What matters is that, before the eyes of all, you worsted him. Therefore let the Trojans keep the oath, sworn by King Priam in their name, and return Helen to you, my brother, so that there may be an ending of this war.'

And so indeed might they have done—for Trojans and Greeks alike were wearied of the years'-long fighting—but that Zeus, watching from his everlasting halls on Mount Olympus, remembered his promise to Thetis, and calling to him his daughter Athene, who gave to men all skill and craft, whether of hands or mind, he bade her go down to earth and put it into the mind of one of the Trojans to violate the truce.

Athene, flashing-eyed and sternly beautiful, answered him, 'It shall be as you say, Father Zeus.' She took up her tasselled shield, terrible to look upon, and wearing her helmet of imperishable gold, immediately she departed from Olympus, gleaming like a star. Well pleased was she to obey the command of Zeus, for she had been ill disposed towards Troy since Paris had awarded the golden apple of Eris to her rival, Aphrodite, and she had no wish to see the war between the Greeks and the Trojans ended until all Troy had paid for Paris's offence, and Priam's city lay in ruins.

On the plain before the city, in the likeness of a young Trojan nobleman, she sought out Pandarus, one of the allies of the Trojans, who had come to the aid of King Priam from Zeleia, at the very foot of the rugged, pine-clad slopes of Mount Ida, south-east of Troy, and she spoke to him with enticing words. 'Brave Pandarus,' she said, 'does it not seem to you, high hearted as you are, a shameful thing that the champion of the Trojans should have been overcome by Menelaus? Should any Greek live to boast of a victory over one of great King Priam's sons? Think you not it would be a good thing, and one which would win you much honour amongst the Trojans, if Menelaus were to fall to an arrow from your bow? Like Prince Paris, you are skilled with the bow, rarely do you miss your mark, as we of Troy well know. Come, my friend, there stands Menelaus, well within reach of an arrow; do not hesitate. Kill Menelaus, and you will win, not only much honour from the Trojans, but, as well, rich gifts and much wealth from Prince Paris. For he will be grateful to the man who is bold and skilled enough to rid him of Queen Helen's lord.'

Flattered by her praise and seduced by her subtle words, in his folly, Pandarus took up his bow, fashioned of the horns of a wild goat which he had slain on Ida, and fitted to it an iron-tipped arrow. Before any standing near him could have prevented him, he had taken aim at Menelaus, with a prayer to Apollo the Archer on his lips.

Swiftly the arrow flew, but Athene was swifter, standing before Menelaus, unseen of any, to turn the arrow from its mark. To his belt of leather set with gold she guided it, and it passed through the belt and pierced the flesh beneath. But the golden clasps of the belt stayed its course, so that no more than the tip of the arrow entered his side, though the blood flowed down, reddening his tunic.

Agamemnon, standing beside him, exclaimed in horror, and put his arms about his brother. 'Menelaus, best of brothers, I have brought you to your death by rashly trusting in the good faith of our enemies,' he cried. 'Ever after will it be said of me that through my folly my brother died. When the war is over and the Greeks sail home again, you will be left alone in alien ground for the Trojans to dishonour your bones, leaping vauntingly upon your burial mound to boast, "Agamemnon is gone home, yet he came to Troy in vain, for he has left Menelaus behind him."'

But Menelaus made light of his wound, saying cheerfully, 'It is no more than a scratch. See, how the barbs of the arrow have caught on the clasps of my belt. There is no need yet to raise the dirge for me. And calm yourself, I beg of you, good brother, or we shall have my men thinking that I am half-way to Hades' land.'

Yet Agamemnon knew too well his brother's courage and his usual bluff manner of speech, to be entirely reassured. 'May the immortal gods grant that you speak truly,' he said. 'But I shall not be satisfied until Machaon, our good physician, has seen the wound and told me so himself.' And he called out to Talthybius the herald to fetch Machaon to them, and, smiling, Menelaus shrugged his shoulders and let him have his way.

When Machaon was come, he cleaned the blood from the wound and laid healing herbs on it, binding it with strips of linen; while Menelaus jested with him.

Once Agamemnon was reassured that his brother was indeed not badly hurt, he turned his thoughts to the Trojans. 'Now that they have broken their oath,' he said, 'surely they will be justly hated of the gods, and victory shall be ours. We cannot fail to destroy them now.' And forthwith he commanded the Greeks to make ready for instant battle, going himself to each leader, urging him to fight his utmost to avenge the broken truce.

First he went to the Cretans, where they were arming themselves eagerly, impatient to take vengeance on the Trojans for their treacherous oath-breaking. Idomeneus, their king, stood before them, calling out to encourage them; while young Meriones, his friend, exhorted the stragglers at the rear. Idomeneus was one of the older leaders of the Greeks, his hair was already a little grizzled, but he was still as handsome as ever he had been, as upright and as strong; and he was, moreover, a rich and important ruler.

Agamemnon, gladdened by the eagerness of the Cretans, praised King Idomeneus for his readiness and thanked him for his support, before passing on to where Ajax of Locris and Ajax, son of Telamon, prepared for battle together, with the Locrians and the men of Salamis, well armed and ready, standing near their leaders.

'You are valiant men, both of you,' said Agamemnon, 'and you need no encouragement from me. If all the Greeks had your daring spirit we should take Troy this very day.'

He found old King Nestor ready armed, his gold shield flashing in the sunlight, as he drew up the men of Pylos in their ranks, ordering the charioteers to keep close together on the field, in one unbroken line, each chariot lending support to the others, and not to fight, each man, selfishly, for his own glory, pressing forward alone against the enemy.

'Good Nestor,' said Agamemnon, 'I wish that your strength were as ageless as your wisdom, or that your old age might leave you and fall instead upon some younger man, giving you his youth, for there is no one of all the kings of Greece like you.'

'Old I may be, great King Agamemnon,' replied Nestor, 'but I can still strike a blow against the Trojans, who have shamefully broken their oath, as they shall learn today. For the rest, I can urge younger men to fight bravely, and set them an example.'

And so Agamemnon went from one leader to another, praising and encouraging, well pleased by the zeal he found. But when he came to those who were farthest from his own men of Mycenae—King Odysseus with his followers from Ithaca, few but brave; and the men of high-walled Tiryns, under young King Diomedes—he found them unarmed and idle, for they had not heard his call to battle, being too far away.

Frowning, Agamemnon spoke to Odysseus. 'Why do you stand here avoiding battle and waiting for other men to do your fighting for you? Full of craft and guile as you are, Odysseus, doubtless you will say that you did not hear me call all men to battle. Yet when I summon the Greeks to a feasting, you never fail to hear me, however far off you may be.'

Odysseus was angry, as well he might be, at being so unjustly taken to task, and he did not hesitate to retort to Agamemnon's words. 'Are you calling me a coward, King Agamemnon, because I did not hear your command? Have you not often seen me in the front of battle? Yet perhaps you were not there yourself to see me.' He made a scornful gesture. 'One should always think well before one speaks, lest one speak foolishly.'

Seeing that he had angered Odysseus by his ill-considered words, and being unwilling to lose the support of another leader of the Greeks, Agamemnon said hastily, 'I do not doubt your courage, Odysseus, nor the courage of your good men. And I am certain that I do not need to urge you to battle.' He smiled ingratiatingly. 'If I have spoken mistakenly, you must forgive me, for I meant no slight.'

Hurriedly he passed on to the men from Tiryns, and, irritated that he had been put out of countenance in his difference with Odysseus, he began immediately to upbraid Diomedes, calling out loudly to him as he approached, 'I have heard, Diomedes, that your father, Tydeus, was a brave man, and one who was ever found in the front of battle. It seems to me that Tydeus' son lacks his father's courage.'

Diomedes, mastering his anger, bit his lip and did not answer, for he was a younger man than Agamemnon and a far lesser king, and would have shown him respect; but Sthenelus, who was at his side, would not stand by and hear his friend insulted, even by the high king of Greece. Flushed and indignant, he stepped forward. 'That is a lie, King Agamemnon, and well you know it. Diomedes is no coward.'

But before he could say further, Diomedes turned on him, speaking, in his anger with Agamemnon, far more harshly than he meant. 'Hold your peace, Sthenelus. It is King Agamemnon's right, as the leader of us all, to rebuke me if he sees fit. For he commands us, and if we take Troy the glory will be his; but if we are defeated, then the shame, also, will be his. So he is both wise and in his rights to exhort and chide us. Come, let us heed his reproach, Sthenelus, and go forth against the Trojans.' And without a word to Agamemnon, he turned away and made ready to go into battle, that he might wash out, in Trojan blood, the sting of Agamemnon's injustice.

When battle was joined, there were many Greeks fought well that day, yet none so fiercely as Diomedes; and few Trojans who came within reach of his spear lived to tell of it.

But while he raged across the plain, and the Trojans fled

from him in terror, Pandarus from Zeleia, who had broken the truce by wounding Menelaus, seeing him come within range of his bow, took aim at him. Straight sped the arrow, and its barbed iron head passed clean through Diomedes' brazen breastplate and on into his shoulder, so that Pandarus, seeing it, cried out in triumph to his comrades, 'Take courage, men of Troy, for I have slain Diomedes, who is the most fearful of those who stand against us today.'

Diomedes withdrew from the fighting to where Sthenelus waited with his chariot and horses, for Diomedes had left him, very early in the battle, to fight on foot. He called, 'Sthenelus, I am wounded. Come to me.' And Sthenelus, hastily tying the reins to the front rail of the chariot, leapt down and ran to him, much distressed.

'Pull out the arrow,' said Diomedes.

Sthenelus set his teeth and drew the arrow out, and the blood streamed down Diomedes' breastplate. Sthenelus staunched the wound as well as he could.

'Can you hear that braggart boasting how he has slain me?' asked Diomedes. 'Not long shall he live to vaunt, if the gods are kind to me.' He prayed aloud to Athene, 'Immortal daughter of Zeus, if ever you stood by my father, Tydeus, in battle, stand by me today. Let Pandarus come within reach of my spear, and grant that I slay him.' And with that, though Sthenelus would have prevented him, he returned into the thickest of the fighting, to seek out Pandarus; while Sthenelus drove the chariot and horses after him, keeping as close as he could, unwilling to lose sight of Diomedes for an instant, lest he neeeded help.

Aeneas, son of a great Trojan lord, and the bravest

warrior of the Trojans after Hector, saw him from his
chariot and called out to Pandarus, who was near, 'Here
comes Diomedes, son of Tydeus, bent on further slaughter.
Loose an arrow at him, good Pandarus, and save many
Trojan lives.'

Pandarus, astonished and disconcerted, exclaimed, 'Does
he still live? My arrow struck him through the breastplate
but a short while ago. Truly, the gods have granted me ill
fortune today. Two kings of the Greeks have my arrows
reached, yet neither have I sent to his death. There is no
luck on my bow. I wish I had not brought it with me. A
chariot and horses would have served me better. In my
father's stables stand eleven new-made chariots, and a pair
of horses to each. He bade me choose from them before I
came to Troy. Yet I thought that, with Troy besieged, it
might not be easy to find fodder for the horses, so I trusted
to my bow instead and came as my men, on foot. If I live
to see my home and my wife again, may some man strike
the head from my shoulders if I do not break this wretched
bow of mine with my own hands and cast it into the fire.'

'Come, do not be downhearted, my friend,' said Aeneas.
'Mount beside me in my chariot and together we will go
against Diomedes. And if he should prove to be too mighty
for the two of us—which I doubt he could be, unless a god
stands by him—why then, my horses are swift and will
bear us safely from him, for they are of the same strain as
King Priam's horses, which are the best in Troy. Come
now, take the reins and whip and I will fight; or, if it is
more to your mind, let me drive whilst you attack him.'

Eagerly Pandarus leapt into the chariot. 'The horses will
answer better to your guidance, noble Aeneas, for they

know your hand and voice. Let you drive, and I will strike at Diomedes with this good sharp spear of mine. It were best we did not risk the horses' running wild at a moment of danger, because a strange hand guided them.'

Aeneas urged the horses on, and together they made towards Diomedes. Sthenelus, close behind his friend, saw them coming and warned Diomedes. 'Here comes Pandarus against you once more. But this time he is with Aeneas. You are tired and you are wounded, and you cannot face the two of them. Come into the chariot and I will take you out of their reach.'

Diomedes' shoulder pained him, and Agamemnon's words still rankled, and he answered sharply, 'I am no coward to fly from battle even if it is you who bid me. I shall meet those two as I am, on foot.' He added, after a moment, in better humour, and with an eagerness hardly hidden by his too casual manner, 'If I should chance to kill them both, Sthenelus, be ready to take the horses of Aeneas, for they are among the best in Troy, it is said.'

As they neared each other, Pandarus leant from the chariot crying out, 'Son of Tydeus, my arrow did not kill you, may my spear have better fortune,' and hurled his spear at Diomedes. The spear passed through Diomedes' shield, and touched his breastplate; but its force was by then spent, and it did not pierce the armour.

Pandarus shouted in triumph, for he saw the point of the spear pass through the shield and he thought that it had passed on into Diomedes' body; but, even as he shouted, Diomedes' spear struck his head and he fell from the chariot. Aeneas, dropping the reins, leapt down after him, and stood with spear and shield to defend his body, lest

Diomedes should seek to strip the armour from it. But
Diomedes remained where he was, and taking up a huge
stone which lay on the ground at his feet, he flung it at
Aeneas with such force that Aeneas fell to the ground, and
everything went dark before his eyes. Diomedes ran forward, sword ready, to take his life, but golden Aphrodite,
unseen, spread a fold of her bright robe over him, and he
vanished from Diomedes' sight.

And so, through the intervention of immortal Aphrodite, Diomedes failed to kill Aeneas; but Sthenelus, leaping
swiftly from the chariot, left his own horses to one of
Diomedes' followers, and took the horses of Aeneas as
spoils for his friend. And very glad were Diomedes and he
to have won so fine a prize.

Across all the plain of Troy the battle raged, with Athene
lending strength and courage to the Greeks, and Aphrodite ever ready to protect the Trojans. And Ares himself,
dread god of war, came down from Olympus to the
battlefield. To him it mattered not who lost or won, so
long as men fought and died; but on this day he fought
beside the Trojans, for he was the lover of Aphrodite, and
she wished the Trojans well.

When Ares was come against them, the Greeks gave
ground and retreated, though slowly, and fighting all the
way, towards the ships; until at last, in wrath, Athene
drove Ares back to Olympus and, for a time, the gods
ceased warring amongst mortal men.

With Ares gone from the field, the Greeks took heart
and rallied, and the Trojans fared ill at their hands. Ajax,
son of Telamon, fought mightily, sparing none, as did

Antilochus, Nestor's son; while Nestor himself forbade his men to cease fighting long enough to strip the slain. 'When all our enemies lie dead,' he said, 'there will then be a time for the taking of spoils.'

Yet, even in the midst of slaughter, there were moments of pity and forbearance. As Adrastus, a rich young Trojan, was fleeing from Menelaus, the wheels of his chariot became entangled in the branches of a tamarisk bush, the chariot pole snapped and Adrastus was thrown to the ground.

Menelaus leapt from his own chariot and came up to him, spear in hand, and Adrastus clasped his knees in supplication, begging Menelaus to take him alive. 'My father has much treasure laid by in his house, good son of Atreus. He will pay you a great price for my life,' he pleaded.

Menelaus hesitated, then, pitying him, turned to call his followers to bind the youth and take him to the ships; but Agamemnon, seeing his brother about to spare a suppliant, came running to him. 'Why so weak and soft-hearted, Menelaus? Have the Trojans done you so much kindness that you should take thought for them? Let us slay them all. Let us not leave one of them alive in Troy.'

Though he was his own brother, Agamemnon was also high king of Greece and leader of all the Greeks at Troy, so Menelaus obeyed him. He unclasped Adrastus' hands from about his knees and stepped aside; yet he did no more than that, and it was Agamemnon who thrust his spear into the young man's body.

More happy was the meeting between Diomedes and

Glaucus the Lycian, who had come to Troy to fight for King Priam with Sarpedon, his friend and fellow-king. The Lycians were a folk who lived far away from Troy, in the south, and were strangely clad, in ungirdled tunics. Yet they were the most respected of all the Trojan allies, and their two brave kings were much honoured.

When all who could were keeping as far from Diomedes as they might, so much were all the Trojans dreading him that day, Glaucus came forth alone and challenged him.

'Who are you, brave stranger, who come so willingly to die at my hands?' asked Diomedes.

'Diomedes, son of Tydeus, why do you ask my name? What matters who I am? Even as leaves upon the trees of the forest are the generations of men. The leaves fall in the autumn and the wind blows them away; and in the spring the trees put forth new leaves. Even so perishes one generation of men, and is forgotten; but another comes to take its place. Yet, since you ask, my father was Hippolochus, and his father was Bellerophon, and I am Glaucus, who rules in Lycia with King Sarpedon.'

Immediately Diomedes thrust the point of his spear into the ground, and leaving it standing so fixed, went towards Glaucus with a smile, saying, 'Then should we be friends, for Oeneus, my father's father, once entertained Bellerophon in his house, and they exchanged gifts. My father Tydeus I do not remember, for he died when I was very young, but Oeneus has often told me of Bellerophon and shown me the golden cup he gave him. So we, too, should be friends, even as they were; and if ever, in happier days, you chance to come to Tiryns, you shall be my guest, and I yours, if ever I am in Lycia. Let us exchange gifts, as our

grandsires did, and keep from each other in the fighting. For surely there are Trojans and their allies enough for me to kill, and Greeks enough for you to slay, without our taking each other's lives.'

So they clasped hands in friendship and pledged faith with each other, and exchanged their armour as a gift. And though the armour of Glaucus was all of gold, while Diomedes' armour was only bronze, and a poor exchange, yet were they both well satisfied, and gladdened by their encounter.

IV

## The Unaccepted Offering

WHILE Hector fought, striving with all his might to resist the Greek advance, Helenus, who was a younger son of Priam and Hecuba—no great warrior, yet a young man of good sense and considered purpose—came to him and said, 'Things go ill with us, brother. Should we not make offerings to the immortal gods, and pray for help? Above all, should we not make an offering to divine Athene, that she may turn from the Greeks and give us her aid? Whilst we others remain here and hold back the enemy, let you, Hector, return to the city and ask our mother to call all the women of Troy to the temple of Athene, and there make her an offering. Then perchance she may spare us from Diomedes' attack, for he seems as mighty today, and as much to be feared, as ever Achilles was, in the days before he held from fighting.'

44

Hector, more used to fighting and to leading men than to devising ways and means, was always impressed by his young brother's quick understanding, and ready to be guided by him in such matters. 'That is well counselled, Helenus,' he said. 'I shall do as you advise.' He leapt down from his chariot and went amongst the Trojans, encouraging them and bidding them fight bravely while he was gone; then, slinging his shield behind his back, he ran swiftly towards the city.

As he neared the great oak-tree, sacred to Zeus, which stood before the Scaean Gate, there came hurrying to meet him along the broad, paved way, a number of women who had been waiting beneath the gate: the wives and mothers of some of those who had gone out to fight that morning, when more of their enemies than ever before, at any one time, had been sighted coming up from the shore against the city. Anxiously the women asked him news of their menfolk: how this one did, whether that one were unhurt, and if he had seen some other.

'Pray to the gods for them, and for all in Troy,' he said, and would not stop to answer further, but ran on through the gateway.

He climbed the wide street to the Pergamus, where stood the palace of Priam, the houses of his sons, and the temples of the gods, and there, at the doorway of the palace, his mother, Queen Hecuba, met him. She took his hands in hers and asked him apprehensively, 'Why have you come from the battle, my son, and alone? Is it to ask help of the immortal gods?' Hector nodded, but before he could speak and answer her, she said, 'First let me fetch you a cup of wine, that, when you have

poured a libation to the gods, you may drink and be refreshed.'

But he shook his head and laid a hand upon her arm
when she would have gone from him. 'Fetch me no wine,
dear mother, lest it make me weak, for I must return to the
fighting without delay. Nor is it fitting that I should pour
a libation to the gods with my hands uncleansed from the
blood and dust of battle. But do you, mother, go to the
temple of Athene, together with all the wives of Troy,
and make her an offering and pray that she will hold back
the Greeks from our city and break the strength of Diomedes, son of Tydeus. While you do this, dear mother,
I shall go to Paris and bid him arm himself and come out
to fight. All this trouble he has brought on us, and yet, too
often, like a coward, he stays at home and lets others fight
to keep Helen for him.' And though she was unwilling to
let him go, he embraced her and hurried on to the house
of Paris, which stood close by the palace.

Having watched him go from her sight with anxious
eyes, Hecuba made haste to call all the married women of
Troy to the temple of Athene, that they might make an
offering to the goddess who, more than any other of the
immortals, had given help and counsel to the Greeks since
they had sailed for Troy. For the offering Hecuba chose
out from amongst her embroidered robes the richest and
most beautiful, of many colours and intricate design, which
had been brought to Troy from Sidon, far across the sea.

Then she and the other women gathered in the temple,
where Theano, wife of old Antenor, Priam's counsellor,
was priestess. There, while the women raised their hands
to immortal Athene and implored her help, Theano took

the lovely robe from Hecuba and laid it across the knees of Athene's statue in the holy place, praying her to hold back the Greeks from Troy and to break the strength of Diomedes.

But Athene loved the Greeks too well to hear the prayers of the women of Troy.

Hector found Paris in his house, busied about his fine armour, polishing here an ornamented breastplate and there a gold-studded baldric or a shield-strap, fitting on his greaves with their silver ankle clasps or trimming the crest of dyed horsehair on a helmet, while Helen sat close by, spinning, in silent discontent.

'Most wretched brother,' Hector exclaimed, 'the Greeks are almost at the gates of Troy, and you disport yourself at home. If you saw another man hold back from battle, you would blame him for a coward who shirks danger. Yet, in this war that is being fought for your sake, little help do you give our people. Put on some of that armour and come out and fight, if you have any pride or courage.'

Paris, with easily assumed penitence, said quickly, 'You rebuke me most justly for my tardiness, good brother, though, truly, it was through grief for the woes that I have brought upon the Trojans, and not through lack of courage, that I lingered here. Indeed, I was even now choosing out my arms to go forth to the fight, and Helen was bidding me make haste.' He smiled beguilingly, very sure of the charm that had so often won him his own way. 'If you will but wait for me, Hector, I will come with you now. Or, if you cannot wait, I will hurry after and overtake you.'

But Hector was no longer to be persuaded by soft words and he looked at his brother in silence, with a contempt that was so familiar that its edge had long been blunted.

Helen flung down the spindle which she held and rose and came to Hector. 'I wish that I had died before I brought so much sorrow on so many people.' Her voice was shrill and biting. 'But if these things are as the gods will them, then I wish that the man for whose sake I left my husband's house had been a better man, or at the least, one who would have paid heed to the censure of others, and felt shame at their scorn.' Then she sighed, and after a moment shrugged her shoulders slightly, smiled at Hector, and said, in a voice more like her own, 'But you look weary, good Hector. Come, sit and rest a little while.'

Hector smiled kindly in return, but shook his head and answered, 'I cannot stay, Helen, for our men need me too badly. Do not try to persuade me, for I must go. Yet, if you can, Helen, put some courage into this brother of mine and bid him hasten after me, that we may go out to the battle together. I shall go first to find Andromache, for things go so ill with us that only the gods know if I shall see her again after today.'

Leaving them, Hector went to his own house, but there he found neither Andromache, his wife, nor his little son, Astyanax. He called to one of the slaves, 'Where is your mistress? Is she gone to the temple of Athene with the queen?'

The woman came forward. 'Our mistress, lord, went in haste to the wall, when she heard that the Greeks had carried the fighting close to the gates.'

Hector turned and hurried from his house, down the

broad street from the Pergamus towards the Scaean Gate; and as he neared the gateway, Andromache saw him and came running to him from the watch-tower beside the gate, followed by the nurse who carried Astyanax.

Hector smiled when he saw the child, but Andromache was weeping. She took hold of his hand. 'Your courage will be the end of you, dear husband. Must you go again to battle? Think of me, if you will not consider yourself. My mother is dead, my father died when the town of Thebe was taken, and my seven brothers Achilles slew. I have no one left but you, Hector. To me you are not only husband, but father and mother and brother as well. If I lose you, what have I left? Have pity on me, Hector, and on our son. Stay with me on the wall today. Call the Trojans together and let them take their stand by the wild fig-tree. For opposite the old fig-tree the wall is weakest, and three times today have I watched the Greeks attack at that place.' She held his hand in both of hers and clasped it close to her.

He put his other arm about her. 'My dearest wife, if I stayed with you and kept from battle, how could I face our people ever again? Indeed, I think that I could not keep from the fighting even if I would; for, all my life, I have learnt only to be valiant and first in danger, to lead other men where they should follow, and to earn honour for my father and myself.' He sighed. 'I think that we cannot win this war, Andromache, and that there must come a day when Troy will fall to the Greeks. My heart is torn when I think of all who will suffer then, my mother, my father, my brothers and sisters, our people; but for none of them do I grieve as I grieve for you, my wife, whom some Greek will take as the spoils of battle. Then, far away over the sea,

in Greece, in the house of a harsh master, someone, some-
day, will see you weeping as you work at the loom or
fetch water from the spring, and he will say, "She was the
wife of Hector, the greatest warrior among the Trojans."
And, hearing, your tears will flow yet faster for the husband who was not able to save you.' He paused and then
broke out, 'Oh, may I be dead and the earth heaped high
above me, before I hear your cries as they carry you off
into slavery.'

Andromache wept; and Hector turned from her and,
leaning forward, stretched out his hands to take Astyanax
from the nurse. But the child was afraid of the great horsehair crest on his father's helmet, and shrank back into his
nurse's arms, so that Hector and Andromache, for all their
grief, had to smile, and even laugh a little, as Hector took
off his helmet and laid it on the ground, and Astyanax,
reassured, came willingly into his arms.

Then Hector kissed his son, and holding him, prayed for
him. 'Great Zeus and all you immortal gods, grant that my
child shall be brave and prove to be, even as I am, the
greatest warrior amongst the Trojans, and grant that he
shall rule mightily, here in Troy. And let there be a day,
when, coming back from battle, it will be said of him,
"He is a far better man than his father," so that he may
gladden his mother's heart.'

He put Astyanax in Andromache's arms, and she smiled
at him through her tears. He held her and the child close to
him, and said, 'Do not torment yourself too much, dearest
wife, for no man can send me down to the land of Hades
before the time allotted by the immortal gods. Now go
home and busy yourself with the household tasks, that you

may forget to fret for me. War is not for women, but for men. And of the men in Troy, for me above all others, who should one day rule here.'

He kissed her, and put on his helmet, while she went up the street towards the Pergamus, turning back time after time to see him, though her eyes were all but blinded by her tears.

Hector hurried on towards the Scaean Gate, and there Paris, running from his house, with all his shining armour on, and laughing as though he had no cares in all the world, came up with him, in a mood more fitted to one who went out to dance than to fight. Hector looked at him with disapproval, but Paris said respectfully, with a sudden change of mood, 'I have kept you waiting. I am sorry.'

For a few moments Hector did not answer, but went on looking at him, yet with an altered expression. Then he said, 'You are not truly a coward, for I have seen you fight well. But you are remiss and slack and careless of your good name. It hurts me and makes me angry when I hear other men speak ill of my brother, and justly.' He smiled a little and laid a hand for a moment on Paris's shoulder. 'But come now, let us go, there is much for us to do. We will make things well again between us, when we have turned this trouble from our city, and the last Greek has left the land of Troy.'

With Paris by his side, Hector made his way back swiftly to the fighting, and the Trojans were glad indeed to see him come, and took heart.

And flashing-eyed Athene came from high Olympus, whilst bright Apollo hastened from his temple on the

Pergamus; the one ardent for the Greeks and the other for
the Trojans, and they confronted one another, unsmiling
and implacable, beside the sacred oak-tree before the Scaean
Gate.

'Why have you come here again, Athene? Is it to
give victory to the Greeks?' asked Apollo. 'Must you forever afflict the Trojans, you and Hera, jealous of Aphrodite?'

'And must you ever protect the Trojans from a fate
which they deserve, and try to ward off ruin from them?'
retorted Athene, with anger.

'The outcome of this war is the will of Father Zeus,'
replied Apollo. 'Yet for today, let both Greeks and Trojans
cease from strife. Let us cause Hector to challenge to single
combat some leader of the Greeks, and so may all other
men, save those two, fight no more today.'

Athene inclined her head. 'It was with that in mind that
I myself came from Olympus. There has been slaughter
enough amongst them for one day.'

So immortal Apollo put it into the mind of Helenus to
go to Hector's side and say, 'My brother, it nears evening
and we are weary. Would it not be a good thing if you
were to call upon both Greeks and Trojans to cease from
fighting, and challenge whoever is accounted the best
amongst them to match himself with you in single combat? Thus might we have a respite from fighting, and you
may win great honour for yourself.'

For the second time that day, Hector took heed of the
advice of Helenus. He bade the Trojans cease from battle
and made it known that he would speak both to them and
to the Greeks; and as soon as Agamemnon was aware of

his intention, he commanded the Greeks, also, to hold back from the fight. The warriors flung down their weapons and sat upon the ground to rest, and Hector stood alone between the two armies and made his challenge. 'Let one of the kings and princes of the Greeks come forward now as their champion against Hector, King Priam's son, to see which is the better man. And let him declare before Zeus and all the immortal gods, that if he chance to slay me, then he will take my armour and my weapons, but leave my body for my people. For my part, I swear that if divine Apollo give me the victory, his armour I shall take and hang up in Apollo's temple, but his body I shall give back to the Greeks, that they may burn it and heap up for him a burial mound upon the shore; so that in days to come, when all we here are no more, some man, sailing over the sea to the land of Troy, may see it and say, "This is the burial mound of a warrior who died long ago, slain by mighty Hector in the olden days." And so shall my fame live on.' Then, having spoken, he was silent, waiting for an answer to his challenge.

Seeing Hector standing there, so strong and eager to do battle, there was no one amongst the Greeks who wished to face him; not even Diomedes, who had done such great deeds that day, for he was wounded and his shoulder gave him pain.

Then, amidst them, Menelaus got to his feet, his tawny beard and hair glinting in the low-lying rays of the late afternoon sun, as he looked all about him. 'Have you become weak women, you men of Greece? Is there no one amongst you with courage enough to meet the son of Priam?' He paused, and when there was no reply, he went

on, 'I am far from being the best warrior here, yet since
no one better has come forward, then I will meet great
Hector and save the honour of the Greeks. The gods will
give the victory as they choose.' And he signed to his
followers to bring his helmet and his weapons.

But instantly Agamemnon sprang up and came to him,
seizing him by the arm and saying urgently, 'Are you out
of your mind, Menelaus? Hector is a far better warrior
than you, and he will surely kill you. You shall not fight
with him, I forbid it. Sit down, and I will find another to
do battle with him in your place.'

At that moment old Nestor rose and stood leaning on
his spear, looking around him frowningly. 'Truly, the men
of today are not what their fathers were. I would that I
were young again, that I might meet Hector and show you
how to fight.'

Shamed by his words, Agamemnon remained standing,
and Diomedes got to his feet, ready, in spite of his wounded
shoulder, to meet Hector if no one else were willing. After
him Ajax, son of Telamon, and Ajax of Locris quickly
rose, and Idomeneus of Crete and Meriones, his friend,
Odysseus, and, too, King Eurypylus, who had come from
snowy-crested Titanus, in mountainous Thessaly, with
forty ships.

Nestor looked at them with approval. 'That is a more
fitting sight,' he said. 'Let us now cast lots so that the immortal gods may decide which one of you shall fight with
Hector.'

They marked their lots and cast them into Agamemnon's helmet, Nestor shook the helmet, and it was the lot
of Ajax, son of Telamon, that was shaken out.

When Ajax knew that the lot had fallen to him, he armed himself saying, 'Now pray to the gods for my victory, my friends; and let Hector beware, for we breed brave men on Salamis.' Then, when he was armed, he took up his huge shield made of seven layers of bulls' hide, covered with a plate of bronze, hanging it about his shoulders, leaving his two hands free to fight with, and strode towards Hector, a tall man with a long shadow, smiling grimly; so that even Hector was troubled at the sight.

And Athene and Apollo, in the likeness of two vultures, sat upon a branch of the sacred oak-tree, to watch the combat with far-seeing eyes.

Ajax stood facing Hector, brandishing his spear, and he cried out, 'Now, Hector, son of Priam, you shall learn that the Greeks have other good warriors besides Achilles. Come, begin the fight.'

Hector raised his spear, and its bronze head reddened in the light of the evening sun. 'Ajax, son of Telamon, I am no woman or untried boy to need your teaching. I have been tested in many a battle, so have a care.' He flung the spear, and with such force, that it pierced the bronze of Ajax's shield and all but passed through to his breast-plate.

At once Ajax cast his own spear, and it passed right through Hector's shield and on through his breastplate, grazing his side. Instantly each of them drew out the spear from his shield and leapt against the other; and this time Hector's stroke failed even to pierce the bronze of the huge shield of Ajax; but the point of Ajax's spear went once again through Hector's breastplate and pricked him low in the neck, so that he gave ground swiftly, but did not cease from the fight. He took a jagged stone and flung it so that Ajax's shield rang loudly with the blow as he held it up before him, and the brazen surface was dented. Thereupon Ajax caught up an even larger stone and flung it with such force that, striking full on Hector's shield, it bore him to the ground. Yet he was up and on his feet again immediately and reaching for his sword, even as Ajax drew his, and they would have fallen upon each other, hacking at shield and helmet, had not the two heralds, Idaeus and Talthybius, come, the one from the Trojan ranks and the other from amongst the Greeks, and parted them with their staves.

'Lords,' said old Idaeus, 'cease your fighting, for you have both proved yourselves mighty spearmen, and now night will soon be on us.'

Lowering his sword, Ajax stepped back, saying to Idaeus, 'Herald, it was Hector who made the challenge. Let him withdraw it, and I will cease from fighting.'

Hector sheathed his sword. 'You are a good fighter, Ajax,' he said, 'and we shall meet again in battle, if the gods so will it. But now the sun has set and it will soon be dark. Let us, therefore, cease our strife. Yet, before we part, let us give each other gifts in token of our mutual respect.'

Ajax willingly agreed, and Hector came forward and gave into his hands a silver-studded sword with a leathern scabbard and baldric; while Ajax took off his richly ornamented crimson belt and offered it to Hector.

And so they parted; and the fiercest day of fighting that

Greek or Trojan had yet known was over, and soon only the dead were left upon the plain, lying all amongst the trampled flowers.

Dusk fell, and from the sacred oak-tree by the Scaean Gate the two vultures were gone; god and goddess, for the moment, reconciled.

V

## *The Wall*

THE Greeks returned to their ships, and Agamemnon feasted all the kings and princes in his own hut, ordering a fine young ox to be killed and roasted, that everyone might eat his fill. There was wine from Lemnos in golden cups, and Agamemnon's slaves standing by with pitchers, ready to refill them the moment they were empty; whilst other slaves went amongst the guests with bread and meat; and a minstrel sang to entertain them. Agamemnon was in good spirits; and for Ajax, who had almost worsted Hector, he had his slaves set aside all the best portions of the meat.

After they had eaten and drunk, old Nestor spoke to them. 'Good King Agamemnon, and all of you, my friends,' he said, 'there is a thing which we have not yet done, which it would be wise to do. In all the long years

since we first came to the land of Troy, we have never yet
built ourselves a wall to protect our ships. We have always
believed ourselves strong enough to guard our ships and
huts with shields and weapons alone—and so, indeed, we
were. But for twelve days now Achilles has not been
fighting at our side, and we feel the lack of his high young
courage and the strength of his Myrmidons, good warriors
all. And today, in the fiercest fighting we have yet seen,
the Trojans sent many of our good comrades down to the
land of Hades. It were well, therefore, that we built a
rampart and a trench before the ships as a defence against
our enemies. Tomorrow, when we have burnt our dead
and raised above them a high burial mound, let us build a
wall to protect our ships and our huts.'

Agamemnon and all the other kings and princes of the
Greeks agreed that his counsel was wise. 'Tomorrow,' said
Agamemnon, 'we shall hold from the fighting and build a
wall. Those are my commands.'

In Troy, meanwhile, on the Pergamus, outside the gates
of the palace, the Trojans held an assembly by torchlight,
and old Antenor spoke before the others. 'Good King
Priam, and all you men of Troy,' he said, 'this war with
the Greeks has gone on long enough, it is time that it was
ended. And so indeed might it have been today, had we not
broken our oath of truce. I say to you, let us give back
Helen, and any treasure she brought with her from Sparta,
to the sons of Atreus, that the one may have his wife again
and the other may sail home to Mycenae, together with
all those whom he called upon to fight against us.'

Having spoken, Antenor sat down again, and there were

many there who murmured in agreement with him; but
Paris, his handsome face shadowed with annoyance, rose
and replied immediately, and with high-handed insolence,
'Lord Antenor, I do not like your words, and I hope that
they were only spoken in an old man's thoughtless moment,
and were not intended to move others to the folly of
approval. I here declare to you, Antenor, before all the
men of Troy, that I will not give up Helen.' He looked
about him, and seeing how few there were who approved
of his assertion, a little of his self-assurance left him and he
went on, almost as though he pleaded with them, 'Whatever treasure she brought with her from Sparta, that shall
I restore willingly to Menelaus, and add to it more of my
own wealth besides, as much as is fitting—or as much as he
demands.' He glanced about him again, then added de-
fiantly, 'But I will not give up Helen.' He sat down, with
his face averted, so that he should not see, in the torchlight, the disapproval—and worse—in the eyes of those
near enough to him.

For several minutes no one spoke, then slowly and
wearily Priam rose. 'Men of Troy, you have heard the
answer made by Paris, my son. I, your king, support that
answer. At dawn let Idaeus the herald go to the ships of the
Greeks with the offer made by Paris. And, further, let him
ask if they are minded to keep from fighting until both
they and we have gathered our dead from the battlefield
and built a burial mound for them.' So Priam spoke,
though, he, too, longed for the war to be over; but
Paris was his son, and it had never been his way not to
stand by his own. And because Priam was their king, the
Trojans agreed with his words, and the assembly was

broken up and each man went to his home for the night, save those whose duty it was to guard the walls.

At the first light of morning Idaeus the herald went to the Greeks and spoke to them, telling them as Priam had bidden him.

When he had done, they sat in silence, and most of them were thinking how they were weary of the war, and there was more than one man there who reflected that, when all was said and done, Helen and her misdeeds were no concern of his, since she was not his wife, but the wife of another man. And everyone was very careful not to look at Menelaus.

But Diomedes was one of the younger kings amongst them, more ready than most for battles and fighting, and, moreover, he had not yet lived long enough to have had to learn to compromise. He then rose and said, 'Are we now to take gifts from Paris and be grateful? Paris need give us no treasure; no, nor need he give us Helen. The Trojans cannot resist us much longer, even a man of little wit could tell us that. If we fight resolutely and with determination, Troy must fall; and then we can take both Helen and all the treasure we want, a hundredfold what Paris offers us.'

And because there was no one there who would willingly have seemed to be of less courage than Diomedes, they all agreed with him, and counselled that the offer made by Paris should be rejected.

Agamemnon rose. 'Herald, you have heard the answer of the kings and princes of the Greeks to the offer of the son of Priam. My own answer is even as theirs. But concerning the dead: let both Greeks and Trojans keep truce on this one day, that their dead may be burnt fittingly.' And in the name of the immortal gods, he swore to keep from fighting for that day.

Before the sun was high, both Trojans and Greeks had gathered their dead and built for them two great pyres, the one near the gates of Troy and the other close by the ships; and when the flames had sunk above the ashes of the pyres, they raised burial mounds above them, that all those whose bones lay beneath might be remembered by their comrades.

Then, for the remainder of that day, as Agamemnon had ordered, the Greeks built a wall just inland of the first line of ships, to be a protection to their camp. First they dug a deep trench and planted it within with sharpened stakes. The earth from the trench, together with stones and rocks and baulks of timber, they built up into a rampart, to the seaward side of the trench; and they worked with such a will, that by nightfall their wall stretched from before the ships of Ajax, at the most eastern point, to the ships of Achilles, at the very west. Here and there in the wall they had set narrow gates, strongly barred, and, at the mid-most point, they had made a wider gateway and a track for their chariots to pass out on to the plain.

Early the next morning, battle was joined once more, and again the plain resounded with the clash of weapons and the shouts and cries of men, and the shrill neighing of the horses as the chariots sped here and there.

But, on Olympus, Zeus called all the gods and goddesses before him and forbade them, on pain of his most fearful wrath, to join in the battle and to fight for either Greek or Trojan.

However unwilling certain amongst them might be, they were silent at his words and bowed their heads in obedience to the command of the king and father of them all, and only Athene dared to stand before him and speak.

'Father Zeus,' she said, 'we know your might and we dread your wrath, yet there are those amongst us here in high Olympus who pity the Greeks, the unhappy Greeks, who fight and perish far from their own homes. We shall hold from battle, as you command us, Father Zeus, yet for their comfort and to their profit, those of us who love the Greeks will offer them our counsel.'

So she spoke, openly and unabashed before him, as was her wont, and Zeus smiled, for he loved her above all his daughters. 'Do not despair for your Greeks, my child,' he said, 'for, in the end, things will be well for them.'

Then, in his chariot drawn by his two immortal steeds, whose hooves were flashing bronze and whose gleaming manes were thin threads of gold, as dazzling as the sunlight, he came from Olympus to Mount Ida, within sight of Troy—Mount Ida of the many springs, where the wild beasts roamed; and there, upon the topmost peak, he sat to watch the fighting of Greeks and Trojans.

Until midday the battle was equal, with neither Greeks nor Trojans gaining ground, nor yet giving way, one before the other. But in the afternoon, in fulfilment of his promise made to Thetis, Zeus filled the Trojans with might and courage, so that they hurled themselves upon the Greeks, who were driven back towards the shore.

One by one, the kings and princes of the Greeks, who

had been foremost in the fighting, turned their chariots and made for safety before the Trojan onslaught. Back towards the ships went Agamemnon and Idomeneus, Ajax, son of Telamon, and Ajax of Locris.

But when old Nestor would have turned his chariot, Paris, from a distance, killed one of his horses with an arrow, terrifying the other, which plunged and reared, so that the chariot was almost overturned, and Nestor's charioteer, thrown into confusion, could make no move to help his lord.

Nestor climbed down from the chariot, sword in hand, to cut the dead horse free; while Hector, from a short way off, seeing him to be at a disadvantage, made towards him, coveting his shield of solid gold, for it would have been reckoned a fine prize in Troy.

Diomedes and Sthenelus, however, saw the old king's plight, and hastened to him, Sthenelus urging on the horses of Aeneas, which he drove. Seeing Odysseus turning for the shore, Diomedes called out to him to come with them to the aid of Nestor, but Odysseus did not hear him and went on, and Diomedes and Sthenelus came to Nestor alone.

'Good old king,' said Diomedes, 'with one of your horses dead, and a worthless weakling for your charioteer, you can never hope to escape death at Hector's hands if you wait here for him alone. Come, instead, into my chariot and see how fleet these horses are that I took from Aeneas two days ago. Well have they served me today. Take the reins from Sthenelus and mount beside me in his place, and he shall take your chariot and your horse safely from the battle to the ships, while we two meet with Hector.'

Sthenelus leapt down and, gladly, Nestor mounted beside Diomedes. He took up the reins, and together they drove to meet Hector's attack. Diomedes flung his spear, but missed Hector, and struck, instead, his charioteer, who fell wounded. Instantly Hector checked his horses, and turned them aside, calling to his followers, and at once a man ran forward to take the place of the fallen charioteer; and Hector once more faced Diomedes' attack.

But that victory that day might be with Hector and the Trojans, Zeus hurled down a thunderbolt before the chariot of Diomedes, and the horses of Aeneas were terrified, and would not move forward a single step, but stood trembling, with wild eyes.

'It was a warning from immortal Zeus,' said Nestor, shaken, 'we would do well to heed it. Let us leave pursuing Hector and return at once to the ships. For no man, however valiant, can prevail against the will of Zeus.'

'That is true, good Nestor,' Diomedes replied. 'Yet I would not have Hector say of me, before the Trojans, that the son of Tydeus fled from him. I would rather the earth opened to swallow me, than that Hector should make such a boast.'

But Nestor rebuked him sternly. 'That is a foolish thing which only a young man would think to say, Diomedes. Let Hector boast in Troy, if he will. And if he calls you coward, will the Trojans believe him, who have seen you in battle? Or will the widows believe him, whose husbands you have slain? No, Diomedes,' he went on urgently, 'it is ill to ignore a warning from the gods. I shall not permit such folly.' And with that he turned the horses, who were only too willing, and drove towards the shore.

When Hector saw them fleeing he was glad, and bade
his charioteer make haste after them, calling himself to his
horses, 'Come, my good horses, pay me now for your
keep. Remember how often my dear Andromache has
herself set corn before you. Many times has she watered
you when you came thirsty from the battlefield—often
before she poured wine for her own husband. Come now,
friends, for old Nestor's golden shield would be fine spoils
to take home to Troy.'

After Hector, across the plain, raced the other chariots
of the Trojans, and, not far behind them, the warriors who
fought on foot. And the Greeks could not withstand their
attack, but retreated to the wall that they had built and
poured in through the gateway and closed it fast; so that
by the time that Hector reached the trench, there were
none but dead or wounded left outside.

Agamemnon came down from his chariot, flinging off
his purple cloak, and hurried to the assembly place, and
standing there, he lifted up his voice, chiding the Greeks
who had fled from battle, and bidding them prove their
courage and go forth to attack before night fell. Those who
heard his words took heart from them, and passed them
on to the others; and, while Hector drove his chariot up
and down before the trench, vowing he would break
down their wall and fire their ships, they rallied and
gathered before the gateway to attack.

Then, on a signal, the gates were flung open and the
Greeks came forth, the chariots first and the men who
fought on foot close after them. First went Diomedes and
Sthenelus, with the horses of Aeneas, and well they carried
their new masters, swerving here and there amongst

the Trojans while Diomedes struck down man after man.

Hard behind Diomedes came the sons of Atreus, Menelaus and Agamemnon himself, then Ajax of Locris, Idomeneus and Meriones, Eurypylus of Thessaly, and Ajax, son of Telamon, with Teucer, his half-brother, a famed archer.

These two sons of Telamon soon leapt down from their chariot and fought side by side, as was often their custom, tall Ajax holding his huge shield to shelter Teucer as he bent his bow, peering out from behind the shield like a tortoise from its shell. Many Trojans fell to his arrows; but it was Hector whom he longed to kill. Twice Teucer aimed at Hector, and twice Apollo turned the arrow aside. Then Hector leapt down from his chariot, and taking up a large stone, he hurled it at Teucer just as he had fitted yet another arrow to his bow and was drawing back the string. The stone struck him on the neck with such force that he fell senseless and the bowstring snapped. But, though Hector leapt forward with a shout of triumph, he could not reach him, for Ajax stood to guard his brother until two of their comrades had borne him back within the wall to safety.

Then once again Zeus put great courage into the hearts of the Trojans, and great strength into their hands, and once again the Greeks fell back before their onslaught and retired within the wall, drawing the gates close after them with difficulty and leaving many dead or dying in the trench or on the plain before the wall.

Within the wall they lifted up their hands and prayed to all the gods for help; but, outside the wall, Hector drove his chariot here and there, rejoicing in his victory and ever threatening to burn the ships:

But it was evening, and fast growing dark; the sun had gone and all battle was over for the day. And never since they had come to Troy had a night been more welcome to the Greeks; though the Trojans would not have had it come so soon.

On Hector's command they withdrew, beyond the battlefield and the slain, to the banks of the River Scamander, and there they made their camp for the night, unharnessing the horses from the chariots and building fires, while some hastened back to the city to fetch food and wine, and fodder for the horses.

Hector stood amongst them and spoke to them, exultingly, 'Men of Troy and brave allies, the night has thwarted us, or we should have made an end of the Greeks this very day. Yet let us eat and drink and rest tonight, and see what the dawn will bring to us. For I do not doubt that tomorrow will be even as today, bringing great glory to us all, and disaster to our enemies. And I think that tomorrow the son of Tydeus shall fall to my spear, for the immortal gods are with us, my friends, and they have abandoned the Greeks. Yet let us not forget to keep our fires burning brightly until the dawn, and hold good watch; not for fear that the Greeks attack us in the darkness, but lest they seek to sail away unseen. They shall not easily leave the shores of Troy, who came here uninvited.'

All the Trojans shouted aloud in triumph at his words, beside themselves with the day's success.

But Hector was not satisfied to chance the Greeks' escaping him. After the Trojans had eaten and drunk their

fill of the good things brought from the city, he called to
him the lords of Troy and the most trusted amongst his
men, asking for someone of them who would go alone to
the camp of the Greeks and spy out, if he could, their intentions: whether they were preparing to set sail, or
whether they would stay and fight again in the morning;
and to learn whether, in their despair at the way things
had gone against them, they had become careless about
keeping guard, or whether, in great fear, they dared not
even sleep, but sat, every man, watchful and alert, afraid
of a surprise attack by dark. 'To the man who ventures this
deed,' said Hector, 'I will give the finest chariot and the
two best horses which we take from the Greeks as spoils.
Now, who out of you all will do this thing for me?'

At this a man named Dolon rose, an ill-favoured man,
but a good runner. 'I will go to the ships of the Greeks for
you, Lord Hector, and spy out their counsels,' he said, 'if
you will swear to me that, as my reward, you will give to
me the chariot and the horses of Achilles, son of Peleus,
which, if all that I have heard of them is true, are immortal
and unsurpassed.'

So Hector swore, by all the gods, that, when the war was
over, Dolon should have for himself the chariot and the
horses of Achilles. And later, when night hung dark above
the plain, Dolon made ready to steal away, down towards
the shore.

# VI

# *The Embassy*

BUT while the Trojans, flushed with the triumphs of the day, waited confidently for the morning, when they might resume the slaughter, Agamemnon, anxious-eyed and sick at heart with his misgivings, sent his heralds to call the kings and princes of the Greeks, and their lords, to the assembly place upon the beach.

When they—as apprehensive as their leader—were all gathered in their places, he stood up before them and spoke. 'My friends, when we set sail for Troy, it was with good omens, and I believed that immortal Zeus would give the victory to us. But Zeus has cheated me, and now he plans to give the victory to our enemies, and we shall all perish here, before the walls of Troy, if we stay longer in this place. So let us rather, while it is yet not too late,

leave the cursed shores of Troy and sail for our homes in
Greece.' He finished, and all the Greeks were silent at his
words, while he looked from one man to another of those
gathered there, scanning in concern each man's face in the
fading light, while he waited for their reply.

But no one spoke, until at last Diomedes stood up. 'It
was not so very long ago, King Agamemnon, that you
taunted me with cowardice, and I did not answer you. A
strange taunt from one who now counsels us to fly from
Troy! You say that Zeus has cheated you, King Agamemnon. I know nothing of that, but I know this, at least:
that, at your birth, Zeus endowed you in unequal propor-
tion. He gave you wider lands and greater riches than any
other king, so that you have leadership over us all; but he
never gave you the courage which a great king should
have. Because we have followed you to Troy and are
subject to your commands, do you think that we are all
cowards like yourself? If you want to go home to Mycenae,
go home. There is the sea, and there are your ships. No
man will hinder you. But I do not doubt that there will
be found few amongst us to follow you. You will have
the whole broad sea to yourself on your return to Greece.'
He paused and looked about him at the others, hoping
for their approval of his words, but they still sat silent.
Yet, though no one spoke in agreement with him,
nor did anyone speak for Agamemnon, and Diomedes
waited.

Then, after a while, his head held high and his eyes
flashing, his voice rang out again across the assembly
place. 'Go home, all of you, with him, if you will. But
when you are all fled, yet will there still be two Greeks left

on Trojan soil, for Sthenelus and I fight on, to the very walls of Troy, until Priam's city falls to us alone.'

As he ceased, a great cheer rose from all the Greeks, and they shouted aloud for him, praising his courage, their former dismay now quite forgotten, while Agamemnon frowned, torn by indecision.

When the cheering had died down, Nestor rose, and he was smiling. 'It does my old heart good to hear a young man speak with courage, as you have done, Diomedes. You are brave in battle, and though you are amongst the youngest of the leaders of the Greeks, yet your words need be despised by none. No, not even by those older and more powerful than you. But now, my friends, all you kings and princes of the Greeks, I would offer you my counsel. I am an old man. I have fought in more battles than you have seen, and had as comrades men finer than any you have ever known, so do not scorn my advice. What I have to say concerns you all, but it is to King Agamemnon that I would address my words. And because I am old, and the old are privileged to speak their minds, do not be angry, great king, if what I say displeases you. For you are the mightiest amongst us and the leader of us all, and there-fore it is your duty, not only to give the best commands, but to listen to the wisest counsel, also. Rashly, and un-advised save by your own folly, and against my words, who sought to counsel you to peace, did you take from Achilles his lawful prize to satisfy a grudge, and he withdrew his help from our most righteous cause. Since that day we have lacked his help against the Trojans, and bitterly have we regretted it, for not only have his courage and his fighting skill deterred our enemies in the past, but his

Myrmidons are all brave, well-tried warriors and we feel their loss most keenly. All the troubles that have lately fallen on us come from this one cause: that you took from another that which was his by right, and put dishonour on a proud and headstrong youth. It was ill done, good king, and it were best you made amends, and swiftly. Send back the woman Briseïs to Achilles and give him gifts, that he may know you are his friend, and may once more bring his Myrmidons into the field against the Trojans, and so give our men new heart and turn the tide of battle for us.'

All were silent again when he had spoken, while Agamemnon's dark thoughts twisted and turned in his mind as he pondered what he should do. But because he was the leader of them all, and their safety rested in his hands, he said at last, bitterly, 'Fool that I was to forget that one man whom great Zeus loves well and honours is worth more to him than a whole army. Zeus and the immortal gods must love young Achilles well—for is his mother not herself a goddess?—and for his sake will see all our mighty army utterly destroyed. No king, however great, can hope to prevail against one so well loved by the immortal gods. For the sake of you all, that you may not perish here, and for the sake of my good brother Menelaus, that he may not be compelled to return to Sparta without the wife who was stolen from him, I will make peace with Achilles. I will return the girl Briseïs to him, and give him goodly gifts besides, and so shall he be won to fight again for us. I will give him gold, and shining vessels, and seven new-gleaming tripods which have never yet been set above the fire; and twelve of my finest horses shall be his. From the spoils we took from the island of

Lesbos, which he himself won for me, I will give to him those seven women, well skilled in weaving and all women's crafts, whom I chose for my share. They shall go to him with Briseïs. All these things will I give him now, from the riches that I have here with me; but when Troy is taken, he shall have more besides. He may make first choice of the captives, even before I myself have chosen; and when I am back home in Mycenae, he shall always be welcome in my palace, and honoured there as though he were my son. And more, he has no wife, and I have three fair daughters. He shall take his pick of them and carry her home to Phthia and pay me no bride-price, but I will, for my part, give her a greater dowry than ever any king's daughter had: seven towns, close by the sea, where the pastureland is good and the harvests rich. All this shall I do for him if he will put away his arrogance and spleen and submit to my authority as well he should, for am I not his elder? Aye, and a far greater king.'

'That is well spoken and generously offered, King Agamemnon. Surely not young Achilles nor any other man could refuse such noble gifts as you have named. Come,' said Nestor eagerly, 'let us send to him at once and tell him of your offer, and bid him forget his anger. Let Odysseus, who speaks well and is skilled at moving men's hearts, go to him, and Ajax, son of Telamon, and your two heralds, King Agamemnon. And, above all, let good Phoenix go with them, for he was Achilles' tutor, and Achilles loves him well and will listen to his words.'

And so, when they had poured libations to the gods and drunk, and prayed that Zeus might have pity on them and turn Achilles' heart, Odysseus and Ajax set out, accom-

panied by the two heralds, with old Phoenix hurrying on
a little way before them, to prepare Achilles for their
coming. They went along the shore in the evening light,
with the sounding of the restless waves upon their right
hand, and they were silent as they went, each man praying
in his heart that Achilles might be easily persuaded.

When they came to Achilles' ships, they passed through
the stout gate, bolted with a fir trunk, which was set in the
palisade of stakes that surrounded the huts of Achilles and
his men. In the wide enclosure they found the Myrmidons
preparing their evening meal, building fires in the open
space and spitting huge joints to roast above them.

Entering the pillared outer porch of Achilles' hut, to go
into the hut itself, they heard from within the sound of a
clear voice singing, and found old Phoenix, a smile upon
his lips, waiting in the doorway as though he were unwilling to interrupt the singer. Still smiling, he held up his
hand for silence as the others came near, and made no
move to enter; but Odysseus looked over the old man's
shoulder to see who it was who sang so sweetly. And there
he saw Achilles with Patroclus, just the two of them,
alone, save for their hounds lying by the hearth; and it was
Achilles who was playing on a lyre and singing to his
friend of the deeds of the old heroes.

Odysseus, noting with satisfaction that Achilles seemed
to be in the best of moods, thought that this promised well
for the success of their mission, and, despite the old man's
protests, set Phoenix gently aside, and went into the hut.

Achilles, glancing up to see which of his men it was had
entered, saw, with astonishment, Odysseus with Ajax
close after him, sprang to his feet, and, still holding his

lyre, went forward to welcome them with unfeigned pleasure. Patroclus turned at the interruption, and then rose also, with equal surprise and gladness. For it seemed long to both of them since they had spoken with any of their former battle-comrades.

Achilles greeted his guests kindly. 'Though you stand by Agamemnon in his quarrel with me, yet are you still my good friends, and very welcome.' He embraced his old tutor and led the three of them to seats spread with purple-dyed rugs, calling cheerfully to Patroclus, 'Fetch a larger bowl for the wine and let us mix less water with it, now that we have companions to drink with us.'

After they had poured libations to the gods and drunk, Achilles said eagerly, 'You are in time to share our supper. Will you stay and eat with us?' And he called for meat to be brought. Automedon, his charioteer, came in with a side of mutton and the chine of a fat pig and laid them on the cutting block which Patroclus had set ready, and Achilles cut a joint from each while Patroclus blew up the fire. Then the meat was sliced and spitted over the hot embers; and when it was cooked, Achilles laid it on platters for his guests, while Patroclus handed round bread in a basket. Then Patroclus cast into the fire the portion which was the offering to the gods, and they all sat down to eat.

When they had eaten and drunk as much as they would, and Achilles was in good spirits, Ajax looked across at old Phoenix, eyebrows raised in query; Phoenix nodded, and Odysseus, watching, knew that the moment was favourable for him to speak. He filled his cup with wine and pledged Achilles, saying, 'The best of welcomes have you given us, and a fine supper, Achilles, and we thank you for it. Yet are our minds not truly set on meat and drink, and our hearts not wholly given up to the good company, for we cannot forget the peril in which the Greeks now stand, and our hearts are heavy for our plight. For the Trojans, led by Hector, whom no man can now withstand, have driven us back to the ships, Achilles, and we lie tonight between their camp-fires and the sea. And Hector, impatient for the dawn, has sworn that tomorrow he will burn our ships. By this time tomorrow, the war may be over and the Trojans victorious, and we, whom you call your friends, may all lie dead, unless you will forget your anger with King Agamemnon and fight with us once more. Good Achilles, when your father, King Peleus, sent you with me to Agamemnon to fight against the Trojans, on that day when he bade you farewell in Phthia, did he not warn you to keep a curb upon your rash temper, and to refrain from quarrelling that you might win more respect from men? I know he told you this, but it seems that you have now forgotten his wise counsel.' He leant forward and spoke earnestly, with carefully chosen words. 'But it is not too late, Achilles. Set aside your anger and forgive Agamemnon's folly. He has admitted he did wrongly, and will send Briseïs back to you, and give you many gifts besides. Seven tripods, twenty cauldrons, and much gold; twelve horses which have won many races, and seven slave women, skilled in all handicrafts. These things will be yours tomorrow; and when Troy has fallen, thanks to your aid, then you shall have the pick of all the Trojan captives and first choice from Priam's treasure house; and evermore in Mycenae you shall be to Agamemnon as a

son. You may choose a wife from amongst his daughters
and pay no bride-price for her, and she will bring you
seven towns in Argolis as a dowry. All this if you forgive
him and bring your Myrmidons to battle in the morning.'

Odysseus paused, and watching closely in the firelight,
he saw that Achilles was not to be won by gifts, and that
Agamemnon could not buy either his forgiveness or his
help, and he said quickly, before Achilles could answer
him, 'Or if you cannot find it in your heart to forgive
King Agamemnon, then have pity on the rest of us. Do
not let the Greeks perish, but fight for them and win their
everlasting love and gratitude, and great glory for yourself. For, who knows, Achilles, you might meet Hector
himself tomorrow in the battle. He would be a worthy
adversary for even you; and the man who kills great
Hector will be remembered for ever with honour in the
minstrels' songs.'

Achilles looked at him. 'You speak skilfully, as ever,
Odysseus. Surely there is not one amongst the Greeks like
you for fair speeches and well-chosen words. But even
your urging shall not move me.' He made an impatient
gesture. 'Come, I have had enough of blandishment and
exhortation, here is my straight answer: I will neither
forgive Agamemnon nor fight for him. I want none of his
gifts. As for Briseïs, let him keep her. She is his now, I do
not want her back. Though she was but a woman I won
by my spear, she was nobly born, and I would have married
her, perhaps. But Agamemnon took her from me. We all
came here to fight in this war for the sake of a man whose
wife had been stolen from him. Are the sons of Atreus the
only men who have the right to cherish their own women-

folk? No, Odysseus. Agamemnon can win back his brother's wife without my help. Or he can perish here on Trojan land. I care not. Go back to him, Odysseus, and you, too, Ajax, and tell him what I say: that I shall never be bought with promises or lured with gifts—not though he offer me twenty times what he has offered, not though his gifts outnumber the grains of sand that lie along the shores of Troy. And as for his daughter, were she as fair as golden Aphrodite and as skilled in women's handicrafts as divine Athene herself, I would have none of her. Let our lord, the great King Agamemnon, who is the mightiest of us all, find a more fitting match for his daughter than Achilles, who will one day rule over no more than little Phthia—if he live long enough. I am doomed to die young, and I have accepted my doom, but my life is too precious to me for me to throw it away for Agamemnon's sake. No, more than that: I would rather lose the glory and undying fame which I was promised with my short life, and endure instead the alternative long days of obscurity, with no man to remember me when I am dead, than that my everlasting fame should be won in dying for Agamemnon. I would sooner set sail tomorrow for Phthia and leave him to perish here. And if the rest of you take my counsel, you will do likewise. Let the sons of Atreus finish their own war alone.' He rose. 'Now, go, my two good friends, and tell Agamemnon what I have said. But you, my dear old Phoenix, you must stay here with me tonight, and then, if I do indeed sail home, you must choose whether you will come with me or remain with Agamemnon.'

There were tears in the old man's eyes, but he answered promptly, 'My child, how could I stay here without you?

The gods never gave me a son of my own, but I have always thought of you as a son. When you were very little, you would not go to a meal in your father's hall unless I were there with you, to set you on my knee and cut your meat for you and hold the cup to your lips. And when your father sent you, still no more than a boy, to lead his Myrmidons to fight at Troy, knowing nothing of cruel war or of the assemblies and councils of grown men, he bade me go with you to guide and help you. No, my child, I cannot stay here without you. If you go home to Phthia, I go with you. But I implore you, Achilles, have pity on the Greeks and help them in their despair. There would be no shame in yielding to their pleas. For not even the gods are unbending, even they will answer prayers, and by sacrifice and supplication can a man who has sinned avert the wrath of the gods. For prayers are the daughters of immortal Zeus. Lame and wrinkled and with downcast eyes, they follow hard on the heels of sin. Sin is strong and swift and runs fast ahead, harming and working ill; but the prayers follow after, stumbling and limping, yet never giving up the chase, and healing all hurts they find. Therefore one should show reverence to these daughters of Zeus when they draw near, and deny them not; and thus, respect the gods. My child, let your heart be moved by Agamemnon's prayers, for he has acknowledged his fault.'

But even by old Phoenix, whom he loved, would Achilles not be persuaded. 'My dear old friend,' he said, 'you wrong us both by your tears and by your pleas for Agamemnon's cause. You should rather hate the man I hate. Come now, it grows late and you must sleep.

Patroclus shall spread a couch for you here, close by the hearth.'

Odysseus still sat undecided whether he should again try to prevail upon Achilles, but tall Ajax rose, saying, 'Come, Odysseus, for we can achieve nothing by staying longer. Achilles will not hear us. He has no pity for his comrades.' He turned to Achilles and said bitterly, 'I have known men accept gold in recompense for the slaying of a brother or a son, and lose no honour by it. But you, for one slave girl, you refuse all a great king's gifts.'

'It is not a question of whether I pity the plight of my comrades,' said Achilles sharply. 'It is not whether I would or would not help the Greeks. It is a question of the wrong that has been done to me. I cannot forget and I will not forgive the slight which Agamemnon put on me. Now go, before I am angered with you, who are my friends.'

And after they had poured a last libation to the gods, Ajax and Odysseus went, heavy at heart, to tell Agamemnon of Achilles' answer, whilst old Phoenix lay down beside the hearth to sleep; and, after bidding him rest well, Achilles and Patroclus went to the inner room of the hut, where they slept.

In the spacious hut of Agamemnon, Odysseus and Ajax found all the kings and princes of the Greeks awaiting their return.

'What answer did he give you?' asked Agamemnon eagerly. 'Will he save the ships from burning?'

'Most noble Agamemnon,' replied Odysseus, 'Achilles will have none of you or your gifts, and he bade us tell you so.'

Agamemnon's face fell, as he saw his last hope gone; and everyone there was silent, wondering what would become of them and whether they were fated, all of them, to perish in the land of Troy.

At last Diomedes spoke. 'King Agamemnon, it would have been best had you not humbled yourself to Achilles or offered him gifts. He has ever been proud, and now you have made him prouder still. But let him do as he will, he and all his men, and let us put him from our minds and think instead thoughts of valour: how well we may acquit ourselves tomorrow. There is no profit in sitting here sadly and regretting what might have been, so let us now go and take our rest, and thereby gain what strength we may to serve us in good stead when day is come.'

Agamemnon sought to hold back no man; and so they went, each to his own hut, and lay down to rest and sleep.

<br>

VII

## *The Spy*

YET amongst the kings and princes of the Greeks there were two who could not rest that night: the two sons of Atreus lay wakeful in their huts.

Menelaus could not sleep through concern for his friends and comrades, who now faced defeat and ruin for his sake, because of Helen, his wife; and at last he rose, meaning to go and wake his brother Agamemnon, to see if he could gain any comfort from him.

But Agamemnon tossed and turned upon his bed, trying in vain to devise some way out of the plight to which he had brought all the Greeks through his vindictiveness and folly; then, thinking that if any man could advise him, wise old Nestor could, he rose and put on his tunic and sandals, flinging about his shoulders a fine lion-skin, and taking up a spear, he went out from his hut even as Menelaus came to him.

'Why are you stirring, brother?' asked Menelaus. 'Is it to call us to council once again? Have you some plan whereby we may avert our fate?'

'No, Menelaus. I can see no way at all to avoid defeat. Truly, the immortal gods are with Hector and have deserted me. Yet let us all take counsel once again, and maybe someone of us—wise old Nestor or wily Odysseus, perchance—can devise a means to save us. So go, Menelaus, rouse Ajax, son of Telamon, and Idomeneus, and the other leaders whose ships lie farthest from here, whilst I go to good old Nestor.'

Willingly Menelaus hurried away to carry out his brother's commands, glad of any action which would empty his mind of its tormenting thoughts.

Nestor was lying asleep on his bed in his hut, with his armour close at hand beside him, and he awoke at once when Agamemnon came to him, carrying a torch lighted at one of the watch-fires. 'Is it Agamemnon? What is amiss?' he asked, sitting up.

'Good Nestor, I cannot sleep. I fear the dawn; I fear an attack by night. Comfort me with your wisdom. Let us go together and see that the watchmen on the rampart are not sleeping, and let us call our friends together for counsel.'

Nestor rose instantly and pulled on his tunic. 'Let us do as you say, good King Agamemnon.' He sat to fasten his sandals, and paused to frown up at Agamemnon in the torchlight. 'I shall chide Menelaus when I see him, that he has left you to rouse us all yourself. He is at fault to lie asleep. He should be with you now when you have need

of him. I know your love for him, great king, yet you must
not mind my saying so.'

Agamemnon smiled. 'This time you do him wrong. I
know that he is easy-going; and often he seems slow to
assert himself, but that is through respect for me, that I
may first make known my opinion and my wishes. Yet
tonight he rose even before I did, and has now gone to call
those leaders whose ships lie farthest from ours.'

Nestor wrapped around himself his thick cloak of
shaggy, purple-dyed wool, and together he and Agamemnon went to arouse Odysseus, who came from his hut to
them, alert in an instant. But, going next to Diomedes,
Nestor found him, in all his armour, lying outside his hut
on an ox-hide, his head resting on a rolled-up woollen rug,
with Sthenelus close by, and all about them their chosen
comrades, in their armour, their heads pillowed on their
shields, and beside each man stood his spear ready to hand,
thrust into the earth: for Diomedes was taking no chances
of a surprise attack. He sat up when Nestor woke him, and
when he heard that he was summoned to an assembly, he
said, 'Must you go all along the shore, good Nestor, calling
the leaders to council? Is there no one younger to run
errands for King Agamemnon?'

'There is indeed one younger,' said Nestor. 'You can go
for me, if you will, and rouse Ajax of Locris.' And Diomedes went at once, snatching up his spear and running
off into the darkness.

Nestor praised all the watchmen whom he found alert
at their posts, knowing full well, in his wisdom, that just
approbation and well-earned approval can do much to
bring courage and confidence to a man.

When all the kings and princes of the Greeks were gathered together, they sat, and Nestor was the first to speak, for it was to him that they all looked for counsel. 'There is nothing,' he said, 'so disheartening as uncertainty. It would be well if we sent forth some brave man to the Trojan camp to spy out, if he can, whether they are stirring and mean to attack tonight, or whether they will sleep and leave all fighting until the dawn. Is there one amongst us who would do this thing and win great honour from his comrades?'

Diomedes said, 'I will go. I am not afraid. But if someone else were to come with me, our advantage would be doubled. For four eyes notice more than two, and what one man misses, another often sees.'

Immediately Ajax, son of Telamon, and Ajax of Locris offered to go with him. Odysseus offered, and Menelaus; Antilochus, Nestor's son, and Meriones the Cretan, the friend of Idomeneus.

Before it could be decided upon who should go with Diomedes, Agamemnon said quickly, 'Good Diomedes, choose which of them you will to be your companion in your dangerous task. Take with you that man whom you know to be most fitted. Do not think that from respect to a man's rank you must choose him to be your comrade and leave a better man behind, because he is less highly born.' So he spoke, because he feared that Diomedes might choose Menelaus, and he did not want his brother to run so great a risk of being taken or slain by the Trojans.

But Diomedes said, 'If I may indeed choose as I wish, then let Odysseus come with me, for he thinks quickly and can get us quickly out of danger. And he is, besides, much

loved by immortal Athene. If Odysseus comes with me, I
do not doubt that, if we had to, we two would pass safely
through even fire and flames, thanks to his cunning and to
divine Athene.'

Forthwith the two of them made ready to go. They did
not need armour and shining helmets, for the metal of a
breastplate would have rung upon the stones if its wearer
had dropped to the ground to hide, while bright helmets
would have caught the light of the Trojan watch-fires.
Instead, Diomedes put on an ox-hide cap, such as was worn
by the common fighting men, and by the slingers and
archers of Locris, and, since he had left his own sword at
his hut, taking up only his spear when he ran to call Ajax
at Nestor's bidding, he borrowed a sword to take with
him. Meriones lent to Odysseus a curious cap of leather,
plated with slivers of boar's tusk, which had been a much-
prized guest-gift to Prince Molus, Meriones' father; and
gave him, moreover, his own bow and quiver, which he
had with him.

Bidding the others farewell, the two of them set out,
and, as they left the rampart and the trench, they heard on
their right hand the cry of a heron. 'An omen from
Athene,' whispered Odysseus, much pleased; and he prayed
to her. 'Divine daughter of Zeus, as you have ever been
with me in the past, so, I beseech you, be with me tonight.
Grant that we may go amongst the Trojans to their cost,
and return safely to the ships.'

And Diomedes, too, prayed to Athene. 'Great daughter
of immortal Zeus, stand by my side and guard me well;
and when I reach the ships again, I will sacrifice to you a
heifer with gilded horns.'

So they prayed to Athene as they moved across the plain, amidst the fallen arms and the dead; and Athene heard and granted their prayers.

Cautiously they made their way towards the Trojan camp, under cover of the rocks and bushes which stood here and there upon the plain. When they were about half-way between the ships and the blazing watch-fires of the Trojans, Odysseus caught sight of a quick and furtive shadow coming towards them. He grasped at Diomedes' arm. 'See there, someone is coming from the camp. It may be no more than someone out to rob the dead, but it may be someone sent to spy upon the ships. Let him pass us by, and when he has gone a little distance, let us turn and follow him. In that way he will be between us and the shore, and cannot escape us back towards the city.'

Thereupon Odysseus and Diomedes lay down amongst the slain, as though they, too, were dead; and after a little, suspecting nothing, Dolon—for it was he—went swiftly past them.

When he was a short way on, they rose and ran after him, towards the ships, and hearing the sound of their steps, Dolon stood and waited, supposing them to be his comrades from the camp, come after him to tell him of a change in Hector's plans. But when they were within a spear's throw of him, in spite of the darkness, he knew them for strangers and fled—straight for the ships, since there was no other direction in which he might go.

Rapidly they gained on him, and Diomedes called out, 'Stand, or I shall kill you!' and with that, flung his spear so that it passed over Dolon's head and stuck in the ground a little way before his feet, missing him on purpose; since they did not want to kill him until he had told them all they wished to know.

Terrified, Dolon stood still, and Odysseus and Diomedes came up with him and seized him by the arms. Instantly he cried out, 'Take me alive, for my father is a rich man, and will pay you a good ransom for his son.'

'Who talks of death?' said Odysseus chaffingly, with seeming friendliness. 'Put such thoughts out of your mind. But come, tell us what you do here, so close to the ships in the darkness of the night?'

Trembling, Dolon said, 'Fool that I was, I let myself be lured by Prince Hector's promises. He swore to give me the horses of Achilles, son of Peleus, if I would go amongst the ships of the Greeks and find out whether they had thoughts of flight, or whether they were determined to fight again tomorrow.'

Odysseus chuckled. 'Truly, my friend, you set your hopes high. The horses of Achilles! Indeed, you would not find it easy, I think, to drive the immortal steeds of King Peleus, which the gods gave to him. But tell me, how is the Trojan camp disposed? What watches do they keep? Where does Hector lie tonight?'

'Hector is not now in the camp. He has gone to take counsel of the great lords of Troy at the burial mound of Ilus, nearer to the city. On the camp there is no special guard, save what is customary, around the fires. The allies are all sleeping, they keep no guard—why should they?— for their wives and children are far away, and safe.'

His face hidden by the night, Odysseus narrowed his eyes and pulled thoughtfully at his dark-red beard. 'The allies,' he asked, 'do they lie amongst the Trojans, or apart from them?'

'They lie apart,' answered Dolon. 'But why do you question me? Do you seek to enter the camp?' In a desperate bid to save his own people, the terrified man said quickly, his words falling over each other with eagerness and fear, 'But why run into more danger than you need? Yonder, on the very edge of the camp, lie the Thracians, newly come to help us, all unguarded, with Rhesus, their king. King Rhesus has the finest horses that I have ever seen, swift, and white as snow, a fair prize for any man. Now take me to your ships and leave me bound to wait for your return, and go and try your luck with the horses of King Rhesus, and see whether I have not told you truly.'

'We shall indeed try our luck with the horses of King Rhesus,' said Diomedes, drawing the sword that he had borrowed. 'But as for you, it is best this way.' And he struck off Dolon's head.

From the severed head they took Dolon's cap of ferret-skin, and the wolf's-hide cloak from his body, and his bow and spear; and Odysseus, taking them into his hands, raised them high to Athene. 'The spoils are to you, great goddess,' he said. 'But now lead us safely to the horses of King Rhesus.'

He hid the cap and the wolf-skin and the weapons in the branches of a tamarisk bush, marking the place with an armful of reeds and boughs, that they should know it again; and then swiftly the two of them made their way towards the spot which Dolon had pointed out to them.

When they were come to the place, they found that it was even as he had said, and the Thracians kept no watch,

but were sleeping, each man alongside his weapons, with
his two horses hobbled close beside him. And in the midst
of his men slept King Rhesus, with his snow-white horses,
gleaming in the darkness, tethered to the side of his gilded
chariot.

'There lies Rhesus, and there stand his horses,' whispered
Odysseus. 'Now we must make speed. Do you kill the
men, whilst I loose the horses and bring them forth.'

Diomedes drew his sword and, like a silent shadow,
striking down left and right of him, he slew all who lay
within his reach; and after him came Odysseus, thrusting
aside the dead men to make a path for the horses. Twelve
men did Diomedes slay, before any woke from sleep, and
the thirteenth was King Rhesus himself, as he stirred, disturbed by a sound.

Swiftly Odysseus freed the horses from the chariot rail,
fastening them together with their reins, while Diomedes
stood, sword in hand, peering all about him through the
darkness, ready to strike down any other man who woke.

Odysseus led the horses safely forth from amongst the
dead and sleeping men, hurrying them along with blows
from Meriones' bow, since he had no whip. Then he
whistled to Diomedes in sign that all was well, and Diomedes rejoined him hastily; and, not without a regret for
the gilded chariot which they had to leave behind, they
each leapt upon a horse and urged it on towards the
shore; while behind them they heard shouts and cries of
dismay, and the neighing of horses, as the Thracians awoke
and found their king and comrades slain.

At the tamarisk bush they pulled up the sweating horses
long enough for Diomedes to dismount and seize their

trophies and hand them to Odysseus, and then they were away again to the ships, where the others awaited them anxiously, before the trench.

Much praise did the two of them win then, as their friends crowded round to admire the horses, asking eager questions; and, as they crossed the trench and passed through the gateway in the rampart, all the kings and princes of the Greeks felt encouraged, and somehow less apprehensive of the morrow.

Diomedes tied the Thracian horses amongst his own, beside those of Aeneas; and the spoils of Dolon Odysseus set up in the stern of his ship until daylight came and he could offer them fittingly to Athene, at the time when Diomedes sacrificed the heifer. Then he and Diomedes stripped off their clothing and washed themselves clean in the sea, and, after they had made a drink-offering to Athene, who had cared so well for them that night, and drunk a cup of good wine themselves, they lay down to rest, for the little time that remained before the dawn.

# VIII

## The Battle

I N the morning, very early, Agamemnon called upon all the Greeks to arm for battle. He himself put on his breastplate of bronze inlaid with bands of gold and shining tin and blue enamelling, with a blue serpent writhing up each side, and took up his fine shield, ornamented with bands of tin and blue glaze about a likeness of the head of the Gorgon, a terrible monster, fit to strike dread into the heart of an enemy.

The daylight had brought courage to him, though he still had little hope of victory; yet he was determined to fight his best that day, that he might be an example to all who had sailed at his command for Troy, even as a high king should.

And so the Greeks gathered together before the rampart

and the trench, and ranged against them were the Trojans, led by Hector and Aeneas, and by Polydamas, a noble Trojan who had been born in the same hour as Hector. And Hector seemed to be first here, then there, and everywhere at once, as he went amongst his men with encouragement and orders.

The two armies met that morning in equal battle, and, for all they had been worsted by the Trojans the day before, the Greeks now held their own, and gave no ground. And so it was until midday, while Zeus, the father of all, in everlasting majesty, looked down upon the city and the ships, upon the flashing weapons, and upon slayers and slain alike.

But when the sun had reached its highest and would climb no more that day, the Greeks began to press the Trojans back towards their city, and many, fearing death, turned their chariots and fled away. The Greeks pursued them across the ford of the Scamander, past the high burial mound of Ilus, crowned by a pillar set up in memory of the ancient king who lay below it, and past the wild figtree, to the very gates of Troy.

Yet, by the sacred oak at the Scaean Gate, the Trojans rallied, and stood to meet the Greeks' attack, and the Greeks could go no farther, such being the will of Zeus, even as he had promised Thetis. For in the fighting near the gate, Agamemnon was wounded in the arm, and though at first he did not cease from fighting, after a while his arm grew stiff and he could no longer hold his spear. So, calling to the Greeks to hold firmly the ground that they had gained, he mounted his chariot and returned to the ships.

When the Trojans and their allies saw that the high king of Greece himself was wounded and gone from the battle, they took heart, and Hector went about amongst them calling out to them, 'See, the leader of all our enemies is wounded. The Greeks will lack the courage to stand against us now, and Zeus will again give us this day's victory.'

The Trojans shouted in answer, and with Hector at their head, they hurled themselves upon the Greeks, driving them back as far as the burial mount of Ilus. There Odysseus, fighting valiantly, was aware of Diomedes close by, and called to him, 'Come, my friend, stand beside me. Together, and with Athene's help, we shall hold off all Troy. For Hector must not reach our wall again today.'

Diomedes came to him willingly, and the two of them together wrought great havoc amongst the Trojans, and many did they kill. Hector, seeing that no other could withstand them, came himself towards them, leaping from his chariot, with his chosen warriors close after him. Yet so eager was he, that he easily outstripped all his men.

Diomedes saw him coming and said, dryly, 'See now, Odysseus, here comes death and destruction upon us: Apollo's well-beloved Hector himself. Let him come; we shall not fly before him.' He poised his spear and waited, and when Hector was near enough, he flung it straight at Hector's head. Nor did he miss his aim; but the spear was stayed by the stout bronze of Hector's helmet, which had been given him for his protection by immortal Apollo himself. Yet, though unwounded, Hector was all but stunned by the blow, and he hastened back to safety amongst his followers, and there, all dazed, he sank to the ground amidst them. But after a very little time he rose again, mounted his chariot, and was driven away, while Diomedes reviled the chance which had saved Hector from his spear.

'Truly,' he said bitterly to Odysseus, 'bright Apollo loves Hector well and guards him constantly. But one day, if Zeus is willing, we shall meet again; and if on that day there stands by me a god who loves me as Apollo loves him, then Hector had best take care.' And so Diomedes had to content himself with killing lesser men, which he did with a will, while Odysseus fought beside him, and Sthenelus waited close by with the chariot and horses.

Yet as Diomedes was stripping the armour from a warrior he had slain, to give it to Sthenelus, he was seen by Paris, who had climbed out of reach of the spears to the top of the burial mound of Ilus, from where he had been watching, leaning idly against the pillar. Paris chose out an arrow from his quiver, and sheltering behind the pillar, loosed it at Diomedes. The arrow passed right through his foot, pinning him to the ground. At the look of pain and surprise on his face, as for a moment he wondered what had happened, Paris broke into laughter, and coming from his hiding-place, shouted down to Diomedes, mocking him. 'That was a good shot of mine, son of Tydeus, yet I wish it had been even better. Had I hit you in the body, the Trojans would no longer bleat before your spear like goats before a lion.'

Diomedes looked up at him, undismayed but furious. 'You cowardly archer,' he shouted back, 'you prattler with your curled hair, stealer of the wives of better men, if you came down here and faced me, you would find your bow

and arrows little use. You boast now because your arrow has grazed my foot, but I take no heed of such small matters. The blows of a coward and a weakling are like the feeble blows of a woman. Not such are my blows.'

Paris laughed at him, yet he did not wait for Diomedes to take vengeance for his arrow, but ran down the farther slope of the burial mound and made his way lightly to where Hector fought, on the far side of the battle.

With Odysseus standing by to guard him, Diomedes sat down upon the ground, broke off the arrow-head and drew the shaft out from his foot. But in spite of his words to Paris, he was forced to heed his wound, and though it grieved him to leave Odysseus with whom he had done so many bold deeds that day, he limped to his chariot, leaning on his spear, and climbed in beside Sthenelus, who immediately turned the horses and drove his friend back towards the ships, greatly distressed for him.

Odysseus, left alone to stand against the Trojans, was torn in his mind as to what it were best to do: to stay and perhaps be slain or captured, or to leap into his chariot and fly to safety. Yet he soon made up his mind, and setting his back against his chariot, prepared to defend himself, for he scorned to fly. And so mightily did he repel the attacking Trojans, who had thought that he would fall an easy prey to them now that he was alone, that before long the Trojan dead lay all about him.

But at last he was wounded by a spear-thrust in the side; though immediately he slew the man who had given him the wound, even as he turned to run to safety after his too daring attack, plunging his spear through the man's back, between his shoulders, while making light of his own hurt. Yet when the Trojans saw that he was wounded, they believed that he could not long resist them, and they fell upon him eagerly. Odysseus, seeing the great danger he was in, shouted aloud for help, in the hope that someone of the Greeks might hear him.

Three times he shouted loudly, and each shout Menelaus heard, where he fought a little way off. He called to Ajax, son of Telamon, who fought beside him, 'That was the voice of Odysseus. He is in danger. Come, let us go to him.' And together they fought their way through the press of men who surged about Odysseus, like jackals around a wounded stag.

When tall Ajax came amongst them, striking about him on every side, with his huge shield slung before him, so that none of their weapons could touch him, the Trojans drew back fearfully, and Menelaus, going to Odysseus, helped him to his chariot, and carried him safely from the fight.

But Ajax, all alone, did great things against the Trojans, putting fear into their hearts, so that none dared stand against him.

On the far side of the battle, Hector fought against old Nestor and King Idomeneus, and Machaon, the physician; and many of their warriors did he cut down, to leave them lying dead upon the plain. Yet the Greeks would have held their own, in spite of Hector's slaughter, had not Paris, guarded safely by his own followers, taken aim at Machaon with an arrow from his bow, wounding him in the right shoulder, so that Machaon could no longer hold a weapon to defend himself. Seeing this, his comrades were afraid that he would be slain, and Idomeneus said to Nestor, 'Good old king, I beg you, take Machaon up with you into your chariot and drive with him to safety, lest he is slain in spite of us. For a physician is worth many men.'

Immediately Nestor, who, old man though he might have been, would not have left the battlefield for any other cause, made his way to where Machaon stood, one hand clasped to his wounded shoulder, the blood trickling between his fingers, and took him up beside him in his own chariot and turned the horses' heads towards the shore, urging them on with voice and whip, out of the press of battle to the safety of the ships.

While Hector fought on against Idomeneus and the men of Crete, Cebriones, a son of Priam and half-brother to Hector, who was Hector's charioteer that day, saw from the chariot, over the heads of the fighting men, to where Ajax fought so mightily amongst the Trojans. 'Brother,' he said, 'I see a warrior who is slaying too many of our men. From the size of his shield, I think he is the son of Telamon. Would it not be well that we should go and prevent him from such mighty deeds? For the Greeks are taking heart from his achievements and our men are being hard pressed.'

Hector was willing, and the horses bore them swiftly through the battle towards Ajax, Hector striking down right and left of him from the chariot as they went, and scattering the Greeks before him.

And Zeus, from where he watched on Mount Ida, mindful of his promise, turned the tide of battle for the last time that day, filling the Trojans with courage and the Greeks with dismay, so that, little by little, Ajax and the Greeks were driven back towards the shore, yet always striving to retain every step they yielded. Right to the trench and the rampart they were driven; and there they sought to make a last stand to hold back Hector.

Ajax, in the forefront of the battle, fought like fifty men, and beside him stood Eurypylus from rugged Thessaly. Yet brave Eurypylus did not fight long at the side of Ajax. For a third time that day, an arrow loosed by Paris at a leader of the Greeks found its mark, and Eurypylus, wounded in the thigh, had to draw off from the fighting, under cover of his comrades' shields, and make for safety. Shouting all the time to the Greeks to rally to the defence of Ajax, he crossed the track over the trench and went through the gateway in the rampart, limping and leaning on his spear, to make his way alone towards his hut, bidding those of his followers who would have gone with him to return to Ajax, who had far greater need of their help.

## IX

## *The Broken Gate*

As the chariot bearing Nestor and Machaon neared
the shore, Achilles, watching the battle from afar,
standing at the high stern of his ship, saw it and
knew it for Nestor's chariot, carrying a wounded man. He
called out to Patroclus, who came to stand by him.

'Things go ill with Agamemnon's advocates today.'
Achilles gave a wry smile. 'Soon, I do not doubt, we shall
have them here again, clasping my knees in supplication
and telling us their need is very great. I have this moment
seen Nestor's chariot, carrying a wounded man. From
here, he looked to me like Machaon the physician, but the
horses were too swift and the chariot too far away for me
to be sure of it. If it is Machaon who is wounded, that will
be a great loss to the Greeks, for, from all that I have seen

of this day's fighting, by evening there will be much work for both physicians. Go quickly, Patroclus, and find out if it was indeed Machaon, and how badly he is hurt.'

Patroclus immediately leapt down from the ship and set off to do as Achilles asked, running along the shore past ships and huts until he reached the place where the ships from Pylos were drawn up, in that line of ships closest to the sea. He went to the hut of Nestor, and there he found Machaon lying, and old Nestor sitting beside him, refreshing himself with wine sprinkled with cheese and barley meal, which he was drinking from a cup which he had brought from home: a fine cup it was, embossed with golden studs, and four-handled, and on each pair of handles were golden doves.

As soon as they saw Patroclus, Nestor rose to welcome him, bidding him sit and drink with them. But Patroclus thanked him and said, 'I cannot delay, for Achilles has sent me to find out if it were indeed Machaon whom you brought wounded from the battle. I see that it is, and with all my heart I grieve for him and for the Greeks.' When Nestor would have pressed him to stay for a little, he answered, 'I must not, good king, for Achilles will be impatient for an answer to his question, and it would be wise not to keep him waiting.' He smiled with an affectionate and understanding tolerance of the ways of his friend, and added gently, 'You know how easily he can be angered, and for how little cause.'

He would have gone then, but Nestor said, 'Why should Achilles trouble himself which of the Greeks lies wounded? Diomedes is wounded, and Odysseus, and King Agamemnon himself. Machaon here was struck by an arrow from the bow of false Paris. But what cares Achilles for our sorrows? He is concerned only with his own glory. He waits, no doubt, until he sees our ships go up in flames and his anger is appeased, not only by Agamemnon's death, but by the death of all the Greeks, his friends and one-time comrades in battle. When we are defeated utterly, then, perhaps, his cold heart will melt and he will pity us—too late. Oh, Patroclus, that time when Odysseus and I were in Phthia, at the house of King Peleus, before you and Achilles sailed with us for Troy, I remember how eager you both were to go with us. And when he parted from him, Peleus bade his son be always brave and let no man surpass him in fighting skill. But your father Menoetius said to you—I myself heard him say it—"Achilles is the son of a greater man than I, and he will one day rule over lands far wider than any I have ever ruled, and, young as he is, he is a finer warrior than you will ever be; but you, my son are the elder and the wiser. Never forget that, and be ready always with guidance and good counsel, for he loves you well and will pay heed to you where he would listen to no man else." Have you forgotten your father's words? Even now, when all is almost lost for us, speak to Achilles and plead with him for all our sakes, and we may yet be saved. If he will not fight himself then let him send his men to help us, for they have held many days from the fighting and they will be fresh, while we have fought long and are weary, and defeat and death seem very close to us.'

Patroclus, much moved, said, 'Good king, I will do all I can for you, you have my word on it.' And he hurried away westwards along the shore, back towards Achilles' ships.

But when he drew level with the ships of Odysseus,

before which stretched the assembly place, there he met
with Eurypylus, alone, limping from the battle with
Paris's arrow-head in his thigh. When Patroclus saw him,
streaked with the sweat and dust of battle, the blood
streaming down his leg to the ground, he cried out with
pity, 'You, too, Eurypylus! What an ill fate the gods have
sent us. How many good Greek warriors will lie still and
cold tonight, robbed of their lives by Trojan weapons.'

'Good Patroclus,' gasped Eurypylus, 'help me to my
hut, for I can walk alone no farther.'

And though he knew Achilles would be waiting for him
with steadily growing impatience, Patroclus did not hesitate, but turned aside, and with an arm about him, supported Eurypylus to his hut. There, a servant saw his
master coming, wounded, and hastily spread rugs upon
the floor for him, and fetched a basin of warm water.

'Cut the arrow-head from my thigh for me, Patroclus,'
said Eurypylus, 'for you have skill in such matters, and our
two physicians can give me no aid, for I saw Podaleirius in
the thickest of the fighting, while good Machaon is himself
wounded and needing a physician.'

So Patroclus cut the arrow-head from his flesh and
washed the wound clean with gentle hands, and bound it
with strips of linen, talking to Eurypylus lightly all the
while, that he might think of other things; and afterwards
stayed beside him until he was eased a little from his pain.

But while Patroclus had been speaking with old Nestor,
the Greeks had been forced to retreat within their wall,
shut fast their gates, and prepare to defend their ships and
huts from the elated and triumphant Trojans.

But though the Trojans might exult in their triumph, they could in no way get their chariots across the trench and over the rampart, and when the first flush of their victory had cooled, they found that they could do no more than fling stones and shoot arrows over trench and rampart, and shout taunts at the defenders. Hector, frustrated, drove everywhere among_t his men, urging them to cross the trench, exhorting and upbraiding, wild at being thwarted. Yet not even his own horses, for all his lashing, could cross the wide trench, but held back on the brink, neighing shrilly, while Hector chafed at this setback to his final conquest.

But Polydamas came to him, and Hector paused to listen to his words; for though Polydamas was a lesser warrior than Hector or Aeneas, his counsel was ever much respected. 'It is folly,' said Polydamas, 'to seek to drive our horses across the trench. At the top it is too wide for them, and at the bottom it is narrow, and set with stakes, besides. And even should Zeus, by his favour, permit our chariots to cross the trench, how could the horses drag them over the rampart? No, good Hector, let us leave our chariots with a single man to guard each one and to hold the horses, while the rest of us, on foot, leap across the trench and climb the rampart. Where Hector leads, all the Trojans and their allies will follow.'

Hector was pleased by the advice of Polydamas, and immediately ordered all his lords and the leaders of the allies to alight from their chariots and lead their men on foot. Then he divided them all into five companies, setting each company a portion of the wall to attack.

One company he and Polydamas led against the

mid-most part of the wall. This company was the most in numbers, and in it were the bravest of the warriors and those most eager to enter the camp. With them went Cebriones, for Hector knew his half-brother's courage and skill too well to leave him with no more to do than guard a chariot and horses.

The second company was led by Paris and Agenor, one of the sons of Lord Antenor, Priam's good counsellor; for, though Paris was not loved by the Trojans, and though such as he was more aptly armed with a bow and arrows than with spear or sword, he was a great prince and King Priam's son, and it was fitting that he should be called upon to lead.

Helenus and Deïphobus, both younger sons of Priam and Queen Hecuba, commanded the third company; while the fourth was led by Aeneas, and with him were two other sons of Antenor. Over the fifth company Hector put Sarpedon and Glaucus, for the two kings of Lycia were the most important of the allies.

Then, shouting their defiance, with weapons ready and brandished, the Trojans leapt across the trench or scrambled over the stakes and sought to climb the rampart beyond; while from the top of the rampart the Greeks flung down stones upon them. They dropped great lumps of broken rock, which they could hardly lift with both their hands, upon the Trojans' heads; and pelted them with smaller stones from slings.

But the Trojans were many and determined, as they swarmed before the rampart, digging away the piled-up earth, rolling stones and rocks aside to uncover the supporting baulks of timber; and these they tore at, that they might make a breach to enter by. And none were more determined in their attack than the men led by Hector and Polydamas and young Cebriones.

Ajax, son of Telamon, and Ajax of Locris went up and down upon the rampart shouting encouragement to the Greeks, taking a hand here or there, wherever the assault was strongest; the tall son of Telamon lifting up great stones, too heavy for any other man to raise unaided, and dropping them down upon the enemy, and Ajax of Locris leaning from the rampart to thrust with his spear at any Trojan who had found a foothold on the exposed wooden supports.

Yet for all the Trojans' furious assault, the wall still held, and the Greeks, not yet entirely despairing, fought with high courage and unflagging determination, for they were now, and for the first time, defending their ships and their own possessions: the huts which had been their homes for almost nine long years, their slaves and cattle, their supplies and stores of grain, and the hoards of booty which were hidden on the ships.

If Hector's attack was the most to be feared, yet not far behind it in persistence was the attack of Glaucus and Sarpedon. In the very forefront of their company's assault, brave Sarpedon called out to his fellow-king, 'Glaucus, why is it that we two are held in honour above all our people? Why are our cups always filled first, and why is it to us that the choicest portions of the meat are always given? Why are we held in reverence above all men in Lycia? Is it that we may prove ourselves to be no better than any others? Come, let us so bear ourselves that our people may say of us, "Truly, they are fine men, these two kings of ours who rule in Lycia. They eat of the best in the land, and drink the richest wine; but so, too, is their might above all other men's, and they excel in deeds of war." Oh, Glaucus, my dear friend, had I my will, and all eternity to live, then would I never again go out to battle, nor would I let you go forth to cruel war. But seeing that things are as they are, let us go forward bravely, whether we win glory for ourselves by our deeds, or whether we win glory for another by our deaths.' So saying, Sarpedon renewed his attack, and Glaucus with him, and after them pressed the army of the Lycians.

The king of the men of Athens, who held that part of the wall where they attacked, was afraid of their might, and he called out to Ajax, son of Telamon, who stood by Teucer on the wall, a short way off, asking for his help. But such was the din of battle, the shouting of the attackers and the cries of the wounded, the clash of shields and the hammering of stones upon the gates as the Trojans tried to break them down, that Ajax did not hear him; so he sent one of his men, though he could ill spare him, running along the walls to Ajax and his brother.

Immediately he heard of the Athenians' plight, Ajax, with a shout to Ajax of Locris to fight for all three of them while he and his brother were gone, set off with Teucer, to find the Lycians clambering up the ramparts, and the men of Athens in confusion.

Teucer fitted an arrow to his bow, and Ajax, his huge shield not now held to shelter his brother, but slung at his back, took up a large jagged rock and flung it at a Lycian warrior, one of the chosen comrades of Sarpedon, shattering his helmet and killing him instantly. Teucer's first

arrow struck Glaucus in the arm, so that he had to drop
back from the rampart to the bottom of the trench. Blood
pouring from his arm, he climbed the farther side of the
trench and made his way towards his chariot, that his
charioteer might bind up the wound for him.

But Sarpedon, half-way up the rampart, found a firm
foothold and thrust upwards with his spear, killing the
man who held that stretch of the wall directly above him.
Then, before any other man could come to take the dead
man's place, Sarpedon, tugging mightily with all his
strength at a large baulk of timber, dragged it down,
making a narrow gap in the rampart.

Yet before he could take advantage of the opening and
leap within the wall, Ajax and Teucer came against him.
Teucer loosed an arrow which struck him on the breastplate but did not pierce it, and Ajax thrust a spear against
his shield and forced him downwards. But he was undaunted. He turned and called out to his men, 'Come, my
Lycians, do not leave me to leap the wall alone and fight a
path unaided to the ships. Come with me, all of you. The
more men who set their hands to it, the easier will be our
task.' And the Lycians crowded about him, clambering up
the rampart to the breach that he had made.

But to brave Sarpedon was not to be the glory of being
the first within the wall, for Ajax and Teucer between
them rallied the defenders, and they stood, a strong line, all
along the top of the rampart at that place, raining down
stones and arrows upon the Lycians, and forcing back with
their spears any they could reach.

Soon it was much the same all along that central portion
of the wall which was being attacked, with the Trojans

and their allies climbing up the rampart, yet never quite
gaining the top, and battering in vain on the strong gates
set here and there; and the Greeks valiantly defending the
wall that they had built, yet never able to do more than
barely to repel the attackers, quite powerless to put them
to flight.

And thus it went until Zeus, who had not forgotten his
promise made to Thetis, gave great glory to Hector, who
stood before the largest of the gates, that which was set in
the very middle of the wall. A broad gateway of double
gates, wide enough for the chariots of the Greeks to pass
in and out from camp to plain, it was built of tree-trunks
and bolted with two huge wooden bars. Against this gate
Hector and Polydamas and their chosen warriors had hurled
themselves time after time, until the timbers had bent and
groaned, yet still the gate had held. Then Hector, in-
furiated and beside himself, snatched up a huge rock torn
from the rampart and struck again and again upon the gate
so mightily that the bars could not hold against such im-
portunate knocking, and at last gave way. With a shout of
triumph, Hector took up his weapons, and thrusting the
gates apart, he leapt within, a spear in either hand, his armour
flashing in the bright afternoon sunlight and the horsehair
crest of his gleaming helmet streaming out behind him.
In that moment of his victory, none but the immortal gods
themselves could have held him back, and no Greek there
dared oppose him. For an instant he stood there alone,
terrible to see, then he shouted over his shoulder to his
men as he sprang forward, and they surged after him,
driving before them the defenders of the gateway.

All along the wall the Greeks leapt down from the ram-

part and fled towards their ships, that they might protect
them with spear and sword and shield and body, now that
the wall had failed; while through the gateway poured the
Trojans and over the rampart they clambered, and everywhere between wall and ships was rout and clamour and
confusion.

The Trojans, thronging after Hector, and already shouting out their triumph cries, did not doubt that they would
take the ships and the camp, and drive the Greeks back to
the very edge of the sea. But, since their wall of wood and
earth and stone was taken, the Greeks drew up, a living
wall, before the first line of ships. Man beside man they
stood, shield touching shield; the bravest in the front rank,
their spears bristling in their hands.

In the centre, opposite the broken gateway, were drawn
up the forty ships of the dead king, Protesilaus, and behind
them, in the second row, lay the forty ships of the Locrians;
and it was here, before the ships of Protesilaus, where the
main attack was made, that Ajax and Teucer and Ajax of
Locris took their stand to await Hector's assault. Ajax, son
of Telamon, and his namesake stood close together, fighting side by side as they had fought so often before, and
behind them and on either side of them stood the warriors
of King Telamon, helmets flashing and spears ready. But
the men who had come from Locris with the other Ajax
did not stand about their leader, for they were men who
wore no crested helmets and carried no spears or shields,
but trusted in their bows and slings, rather than in close
fighting; and now they stood behind the ranks of the men
from Salamis, sending their sharp arrows and their stones
high over their heads against the oncoming Trojans.

Surprised that the Greeks had rallied, and seeing how, quite unexpectedly, they were ready for him, Hector, meeting with a hail of stones and a rain of flashing arrows, paused in his wild advance towards the ships, and drew back a little, halting his men and calling out to them, 'Be resolute, my friends, and we shall conquer. For all that the Greeks have ranged themselves as a wall against us, with the help of Zeus, we shall break through that wall as we broke through the other.' And he sent word to the charioteers who waited beyond the trench, that they should drive the chariots through the gateway and hold them ready, in case they should be needed.

A little way beyond where Hector stood, from amongst the Trojan ranks, Deïphobus, his younger brother, stepped forward, his shield held before him, meaning to hurl his spear against the Greeks. But Meriones the Cretan marked him, and hurled his own spear more quickly, so that it struck, resounding, against Deïphobus' shield; and for one appalled moment, Deïphobus feared for his life. But the shield held and the spear fell to the ground, the head breaking from the shaft with the violence of its impact.

Meriones stepped back amongst his companions, angry that he had lost his last spear to no purpose; and, since he had no other weapon left, he thrust a path through the ranks and made his way along the narrow lanes between the ships, towards the vessels of the Cretans in the second row, that he might fetch another spear from his hut. As he reached the king's hut, which stood before those of the lesser lords, he met Idomeneus himself, a spear in either hand, returning to the battle after seeing how the Cretan wounded did.

Finding Meriones there, so far from the fighting, Idomeneus was greatly concerned. 'Are you wounded, Meriones?' he asked anxiously. 'Or have you come only to call me to the fighting?'

Meriones smiled at him and shook his head. 'I have but come to fetch a spear, lord. I broke mine, throwing it at the shield of that vainglorious, empty boaster, Deïphobus. I wish that it had killed him, before it broke.'

'There are twenty spears, at least, leaning ready against the wall of my hut. Take one of those, for they are nearer at hand than yours, and I will wait for you.'

Meriones fetched the spear and came running back with it, and together he and Idomeneus hurried towards the fighting.

'At what place shall we join the fighting, lord?' asked Meriones. 'I think that our defence is weakest to the left. Should we go there?'

'When I left the battle, the two sons of Telamon and Ajax of Locris were drawn up in the very centre, facing Hector. They should be a strong enough defence against him. So let us go to where we are most needed, on the left,' replied Idomeneus.

When the Trojans saw the two Cretans approaching to join the battle they attacked them with a will, hoping to slay them both before they had time to strengthen the Greek defence. But they were too slow for Idomeneus, who was as quick and agile as many a younger man, leaping forth from amongst the Greeks to strike down Othryoneus, an important ally, newly come to Troy, one to whom King Priam had promised his daughter Cassandra for a wife, as the price of his aid. Yet he never lived to wed

Cassandra, for he died, slain by the spear of the Cretan king.

Then Antilochus, the son of Nestor, came to join the fighting at that place; and Deïphobus came amongst the Trojans, since he had won no glory against Ajax and his comrades. The battle grew fiercer as the Greeks were heartened by the boldness of Idomeneus; and when he called out a challenge to Deïphobus, Deïphobus did not dare to face him, but went in search of Aeneas, to bid him stand beside him. Aeneas came willingly, and with him came Paris and Helenus, and Agenor, Antenor's son, and all their followers.

When Idomeneus saw them coming, he called out, 'My friends, here comes brave Aeneas against me, a younger man than I. Do not let me have to stand against him all alone.'

Almost before he had finished speaking, Meriones was at his side, and after him came Antilochus, and so they awaited the attack. Fierce was the fighting between them, and in it young Meriones did great deeds, to the pride of Idomeneus. Amongst others, he wounded Deïphobus in the arm, so that Priam's son, in much pain, was led from the battle to where his chariot waited, just within the wall. He mounted into it and was carried back to the city, bewailing his misfortune.

Then Menelaus came from the fighting farther along the line, and Helenus, seeing him and hoping to gain honour by his death, fitted an arrow to his bow. But even as he drew back the bowstring, Menelaus saw him and threw his spear. The flying arrow rebounded from Menelaus' breastplate, but the spear pierced the hand that held the bow, and Helenus darted quickly back amongst his men, hand and bow alike reddened with his blood. Agenor went to him, and taking from one of his followers the sling he carried, with its cord of twisted wool, he bound the wool tightly about Helenus' hand, preventing further bleeding and making a rough bandage to serve until a better could be found in Troy.

Soon after, Hector left the fighting at the centre of the battle, to see how the Trojans fared to the left and right of him. When he came to where Idomeneus and Menelaus were, he found many of the Trojan lords and allies gone from where he had believed them still to be. And on the very left hand of the battle there remained only Paris, encouraging his followers and those of his two brothers.

Anxious and ill pleased, Hector said, 'Most wretched brother of mine, where are all our good comrades who fight in this war for your sake? Where are Adamas and Asius and Othryoneus, who is to wed Cassandra? And where are our brothers, Helenus and Deïphobus?'

Paris's handsome face was haggard beneath his rich-wrought helmet. 'Why do you rail at me now?' he asked wearily. 'I have been fighting ever since you breached the wall. Many other times have I kept from battle, but not today. Adamas and Asius are dead, and Othryoneus is slain by Idomeneus the Cretan. Our brothers are wounded and returned to the city, but, by the grace of Zeus, they are not dead.' Then, seeing Hector's frown and his distress, as he learnt that other, better men had died, while the king of Sparta's false guest still lived and was not even wounded, he made an effort to appease him. With his ready, charming smile he stepped closer, saying, 'But now that you have come to me here, dear brother, tell me what you would have me do. Tell me where the battle is fiercest and where you would have me fight, and I shall do my best for you.'

'The fight is fiercest where good Polydamas and Cebriones stand against the sons of Telamon,' said Hector shortly. But his anger had been turned aside and he went peaceably enough with Paris, back to the fighting at the centre, and did not chide him further.

When Ajax saw Hector returning to the fight, he called out to him, above the noise of clashing weapons, 'Welcome, son of Priam. Come nearer. Do not keep so far away. You thought to take our ships, but you have not won them yet. Soon will come the moment, Hector, when you stand trembling in your chariot, praying to Zeus and to all the immortal gods that your horses may be swifter than hawks, as they bear you from the battle to the safety of your city.'

So Ajax mocked him, and Hector shouted back, 'You speak nonsense, son of Telamon, braggart and boaster that you are. I shall kill you yet—if you stay and do not fly from me.'

And, once again, he led the assault against the Greeks; and battle broke out afresh, with renewed might.

# X

## The Fighting at the Ships

AFTER Patroclus had left them, the din and clamour
of the battle reached to where old Nestor rested in
his hut, in company with the wounded physician,
and he listened to it, much disturbed.

'The noise sounds close,' he said to Machaon, 'closer than
it should be. May the immortal gods grant that the Trojans
have not won through our wall.'

Bidding Machaon stay where he was and not move,
because of his wound, Nestor took a spear and went from
the hut. Hastening up one of the narrow lanes that ran
between his ships, and crossing the wider way which
divided the second row of ships from that which lay nearest
to the shore, he hurried into another shadowed lane between high hulls towards the first line of ships, with the

uproar of the battle growing ever louder in his ears. Even before he saw the fighting, he knew that what he feared had happened, and the Trojans had indeed crossed over trench and rampart and had reached almost to the ships.

For a moment Nestor hesitated, a sturdy, upright, grey-haired figure, standing beside the sheltering hull of someone else's ship, anger and pity urging him to fling himself, without either shield or breastplate, helmet or greaves, and armed only with a spear, into the battle in defence of the ships and huts; while prudence and duty counselled him first, at least, to go and arm himself and acquaint Agamemnon, as leader of the army, with the way things were going. For, Nestor reflected, Agamemnon, having left the battle wounded, long before the Trojans reached the wall, might well still be ignorant of the plight of the Greeks. As always with good Nestor, duty and better judgement won, and he hurried back towards the shore and the third line of ships, where Agamemnon had his huts.

But when he came to the broad way between the third and second rows of ships, he met the three wounded kings, Agamemnon, Odysseus, and Diomedes, coming, all together—Diomedes limping, and each of them leaning on a spear—to learn what they could of the battle. For all of them, having, like Nestor, their huts behind the row of ships nearest to the shore, had heard and been made uneasy by the sudden nearness of the sounds of fighting.

Seeing Nestor hurrying towards them, Agamemnon called out, 'Why have you left the battle, worthy Nestor? Surely Hector has not made good his boast to break down our wall? Such a thing could not be possible unless all the gods were with him. Or are there yet others amongst the kings and princes of the Greeks who, like arrogant, spiteful young Achilles, refuse to fight any longer under my command?'

'It is true, great king, our wall is indeed broken down,' replied Nestor, 'and Hector and the Trojans have driven us back even to the first line of ships. We must take counsel quickly as to how best we can help in the defence.'

Odysseus and Diomedes exclaimed in distress at his words, but Agamemnon, pale and dismayed, said, 'Truly, the immortal gods are against us and would destroy us utterly. The Greeks have now no hope of ever taking Troy. They must endeavour instead, as many as may, to save themselves and their ships. Come now, let us, whose ships lie in the line nearest to the sea, have them dragged down to the water immediately. There let us anchor them just off the shore until tonight, and then, under cover of darkness, let us set sail. At sunset—if then by the grace of Zeus the Trojans leave off fighting—those whose ships lie farther from the shore may drag them down to the sea and set sail with us. For when all things are against one, and even the immortal gods stand with one's enemies, there is no shame in flying from utter ruin.' So he spoke, thinking in his heart that at least his ships and all the treasure they held, and those of Menelaus, which lay by his, would be safe; and reflecting further that, if he sent word at once to Menelaus and bade him call his men from the fighting and make ready to embark, Menelaus, however unwilling, would obey him, as he always did; and so, come what might, the two sons of Atreus would see Greece and their homes again.

After the first shocked instant of silence that followed their understanding of Agamemnon's proposal, it was Odysseus who spoke before the others, and for once he did not stop to choose the words he used. 'By all the gods, King Agamemnon, would you have us basely abandon our friends? You should have led an army of cowards and little men, not such as we are who have fought in the land of Troy for the sake of the sons of Atreus for all but ten years. You had best take care that no more than we, who are beside you now, hear you speak words which no great king should ever be heard to utter.'

Agamemnon glanced at Nestor and Diomedes, seeking support and finding none, then he looked quickly down to the ground at his feet, unwilling to meet again the angry scorn in Odysseus' eyes, old Nestor's expression of pained and stern disapproval, and the contemptuous stare of young Diomedes. He said, as composedly as he might, 'You speak with passion, Odysseus. If you believe that, even hard pressed as they are, the Greeks will not wish to sail from Troy, why then, I will not command them to do so against their wishes.' He paused, and no one spoke. Recovering his self-possession, he looked up at them. 'You have heard my counsel, the best that I can offer. Now gladly will I listen to the counsel of any other man, if he can offer advice that is found more acceptable than mine.' He waited for their answer, outwardly aloof and a little condescending, in the manner of a great king, and inwardly resentful and afraid.

Diomedes looked at Nestor, but saw only a worried frown on his thoughtful face, then at Odysseus, and saw that he was still angry, so, after a moment or two, he spoke.

'I am amongst the youngest of the kings and princes of the Greeks, but since neither Nestor nor Odysseus—both better men than I—has spoken, I shall offer my counsel. I say that there is nothing left for us to do save arm ourselves and go to where our comrades fight, holding back Hector from the ships. Those of us who are already wounded, would do best not to join the fighting, lest we bring more affliction upon our men, by our deaths or capture. But we can at least give them encouragement and exhort them to fight bravely; and the presence of the leader of us all will be some comfort to them. And if—which may the immortal gods forbid—the Greeks should be doomed to perish here, between the Trojans and the sea, why then, we, too, can perish with our friends.'

Nestor and Odysseus received his words with approval, praising his courage; and Agamemnon, seeing there was no help for it, added his assent. And so the four kings hastened to arm themselves and join the Greeks, who fought before the first line of ships, still valiantly holding off the Trojans. There they went, amongst the warriors, urging them on to mightier deeds, and encouraging them greatly.

Before the ships of Protesilaus, where the fighting had all the time been fiercest, and where Hector led the re-newed assault, with Paris close beside him, and he and Ajax taunted one another, Hector followed his words with weapons, stepping forward to fling his spear at Ajax, striking him, but failing to pierce his armour.

Before Hector could draw back amongst his men, Ajax bent and took up one of the huge stones upon which the keels of the ships were resting, and which had been dislodged by the press of men about the ships. This stone he flung at Hector, and it struck him on the chest, passing over the rim of his shield. He staggered, gasping for breath, dropped his spear, twisted about, and fell.

The Greeks, with shouts of triumph, immediately ran forward, but Hector's comrades reached him first. Polydamas, Aeneas, and the two Lycians, Sarpedon and Glaucus, covering him with their shields, fought off the Greeks until he had been borne to safety behind the fighting line. Still senseless, he was laid in his chariot, the charioteer whipped up the horses and drove out through the broken gateway in the wall, and across the plain as far as the bank of the River Scamander, followed by a number of Hector's men, grievously distressed, and fearing that he was dead.

They carried him from the chariot and laid him on the ground, in the shadow of a tree, and taking off his helmet and armour, they poured water over him. Hector revived a little and sat up; then he fell back again, overcome by the effort.

But it was not the will of Zeus that the Greeks should be victorious without Achilles, so when he saw Hector hurt and lying amidst the green rushes on the river's bank, far from where the battle raged, he sent Apollo to him, saying, 'Go now, and put great might into Hector, son of Priam, and be beside him in the battle, that he may have the victory against the Greeks this day.'

Apollo, glad that Zeus no longer forbade him from the battle, went willingly to the help of Hector. He roused him, putting great hope and great determination into his spirit, and great strength into his limbs; and Hector armed

himself and leapt on to his chariot and drove swiftly towards the shore, his elated followers running after him.
And before him went Apollo, the Bright One, wrapped in
cloud, bearing disaster to the Greeks.

At the ships the Greeks had taken heart, hoping that
their most dangerous enemy was slain, and Ajax had done
yet more great deeds. But the Trojans, believing Hector to
be dead, were in despair, and by far the greater number of
them had been driven back from the ships and through the
gateway in the wall, their chariots with them; and they were
fighting just beyond the trench when Hector came amongst
them once again.

The Greeks, seeing him, said, 'It is Hector come again,
whom Ajax slew. The immortal gods are with him or he
would not still be living. Let us go back within the wall, and
once more prepare to defend our ships.' And they retreated
within the wall and made towards the ships, all save the
very boldest, who remained with Ajax and Teucer, Idomeneus and Meriones, to hold back the Trojans at the
trench for as long as they might.

But with the coming of Hector the Trojans were beside
themselves with joy, seeing him alive. And the presence of
Apollo filled them with courage, so that they fought
mightily; yet on the Greeks Apollo cast despair and
terror, so that, at last, even the bravest of them turned and
fled within the wall.

From his chariot, Hector shouted to his men, 'On to the
ships, and leave the spoils till later. Let no man stop to strip
the slain until the day is won. And let no man hold back
from the fighting, or I myself will take his life in that

moment when he falters.' He drove his horses straight at the wall; and after him came the chariots of the Trojan lords and allies, and after them the men who fought on foot; and every man shouted, raising his war-cry.

And immortal Apollo, before them, lightly cast down the rampart into the trench for the length of a spear's throw, making a bridge. And over it the chariots thundered and the Trojans poured, rank on rank, on towards the ships.

The Greeks, once more caught between the Trojans and their ships, and filled, this time, through the all-pervading ill-will of Apollo, by dread and a foreboding of disaster, could only pray to all the gods—in the hope that one at least would answer them—and wait for the attack. Like a wave, the Trojans swept upon them, and the Greeks could not withstand their onrush, but were driven back, close pressed against the tall sides of the ships, so that many of them clambered on the decks and fought from there, leaning down to thrust with their spears at the Trojans in their chariots below.

And yet once again Hector and Ajax met, in the midst of the line of battle, at the ships of Protesilaus, yet neither would give way before the other. Hector called for fire to be brought, that he might burn the ship which Ajax and Teucer defended, but no one could come near enough to fling a torch and yet still be out of reach of the spear of Ajax or the bow of Teucer, who stood high on the deck, never missing his aim. Yet when Teucer set an arrow to his bow for Hector, his bowstring snapped as he was drawing it back, for it was not the will of Zeus that Hector should die that day. Teucer, shaken, said, 'I restrung my

bow this morning. This should not have happened. There
is indeed a god against us.'

'Then leave your bow and arrows, and take up a spear
and come and stand beside me,' replied Ajax. 'If they are to
have the victory, let it not be without a struggle.'

But when Hector and the Trojans saw Teucer's broken
bow, they cried out, 'See, the gods are with us!' and flung
themselves against the ships, so that the Greeks were,
little by little, forced back into the narrow lanes between
the ships, and along them, to take their stand before the
huts at the rear. And there good old Nestor went up and
down amongst their ranks, heartening them and bidding
them fight bravely.

Ajax alone would not leave the ships, but holding a long
grappling-iron in his hands, he leapt from the stern of one
ship to the next, thrusting down with the grappling-iron
any Trojan who tried to climb upon the decks, shouting
all the while to hearten those of his men who still fought
between the ships, 'My friends, have courage and give no
ground. For there can be no retreat for us, who have only
the sea at our backs.'

Yet at last, for all Ajax's untiring efforts, Hector and his
followers seized the stern of one of the ships of Protesilaus and held it, while Hector shouted again for fire to
be brought. And several, seeking to please him, brought
torches and tried to set the ship alight, but Ajax was there
to prevent them while he yet could, his spear ready in his
hand. Twelve men he killed before the ship caught fire.

XI

# *The Parting*

As the sounds of battle from around the ships grew
ever louder, Patroclus came out from the hut of
Eurypylus to learn what had befallen. When he
heard that the Trojans were at the ships, he returned, much
distressed, to Eurypylus, and said, 'My friend, I can no
longer stay with you. Things go ill with the Greeks and
I must hasten to Achilles. With the help of the gods, perhaps I can persuade him to forget his anger. If he can be
persuaded by anyone, then surely I can do it.'

He went from the hut and hurried towards Achilles'
ships, hearing the sounds of battle grow fainter behind him
as he made for the most western point of the camp, where
the battle had not reached. But as he came out from behind
the first line of ships, into the open space which stretched
before them as far as the wall, turning to look, he could

see how fiercely the fight was raging farther along, to the centre; and he could see, too, how close to the ships the Trojans had won; and at the sight, tears came to his eyes, and he wept for the sorrows of the Greeks.

Achilles was waiting where Patroclus had left him, at the stern of his own ship, from where he could clearly see the fighting. He saw how hardly pressed the Greeks were, and how many of them had fallen, and in his heart he pitied them and—though he would not have admitted it, even to Patroclus—felt himself in some measure to blame for their present plight. He pitied them, but he was determined that not for anything in the world would he be reconciled with Agamemnon and fight for him again.

He turned as Patroclus approached him, climbing on to the deck of the ship, and marked his tears and read in them a reproach which, he felt, was not unjust, and, defensively, he spoke with a scorn he did not feel, 'Why, Patroclus, what are you weeping for, like some silly little girl? Have you had bad news from Phthia? Is your father dead, or mine? For surely you do not weep for the Greeks, who have brought their own misfortunes on themselves by upholding Agamemnon when he slighted me?'

But Patroclus knew and loved him too well to fail to perceive the doubts which lay beneath the words, or the carefully hidden pity which his light and mocking tone would have denied. 'I do indeed weep for the Greeks,' he said quietly, 'and it need not make you angry with me. Any man who had not a heart of stone would pity them. Brave Diomedes is wounded, and Odysseus, and even Agamemnon; Eurypylus and Machaon, and I know not how many besides of our friends and former comrades.'

He broke off; but Achilles said nothing, and only looked
at him, his lips set firmly and his eyes unyielding. Patroclus
exclaimed, 'Oh, Achilles, how can you be so pitiless? I
think that good Peleus—who was always kind to me, from
the day when I first came to him, young and friendless, an
exile in his land—I think that he cannot be your father, nor
lovely gracious Thetis your mother; surely, rather, you
were born of the cold grey sea and the stark cliffs that
tower above it, so hard your heart seems.'

Achilles, moved by his words, came down to him on the
deck and would have spoken, but Patroclus, stepping forward, grasped both his hands and cried out, 'Achilles, if
you will not go to fight and save our friends, then let me
go alone and lead the Myrmidons. Lend me your armour,
that the Trojans may see me and think that you have come
to the battle, and they will fear for their lives and retire to
the city.'

'Not for any reason in the world will I be reconciled
with Agamemnon: I have sworn it. And I will not fight
again for him. But you know I would deny you nothing,
Patroclus.' Achilles smiled. 'Take the Myrmidons and
take my armour, and may the gods go with you and give
you a great victory.' Impetuously, he went on, 'Drive the
Trojans back from the ships and save the Greeks. Show
Hector that we are mighty still and do not fear him.' His
eyes shone as he talked of fighting, and his voice was eager at
the thought of battle. 'Oh, Patroclus,' he cried, 'I wish all
the Greeks had sailed for home and all the Trojans were
lying dead before us, that just to you and me alone might
fall the glory of taking Troy. That would be a day worth
having lived to see.' He paused, and his eager smile faded

to a wistful self-mockery. He shrugged his shoulders and sighed a little, then said, 'But go now, Patroclus, and come back soon to me: and come back safely. I will call the men together whilst you arm yourself.'

The Myrmidons raised a great shout of joy when they heard that they were to go to battle once again, for they were weary of idling on the shore, and they grieved for the misfortunes of the Greeks.

Automedon, the charioteer, harnessed Achilles' horses to his chariot. Two of them, Xanthus and Balius, were immortal steeds; their sire was the West Wind, they were the swiftest of all horses, and had been given by the gods to King Peleus, on his marriage. Their manes were combed and shining, and their trappings rich, as befitted them: reins and bridles ornamented with ivory, and carved ivory cheek-pieces. With Balius and Xanthus, in the side traces, was Pedasus, who, though no god-born creature like the other two, was yet well matched with them.

Patroclus put on Achilles' armour: the stout leather greaves with their ankle clasps of silver, the engraved and studded breastplate and the helmet with its flowing crest of horsehair: gifts, also, from the gods to Peleus. About his shoulders he slung Achilles' shield and Achilles' brazen sword with its silver-ornamented hilt, and took up two spears of his own, favourites and well-tried; for, besides Peleus himself, only Achilles might use the spear which the gods had given his father.

When the Myrmidons were armed and ready, Achilles stood up before them and cried out to them, 'For many long days you have grumbled that I kept you from the fighting, and boasted of all that you would do if you might meet the Trojans. Now the time has come for you to make good your vaunting. I shall wait for you to return to me with news of a great victory.' And they answered him with a mighty shout, raising high their spears.

Then Achilles embraced Patroclus, and Patroclus mounted into the chariot with Automedon beside him, the long reins in his hands, and, at the head of all the eager Myrmidons, they led the way to where the fighting raged about the ships of Protesilaus.

But Achilles went alone into his hut, and from a coffer which his mother Thetis had given him he took a cup of finest workmanship, from which he would pour offerings to none save only Zeus himself. This cup he now filled with wine, after he had first cleansed his hands with water, and, standing before the doorway of the hut, he poured out the rich crimson stream to Zeus, and prayed to him for Patroclus, his friend. 'Great Zeus, you who dwell on high Olympus and rule all things, hear and answer my prayer. Today I have sent my friend alone to battle. Let Hector learn to his cost that Patroclus is a strong and fearless warrior even when I am not fighting by his side. Grant him victory and give him glory, and when the battle is over, send him safely back to me.' Then, having made his offering and his prayer, Achilles laid away the cup in the coffer and went once more on to his ship, that he might see all that was to be seen from there of how the battle went.

With an eager anticipation, like that which he had felt before his own first battle, he watched and waited confidently for Patroclus to prove himself, before all the Greeks, to be a great warrior in his own right, and worthy of their respect. For ever in the fighting, until that day, they had fought side by side; and Patroclus, for all his skill and courage, had always been outshone by Achilles, as any man would have been by one who was the finest warrior amongst the Greeks.

Close by the ship which had been fired, where the flames now rose high whilst the Trojans shouted out their triumph, Automedon halted Achilles' chariot and Patroclus turned and spoke to the Myrmidons. 'My friends,' he called to them, 'let us fight today as we have never fought before, and win great honour for our lord, Achilles. Let us show King Agamemnon what manner of man he is whom he has slighted.' They shouted their war cries, stirred up by his words, while Automedon lashed on the horses; and so they fell upon the Trojans who were gathered around the blazing ship.

Patroclus was the first to strike down an enemy. He leant from the chariot and flung his spear at the king of the Paeonians, an ally of the Trojans, who, with his men, stood close about the stern of the burning ship. The aim was true, and the Paeonian king fell to the ground, and never saw his far-off land again.

Utterly dismayed by their leader's death, and believing at first, from the sight of his armour, that the dreaded Achilles had come into battle once again, the Paeonians fled before the Myrmidons' attack, whilst the weary Greeks raised a cheer at the sight of the help which had come so unexpectedly to them, and took fresh heart and set upon their enemies and did great slaughter.

Some of the Myrmidons swarmed upon the blazing ship, and with sand and sea-water they quenched the flames to smoke and smouldering spars, then, leaping from the blackened hull, they joined their comrades in forcing back the Trojans to the rampart and the trench.

Menelaus, Antilochus, Ajax of Locris, and Idomeneus flung themselves into the fight with renewed strength, and many Trojan leaders they killed, throwing into confusion their followers, who fled, in wild disorder, towards the wall, clambering up the rampart and flinging themselves down into the trench.

But many Trojan warriors, though they escaped from the Greeks, did not live to reach the rampart, for they were ridden down by their own chariots, crowding towards the gap that Apollo had made, overturning each other as wheel interlocked with wheel and horses plunged, until the gap was all but blocked by the turmoil of chariots and horses. Soon the trench was filled with shattered chariots and broken wheels and men's bodies; while terrified horses, dragging after them splintered chariot poles, galloped wildly over the plain.

Only Hector, whom Ajax, son of Telamon, still sought to kill, bravely stood his ground with a handful of bold comrades and sought to cover the Trojans' retreat. But at last even he saw the hopelessness of staying longer to fight against Achilles' men, who were fresh and unwearied; and he leapt into his chariot and fled, along with his men, through the gap, now clear, save for the broken chariots and the dead.

And after them came the Greeks, with Patroclus at their head, ever shouting encouragement to those behind him; and Achilles' immortal horses, with brave Pedasus beside them, leapt straight over rampart and trench, and on, amidst the fleeing Trojans, to cut off their retreat. And though Hector in his chariot went safely past, on towards the walls of Troy, many of the Trojans were turned back by the overtaking Greeks, and, hemmed in between the trench and the enemy who had caught up with them, they were forced to stand and fight. And so the battle went on, all across the plain.

Ajax, son of Telamon, and Ajax of Locris, come from the ships, fought with a will, weary though they were; and young Meriones, too, seemed tireless.

Meriones met with Aeneas, fighting over the body of a Trojan warrior whom he had slain. Aeneas aimed a spear at him, but Meriones jumped swiftly and lightly aside, so that the spear missed its mark. Aeneas, disappointed, shouted out, 'You are nimble on your feet, son of Molus, and you are, no doubt, a good dancer, but had my spear reached you, you would not have danced again in battle, or anywhere else.'

Meriones laughed at him and taunted in return, 'Conceited though you may be, Aeneas, you can surely not hope to kill every Greek you meet. You, too, are only mortal, and if you were to stand still and await my spear, you would quickly be gone to Hades' land.'

But Patroclus, who was near, heard him and rebuked him in a friendly manner, saying with sincerity, 'Good Meriones, you are brave and skilled enough to have no need of words to strengthen your blows. Words are for the assembly place: blows are for the battlefield. Words waste breath and kill no enemies, therefore it is always best to fight and say nothing.'

Wherever the fighting was thickest, there Patroclus was.

He fought that day as he had never fought before, and put terror into every Trojan heart, killing leader after leader of the Trojans and their allies. Thus did immortal Zeus, father of gods and men, grant one half of Achilles' prayer.

When brave Sarpedon, king of Lycia, saw how many Trojans fell beneath Patroclus' spear, he cried out to his fleeing men, 'Shame on you, you cowards. Will you desert the Trojans for whom we came to fight from so far away? This man, who wears great Achilles' armour, has done much harm to us today. I will meet with him myself, and learn who he is.' And with that he leapt from his chariot, a spear in each hand, and ran towards Achilles' chariot; and with him ran young Thrasymelus, one of his followers, who would not see his lord go alone into danger.

When he saw Sarpedon coming, Patroclus, too, leapt to the ground and stood awaiting his attack. Each of them cast a spear at the same moment. Patroclus aimed at Thrasymelus, and his spear struck the youth in the middle of his body, and he fell dead even as he was running forward. But Sarpedon's aim flew wide and missed Patroclus. The spear passed to one side of him and struck Pedasus instead, and with a shrill cry the horse sank dying to the ground, while Xanthus and Balius reared and plunged at his fall. The reins became entangled and the chariot pole creaked as though it would have snapped; but quickly Automedon drew his sword and cut free the dead trace-horse, and calmed the others.

Meanwhile, Sarpedon threw his second spear; but once again he misjudged his aim, and the spear passed over Patroclus' shoulder. But Patroclus' second spear pierced Sarpedon below the heart, and he fell to the ground almost beneath the hooves of his own horses. His hands clutched at the dust as he tried to raise himself, and with his last breath he called to Glaucus, his friend and fellow-king, saying, 'Glaucus, dear comrade, now must you alone lead the Lycians, since they have lost one of their two kings. Be valiant for my sake.' And then he spoke no more, for Patroclus ran up and pulled the spear from his breast; and so Sarpedon died, far from his own land.

Glaucus, for all he had been wounded in the arm by one of Teucer's arrows, while trying to climb the rampart, prayed to Apollo for strength to do as Sarpedon had bidden him, and he went from one to another of the Lycian lords, seeking to put heart into them. And to Hector he appealed, saying, 'Sarpedon was the noblest of your allies, and the first, save you, over the Greek wall. Help me now to avenge his loss.'

But they were utterly dismayed by Sarpedon's death, Lycians and Trojans alike, and did not fight for long before they fled, Hector with the others; and the Myrmidons stripped the shining armour from Sarpedon's body and sent it to the ships as a rich prize.

But Sarpedon had been a brave warrior and a good king, and well loved by the gods; and Zeus sent Apollo to fetch his body from the battlefield. Like a cloud from Mount Ida, Apollo came swiftly down, took up Sarpedon from the blood-soaked dust, and gave him to the divine brothers, Death and Sleep, who bore him far away to Lycia, that his own kinsmen might bury him in his own beloved land.

Patroclus, overjoyed by the triumph of the Greeks, for-getting that Achilles waited for his quick return, called to Automedon and leapt into the chariot, and pressed eagerly after the flying Trojans, even to the walls of Troy, slaying all he overtook. Followed by the Myrmidons, he flung himself against the walls at that place, near the old fig-tree, where they were weakest. Three times he charged, and three times Apollo thrust him back; until Patroclus, knowing a god to be against him, desisted and withdrew.

Through the Scaean Gate poured in the Trojans, their shields cast aside that they might run the faster, and Hector in his chariot came after them. In the gateway he waited, wondering whether he, too, should seek safety within the city walls, or whether he should go out and meet Patroclus. And Apollo put new courage into his weary heart and new strength into his tired limbs, and he bade Cebriones, his half-brother, turn again and drive the horses once more into battle, and seek out Patroclus. Back towards the oncoming Greeks the chariot raced; but against no lesser warrior Hector raised his weapons, for he coveted the glory of being the one who should slay Patroclus, whose deeds that day had been unmatched; and he sought, besides, to bring hurt to Achilles, most hated and dreaded of all the enemies of Troy, by killing his best-loved friend.

Patroclus saw Hector's chariot nearing him, and he leapt to the ground, a spear in his left hand, and snatched up from the earth a large, jagged stone. When the chariot came near enough, he flung the stone at Cebriones, and struck him on the brow, so that he fell dead from the chariot, head first, the reins still clutched in his hands, and the horses were halted. Patroclus ran towards him as Hector sprang down, and they fought together over the body of Cebriones, until they were separated by the press of men, both Greeks and Trojans, who crowded about them, parting Patroclus, also, from Automedon and the chariot.

Then those Trojans who had followed Hector drew back with him, little by little, in a group, until they were out of range of the weapons of the Greeks; while those Greeks who had been closest after Patroclus gathered about him. Three times Patroclus ran forward alone from amongst his companions, upon the retreating Trojans, and each time he slew many men. And so, in his last fight, he gained great glory for himself.

But as he was running forward alone for a fourth time, Apollo smote him with confusion, so that his senses reeled and he staggered blindly, stunned and bewildered, close upon his enemies. He bent his neck and Achilles' shining helmet dropped from his head into the dust and rolled beneath the hooves of the Trojan horses, and his long hair fell about his face. The shield-strap broke and his spear slipped from his grasp, as he stood unseeing and all amazed.

And while he stood there, alone and unprotected, a Trojan warrior ran forward and struck him from behind, driving his spear deep between the shoulder-blades. Yet such had been the fighting of Patroclus that day, that the Trojan dared not wait to strike a second blow, but snatched out his spear and fled back to his comrades.

In spite of the fearful wound, Patroclus did not fall, but tried, with faltering steps, to make his way back towards the Greeks. Hector, seeing how he was hurt and defence-less, ran forward, and finding him still standing, thrust his spear into his body and felled him to the ground. Standing over him, he laughed in triumph. 'You fool, Patroclus!

You thought that you could take Troy today, but you forgot Hector, whose spear is ever ready to protect Troy's walls. You thought to take Troy and end the war, but instead the vultures shall tear your flesh before the walls you never reached. Unlucky Patroclus,' he jeered, 'whom Achilles sent out to kill me, while he remained in safety by his ships. Much good his love is to you, now that you are dying at my feet, slain by my spear.'

Patroclus, lying before him, twisted on the ground, his hands scrabbling at the spear-shaft, looked up at him, and saw him only through a mist of pain. 'You need not boast of having killed me, Hector,' he said, 'for you only finished what others had begun. The immortal gods, who took away my strength and disarmed me, were before you, and the man who struck me from behind. You were no more than the third. Yet you have doomed yourself to a short life, Hector, by this deed, for Achilles will avenge me.' His voice grew fainter. 'Remember this moment when he comes soon—very soon—to seek you out.' He gave a last shudder before he lay still, and so died.

'Perhaps, for all you know, I may slay Achilles, as well as his friend,' said Hector. But Patroclus could not hear him. Hector set his foot upon Patroclus and pulled out his spear, and spurning aside the body, he leapt forward to find Automedon and the chariot, thinking to kill yet another whose life Achilles prized, and to win for himself the immortal horses; but Automedon, seeing that Patroclus was dead and beyond his help, overcome by horror, turned the chariot, and Balius and Xanthus carried him swiftly out of reach of Hector's spear.

## XII

## *The Dead Warrior*

FROM where he was, a short way off, hearing the Trojan's shouts of triumph at Hector's victory, and wondering what they meant, Menelaus came closer and beheld how Patroclus was fallen, and instantly he ran forward.

But as he reached the body, the man who had struck Patroclus from behind came from amongst the Trojan warriors, his spear held ready. 'Stand aside, King Menelaus, son of Atreus,' he said, 'and let me take my spoils. For I was the very first who dared to strike Patroclus today, and his body should be mine to take to Troy to win me honour from the people. Stand aside, son of Atreus, unless you would lie beside him, with my good spear through your heart.' And he raised his weapon as though he would have thrown it.

Menelaus did not move. His shield well before him and his spear grasped in his hand, he stood above the body of Patroclus to save it for Achilles. 'It is an ill thing,' he said, 'for a man to boast when the gods have given him some small measure of glory. Go back to your comrades and taunt me not, lest you do not live to boast in Troy.'

The Trojan flung his spear, but Menelaus caught the blow upon his brazen shield, and the good shield held firm, so that the spear did not pass through. Then Menelaus stepped forward swiftly and thrust the point of his own spear through the Trojan's throat, and the man fell dead.

Then might Menelaus very easily have borne the body of Patroclus safely from the battle, for the other Trojans standing near saw with consternation how their comrade was slain, and no other one of them dared face the king of Sparta at that moment. But Hector, finding the horses of Achilles too fleet for him to catch, and looking back and seeing that he was likely to lose the body of Patroclus to Menelaus, turned and hastened towards him, calling out to the Trojans as he came.

When Menelaus saw how he would be ringed about by enemies, his mind was torn two ways. 'How can I fly and save myself,' he thought, 'and leave good Patroclus, who has died for my sake? Yet if I stay and fight alone against Hector and all the Trojans, then soon I shall lie beside Patroclus, and there will be two of us to bring joy to our enemies.' Yet he stood his ground and would not go, but instead called out to any Greeks who might be near enough to hear him, to come to his aid; and most of all to Ajax, son of Telamon, for he believed him to be not far away. 'Together, just the two of us, Ajax and I,' he thought, 'we could hold back these Trojans and save Patroclus for Achilles.'

But Ajax did not hear him, and no one came to his aid; and at last, for all his courage, he was driven back and had to leave the body. He turned and fled swiftly, to seek out Ajax; while Hector triumphantly stripped Achilles' armour from the body of his friend.

Menelaus found Ajax, his huge shield slung about him, urging on his men, for they had been greatly dismayed by the Trojans' recovered strength.

'Come quickly, good Ajax,' cried Menelaus, 'and save the body of brave Patroclus from the Trojans. His armour they will have by now, but we can at least try to take his friend's body back to Achilles.'

At once Ajax went with him to where Hector, the armour safely stowed in his chariot beside the helmet which Patroclus had dropped, was drawing his sword. 'This carrion,' he said, 'shall feed the dogs of our city, but his head I shall have as a trophy to set on a stake upon the walls of Troy.' He lifted Patroclus' head by the long, bright hair, and raised his sword, but with a shout tall Ajax leapt towards him, brandishing his spear, and Hector gave way before him.

Then Ajax, with Menelaus at his side, stood over the body of Patroclus, and the huge shield which had so often sheltered Teucer when he loosed his unerring arrows, now covered dead Patroclus. And so resolutely and firmly the two of them stood there, side by side, that for a time there was no one of all the Trojans that dared oppose them.

But Glaucus the Lycian, grieving for the death of Sarpedon, came to Hector and said scornfully, 'Think now how best to save Troy by Trojan arms alone, for of your allies, the Lycians, at least, will fight for you no longer. For seeing that you left one of their kings alone to die for you, what help from you could any lesser man expect? Sarpedon was a good friend to you, and your guest, and now I cannot even find his body, that I may raise a burial mound above it. No doubt the Greeks have borne it to their ships, that they may show it forth and boast how they have killed a king of Lycia. That man who lies there dead, guarded by but two others, he was the dearest friend of the greatest warrior of the Greeks. If we can take his body into Troy, then we can use it to ransom Sarpedon and his armour. For, if all that I have heard is true, Achilles loved his friend so well that he will pay any price to save his body from dishonour. A fitting burial, at least, you owe to King Sarpedon, the best and bravest of your allies; but you have not the courage to stand face to face with Ajax, for he is a better warrior than you.'

Hector answered him angrily, 'Your wits have left you in your grief, Glaucus, else you would not speak such words. I fear Ajax! I will show you how little I fear him, or any other man.' And in his pride, he put off his armour, and put on the armour of Achilles, which the gods had given to Peleus, and exulting, he stood up before all the Trojans and their allies and cried out, 'To that man who drags the body of Patroclus into the city, I will give half the spoils of this day's fighting, and he shall have equal glory with me today.'

The Trojans cheered his words, and with a great shout

they surged forward against Ajax and Menelaus, until the two were likely to be overwhelmed, for all their courage and determination.

'My friend,' said Ajax, 'in a very little while will the vultures and the ravens and the dogs of Troy be tearing not only the body of Patroclus, but our bodies, too, unless help comes to us, and speedily. Call loudly, Menelaus, for your voice carries far, and bid someone come to us.'

Menelaus cried out with a loud voice, and Ajax of Locris heard him and came running, and after him Idomeneus and Meriones and several others. They formed a ring about the body of Patroclus, and stood, shield touching shield, and faced the Trojans on all sides. And so they fought, for a long while, until some were fallen, and all those who still stood were weary beyond measure; while ever around their wall of shields, the number of the Trojan dead grew greater.

Through all the afternoon they fought to save the body of Patroclus for Achilles—Achilles, who, all unknowing, waited on the shore for his friend to return to him; for the fighting was now close about the walls of Troy, too far away for him to see clearly from his ship how things were going.

Meanwhile, as soon as Automedon had found himself no longer pursued by Hector, he had ceased his headlong flight towards the ships and reined in the horses, and would have turned the chariot once more towards the battle. 'Alas,' he cried out, 'that brave Patroclus should be dead and that I should have lived to see him fall and been powerless to help him. But I may at least try to save his body from the Trojans.'

But when Xanthus and Balius learnt that Patroclus was dead, they would not move, either for the lash or for Automedon's coaxing, but stood there, like two steeds of stone, their heads bent low and their long, silken manes trailing in the dust, and large tears dropping from their eyes. And so they stood and wept for Patroclus, who had so often driven them, and would now never drive them again; and they would carry Automedon neither to the ships nor back into the fighting, until Zeus, watching the battle from far-off Olympus, took pity on them.

'Unhappy ones,' he said, 'why did we gods give you, immortal as you are, to Peleus? Was it only that you might share men's sorrows? For indeed, of all creatures that move and breathe upon the earth, there is none more miserable than man. But you shall not fall into the hands of Hector.' And he breathed strength and courage into the immortal horses, so that they raised their heads and shook the dust from their manes, and neighing shrilly, galloped once more into the battle.

Automedon, distractedly, in vengeance for Patroclus, tried to thrust with his spear at any Trojan within his reach, guiding the horses the while with only one hand; but, impeded as he was, for all his zeal, he succeeded in slaying not one single man; though he came near to death a hundred times himself.

At last a comrade, Alcimedon, saw him and called to him to stop. 'Have the gods robbed you of your wits, Automedon,' he asked, 'that you venture with a chariot in the forefront of the battle all alone?'

'Patroclus is dead,' replied Automedon wildly, 'and I would strike a blow in vengeance for him. Save only he and I, there is no man, besides our lord Achilles, who can drive Balius and Xanthus. But you have some skill with horses. Take the whip and the reins, good Alcimedon, so that I may dismount and fight.'

Alcimedon did as he was bidden, and Automedon leapt eagerly from the chariot, with spear and sword, crying, 'Keep the chariot close behind me as I fight, Alcimedon. Let me all the time feel the breath of Balius and Xanthus on my neck. We must not be parted in the press of battle, for there are many who would wish to take from us the fine chariot of our lord Achilles and the immortal horses.'

Indeed, he spoke truly, for, from where they fought about the body of Patroclus, Hector, seeing the chariot approaching, said to Aeneas, 'Look, my friend, yonder is the chariot of Achilles with the horses which the gods gave to old King Peleus. No more than one man guards it, while he who holds the reins seems to me to be unpractised in managing the horses. The immortal horses should fall easily to our hands if we go together against them. Two such weaklings as those men of Achilles' will never stay to face Troy's two greatest warriors.'

Aeneas laughed, as though the horses were already won, and together he and Hector made their way towards the chariot; and with them went two young Trojans, Chromius and Aretus.

Automedon looked up and saw them coming, the two greatest warriors amongst the Trojans, and he feared for his life and the safety of Achilles' horses, and raised his voice in a shout for help to those Greeks who stood around the body of Patroclus. Yet he did not wait for their aid, but instead, with a prayer to Zeus, he took aim with his spear and hurled it with all his might against Aretus, so that it passed right through the young man's shield and on into his body, and he fell dead. Immediately, Hector cast his spear at Automedon, a well-aimed throw which would have killed the charioteer had he not marked the spear as it came and crouched low to the ground before it reached him, so that it passed harmlessly over his head and struck quivering in the ground behind him.

Upon that the three Trojans ran forward with drawn swords and fell upon Automedon, and he would indeed have been slain in that moment, had not Ajax, son of Telamon, and Ajax of Locris come hurrying towards him, having heard his call. So fierce was their attack, that Hector and Aeneas and Chromius drew back, leaving their dead comrade.

Automedon stripped the armour from the body of Aretus and flung it into the chariot. 'One man at least have I killed in vengeance for Patroclus,' he said. 'And though he was far from being his equal, I have eased my heart a little for the loss of a good comrade.'

Seeing that Achilles' horses were not to be lightly won, Hector and Aeneas returned to the fight about the body of Patroclus with renewed strength, for it irked them that they should be held off from their spoils for so long by so few. And though Ajax, son of Telamon, and Ajax of Locris came swiftly back to the fight, the Greeks were sorely pressed by the Trojans' latest attack, and saw that they could not hold their ground for much longer.

Ajax, son of Telamon, then said to Menelaus, 'It is time that someone bore word to Achilles that Patroclus is dead and lying beneath the walls of Troy, for truly, soon will the rest of us be slain, and all for the sake of his friend.'

'I will go,' said Menelaus, 'and find Antilochus, for he runs fast, and bid him go to Achilles at his ships; though I would by far prefer to remain here with you, where I am so sorely needed. But, good Ajax, and all of you, my friends, while I am gone, do not weaken your resolve to save the body of Patroclus from the Trojans. Now, if ever, remember how good a man he was, how kindly spoken and how gentle to all, and do not leave him for the dogs of Troy to tear.' And turning from them, Menelaus fought a way through the Trojans who pressed them round, and the gap left by his going was closed as his comrades drew nearer together.

Over the plain hurried Menelaus, stopping for no man, until he caught sight of Nestor's son, on the left of the battle, urging on his men to fight. Menelaus came up to him, breathless and weary, and gasped out, 'Ill tidings I bring you, Antilochus. Patroclus is dead. Run to the ships and tell Achilles, that he may come and fetch the body of his friend. As for his armour, Hector has taken that.'

At first, for shock and grief, Antilochus could not move or speak; for, out of all the kings and princes of the Greeks, he had ever held Achilles and Patroclus in the greatest admiration and friendship, and now one of them was slain. But when at last he could use his limbs again, with tears he put off his armour and gave it to his charioteer, that he might run the faster; and so, weeping, he set off with speed for the shore.

Menelaus did not delay, but returned immediately to the comrades he had left, and fought his way once more to the side of Ajax, son of Telamon, who said to him, 'I doubt that we can wait long enough for Achilles to come to us. You fought safely through the Trojans to find Antilochus, so do you and Meriones now take up the body and bear it towards the ships, while Ajax, my good namesake, and I cut a path for you and hold off the enemy. We shall not fail you, for we are old comrades and often before have fought side by side.'

So Menelaus and Meriones took up the body of Patroclus and held it high above them, while Ajax, son of Telamon, and Ajax of Locris, with spear and sword, cut a path for them through the encircling Trojans, who, as they saw their spoils being taken from them, shouted with anger and dismay, remembering Hector's promise of all that he would give to the man who brought the body of Patroclus into Troy.

Step by step, the Greeks fought their way back towards the shore, all the time harassed by the Trojans, and menaced by Hector and Aeneas; until, within sight of the trench and rampart, they were almost overwhelmed.

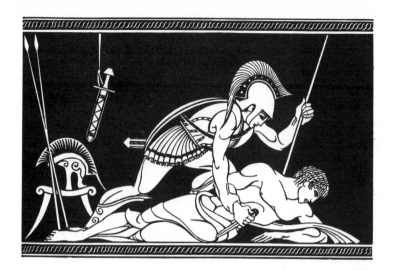

# XIII

## The Preparation

ANTILOCHUS found Achilles waiting outside his hut, a troubled frown between his brows, for it was fast drawing close to evening, and Patroclus had not yet returned. Moreover, Achilles had learnt from others who still watched that the Greeks were once more being driven back towards the shore; and he feared for his friend. When he saw Antilochus, without his armour, breathless from running, tears wet upon his cheeks, his heart was gripped with dread.

Antilochus, gasping, leant against a pillar of the outer porch. 'I wish it were another man who had to tell you what I now have to say. Patroclus is dead, Achilles, slain by Hector, and Hector wears your armour and boasts how

he will have his body, too. Not easily will the Greeks keep
it from him.'

Achilles put his hands before his face and flung himself
upon the ground, writhing and twisting in his sorrow and
tearing at his hair. The captive women, who had been
making ready his evening meal, came from his hut and
watched him, perturbed and apprehensive. When they
knew that Patroclus was dead, they wailed and beat their
breasts; for Patroclus had ever been kindly towards them,
and much liked.

Antilochus stood there in tears and watched Achilles
with pity; until he saw Achilles reach for the dagger at his
belt, then he dropped to his knees beside him and grasped
his wrists, that, in his agony of mind, Achilles might not
take his own life.

And in his wild grief Achilles cried aloud, and his mother
Thetis heard him where she sat deep below the sea with
her nine and forty sisters, the daughters of blue-haired
Nereus, to whom the sailors prayed. Immediately she rose
up through the water, and coming swiftly over the sands
on her bare white feet, she went to where her son lay and
gently touched his head; while up from the sea after her
came her sisters, all nine and forty of them, and each one's
wailing was the thin sound of the wind upon the waves.

'My son,' asked Thetis, 'why do you weep? For all
things are as you wished, and Zeus is giving victory to the
Trojans, even as he promised me, when I asked him, for
your sake.'

Achilles raised his head from the ground a little way and
answered her. 'What good has it done me, mother, that
Zeus has granted your prayer? For Patroclus is dead, whom

I honoured above all men and loved more than my life. He is slain by Hector, who now wears my armour and boasts of his deeds. Oh, mother, Patroclus is gone, and what have I left to live for, save to take Hector's life?'

Gently she stroked his hair, saying sadly, 'My most unhappy son, that in your short life you are destined to so much sorrow.'

'I have lived too long already,' said Achilles, 'since I was not there to stand beside Patroclus when he needed me. Oh, that there might never more be strife or quarrelling amongst gods or men, for it was my accursed quarrel with Agamemnon that led to this day's grief. But now I shall go forth to battle once again, and bitterly shall the Trojans rue my coming. Let me die when I must, as soon as it pleases the gods, so long as I have lived to see Hector lying dead.'

Thetis gave a sigh, like the wind that ripples the sea. 'As you will, my son. Yet do not go forth to battle today, for Hector wears your armour, that the gods gave to Peleus. In the morning I shall come again, and bring new armour for you. Then may you seek out Hector and slay him, if it is the will of Zeus.'

She rose from beside him and went swiftly to high Olympus, to the house of Hephaestus, the craftsman of the gods; whilst, one by one, her sisters slipped below the waves, their wailing fading on the evening air; and, in its place, from beyond the rampart and the trench, came the clash of battle, as the Trojans flung the Greeks back on to their own defences.

Achilles heard it where he lay, and Hera, queen of all the gods, sent it into his mind to go upon the rampart and show himself to the Trojans, that they might see he no longer held from the fight; though because of his mother's command, he would not enter battle that day.

He went upon the rampart and looked down on the fighting, and he shouted aloud with a mighty voice, to encourage the Greeks. For a moment the strife ceased, and the Trojans looked up and saw him there, against the evening sky, with the rays of the setting sun glinting in his long, golden hair, and a great light about his head, as though he had been a god.

Three times he shouted, and a great fear came upon the Trojans, so that they fell back from the wall, and Hector withdrew from the struggle about the body of Patroclus, which once again he had almost won, so that the Greeks were able to take it up. Triumphantly they laid it on a litter and brought it within the camp and set it down with lamentation.

And coming from the rampart, Achilles flung himself across the body of his friend and wept, as darkness fell.

A short way out on the plain, the Trojans gathered in the fading light, to debate what it were best to do; for they were weary from fighting, and afraid, now that it was certain that Achilles would once again take arms against them.

First Polydamas spoke, whose counsel was much respected. 'It were best,' he said, 'that we returned at once to Troy, and tomorrow prepared to defend its walls; since it seems that Achilles, who in the past has made so many Trojan women widows, and taken so many captives, will come once more against us. This time there will be little pity in his heart. He will exact vengeance to the uttermost for his dead friend, and we had best beware of his wrath. Let us return to Troy and guard our city well tonight, and in the morning take our stand upon the walls; and it will be the worse for Achilles or any other Greek who tries to enter Troy.'

His counsel was wise, as his counsel always was, but Hector said angrily, 'You are a coward, Polydamas, and I will not hear your words. No, nor shall any other man of all the Trojans, for I forbid it. We shall camp here tonight, upon the plain, and eat our fill and take our rest; and in the morning we shall again attack the ships. And if Achilles does indeed come once more into the battle, then it is he who had best beware, for I shall be ready to meet him, with my good spear in my hand; and if the gods so will it, he shall end even as his beloved friend, and they can go together to the land of Hades.'

There were many Trojans who praised his bold words and shouted out their agreement with him, scorning Polydamas for a coward. But those others who would have done as Polydamas advised, they kept silent, for they feared Hector's anger.

The Myrmidons bore the body of Patroclus to Achilles' hut, and there they warmed water in a cauldron and fetched out rich unguents and soft woven cloths. And when they had washed away the blood and dust and anointed Patroclus with sweetly scented oils, they wrapped him in a cloth of fine white linen and laid him on his bed in the inner room of the hut, mourning for him all the while they did so.

Achilles, laying his hands upon him, said, 'Here shall you lie unburied, Patroclus, until I have brought you Hector's head. You will not have long to wait, I promise you.'

And all the night Achilles sat beside his friend, unsleeping, his heart within him desolate and aching with grief.

On snow-crowned Mount Olympus, Thetis came to the house of Hephaestus, fashioned of imperishable bronze, all set with stars, which the lame god had built for his own pleasure.

She found him in his smithy, fashioning twenty tripods to stand around the gleaming walls of his hall. Beneath each tripod he had set little wheels, so that they might go of themselves to the feasts and assemblies of the gods, and return again of themselves to his own house, as he wished.

Charis, his fair wife, came forward to greet Thetis and led her to a silver-studded seat and set a footstool at her feet, calling to Hephaestus to come and speak with his guest.

Hephaestus set aside his bellows and laid his tools in a silver chest, and taking up his staff, he limped towards Thetis; and there came with him, to support him, handmaidens fashioned all in gold. So cunningly had he wrought them, that they might indeed have been real maidens.

He took Thetis by the hands and welcomed her, then sat beside her and asked her why she had come to him. 'For if there is any way in which I can serve you, good Thetis, gladly will I do it, whatever you ask of me.'

With sorrow Thetis told him of her son's great grief, and begged that he would make armour for Achilles to take the place of that which he had lost to Hector. 'For my son has but a short life to live—such was his choice—yet I would wish him to have glory in his few brief years.'

'Grieve no more,' said Hephaestus, 'for I shall make for brave Achilles, your son, armour that shall be the wonder of all men who behold it, as I have the skill to do. Yet I would that, when the time comes, I could hide him from death with equal ease.'

With that he limped back to his fire and bade his bellows, twenty in all, to blow their hardest upon the flames; and into the fire he threw strong copper, shining tin, and precious silver and gold; and set his huge anvil on its block and took up his hammer and his tongs.

First, he fashioned a shield in five layers of shining metal, great and strong, with a baldric of silver; and this shield he ornamented with many a cunning design: the sun and the moon and the stars, and figures of beasts, and of men, fighting, dancing, reaping, and gathering rich grapes for wine, a wonder to behold; and all about the rim of the shield was the likeness of the great river, Oceanus.

And when the shield was ready, Hephaestus made a breastplate that was brighter than the blaze of his fire, and two shining greaves and a helmet with a crest of gold.

These arms he gave to Thetis, and she took them up, and like a falcon, she swooped down from high Olympus as the dawn glowed redly in the sky; and as she entered the hut of Achilles, all glorious, bearing the arms, the Myrmidons drew away from her in awe, and she called to her son.

In the inner room of the hut, Achilles, haggard-eyed and pale, looked up from where he lay across the body of his friend, and Thetis set down the arms before him and took him by the hands and raised him. 'My son,' she said, 'for all your sorrow, you cannot bring Patroclus back to life, for he died by the will of Zeus. Let him lie there, and take the armour which Hephaestus has wrought for you alone. No mortal man ever bore finer armour than this.'

His followers turned away their eyes from the splendour of the arms which had been made by a god; but Achilles looked long at them, while his hands clenched at his sides and a fierce light burnt in his eyes. At last he spoke. 'I thank you, my mother, for your care of me, and I thank Hephaestus, also, for his gift. Soon I shall arm myself for battle, and I think that I shall not dishonour this god-wrought gift.'

'Have courage, my son. You will do great deeds today,' she said. And in the next instant she was gone, back to the depths of the sea, and only the armour, lying there before Achilles, showed that she had ever been with him.

Achilles looked once more upon his friend, then went from his hut along the shore towards the place of assembly, calling out to every man he met to join him there.

All the Greeks hurried after him, crying to each other to make haste. Not the warriors alone, and their leaders, who were wont to come, but the pilots, and the helmsmen, who usually remained on their ships, and even the men who had charge of the stores, hurried to the assembly which he called. For Achilles had held himself so long from the war and from the counsels of the Greeks, that all men were curious to hear what he would say, remembering how he had sworn never to take up arms again for Agamemnon in any cause.

Yet now the one thing had happened which, to Achilles,

made all his oaths as nothing: Patroclus was dead and must be avenged.

Odysseus came, and Diomedes, each leaning on his spear, for their wounds were still unhealed, and took their places in the assembly with all the other Greeks. And Achilles sat in his wonted place; for the first time without Patroclus by his side. Last of all, and reluctantly, came Agamemnon, for he had little inclination to face Achilles, now that he had lost his friend.

As soon as all were gathered, Achilles rose, and stepping forward, spoke shortly. 'King Agamemnon, I wish that Briseïs had died on the day we sacked Lyrnessus, before ever I chose her for my share of the spoils. Then would we not have quarrelled over her, and so much sorrow would not have come on all the Greeks. But what has been, has been; and it is over now and done with, and I am ready to fight again. So call the Greeks speedily to battle, that the fewer Trojans shall escape my spear.'

He sat again in his place, and the Greeks made plain their gladness that he was with them and willing to fight once more, by shouting out their approval of his words.

Agamemnon rose to answer him, but in the shouting he could get no hearing, and his words were lost in their cheers. When at last the uproar had died down, he spoke from his place, not coming forward before them. 'My friends, good warriors all,' he said, glowering irritably about him, 'it is fitting to listen when a man stands up to speak, if you do not wish him to confuse his words.' He hesitated, then went on, 'Often enough you have blamed me for my quarrel with Achilles and all that it has cost us, yet these things come from the gods. It was not my fault.

The gods order all things as they please and send what they choose to mortal men. And if I acted foolishly, why, not even the gods are always without folly, as the old tales tell us. Yet, though I am not to blame, to you, Achilles, I shall make amends. I shall send to your ships immediately all those gifts which through Odysseus I promised you two days ago, so that you may see the gifts for yourself and be satisfied.'

Achilles flung out his hand with an impatient gesture. 'Send me your gifts or keep them, as you please. I care not. This is no time to talk of trivial matters. There is a deed yet undone which I must do, so bid the Greeks arm and go to battle.'

Agamemnon scowled, resenting Achilles' scant respect, but quickly Odysseus rose, smiling. 'Come, Achilles, have patience for a little longer. You cannot expect the Greeks to fight fasting. Let us all hearten ourselves and strengthen our courage with good food and drink, before we go out to battle. For he ever fights better who has first taken his fill of meat and wine. And while our meal is being made ready, let our good leader, King Agamemnon, set out the gifts he means to give you here in our assembly place, that we all may see how nobly he has recompensed you, and that you may be gladdened by the sight of all the riches that are to be yours. Let him hand them over to you with goodwill, and then with goodwill, also, let him feast you, Achilles, that the quarrel between you may be done with in the sight of all.'

'That is well spoken, Odysseus,' said Agamemnon. 'I shall do even as you have said.' He turned to Achilles. 'Curb your impatience for a while yet, and accept the gifts

I offer you. Let us make sacrifice to the gods together, and take our meal in friendship.' He quelled his dislike and smiled at Achilles with sullen condescension.

But Achilles exclaimed, 'King Agamemnon, deal with this matter at some other, and more fitting, time. When there is a truce perhaps, or no fighting to be done; or when I am in the mood. Patroclus has been slain by Hector, and you invite me to a feast! If I had my way, the Greeks would fight hungry, and gorge themselves, if they will, tonight, when the dead have been avenged. Yet let them eat if they must, but let them do it quickly. For myself, I cannot think of food or drink, but only of death and vengeance. Patroclus lies in my hut, cold and dead, with his body hacked and torn; I will not eat or drink until I have avenged him.'

Once more Odysseus sought to calm him with lightly spoken words. 'Achilles, you are the mightiest warrior of us all—far better than I in battle—but I am older and have seen more of life, and so must be better in counsel. Pay heed to my advice, therefore. Let us mourn our dead with our hearts, not with our bellies. For, in time of war, men die continually. If things were as you wished them, their comrades who were left would have little chance of eating or drinking, and would speedily fall to the weapons of the enemy, all weak as they would be from fasting.' He smiled and went on, 'No, rather let us mourn our dead and eat and drink our fill as well, that we may be the stronger to avenge our fallen comrades.'

Achilles shrugged his shoulders and wasted no further time in argument, but waited while the promised gifts were brought from Agamemnon's ships and laid before him: seven tripods, twenty shining cauldrons, and much gold. Twelve of Agamemnon's finest horses were then led into the assembly place, and the seven serving women, skilled in handicrafts; and last of all came Briseïs.

Then Talthybius, the herald, brought a boar to the altar in the midst of the assembly, and calling upon the gods to witness his good faith, Agamemnon slew it. Talthybius raised it up, and carrying it down to the sea, he flung it far out into the waves, a sacrifice to the immortal gods.

Immediately he had done, Achilles rose. 'As King Agamemnon says, no doubt it was the gods who robbed him of his wits and sent this trouble upon us.' He spoke in haste, with indifference, adding with more feeling, 'And now, my friends, go to your meal with no more profitless delay, that we may the sooner be at fighting.' And without a glance at the gifts, he turned and walked back to his hut, and the assembly broke up.

The Myrmidons gathered together the gifts and carried them to Achilles' ships, and led away the horses and the women. When Briseïs came to Achilles' hut and saw Patroclus lying dead, she wept and knelt beside him, crying out, 'Dear, good Patroclus, who was always kind to me, will there never be an end to my sorrows? I have seen my husband slain, and my three brothers, and now I lose my kindest friend amongst the Greeks. Unhappy Patroclus, I shall always remember you and your kindness to me, and always mourn your death.'

And when the other seven captive women saw him lying there dead, young, and good to look upon, they, too, pitied him and wept for him; and as she wept, each remembered her own sorrows, and so wept the more.

## XIV

## *The Slaughter*

THROUGHOUT the camp the Greeks ate and drank and
armed themselves in readiness for the battle that was
to come, all save Achilles, and he would touch
neither food nor wine. When his followers would have
persuaded him, he only said, 'Patroclus is still unavenged.'

Old Phoenix, who had watched them both grow up,
stayed with him and tried to comfort him; but Achilles
turned away from him, saying, 'Let me be. Ever before,
when I prepared for battle, Patroclus himself would make
ready a meal for me, and we would eat and drink together
before going together to meet the enemy. He lies there
dead. Would you have me eat and drink alone?' He put his
hands over his face and a sob shuddered through him. 'Oh,
Patroclus, no man has ever had a better friend than you.

Never again shall I know another sorrow like this; not though I live to learn from Phthia that my father has gone down to Hades' land, not though I hear that in Scyros my little son is dead. I have known and accepted my doom, that I shall not leave Troy alive; but I believed that you, at least, would go home to Phthia to tell my father how I died, and to fetch little Neoptolemus from Scyros and take him to my own land and care for him for me and teach him battle skill and courage. But it is not to be.' And once more he fell to weeping.

But after a time he raised his head as he heard from all about the camp the sounds of clashing arms and the neighing of horses and the eager shouts of men, as the Greeks gathered under their leaders, confident that they would drive the Trojans back to their city, now that Achilles was come to battle once again. The time for tears was over.

Achilles rose and armed himself in the armour which Hephaestus had made for him: the greaves with their silver ankle clasps and the shining breastplate. He slung the sword and the shield about his shoulders, then, twisting up all his long, yellow hair, he set on his head the helmet with the golden crest. He moved and flexed his limbs, testing the arms and armour, and found them good, and perfectly fitted to him. Then, taking the great spear which had been given to King Peleus by the gods, he went out from his hut to where his chariot waited, with Xanthus and Balius ready harnessed and Automedon beside them; and beneath the flashing, crested helmet, his young face was grim and set, and his eyes were without pity.

Automedon sprang into the chariot and took up whip and reins, and after him Achilles mounted, his armour gleaming like the sun. He stood a moment thus, looking down upon the immortal horses, and then said, bitterly, 'Today, Xanthus and Balius, when the battle is over, bring me safely away. Do not leave me lying dead upon the plain, as you left Patroclus, yesterday.'

Xanthus bent his arched neck beneath the yoke until his long, chestnut mane hung in the dust, and spoke. 'Lord Achilles,' he said, 'this time we shall bring you safely away. But there will come a day when you return not from the battle, for so have the gods ordained. As for Patroclus, he died because the Bright One was against him, and not through our fault or failure, for we are as swift as the West Wind, who is our sire.'

Achilles shook his head and answered quietly, 'Why do you remind me of my doom, Xanthus? There is no need. I know of it already. Nevertheless, I shall not cease from fighting until Patroclus is avenged and the Trojans have had their fill of war.'

Then with a great cry he urged them forward, and after him pressed the Myrmidons, and all the army of the Greeks. And so, for the first time, Achilles went out to fight the Trojans without Patroclus at his side.

From his high throne on Mount Olympus, Zeus looked down on Troy and all the wide Trojan plain; and since this was the day on which his promise to Thetis was to be fulfilled, he no longer forbade any of the gods who would, from joining in the battle. And forthwith Hera, their queen, and Athene with her flashing helmet, brighter than the sun, and lame Hephaestus with them, went from Olympus to watch over the Greeks, bringing to them redoubled courage; while Apollo of the silver bow and golden Aphrodite, as always, were ready to defend the Trojans, and, once again, dread Ares was with them, dark as a thundercloud.

And so the Greeks, led by Achilles, came from the ships against the Trojans, who were awaiting their attack, drawn up upon the plain; and Hector, wearing Achilles' armour, went up and down along their lines, encouraging his men and their allies to fight boldly. But when he saw Achilles approaching, Hector withdrew himself from the front of the battle; for he knew why Achilles had at last come out to fight again.

Within spear-casting distance of the Trojans, Achilles leapt from his chariot, calling to the Greeks to follow him, and he sprang amongst the Trojans so fiercely that none could withstand him, bringing death to many.

Almost twenty of the finest Trojan warriors he slew in that first short space of battle, showing mercy to none. One of them, who was young and of his own age, cast aside his weapons and knelt and clasped his knees in supplication, and would have pleaded for his life and offered much gold as a ransom. Yet Achilles did not give him even time enough to speak; his sword was in his body and the young man's life was gone, before ever the appeal was made.

Yet it was always Hector whom Achilles sought, looking about for him in the press of battle. But Hector, with prudence, kept afar from him, until that moment when Polydorus was slain.

Polydorus was King Priam's youngest son, a half-brother of Hector. His father had forbidden him to fight, but being young and foolish and eager to prove his courage, he came now to the front of battle, running here and there amongst the fighters, trusting, by the fleetness of his foot, to go unscathed, for he was the fastest runner in Troy.

But Achilles saw him, and swift as he was, Achilles was yet swifter and flung his spear as Polydorus turned to flee from him, so that it struck him full in the back, and he fell to his knees with the spear right through his body.

When Hector saw his young brother dying, he cast aside all caution and strode forward through the Trojan ranks to where Achilles stood. Achilles, looking up, saw him come, flaunting the armour he had taken from Patroclus, and his anger was like a tight hand clasped about his heart. 'Come closer, Hector,' he called out. 'Come closer, that Patroclus may be avenged the sooner.' And he stood waiting for him, his knuckles white about the ashwood shaft of King Peleus' long spear.

'You need not think I fear you, for all you are the greatest warrior amongst the Greeks. I, too, have a sharp spear, as maybe you shall learn.' Hector raised his spear and flung it at Achilles.

But divine Athene breathed upon it gently and turned it aside from its course, and with a shout, Achilles leapt forward and thrust with his spear at Hector. But in that moment Apollo let fall a thick mist all about him, so that Achilles could not see where he should strike. His blow fell wide, and Apollo drew Hector, unharmed, through the mist and away to safety.

Four times Achilles struck into the veil of mist, until at last it cleared, so he could see that Hector was not there, and he cried out in anger, 'This is the doing of one of the immortal gods. No doubt you make rich sacrifice to Apollo before you go amongst the spears, Hector. This time you have escaped me; but there will surely come a moment when no god stands by your side, and in that moment I shall make an end of you.' And forthwith Achilles went to seek out others whom he might slay, until that time when he should again meet with Hector.

He fought ceaselessly and without mercy, until his hands were as red as his spear, and the wheels of his chariot which followed him, and the hooves of the immortal horses, dripped with the blood of those he had slain.

The Trojans gave way before the onslaught of the Greeks, and retreated towards their city; at first in order, making for the ford of the River Scamander, and then, as the Greeks pressed harder on them, in a wild rout.

The ford was not wide enough for a great number of chariots and men to pass over at one time, and in their terror many of the Trojans fled into the deeper water and were drowned, and many drove their chariots over the high banks of the river, so that they sank. Soon the waters of the river were filled with the bodies of men and with the arms that they had cast away as they sought to save themselves.

Achilles set his spear against a tree, and with his sword alone went here and there upon the river's edge, striking down those who would have climbed to safety up the steep bank, clinging to the roots and branches of the willows and the tamarisks that grew there. One after another he cut them down and they fell back into the water, until the river flowed red with their blood.

Many Trojan lords he slew there, beside the river, and

many of their allies. One, amongst so many, was Nastes, leader of the Carians, men who spoke in a strange tongue. Nastes, who had brought his men to Troy, ever went out to battle all decked with jingling golden ornaments, like a young girl. But he lost all his gold when Achilles killed him beside Scamander, and stripped it from his body before flinging him back into the river.

After a time Achilles sheathed his sword and picked out from amongst the others twelve noble Trojan youths, whom he took alive, overpowering them easily, half-drowned and all dazed as they were; and binding their hands behind them with their own girdles, he gave them to his men to be taken to the ships, that they might die on the funeral pyre of Patroclus.

One of those who sought to save himself from the rushing waters of the river was Lycaon, one of King Priam's many sons, the elder brother of Polydorus. Achilles had taken him alive some months before, one night when the youth had stolen out from the city to cut himself the pliant branches which he needed to repair the sides of his chariot. That time Achilles had not killed him, but, for the price of a hundred oxen, he had sold him into slavery in Lemnos. There, at great cost, he had been ransomed by one who had once been King Priam's guest, and wished well to him and to all his family; and so Lycaon had returned to Troy, but eleven days before, to be received in his father's palace with great rejoicing. And now, on the twelfth day after his homecoming, he fell once more into Achilles' hands.

Achilles knew him again as he saw him scramble up the river's bank, unarmed and exhausted, and exclaimed in surprise to see him there. Bewildered, Lycaon stared back at him, standing dripping amongst the rushes and the flowers, dismayed at the ill chance that had given him once again into the power of so mighty an enemy.

'So,' said Achilles, 'a second time we meet, Lycaon, son of Priam. Come, and feel the sharpness of my spear.'

But Lycaon stumbled forward, hands outstretched, for he would have begged his life a second time. Achilles raised his spear, but Lycaon stooped and ran beneath it, so that the spear stroke missed him and the bronze head was buried deep in the ground behind him. Lycaon knelt and grasped Achilles' knees with one hand as a suppliant, while with his other hand he reached back and took hold of the spear-shaft, holding it firmly, so that Achilles might not draw it from the earth too easily.

'Have pity on me, great Achilles,' he pleaded, 'for it must be that I am hated by the gods that they have delivered me into your hands a second time. Spare me now, as you did once before, and take a ransom for my life, for I have eaten bread in your own hut.' He wept. 'Spare me, Achilles, for though we are both sons of Priam, I was not born of the same mother as Hector, who slew kindly, good-hearted Patroclus, your friend. Must I die for Hector's offence?'

But Achilles was moved neither by his tears nor by his entreaties. 'You are too late,' he said. 'Gone is the day when I would have taken a ransom for any son of Priam. They shall all die, all whom I meet with, to pay for the man whom Hector slew.' He gave a bitter little smile. 'Come, my friend, why should I spare you? Patroclus died. He was a better man than you.'

In his cold eyes Lycaon saw no mercy, and he let go of Achilles' knees and unclasped his hand from about the spear-shaft, and with a sob he crouched at Achilles' feet, his hands outstretched amongst the sedges, waiting for the blow which should end his life.

Achilles drew his sword. 'And I, too,' he said, 'I am tall and beautiful, and I am young. My father is a king, and my mother is a goddess. Yet I, too, must die. One day soon there will come a dawn or an evening or a noontide when some man will take my life in battle, with sword or spear or arrow.' He raised the sword and struck Lycaon on the neck, and his blood spattered the flowers and all the green reeds.

Then Achilles threw his body into the river. 'Let the fishes mourn for you, if they will,' he said. 'For your mother will never see you again, to weep over you.'

So it went on, with Achilles slaying all whom he found, as though he could never have enough of killing; until the waters of the river, red with Trojan blood, were choked with Trojan bodies, and still Achilles ranged upon the bank, seeking for more men to slay.

And then at last, in wrath, Scamander, the god of the river, rose up, and in a voice that filled all men with terror, he bade Achilles cease his slaughter. 'Rash and wretched mortal,' he said, 'you have choked my fair stream with dead men and my waters can no longer flow down into the sea. Come, kill no more of the Trojans. They are my people, who, in the past, in time of peace, have offered rich sacrifice to me.'

Achilles, unflinching, answered him, 'I will not cease from slaying the Trojans until they are all fled into their city and until I have met with Hector face to face.'

Scamander rose up in a rushing flood, casting forth on to the land all the Trojan dead, and towering above Achilles, who sought to stay him with his shield, and could not. With the waters swirling about him he grasped the trunk of an elm-tree which grew upon the bank, but with a mighty roar Scamander uprooted the great tree and swept Achilles backwards before him.

Then, because a mortal cannot strive with one of the immortal gods and live, Achilles turned and fled; but the waters of the furious river pursued him across the plain, now washing about his feet and now rising above him as though they would have engulfed him, while he turned and twisted here and there, and tried to reach a place of safety.

But for all his matchless speed, he could not outstrip an immortal, and fearing that he might die there, upon the plain, drowned in the waters of Scamander, with Patroclus still unavenged, he cried out to the other gods for help against the river, and then, since he could run no farther, turned at bay, holding the sword which Hephaestus had forged for him.

Scamander rose higher and higher to engulf him, his torrents roaring mightily. 'Here shall you perish, son of Peleus, you who thought to stand against one of the immortal gods. Neither your arms nor your armour shall protect you, made though they were by a god, but under my waters they shall lie in the slime, and over your body shall I dredge up sand and shingle, so that your comrades will not find your bones when they come to look for them, nor will they need to build any other burial mound for you.'

Then indeed would Achilles have been overwhelmed, but lame Hephaestus, urged on by Hera, came swiftly with flames and kindled fire upon the plain, burning bush and tree, and driving back the waters of Scamander even to his banks. There, on the green margin of the river, the willows and the tamarisks and the cypresses were blackened by the flames, and the flowering rushes and the parsley and the lilies were shrivelled and scorched in the heat, while the stream boiled and steamed, so that Scamander cried out to Hephaestus, 'Cease your burning, for I cannot fight with you, you are too strong for me. Cease your burning, and I will swear an oath that never again shall I help the Trojans, not though I see your flames about their city.'

Hephaestus stayed his fire; and once more Scamander flowed within his banks, down to the sea; and the two gods strove no more together.

But Achilles, delivered by Hephaestus, again attacked the Trojans, slaying ceaselessly, and ever seeking for Hector. While over the plain, towards the city, fled those Trojans who had safely crossed the river, hoping to hide themselves within the walls.

XV

## The Vengeance

KING PRIAM came upon the walls of Troy, and from the watch-tower beside the Scaean Gate, he saw his people driven in rout before the spears of the Greeks and he called down to the gatekeepers, bidding them fling wide the gates, that the fleeing Trojans might win through to safety.

Through the Scaean Gate the Trojans poured, with the Greeks coming after them across the plain. But their fear gave them speed, and of those Trojans who had lived to cross the river all passed safely through the gates. All save Hector. He stood before the gateway, watching the on-coming Greeks, and wondering what it were best to do: to save his life and live to fight again, or to stay and face Achilles.

It was Priam, from the watch-tower, who first saw Achilles as he drew near, his god-given armour shining in the afternoon sun, and in fear the old king called down to Hector, 'My son, I beg of you, come within the walls. Do not stay to meet with Achilles. Many of my people has he slain since first he came against Troy, and many sons have I lost to his pitiless spear. Today Lycaon went forth and, against my will, young Polydorus, and I have not seen either return. Oh, my dearest and my best and eldest son, who should be king in my place when I am gone, do not let me have to mourn the death of a third son in a single day.'

Hector looked up at him, and his heart was filled with pity, but he shook his head and set his heavy shield against the wall, and remained where he was, before the gates, alone.

King Priam tore his grey hair and pleaded with his son, and, while he spoke, those who stood near him on the wall moved aside to let Queen Hecuba come by. When she came to the watch-tower, to her husband's side, and looked down and saw Hector standing there alone, she gave a great cry.

'If you are slain, my son,' said Priam, 'who will be left to guard the men and women of Troy? For you are our strong shield and our safety, and if you are killed we shall be left defenceless. Troy will fall to Achilles and the Greeks, and I, your old father, shall be slain, my naked body left for the dogs and the vultures, as though I had not been a king.'

So Priam spoke with tears, yet he could not persuade his son. Nor could Hecuba prevail with him, though she, too, wept and said, 'Have pity on me, my child, if on no other. I gave you life: must I now see that life taken from you with my own eyes?'

But Hector, torn between two duties, stood where he was until he, too, could see Achilles coming, in the forefront of the Greeks. Then he almost turned and fled in through the gates, but checked himself, thinking, 'If I go within the walls to safety now, I must face Polydamas, who gave me such good counsel, bidding me order the Trojans back to the city when he knew that Achilles was to fight again: and I would not hear him. He will reproach me, that by my folly so many men have died who did not need to die. How can I go into the city now, to hear some wretch of no account say of me, "Hector, in his pride, has brought ruin on his people"? No, I would rather stay and meet Achilles and either kill him or die gloriously.'

Then he thought how, perhaps for the Greeks as well as for the Trojans, the war had lasted long enough. 'What if I were to lay down my weapons and strip off my armour and go all unarmed to meet Achilles, offer him Helen for Menelaus, and half of the great wealth of Troy, that the war between us might be over and our two peoples be at peace?' For a moment he was eager and hopeful; and then he remembered that it was he who had killed Patroclus, and that there could be no mercy for him from Achilles, though he offered him the whole of Troy and all its riches, for himself alone. 'He would kill me as I stood unarmed before him. For between Achilles and myself there can be no pretty speeches, such as loving youths and maidens toss lightly to one another—fool that I was to think it.' He shrugged his shoulders and took up his shield again.

Moving forward from the Scaean Gate, he saw Achilles running towards him, brandishing his father's long spear, and knew that the time was very close when Patroclus might be avenged.

Then suddenly he thought, 'By all the immortal gods, I do not want to die,' and a great fear came upon him, and he turned and fled along the walls; and with a shout, Achilles was after him, signing to his men to keep away, for Hector was for him alone.

Past the watch-tower Hector fled, and by the old fig-tree, and on to the smoother surface of the wagon track, a short distance from the walls, where the going was easier; and close after him came Achilles. They reached, and passed, the two springs and the washing-troughs of stone, where, in the days of peace, before the Greek ships had come, the wives and women of Troy had brought their clothes to wash. On, on, they ran, as though it were a race that they were running, and for a prize. A prize there was indeed, and it was Hector's life.

Right around the city they ran; and ever Hector sought to run close in beneath the walls, so that the watchers might drop stones and weapons down on Achilles. But Achilles saw his intention, and always contrived to keep between him and the walls, to prevent him. Three times about the city they ran, and each time, as they passed the Scaean Gate, Hector tried to turn aside to escape within; and each time Achilles was there to intercept him and drive him back again on to the track.

But when they came for the fourth time to the springs and the washing-troughs, the immortal gods, beguiling him—for he was doomed—sent Hector's fear from him, and he stood and turned to face Achilles. And in that moment, bright Apollo, till then his constant protector, abandoned him, leaving him, at last, to stand alone.

Breathlessly Hector called out to Achilles, 'I will fly from you no longer, son of Peleus. Here let one of us make an end of the other. But first let us take an oath together that whichever is the victor will respect the other's body. I swear to you, Achilles, that if the gods are with me today and let me take your life, your armour I shall keep for myself, but your body I shall give to the Greeks, that they may burn it as befits the son of a king. Give me your oath to do likewise for me.'

Achilles stood a short way off and leant upon his spear, his breast heaving underneath the shining armour. When he had breath enough to speak, he said, 'You must be mad to talk to me of oaths. There are no oaths made between men and beasts of prey. Wolves do not swear oaths with the sheep within the fold. There can be no oaths between us, Hector.' He straightened up and moved his hand along the spearshaft. 'Now show if you have courage, son of Priam, or whether all your great fame is undeserved, for the time has come for you to pay me for the death of Patroclus.' He raised his spear and flung it; but Hector, watching carefully, crouched down, so that it passed over him and lodged, transfixed and quivering, in the ground behind him.

'Your aim was poor, Achilles. Now may the gods speed my spear and may it find its mark, for of all Troy's enemies, you are the one most to be feared.' Hector cast his spear and his aim was true, for the bronze head struck, ringing, full upon Achilles' shield; but the shield made by immortal Hephaestus held and was not pierced, and the spear fell harmlessly to the ground.

Hector stood dismayed, for he had no second spear; then he drew his sword and stepped aside, ready to fall upon Achilles, who leapt forward to snatch up once again his father's spear: and Athene herself, unseen, put it into his hand. And so the two of them stood close and faced each other, Achilles in the armour which a god had made for him, and Hector in Achilles' armour which the gods had given to Peleus; and each watched the other warily to see where he should strike, for on that next blow would hang the outcome of the combat.

But Achilles knew the weak place in his own armour that he had brought from his father's house and worn so many times: a gap between the breastplate and the cheek-piece of the helmet. And there he thrust his spear, into Hector's neck, and Hector fell to the ground, gasping out his life.

Achilles laughed to see him. 'Fool that you were, Hector. You forgot me when you killed Patroclus. Did you think that I would not remember you?'

Weakly, with fast ebbing breath, Hector whispered, 'I beg of you, Achilles, accept a ransom for my body, that my people may burn it fittingly. Do not leave me for the vultures.'

Angrily and bitterly Achilles answered him, 'Ask me no favours, Hector. Was it not you who would have set the head of Patroclus upon the walls of Troy? By all the gods, I wish that in my hatred I might tear and devour your flesh myself, for the grief that you have brought to me. There does not live the man who could pay me ransom enough for your body. Let your father offer your weight in gold.

He shall never look upon your face again, nor shall your mother lay you on a bier and weep for you.'

The blood dripped from the wound in Hector's neck, and his voice was no more than a murmur. 'Your heart is hard as iron, Achilles, how could I have hoped to move you?' His voice rattled in his throat, his head sank down, and he was dead.

Exulting, Achilles raised the triumph cry and bent to strip his armour from Hector's body; and the Greeks ran forward, rejoicing that the Trojans had lost their greatest warrior. And there were many, seeing Hector lying there defenceless, thrust their sharp spears into his body, who would not have dared to face him while he lived.

Watching, helplessly and with horror, from the walls, the Trojans cried aloud and lamented that their best protection against the enemy was lost. Queen Hecuba shrieked and tore her veil; and it was all that they could do to hold back old Priam, who would have run out through the Scaean Gate in frenzy to reach his son.

Hector's wife, Andromache, was in her husband's house, working at her loom on a strip of purple cloth, adorning it with flowers of every colour. She had just called to her women to set the great tripod and cauldron upon the fire, so that there should be hot water ready for a bath for Hector when he came from the battlefield, for it was nearing evening.

They were hastening to do her bidding at that very moment when she heard the sounds of lamentation from the walls. Her cheeks grew pale and her hand shook, so that the shuttle fell to the floor, and she ran out from the house and through the streets to the wall, and the people

made way for her. She looked down upon the plain, gave one cry, and fell senseless into the arms of those about her.

When she came to herself again, she wept and exclaimed, 'To what an ill fate were we born, you and I, Hector. And to what an ill fate has our little son been born, that he is left fatherless while yet a babe.' And so she wept, and her women wept with her.

There were some amongst the triumphant Greeks who were for attacking the city at that very moment, sure that it would fall easily to them while the Trojans were all confounded by the calamity that they had seen and crushed by their great loss.

And though at first Achilles agreed with them, he then said, 'Let Troy be. I have done what I came out to do. Let us return to the ships, for we have had a great victory today. Shall Patroclus lie longer unburied, unmourned and forgotten? I shall not forget him so long as I still live; and even if, in the land of Hades, men forget their dead, yet I shall remember Patroclus, even there. Come, let us go.'

And Achilles, in his hatred, pierced the sinews of Hector's feet from heel to ankle and bound them together with a thong, and made fast the body to the back rail of his chariot, so that the head lay along the ground. He flung in Hector's weapons and his own armour, then leapt himself into the chariot, and snatching the reins and the whip from Automedon, he turned the horses' heads for the shore. He lashed them to a gallop, and Xanthus and Balius went like the West Wind, who was their sire; and so Hector's body was dragged behind the chariot all across the Trojan plain, with his dark hair trailing in the dust.

# XVI

## *The Funeral*

BACK at the camp, each leader of the Greeks, with his own men, went to his ships, there to feast the day's great victory. But Achilles had the body of Patroclus, lying on a bier, brought out from his hut and set upon the shore; then three times about the bier the Myrmidons drove their chariots, to pay honour to dead Patroclus. Then they unharnessed the horses from the chariots, and prepared a feast beside Achilles' ships.

Achilles cut the thongs which tied the broken body of Hector to his chariot and dragged it to the bier and flung it at the feet of Patroclus. He laid his hand, still stained with Trojan blood from the day's slaughter, on the cold breast of his friend, and said with tears, 'I have kept my promise,

Patroclus, and brought you Hector's body. Rest well in the land of Hades, for you are avenged.'

Then, though he had no heart for it, he ate and drank with the Myrmidons, for it was more than only the celebration of that day's deeds, it was the funeral feast of Patroclus. But when the others, having eaten and drunk their fill, had gone to rest, he went apart and walked along the shore, where the waves lapped on the sand, and there, alone, he sat crouched in the darkness, his cloak pulled close about him, his head in his hands, and wept.

But he was weary from the long day's fighting, and from his chase around the walls of Troy, and at last, in the silence of the night, that was broken only by the murmuring of the sea, he fell asleep.

Yet his sleep was not untroubled, for while he slept he dreamt. In his dream he saw Patroclus standing beside him, just as he had been in life, with his same smile and his kindly eyes. Looking down at Achilles, he said in that loved and gentle voice, 'You sleep, Achilles, and I am forgotten. While I yet lived, I was ever in your thoughts, but now you think of me no longer. Bury me soon, that my spirit need no more linger on the bank of the dread River Styx, but may pass over into the land of Hades. And give me your hand, Achilles, for one last time, since I shall not come to you again. Never more shall we sit together, apart from all others, and take joy in each other's company. And one final thing I would ask of you, Achilles. You, too, will soon be dead. Do not let our bones be laid apart, but let them lie together in one urn. Many years were we together while we both lived; do not let men part us when we are dead.'

In his sleep Achilles sat up and cried aloud, 'Why do you bid me do for you as I would have done, without your asking? All shall be as you wish. Oh, Patroclus, never before has there fallen on us a sorrow we might not bear together. Come closer to me. Though we have but a moment left to us, put your arms about me and let us find some comfort in the sharing of our grief.' He stretched out his hands, but clasped only the empty air, and woke in tears to find himself alone on the shore, trembling and cold, in the cold light of early dawn.

When day was come, the Greeks brought wood and built a high pyre close by the sea, and the sorrowing Myrmidons carried to it the body of Patroclus, lying on the bier, with all their chariots coming after; and one by one his comrades cut a lock of hair in mourning and laid it on the bier as each took his last farewell.

After all the others came Achilles, who said, 'On the day I left my father's house he promised my hair to the god of our fast-flowing River Spercheius, if I should return safely home. Since I shall never see my land again, my father cannot fulfil his vow, so I shall give my hair to Patroclus, to take with him as a keepsake.' And he cut off his long, yellow hair and laid it in his friend's cold hands.

Then was Patroclus laid high up on the pyre, with painted jars of oil and honey about him; and from his nine hounds, Achilles chose out his two favourites, that they might go with their master down to the land of Hades. And four swift horses, also, he slew, and they were laid about the pyre with the bodies of the hounds, that Patroclus should be well attended on his journey. And lastly, Achilles had brought to him the twelve noble Trojan youths whom he had taken alive from the battle. They came with fear in their wide eyes and reluctant feet; and he cut the throat of each one and cast him on the pyre.

Then, evening being come, with tears he set a blazing torch to the pyre and kindled it, praying to the winds to blow upon the fire. And the flames rose high, blown by the North Wind and the West Wind.

All night the pyre burnt, and all night Achilles went about it, pouring wine upon the ground from a golden bowl and calling upon Patroclus with many sighs. And at that time when the Morning Star begins to herald the approach of dawn, the flames dropped and the fire died down; and Achilles, wearied out, sank to the ground, and, for a short while, forgot his grief in kindly sleep.

When morning was come, he and the other kings and princes of the Greeks quenched the smouldering ashes of the pyre with wine, and gathered up the charred bones of Patroclus. Achilles placed them in a golden urn which he wrapped in a linen cloth and set in the inner room of his hut. 'Let them lie there,' he said, 'until that day when my bones shall be mingled with them. Now let us raise a burial mound for Patroclus. There is no cause to build it high, for it need do no more than mark the place where our ashes shall one day lie together. But when I am dead and gone to join Patroclus in the land of Hades, then let those of you, my friends, who are still left to do the service for us, build it both high and wide.'

They marked off the circle for the burial mound around the ashes of the pyre, and heaped up earth and stones; and when they had done, they would have gone, but Achilles prevented them. 'It is not fitting,' he said, 'that we should hold no funeral games for one who was my friend.' And he ordered a course to be laid out for the races, and had many fine prizes brought from his ships: bronze cauldrons and tripods, and bars of iron, much valued for its scarcity; and horses and slaves, also, for the winners.

All that day Achilles directed the funeral games in remembrance of his friend, commending the skill of the contestants, and, with praise, awarding the rich prizes. But his heart was heavy, and he cared nothing for it all, save that it honoured Patroclus.

In the chariot races the winner was Diomedes, with the horses of Aeneas, and his prize was a tripod and a slave. Ajax, son of Telamon, and Odysseus proved themselves the best at wrestling, yet could neither throw the other; so Achilles gave them each an equal prize. Of the three who could run the fastest, Ajax of Locris, Odysseus, and Antilochus, Odysseus outstripped the others, and won a huge silver mixing-bowl for wine; though, had Achilles been competing, Odysseus would not have won, for no one of all the Greeks could run faster than Achilles.

The arms and armour of King Sarpedon of the Lycians, which Patroclus had taken from him when he killed him, were the prize for that warrior who should be found the best at fighting with a spear. But Ajax, son of Telamon, and Diomedes both fought so mightily against each other that the prize was divided between them. For his skill with the bow, Meriones the Cretan won ten double-edged axes.

To Nestor Achilles gave as a gift a two-handled urn, saying, 'Good old king, you can have no part in the contests with younger men, though once, I do not doubt, you were as skilled and agile as any here. Therefore, since you cannot win a prize, I give you one. Accept this, Nestor, in memory of Patroclus, for you will not see him again.'

And so it went on throughout the day; and in the evening, when the games were done, they parted, and each man went to his own hut, and having supped, slept peacefully.

But Achilles lay sleepless on his bed, tossing from side to side, weeping and longing for Patroclus as he remembered all that they had done together since they had been children: the journeys they had made by land and sea, their coming together to Troy, and all the many times they had fought side by side.

All night sleep kept from him, and, at the first faint light of dawn, he rose and went out from the hut, weary and heavy-eyed with grief. Seeing the body of Hector where it still lay beyond the palisade about the huts, and thinking how it was to Hector that he owed his sorrow, he yoked Xanthus and Balius to his chariot, and once again, in his hatred and misery and anger, he fastened Hector's body to the chariot and dragged it three times about the burial mound of Patroclus; then left it lying there, outstretched upon the ground, and returned once more to his hut in search of rest, his anger a little blunted, but his heart uncomforted.

And every day, at dawn, he did the same, until eleven days were passed.

XVII

## *The Ransom*

ON the twelfth day after Patroclus had been avenged, great Zeus, father of gods and men, put it into the mind of King Priam that he should go alone to Achilles with a ransom for the body of his son. He rose up from the floor where he sat, with hair dishevelled and garments disarrayed, and through his palace—which yet resounded with the lamentation of his daughters and the wives of his sons, who still wept for Hector—calling as he went for Queen Hecuba, he made his way to his vaulted treasure chamber, with its walls and pillars of fragrant cedar wood, where all his royal wealth was stored.

Goblets and vases of gold and copper, gold and silver cups and dishes were there; chests of rich, embroidered garments, woven rugs, bars of gold and silver; and, laid in wooden coffers, ornaments fit to adorn those who lived in the house of a king: diadems of hanging golden leaves, fillets of beaten gold; bracelets, thin, of twisted gold, or broad and decorated with formal little flowers; necklaces of golden beads, or silver beads and ivory; golden ear-rings in the form of coiled serpents, or with hanging tassels of gold; cunningly wrought brooches to fasten a rich cloak, and pins of gold and ivory, for long, dark hair. All these things, and many more, there were in Priam's treasure chamber.

As he entered, Hecuba, pale and wearied from much weeping, came to him, asking, 'Why did you call me, lord?'

'Immortal Zeus has put it in my heart that I should go to the ships of the Greeks and offer a ransom to Achilles for the body of our son. Tell me, wife, does this not seem good to you?'

But Hecuba flung wide her arms and cried out in horror, 'Through our great grief you have lost your wisdom, lord, that wisdom for which you have ever been honoured. Gone is it utterly, or you would not think to put yourself in the power of Achilles, who is cruel and merciless and has a heart of stone. Remember how many of your sons he has slain. Remember how he dealt with Hector. He will have no respect for your age, nor care that you come to him as a suppliant. No, my husband, let us rather mourn Hector here in our own house. Do not give Achilles, who has slain so many of your sons, cause to boast that he has slain their father, also.'

'My mind is made up,' said Priam, 'and I will go, for I believe that the immortal gods are with me in this thing.

But if I am mistaken and Achilles kills me—well, I am an old man now, and I shall die gladly if first I have looked once more upon my dear son's face and bidden him farewell.'

He would listen to no more of Hecuba's entreaties, but, opening chests and coffers, he took out the finest of the garments that lay in them, and costly woven stuffs, and golden ornaments. Ten talents of gold he weighed out, and chose two shining tripods and four cauldrons, and a Thracian cup, the most precious that he owned.

Then he called to his sons, Paris, Deïphobus, and Helenus and those others who were still left to him, and bade them take the treasures and lay them in a wagon. And when they would have protested, he grew angry and rebuked them. 'Make haste when you are bidden, worthless ones. I would that you had been slain in Hector's stead. All my good, obedient sons are dead: brave Cebriones, young Polydorus, Lycaon; and Hector, the best of them all. While you still live, idle wretches who are fit for nothing but for dancing and the telling of lying tales. Do as I bid you, and with no more delay.'

They hastened to obey him, though they thought that he was indeed crazed with grief, in that he meant to go alone to the ships of the Greeks. They harnessed mules to a new-made wagon and laid upon it the treasure he had chosen out, and brought a chariot for their father, and his best horses.

Priam called to him Idaeus, his old herald, and bade him drive the wagon on ahead; but when he would have mounted the chariot, Hecuba came out to him, carrying wine in a golden cup. 'Make the drink-offering to immortal Zeus before you go, lord, and pray that he may send you safely home from amidst our enemies. Ask of him a sign, I beg of you, that you may be certain of his favour. Ask that he may send an eagle. flying upon your right hand, as a sign that the gods are indeed with you in this thing.'

'That is well thought of, wife,' said Priam. And when he had washed his hands in clear water, he took the cup and poured out the wine and prayed to Zeus for a sign; and then, as he and all the others there anxiously watched the sky, they saw an eagle with wide, dark wings flying across the city, on their right; and even Hecuba was cheered a little by the sight.

Then Priam mounted on to the chariot and took up the reins and went out through the gateway of his palace, with old Idaeus going on before him in the wagon with the ransom.

Down from the Pergamus and on through the wide streets of Troy they went to the Scaean Gate; and Priam's sons and the husbands of his daughters followed them, mourning as for one going to his death. But once through the gateway and beyond the sacred oak, the young men turned back, and Priam and the herald went on alone. Past the burial mound of King Ilus they went and on towards the River Scamander, and close by the ford they stopped to water the horses and mules.

And there, by the river, Hermes, swift messenger of the immortal gods, met them in the likeness of a youth. Idaeus, looking up, saw him come, and said fearfully, 'My king, there is a young Greek coming towards us. Shall we flee, taking the treasure with us, or do we stay and implore his mercy? For though we are two, we are both old, and he is young and armed.'

But Hermes greeted them kindly and asked them whither they were bound; and when they had told him, he said, 'I shall myself conduct you to Achilles' hut, for it is not well that you should be alone and unescorted, bearing such rich treasure with you. Trust yourself to me, and have no fear, good king.'

'Truly,' said Priam thankfully, 'the gods are indeed with me in this, that I should have met with one so kindly and courteous as yourself.'

So Hermes went with them, and when they were come to the ships of Achilles, Hermes caused the wagon and the chariot to pass, unseen of any man, through the gate in the palisade and on into the wide enclosure where the Myrmidons were making ready their evening meal. There he leapt down from the chariot, saying, 'Go quickly in, good king, and ask your boon of Achilles, entreating his mercy in the names of his old father, Peleus, and of silver-footed Thetis, his immortal mother.' And with that he was gone from them, back to snow-crowned Mount Olympus.

Priam came down from his chariot, and leaving Idaeus to hold the horses and the mules, he went alone into the hut of Achilles.

Achilles, having at that moment finished his meal, was sitting, unsmiling, apart from his companions, and only Automedon was near him, to pour more wine for him, or fetch more meat, should he demand it. Straight to Achilles old Priam went, unhesitatingly; and before he could be prevented, knelt in front of him and clasped his knees in supplication, and kissed the hands which had slain his son.

Achilles looked at him with amazement; whilst all his companions in the hut fell silent, watching the stranger who had come amongst them, and wondering who he might be.

'Great Achilles, I beseech your mercy in the name of King Peleus, your father, whose years equal mine, and who, even as I, stands now on the sad threshold of old age. Yet, unlike me, he lives with hope, hope that one day soon he will see his dear son return to him, victorious after many battles. But I, I have no hope to lighten my remaining days. The dearest and the best of all my sons is gone, and I shall never speak with him or hear his voice again. Nor will he ever return victorious to his father's house. Yet one little grain of comfort would it bring to me, in my last years, if I might look upon his face once more and touch him with my hands; and a great solace would it be to me if, in the sad and lonely, unprotected days which yet remain to me, I could remember how his body had been burnt with all honour as befitted the son of a king, and if I could look upon the burial mound which his mourning comrades had raised for him. In the name of your own father and in the name of immortal Thetis, your mother, have mercy, great Achilles, and give back to Priam, that most wretched king, the body of Hector, his son. A great ransom have I brought you for him; do not refuse it.' The tears streamed down his cheeks and he could hardly speak for weeping. He clasped Achilles' hands and said, 'I implore you, have pity on an old man who must humble himself and kneel to one who has slain so many of his sons.'

Achilles, much moved, gently loosed the old king's clasp and put him from him. His eyes were filled with tears and he turned his head away, thinking how his father Peleus would wait in vain for his homecoming. 'I shall never see my father or my own land again,' he thought. Then he thought how he would never again see Patroclus, a far greater grief than any other, and the tears would not be denied. And so they wept together: Achilles for his father and his friend, with the old king crouched at his feet, weeping for his son.

But at last, as Achilles' tears grew less, he was once again aware of Priam, and immediately he stood and raised the old man kindly, saying, 'Your courage is indeed great, King Priam, that you ventured alone amongst your enemies to seek me out. But, come, sit here upon this seat and let us put aside our sorrowing. For of what avail are tears? They cannot bring back the dead. That is a thing which I have learnt.' And he led him to a chair.

But Priam shook his head sternly. 'Should I sit and take my ease, son of Peleus, while Hector lies in the dust amongst his enemies? No. Give him back to me and let me see him. Take the ransom I have brought you, it is a fitting price for the son of a great king.'

For a moment Achilles frowned, then with an effort he forced down his rising anger and answered, 'Do not provoke me with ill-chosen words, good king. I shall give you Hector's body, as you ask, for I think that you came here today by the will of the gods, else could you not have reached my hut unharmed.' He signed to Automedon to follow him, and quickly left the hut.

Outside, he called Idaeus, bidding him go in to his master and rest himself; then he ordered Automedon to unharness the mules and the horses from the wagon and the

chariot, and to carry the ransom into his hut. 'But leave a
tunic and two cloaks to wrap the body in,' he said, 'lest
Priam, seeing his son's wounds, should reproach me, and I
should grow angry at his words and do what I would afterwards regret. For I would not dishonour the gods by mis-
treating a suppliant, and he a grey-haired king.'

He bade the captive women take Hector's body from
where it lay, and, in some place apart, where Priam could
not see them, to wash it and anoint it with oil and wrap it
in the tunic and the cloaks. And when all had been done as
he commanded, he himself helped to lay Hector's body on
the wagon; and as he did so, in his heart he cried out, 'Do
not be angry, Patroclus, if, even in the land of Hades, you
hear that I have given Hector's body to the father who
loved him. Do not be angry with me, but understand why
I have done it, even as you would have understood while
you yet lived.'

Then Achilles returned once more into his hut. 'I have
done as you asked, King Priam. Your son lies on your
wagon. Tomorrow you shall bear him back to Troy. But
now you shall eat and drink with me, and for tonight you
shall lie safely beneath my roof.'

Priam sat, and Achilles gave him roasted meat upon a
platter, and Automedon brought bread to him in a basket;
and in silence they ate and drank together peaceably, the
old king and the young warrior who had slain his son.

When the meal was finished, it had grown dark, and a
slave set torches on the walls, and Priam, rested and refreshed, looked well for the first time at Achilles, all golden
in the flaring torchlight, and saw how all that he had heard
of his peerless beauty was true, and he thought, 'Truly,

rumour has not lied. He is like one of the immortal gods to look upon.'

Achilles, watching, marked how Priam gazed at him, but he said nothing; and it was Priam who broke their silence.

'This is the first time in twelve long days,' he said, 'that I have sat to eat and drink with other men, for I have cared nothing for food or wine since Hector died. As little as I have tasted, so little have I slept for grief. But this evening, son of Peleus, I have eaten and drunk with you, and now I am weary and would sleep.'

At once Achilles ordered beds to be prepared for Priam and Idaeus in the outer porch. 'Forgive it, good king,' he said, 'that I put an honoured guest to sleep outside. But if any leader of the Greeks should come here through the darkness to speak with me tonight—as well might be—he would see you, should you be lying near the hearth, and know you for the king of Troy. And if word reached Agamemnon that you were here, no doubt, to spite me, he would try to make it difficult for you to take with you the body of your son, which I have given you leave to take. But now, before we part tonight, tell me, how many days do you need to celebrate the funeral rites of Hector? For I doubt, with matters as they are, that the Greeks will go out to fight unless I go with them; and I shall keep from battle for as many days as you need.'

Priam, touched by his offer, said, 'I am grateful for your kindness, son of Peleus. May the gods reward you for it. You must know that it is not easy for us, pent up in our city as we are, to venture far from the walls to fetch wood. Give us eleven days, good Achilles. Nine days to mourn for Hector and to gather the wood we shall need for his pyre; on the tenth day we shall burn him and keep his funeral feast, and on the eleventh we shall raise the burial mound above him.' He paused, then added, 'On the twelfth day, if need be, we shall fight again.'

Achilles smiled a little. 'You shall have your twelve days' truce, King Priam, I give you my word on it.' He laid his hand for a moment upon the old king's arm in reassurance, saying to him, 'Now lie down and sleep, you and your herald, and have no fear, for you will be safe beneath my roof.'

And so, amongst his enemies, Priam slept calmly and in peace; but long before dawn Hermes, once again in the likeness of a Greek youth, woke him, saying, 'You came to Achilles as a suppliant, and as a guest he has received you. Him you can trust, for you sleep beneath his roof; yet you can trust no other amongst the Greeks. Do not delay here, close by the ships. A great ransom you have given for your son, but it would be a ransom three times as great that the people of Troy would need to pay to buy your freedom, once Agamemnon knew that you were here.'

Hastily, and in fear, Priam roused Idaeus, and they hurried from Achilles' hut, while Hermes himself harnessed the mules and the horses and, once again, led them safely past the ships and across the plain. At the ford of the Scamander he left them and returned to high Olympus.

As the sun was rising, the wagon and the chariot came slowly along the track towards the Scaean Gate. Cassandra, Hector's sister, watching from the walls, beheld, in the first light of day, her father and Idaeus, and saw that they had returned with him whom they had gone to fetch, and with

a loud cry she roused all the people. 'Come, all you men
and women of Troy. If ever you welcomed back Hector,
living, from the battle, come now and welcome him, dead.
For he died to save our city and us all.'

Out from their houses and out from Priam's palace came
the people of Troy, crowding about the gates as Priam
brought home his son, and with tears and wailing they
welcomed him, following the wagon up the wide street to
the Pergamus.

In the palace Hector was laid upon a bier, and about him
stood the singers to sing his dirge; and one by one the
noble women of the household made lament for him.

First spoke Andromache, his wife, with her arms clasped
about her husband's head. 'Oh, Hector, ill fated are we
whom you have left defenceless, and ill fated is your little
son, but most ill fated of all am I, your unlucky wife; for
you did not stretch out your arms to me when you were
dying, nor speak to me in words which I might have remembered with tears and treasured in my heart for all my
life.'

Beside her stood Queen Hecuba. 'You were the eldest
and the dearest to me of all my children, Hector,' she said.
'And while you lived divine Apollo, the Bright One,
cared well for you. Yet even in your death the immortal
gods did not utterly forsake you; for, though I dared not
hope to do so, I have seen your dear face once again, and
in all honour do you lie in your father's house, and in all
honour shall we celebrate your funeral.' But, after that, she
could say no more for weeping.

Then Helen came to them, and the women drew aside
as she passed and would not look at her, walking slowly

until she stood beside the bier, looking down on Hector. 'Kind Hector,' she said quietly, 'of all the brothers of Paris, you alone never reproached me for the trouble that I brought on Troy, and always would you defend me against the harsh words of others. Now that you are gone, in all Troy I have no man to speak for me, save your father, who, with you, alone was kind.' And she drew her veil across her face to hide her tears.

For nine days was Hector mourned; and on the tenth day, when dawn was come, they laid him on a tall pyre and fired it. All day it burnt, and through the night the ashes smouldered; but on the morning of the eleventh day they poured wine upon the ashes and gathered up the dead man's bones and laid them in a golden urn and set upon it stones and earth, raising a high burial mound.

And so, by the compassion of Achilles, was Hector buried, who had slain Patroclus and brought Achilles so much grief.

## EPILOGUE

# How the War with Troy was Ended

AFTER the death of Hector, the war with Troy went on, though things were hard for the Trojans without their finest warrior; and many times the Greeks carried the battle right to the very walls of Troy.

It was on one such day that the doom foretold for Achilles fell on him. Leading the Greeks against the hard-pressed Trojans, he was fighting close to the Scaean Gate, where Paris, loath as ever to face the dangers of battle, stood with his bow in the shelter of the gateway. When he saw Achilles come within bowshot's range, with a prayer to Apollo the Archer, who had shown himself such a good friend of Troy, he loosed an arrow. Never had his aim been surer, and Achilles, whom Paris would not have dared to face, fell dead. And so was the greatest warrior of them all slain by a man of little courage and no worth.

After a great fight in which Ajax, son of Telamon, slew Glaucus of Lycia, Ajax and Odysseus saved Achilles' body from the Trojans and carried it back to the ships and laid it upon a bier on the shore. There all the kings and princes of the Greeks gathered with Achilles' own Myrmidons to mourn him. Then up from the sea came his mother Thetis with the nine and forty daughters of Nereus, all wailing for Achilles. At the sound, and at the strange sight of the immortal sea-nymphs, a great fear came upon the Greeks, and they would have fled, but old Nestor, in his wisdom, called to them to stay. 'We have no need to fear,' he said. 'It is immortal Thetis and her sisters come to weep for her dead son.' And the Greeks were afraid no longer, but remained to weep with the goddesses; and so they mourned for great Achilles, mortal men and immortal goddesses, for seventeen long days. And on the eighteenth day the Greeks burnt the body of Achilles on a high pyre with jars of sweet oil and honey. The next day they took his bones from the ashes and laid them in a two-handled golden urn which Hephaestus had given to Thetis. And into this urn, also, they put the bones of Patroclus, and above the urn they raised, even as Achilles had asked it of them, a high burial mound on a headland which overlooked the sea.

At the funeral games in his honour, Thetis declared that the god-wrought arms of her son should be given to the bravest of the Greeks. Because they had, together, brought his body safely from the fighting about the Scaean Gate, both Odysseus and Ajax, son of Telamon, claimed them. But Agamemnon, who wished to please Odysseus, awarded the arms to him, and Ajax, disappointed and angry, went out of his mind and fell upon his own sword, and his half-brother Teucer raised a burial mound for him close by the ships of Salamis.

Paris did not survive long to boast of his triumph. Wounded by a Greek archer, he died, later, of his wounds, and Helen, now quite alone and friendless in Troy, and bitterly regretting that she had ever left Menelaus and her home in Sparta, was grateful for the protection of Deïphobus, the brother of Paris, and went to live in his house.

With Achilles and Patroclus both dead, the Myrmidons were without a leader, so Agamemnon sent to Scyros for Neoptolemus, Achilles' young son, without whom, so Calchas the prophet had said, Troy would never be taken. Though he was still a boy, Neoptolemus had inherited his father's courage and much of his battle skill. He came willingly to the war, and willingly the Myrmidons followed him as their leader; and Odysseus gave up to him the arms of his father which Agamemnon had awarded him.

Yet still the war with Troy dragged on, and the Greeks, seeing that they could not take the city by force, decided to take it by a trick. Many say that it was Odysseus who was the author of the cunning ruse by which Troy fell, and indeed, from all else that is told of him, this seems most likely.

The Greeks built a huge horse of wood, all hollow within, and in the body of this wooden horse fifty of their boldest warriors hid; amongst them Menelaus, Diomedes, and Sthenelus, Odysseus himself, and young Neoptolemus.

The Greek army, led by Agamemnon, then dragged the ships down to the water's edge, burnt the huts, and set sail, as if for Greece and home, leaving the wooden horse alone on the beach. But the Greeks sailed no farther than the island of Tenedos, a little way along the coast, and there they cast anchor and waited.

Amazed and joyful that the long siege seemed to be over, and their city free once more, the Trojans poured through the Scaean Gate and across the plain to the shore. There, amongst the ashes of the camp, stood the horse, and the Trojans wondered at it. 'It is an offering to the gods,' said some. 'It is a trap,' said others. 'Let us destroy it,' they cried.

But King Priam said, 'It is a sacred offering. It must not be harmed. Let it be taken into our city.' And he would not listen to the protests of those who would have advised him against such a course.

So the horse was dragged into the city and honoured as an offering to the gods. And there in the assembly place it stood all day, garlanded with flowers, and with petals and green boughs strewn beneath its hooves. And all day the Trojans made merry and rejoiced that the war was over at last, and their city safe.

That night, when darkness had fallen, the Greeks opened the hidden door in the side of the horse and leapt out. Meanwhile, Agamemnon had sailed back with the army from Tenedos, and landing once more on the Trojan shore, hastened across the plain. The Scaean Gates were opened to him by those Greeks already in the city.

The Trojans, for the first time in ten years, sleeping soundly, with no more watchmen to guard the walls than they would have had in time of peace, were taken by surprise as the Greeks swept through the city, killing, plundering, and burning.

King Priam was slain on the steps of his own palace; Odysseus and Menelaus killed Deïphobus; Hector's little son, Astyanax, snatched from his mother's arms, was flung to his death from the walls, lest he should live to avenge his father. By morning, there were few Trojan warriors left alive; though Aeneas, second only to Hector in battle, escaped and fled from the city.

Now that there was no one left to defend Troy, the Greeks tore down the walls and divided the spoils between them: all the great wealth from Priam's treasure chamber, and the women of his household.

Queen Hecuba fell to the lot of Odysseus, but she did not long survive her husband and her children. Unhappy Andromache was claimed by Neoptolemus, and so she found herself a slave to the son of the man who had killed her beloved husband. He took her with him to his grandfather, King Peleus, and treated her well enough. Old Phoenix sailed with them, but he did not live to reach Phthia, for he died on the way home.

Helen, dragged from the house of Deïphobus by her husband Menelaus, expected no mercy. But Menelaus was ever generous and warm hearted, and she was still the most beautiful woman in all the world, and so he forgave her, and they returned to Sparta together, where they lived in accord and happiness for many years.

With the war over and the spoils shared out, the Greeks set sail for home, but the wrath of Aphrodite still followed many of them. Ajax of Locris was drowned on the voyage, and Diomedes came to Greece to find his kingdom lost to him; but he won himself another kingdom, and lived to an old age.

When Teucer reached Salamis, his father, King Telamon, cast him forth, for he had come home alone, without his brother Ajax.

Agamemnon returned to Mycenae, taking with him great riches, and Cassandra, Priam's daughter; and there, in his splendid palace, he was murdered by his wife Clytemnestra, and by Aegisthus, his cousin, with whom he had inherited a family feud; and Cassandra was killed with him.

Idomeneus was shipwrecked on his way to Crete, and when, at last, he came home, it was to find a usurper ruling his rich kingdom.

Odysseus returned to his little kingdom on the island of Ithaca, but only after ten long years of wandering, and many strange adventures.

Wise Nestor alone, who was much loved by the gods, reached home after a short and fair voyage and lived, respected by all, to a very old age in sandy Pylos, with his many sons about him. Yet he, too, had his sorrow, for he had left his eldest son, Antilochus, dead in the land of Troy.

So ended the long war of the Greeks and the Trojans, a war which, in the end, brought as little good to the victors as to the vanquished.

# THE
# ODYSSEY

# PREFACE

SOMEWHERE around three thousand years ago, Homer wrote his great epic poem *The Odyssey* in which he told of the adventures and wanderings of Odysseus, one of the Greek heroes. Since that time, the poem has been translated from the Greek dialect in which it was written, or the story retold in another writer's words, countless times. Every boy and girl knows at least one of the adventures of Odysseus; how he heard the Sirens sing, perhaps, or how he outwitted the Cyclops, Polyphemus; and there have been published numerous volumes of stories for children taken from *The Odyssey*. But there does not seem to have been a complete retelling of the entire story of the poem for young people.

The story is so good that it seems a pity that boys and girls should not read the whole of it; and what I have tried to do in this book is to give the whole tale of *The Odyssey* as the exciting and wonderful adventure that it was.

None of the characters in *The Odyssey* was created by Homer. They are all either legendary figures and great heroes well known to the people of his day, or they are the gods and goddesses of the Greeks.

The Greeks did not believe in one god, but in several, each with his or her own particular attributes. To the Greeks, the sky, the sea, and the earth were divided up between the three divine brothers, Zeus, Poseidon, and Hades. Zeus, the father of gods and men, and the most important of all the Greek deities, ruled over the earth and the sky; Poseidon was lord of the seas and rivers, while

Hades was the god of all that is found under the earth and the guardian of the spirits of the dead. Hera, the wife of Zeus, was the queen of the gods; and the other chief deities were Apollo, the god of art and learning and all the daylight things of the world; his sister, Artemis the huntress, who was goddess of the chase and all wild creatures; Aphrodite, goddess of love and beauty; Athene, goddess of wisdom, who presided over all craft and skilfulness, whether of the hands or the mind; Ares, the god of war; and Hermes, who was their messenger. In the north of Greece is a mountain called Mount Olympus, and here, on the very summit of the peak, the Greeks believed the gods lived, in everlasting peace and joy.

But there was one occasion on which their peace was broken for a while, when the three goddesses, Hera, Aphrodite, and Athene, quarrelled among themselves as to which of them was the most beautiful. The gods could not decide for them, so they went down to earth, and in the land of Troy they found Paris, the young son of the king of that country, and asked him to say which of the three he considered the loveliest. He chose Aphrodite, and as a reward, she promised him the most beautiful woman in the world for his wife. Unfortunately, the most beautiful woman in the world was the Grecian, Helen, and she was already the wife of Menelaus, the king of Sparta. But Aphrodite kept her promise, and when, later, Paris was travelling through Greece, he became a guest in the house of Menelaus, and there Helen saw him and fell in love with him. When he returned home to Troy she went with him. Menelaus appealed to his brother Agamemnon, the greatest of all the kings in Greece, to help him recover his wife; and

Agamemnon called together all the leaders of the Greeks and with a mighty fleet they sailed for the Trojan coast, and laid siege to the city of Troy. The siege lasted for ten years, and at the end of that time the city fell. Most of the Trojan leaders were killed, and Menelaus won back Helen.

When the war was over, the Greeks set sail for their homes, and among them was Odysseus, the king of Ithaca, and it is the story of his eventful voyage that Homer tells in *The Odyssey*.

*Barbara Leonie Picard*

# CONTENTS

# PART ONE

# Odysseus sails for Ithaca

# I

# *Polyphemus the Cyclops*

AFTER their ten-year-long war with the men of Troy
was ended and the Trojan city had fallen in flames
and smoke, the victorious Greeks gathered together their booty and their prisoners; and when the great
King Agamemnon, who was in charge of all the Grecian
host, had given the word, one by one all those leaders of
the Greeks who had survived the fighting boarded their
ships and set sail for home.

Among them was Odysseus, king of the little island of
Ithaca, lying off the mainland of Greece. He and his men
put out to sea in twelve ships of fifty oars, their white sails
unfurled and their blue-painted prows thrusting through
the waves as the wind filled the sails: nigh on sixty men on
board each ship. And the heart of every man was happy

as he thought how at last, after ten weary years of battle, he would once again see Ithaca, which was his home.

After a few days at sea, Odysseus and his men landed in the country of the Cicones, and because for ten years their minds had been filled with thoughts of war and strife, it did not seem to them an evil thing to fall unprovoked upon the Cicones in their coastland city, killing the men and driving off their cattle.

On the beach they divided the spoils so that each man in the twelve ships had an equal share; and when this was done, Odysseus urged that they should set sail at once. But they were arrogant in their success, and gave no heed to his advice; instead they built fires upon the shore and roasted meat and broke open the Cicones' wine-jars. And feasting their victory with looted food and drink all night, they gave no thought to the people whose city they had that day despoiled.

But the Cicones sent for help to others of their race, finer warriors than themselves, who lived inland and fought from chariots; and in the first light of dawn they swept down upon the Greeks as they camped on the shore. All the morning, fighting with their backs to the sea, the men of Odysseus held their own, but in the hours after midday they were overwhelmed by the Cicones and, fleeing to the ships, they put out to sea leaving the Cicones masters of the day. And when their numbers were counted Odysseus found that he had lost six men out of every ship.

Not many days later, the ships ran into a strong north wind which blew them from their course, and after nine days' sailing in the wrong direction the land of the Lotus-eaters came in sight. They put in to shore, and Odysseus,

ever curious as to the customs of other lands, sent out three
men to discover what manner of people dwelt in this
country.

They found them a peaceable and lazy folk, who desired
nothing more in life than to eat of the fruit of the lotus
plant and dream away their time. The Lotus-eaters received
the Greeks kindly, as was their way with strangers, and
gave them lotus fruits to eat. Immediately they had tasted
of this food, Odysseus' men lost all wish to return to their
comrades on the shore and toil once more upon the waves
on their voyage to Ithaca. Indeed, they cared no longer for
their homes and wished only to remain in the country of
the Lotus-eaters, idly eating the lotus fruits and dreaming
the days away.

When they did not return to him, Odysseus went with
others of his men to find what had befallen them. 'Perchance they may have met with savage folk who hold them
prisoner, or perchance they may be slain,' he said. 'We may
yet be in time to save them, or we may avenge their deaths.'

But he found his men sitting with the Lotus-eaters in
quiet content, with no wish in the world but to remain
there evermore. Odysseus and his followers dragged the
three men back to the ships, protesting and wailing, and
bound them firmly, lest they should return to the Lotus-
eaters and be lost to their comrades for ever. Then with all
speed he ordered the ships to set sail again, before any more
of his men should taste of the fruit of the lotus and forget
their homes.

The next land that they reached was the country of the
Cyclopes, a simple, savage folk, of more than human size,
who never tilled their land, or built ships or houses, or

traded with other nations. Instead they lived in caves in the rocks and spent their time pasturing their flocks on their rich green fields.

Just off the mainland lay a wooded island, the home of many wild goats, and to this island the twelve ships came on a misty night. The men disembarked and slept; and in the morning, when the mist had cleared, they saw opposite them the land of the Cyclopes, and were surprised, for in the fog they had not imagined the mainland to be so close.

All that day they rested from their labours on the sea and feasted on the flesh of the island goats. Keeping a careful watch upon the land, Odysseus was just able to make out the huge flocks of sheep and the cattle of the Cyclopes, browsing in the fields, and the smoke from the fires of the herdsmen. 'Tomorrow', he said, 'I shall go with one ship to the mainland and see who lives in that rich country. It may well be a friendly folk who will give us welcome hospitality after our days at sea.'

Accordingly, in the morning Odysseus sailed to the mainland and beached his ship on the shore below a rocky cliff which towered above their heads, with shrubs growing among the rocks and little yellow wallflowers springing from every cleft.

Close by, half-way up the cliff and approached by a zigzag pathway, was the opening of a wide cave, half-hidden by laurel bushes and surrounded by a wall of huge stones. It was plain to see that the cave was someone's home, and picking out twelve of his best men, Odysseus set off up the cliff carrying a skin of the finest wine he had on board, as a gift for whoever might live there.

Beyond the wall they found a courtyard with pens for sheep and goats; though the pens were empty when they saw them, for the flocks were out at pasture with their owner.

'There is no one here,' said Odysseus. 'Let us wait in the cave for the shepherd to return.' And they passed beneath the glossy foliage of the overhanging laurels and went inside.

Within, the light was dim, but when their eyes grew used to it, they saw that the huge cave held many pens of lambs and kids, all separated according to their ages. There were, too, great pails of milk, and cheeses stacked in baskets hanging from the roof. But for all this abundance of good food the cave did not seem a friendly place, and Odysseus' men urged him to let them take as many cheeses and lambs as they could carry and return at once to the ship. But he would not hear of this. 'We could not rob a stranger in his absence,' he said. 'Besides, when he returns it may please him to give us far more gifts than thirteen men can carry off, and it would be folly to miss the chance of filling our ship with savoury cheeses and tender kids which we might share with our comrades waiting on the island.'

So they remained in the cave, and towards evening the herdsman returned with his flocks. He was as tall as three men and broad, with but one eye in the middle of his forehead; and as soon as Odysseus and his men caught sight of him, they knew that they had been unwise to wait.

He came to the entrance of the cave and flung inside a huge bundle of logs, large branches lopped from tall pines and oaks, as faggots for his fire; and in terror the Greeks fled to the darkest corner of the cave and hid themselves. The monster penned his rams and goats in the courtyard.

and drove the ewes and she-goats into the cave for milking, blocking the entrance with a great stone. And even his sheep and goats were larger than any Odysseus had ever seen before.

When the milking was over, the monster penned the ewes with their lambs and the goats with their kids, and set himself to make a fire from the wood he had brought home. As soon as he had a blaze, he was able to see, by the light of the leaping flames, Odysseus and his men, crouching in the very farthest corner. 'Who are you, strangers?' he asked in a voice like thunder.

For all his terror Odysseus stepped forward and answered boldly enough. 'We are Greeks, sailing home to Ithaca from the war with Troy. The winds have carried us somewhat from our course, and we have come to you in the hope that you may be our host until we can set sail once more.'

The giant roared, 'I am Polyphemus the Cyclops, and I entertain no guests unless it pleases me. But tell me this, where have you beached your ship? Is she close by?'

Odysseus suspected the question and guessed the Cyclops meant harm to his ship and the men guarding her, and he answered cunningly, 'Our ship was wrecked upon your shore, and only I and these twelve men escaped alive from the sea.'

But Polyphemus gave no word of sympathy in reply. Instead, he seized a man in each hand, and dashing out their brains against the rocky floor, he tore them in pieces and ate them for his supper before the eyes of their horrified comrades. Then after drinking several large pailfuls of milk, he lay down by the fire to sleep.

Odysseus would have drawn his sword and crept upon him while he slept and killed him, but that he knew it would be impossible for him and his men to move away by themselves the great stone that blocked the opening of the cave. So, terrified, they waited all night, whispering together and trying to devise some means of outwitting the cruel monster.

At dawn Polyphemus rekindled the fire and milked his ewes and goats again. That done, he snatched up two more of Odysseus' men and ate them as a wild beast might have done. Then he rolled aside the great stone from the mouth of the cave and drove out his flocks; and replacing the stone once more, he went towards the mountain pastures, whistling cheerfully at the thought of the good supper which awaited his return.

Odysseus and the eight men left to him sat down beside the fire to think how they might escape the fate which would surely be theirs unless they could find a way to leave the cave; and at last a plan came to Odysseus. In the cave there lay a long pole of green olive-wood, drying so that it might serve the Cyclops for a staff. From this pole Odysseus hacked off with his sword a piece the length of a tall man, and set his companions to sharpen one end into a point and harden it in the fire.

'Tonight,' he said, 'when the monster sleeps, we will heat the wood red-hot and with it put out his single eye.'

When the point of the stake was hard and sharp, they hid it, and then chose by lot the four men who should help Odysseus use it in the night.

When evening came the Cyclops returned with his flocks, and this time he drove all the sheep into the cave, rams and ewes alike, and penned them safely. When he had milked the ewes and goats he thought of his own supper, and seized two more men. While he sat by the fire eating them, Odysseus poured out a huge bowlful of the wine he had brought with him, and coming forward, offered it to Polyphemus. 'Such wine as this our ship held before it was wrecked upon your shores,' he said. 'Come, taste of it and tell me if you think it is not good.'

The Cyclops took the wooden bowl and drained it at one draught. He held it out to Odysseus. 'Give me more,' he said.

Odysseus filled it a second time, and again the monster drank. 'Give me yet more of your wine, stranger,' he demanded, 'and tell me your name, that I may give you a gift in return.'

A third time Odysseus filled the bowl and the Cyclops drank. 'My name is No-one,' said Odysseus. 'Tell me now what gift you will give to No-one in exchange for his good wine.'

'I will eat you last of all your comrades. A few more hours of life, that shall be my gift to you.' And with a mighty laugh that echoed through the cave Polyphemus lay down beside the fire; and made drowsy by the wine, he fell deeply asleep at once.

Odysseus thrust the stake into the embers and held it there until it was red-hot, then taking it, he and the four men on whom the lot had fallen drove it deep into the Cyclops' eye.

With screams and with shouts of rage Polyphemus awoke and pulled the stake from the socket of his eye, and wildly flinging his arms about and stumbling around the cave, he tried to catch Odysseus and his friends, who crouched trembling against the wall.

The neighbouring Cyclopes who dwelt in caverns nearby heard his cries, and coming to his cave, stood outside the great stone and called to him. 'What ails you, Polyphemus? Why do you wake us with your cries? Does someone steal your sheep or kill you?'

'Good neighbours,' said Polyphemus, 'it is the cunning wiles of No-one that are killing me.'

'If no one is killing you,' answered the neighbours, 'you must be sick, and illness comes from the gods, and we can be of no help to you. You have woken us in vain. May your sickness have left you by the morning.' And they returned to their own homes.

But the Cyclops groped his way to the entrance of the cave and pushed away the great stone, and sitting down in the doorway, waited to catch any of the men who might try to pass him; so that they saw that there was no escape for them that way.

At the far end of the cave Odysseus and his companions made whispered plans; and taking reeds from Polyphemus' bed, Odysseus bound together eighteen of the finest rams in threes, with one of his six men tied beneath each middle ram. Then he himself laid hold of the largest ram of all, a great creature with a splendid fleece, and lay underneath it, clinging on and hidden by the shaggy wool that hung down from its broad sides.

By that time it was dawn, and the rams were eager to be grazing in the rich pastures. Bleating, they moved together to the entrance of the cave, where Polyphemus felt across the back of each one as it came to him, before passing it through into the courtyard. But he never thought to feel beneath the animals, so the six men went safely out. Last of all to come was the leader of the flock, walking slowly under the weight of Odysseus, clinging to its fleece.

As Polyphemus felt its back he spoke to it. 'My good ram, you are ever the foremost of the flock, leading the others to their grazing ground. Why are you last today? Are you grieved for your master, blinded by wicked No-one, and would stay to comfort him? I would that you could speak and tell me where he hides, that wretch who took away my sight. But go, dear ram, join your companions in the fields.' And Polyphemus moved his hand aside and the ram stepped through the opening into the sunlight, bearing Odysseus.

Once outside the courtyard, Odysseus freed himself from his hiding-place and went to release his companions. Then hastily they drove the sheep down to the ship and their comrades waiting on the shore. With no delay they stowed the flock on board and set out to row back to the island where the fleet was moored.

A little way from the shore Odysseus stood up in the ship and shouted with all his might, 'Now indeed, wicked Cyclops, do you know what ills your cruelty to helpless strangers has brought to you.'

Polyphemus heard him and came out from his cave in fury, and breaking off a huge piece of rock he flung it into the sea in the direction of Odysseus' voice. It fell in the water by the bows and the great waves made by its fall washed the ship back towards the shore; but Odysseus seized a long pole and pushed off again, and his men fell to rowing hard once more.

Again Odysseus stood up to shout his taunts to the Cyclops, and though his men tried to restrain him, for they feared another rock might be cast at them, he called out, 'Polyphemus, if anyone should ever ask you how you lost your sight, you may tell him that Odysseus, king of Ithaca, put out your eye.'

And Polyphemus cried out with a loud voice, 'Alas, it was foretold that great grief would come to me through Odysseus, king of Ithaca, but I had thought he would be a fine big man, a worthy enemy for me, not a tiny weakling like yourself. But evil will come to you as well from this, for Poseidon, god of the sea whereon you sail, is my father, and he will avenge my eye.' And he held out his hands over the water and prayed to his father for vengeance. 'Great Poseidon, lord of all the seas, grant your son this one request. May Odysseus and his men never reach their home in Ithaca. But if, in spite of all his misdeeds, it is the will of the gods that Odysseus should gain the shores of his own land, let it be alone and friendless, and may he find sorrow awaiting him in his house.'

And again Polyphemus tore off and hurled into the sea a rock. But this time it fell to the stern of the ship, and sent her rushing forward to the island.

Once safely with the men from his other ships, Odysseus divided the sheep among them, a fair share to each. But his companions allotted him the fine ram by the help of which he had escaped, as an extra gift, because he was their leader and because he had saved six of his men from the Cyclops.

All that day they feasted on the island, and in the morning they set sail once more. But mighty Poseidon had heard the prayer of Polyphemus the Cyclops, and he brought great trouble on Odysseus and his men.

They came next to the floating island of Aeolia, around which ran a mighty wall of cliff surmounted by a wall of bronze, and within these brazen walls lay the lands of Aeolus, guardian of the winds. In his vast palace he lived with his wife and twelve children, six sons and six daughters, feasting continually. Every day on Aeolia was a holiday with banquets and rejoicing, abundant food and everflowing wine. And far from the palace could the savoury smells of roasting meats be marked, and the sounds of revelry.

Aeolus and his family welcomed Odysseus and his men with kindness and willing hospitality; and for thirty days they lived in the palace, joining in the feasting and gaiety of their hosts. At great length Odysseus related all the deeds of the Greeks at Troy; and there was no end to the questions that Aeolus asked of all that he had seen and done in the ten years after he had left his home in Ithaca.

Since Aeolus had all the winds of the world in his keeping, when the time came for Odysseus to depart, he asked his host for a favourable breeze, that his ships might reach the coast of Ithaca with all speed. Aeolus promised him a brisk west wind to make his voyage short, and gave him besides, all the contrary winds tied in a leathern sack; so that until the sack was opened when he was safely home, not one might blow and drive him from his course.

This sack Odysseus kept close beside him, never permitting any of his followers to touch it, nor telling them what it contained; until, on the tenth day after they had left Aeolia, the coast of Ithaca came in sight. Then indeed did

Odysseus and his men rejoice, when they came close enough to see the herdsmen's fires upon the hills; and then at last Odysseus relaxed his eager watching for the first sight of land, and lay down to rest. Thinking of his wife, Penelope, whom he had left ten years before with her tiny babe in her arms, he smiled, wondering if she would have altered in his absence; whether she was now as beautiful as a woman as she had been as a young maiden; and reflecting that the babe would now be a sturdy little boy of ten years old, to whom his father would seem a stranger. 'To see them both again,' thought Odysseus, 'could any joy be greater?' And thinking pleasantly of their happiness and of all he had to tell them, he fell asleep.

While their leader slept the men in Odysseus' ship talked. 'It will be good to see our homes again,' said one. 'And we have spoils in plenty to gladden our families.'

Another glanced at the leathern sack beside Odysseus. 'He has more than we,' he said.

'He is our king,' said another, 'it is only fitting that his portion should be greater.'

'Our voyage has been as long and perilous as his,' grumbled the man who had spoken second, 'but good Aeolus gave us nothing. That great sack Odysseus guards so carefully is doubtless filled with gold and silver; cups and platters and finely wrought bowls to hold the sparkling wine. I would that we had gifts as fine to carry home.'

And they stared at the sack until envy made them rash and they spoke foolishly. 'Let us open the sack and see what may be in it. Perchance there will be inside some small thing apiece for us which will not be missed.' And one of them opened the sack quietly to look inside, and all the winds rushed out, filling the sky and beating the sea into mighty waves and driving the ships back the way that they had come.

Odysseus awoke at the despairing cries of his men, to see the coast of Ithaca vanish from sight as the ships were borne swiftly towards the island of Aeolia.

Landing on Aeolia, Odysseus went with two men to the palace, to ask if Aeolus might not help him once again. He entered the hall where Aeolus feasted with his family and friends, and sitting down by the doorway he waited silently.

Aeolus saw him with amazement. 'Odysseus, how have you come here? I thought that by this day you would have been in your own home. Did I not make your return to Ithaca certain by my help?'

Then Odysseus told them what his comrades had done, and he pleaded, 'Give me your help once again, good Aeolus, for we are indeed the most miserable of men.'

But Aeolus and his sons rose up and drove him from the hall, saying, 'Go from the island instantly, for you must be the unluckiest of all mortals, and carry ill fortune wherever you set foot. Begone, for we want here no bringers of calamity.'

And Odysseus and his ships put out to sea once more, and this time Aeolus kept the winds prisoned on the island and the sea was calm; so calm that for six days and nights the men were forced to row unceasingly.

On the seventh day they reached Telepylus, the home of the Laestrygonians. In this land there was no night, but the sun shone unendingly; so that a man who needed no sleep could have earned two men's wages, as a shepherd by day, and as a cowherd during the sunlit night.

In Telepylus they found a fine harbour, a cliff curving around like a horn on either side of it, with a narrow passage out to sea. In this calm bay eleven of Odysseus' ships moored, so that the men might have rest after their toil at the oars. But Odysseus made fast his ship at the point of one of the curving horns of land, for he wished to climb the cliff to see if he could gain a glimpse of the inhabitants of the country.

From the topmost rock of the cliff all he could see was the smoke from a few fires; no dwellings, no herds, no men. So he sent out three of his followers to bring back tidings of the Laestrygonians, and of their chances of finding in that land the provisions they needed, and perhaps news of a kindly host to welcome them at his house.

The three men found a well-made road leading from the shore, and a little way along it they met a maiden, tall and handsome, drawing water from a spring. They asked her who was king of the land and where he lived, and she replied, 'My father is King Antiphates and yonder is his house.' And she led them to a lofty building near a town of great houses, the largest they had ever seen. In the house a woman of enormous size, Antiphates' queen, came to them, and with fair words beguiled them and made them sit and eat, while she sent for her husband to come home at once.

Already filled with fear at the sight of the queen, who seemed to them to be as tall as a mountain, the three men were struck with terror at the appearance of King Antiphates, striding into his halls with a mighty roar, for he was even taller than his wife.

Immediately he seized one of the unfortunate men, and

killing him with one blow, tossed him to his wife. 'Make him ready for my supper,' he said.

Before he could catch them also, the two others rose and fled back to where Odysseus waited by his ship, but almost before they could stammer out their story, Antiphates had called up his men; and standing on the cliffs the Laestrygonians hurled great rocks upon the ships, pent up in the harbour and unable to pass with any speed through the narrow way to the open sea beyond. The timbers of the ships were shattered and the men struggled in the water, seeking to reach the safety of the shore before they drowned. But the giants rushed down to the beach and speared them as they swam and carried them in triumph to their homes to cook and eat.

Seeing that there was no way of saving the remainder of his ships from the Laestrygonians, Odysseus cut through the cables of his own ship with his sword and shouted to his men to row out to sea with all their might; and thus he saved them from the slaughter.

But of all his fleet that had sailed so joyfully from Troy, that one ship alone was saved.

# II

## *Circe*

ODYSSEUS and his companions sailed on, glad to have escaped alive from the cruel Laestrygonians, but with their hearts heavy for their slain comrades. After many days they sighted the shores of Aeaea, a fair green island in the waste of blue sea.

Thankful to be within reach of land again, they put in to the shore at a spot where the coastline made a safe harbour for the ship, and cast themselves down upon the golden sand, weary and dispirited. For two days and two nights they sighed and sorrowed for their friends whom they had lost, and for the homes and families they feared they might never see again; and Odysseus, as full of grief as any of his men, sat crouched beside a rock, his cloak drawn across his face.

But it was not Odysseus' way to remain long inactive

and despairing; and on the morning of the third day, when
he saw the sun rise in a blaze of rosy light, making a golden
path across the sea from the far horizon to the very shore
where he lay, he jumped to his feet, flinging aside his slug-
gardly sorrow with his cloak. 'For shame,' he thought,
'shall I remain here idle while there are yet things which I
could do to help my men?' And taking his sword and his
spear he turned his back upon the sea and walked away to
where the beach sloped upwards towards a hill, thinking
that from this higher land he might gain a sight of the
island and perhaps judge what manner of people dwelt
upon it.

He climbed hopefully up the rocky hillside where the
little pink cyclamen with their silver-mottled leaves un-
twisted their buds in the morning sunlight; and at the top
he stood and looked out across the whole isle. He saw that
inland of the rocky hills that ran around the coast, Aeaea
was a pleasant wooded valley.

As his sharp eyes wandered over the treetops, Odysseus
suddenly caught sight of a streak of blue-grey smoke that
rose up through the trees into the calm morning air.
'Where there is smoke', he said to himself, 'there is a
hearth; and where there is a hearth, there someone has his
home; though what manner of man he may be, whether
friendly to strangers or of ill intent, no one may guess.'
And he wondered in his mind whether to go alone among
the tall trees to spy out the chances of friendly entertainment, or to return to the shore and rouse his men, and bid
them come with him into the wood.

But while he stood undecided, he saw a fine stag step
from the shelter of the trees to drink at a little stream which

ran below him. His heart leapt up at the sight. 'Fresh meat', he thought, 'will put new courage into my men. A good meal will make them bold once more.' And carefully and silently he poised his spear and hurled it at the beast. His aim was perfect and the stag fell dead. Rejoicing, Odysseus ran down the slope; and plucking reeds from the banks of the stream, and cutting pliant branches from a nearby willow, he plaited a strong rope with which he tied the legs of the stag together, and heaved the animal across his shoulders. With his burden he climbed slowly to the top of the hill, and from there descended once again to the shore.

He woke his men with a great shout, and when they saw the stag they came running eagerly. 'Come, my friends,' said Odysseus, 'let us not give way to grief while we yet have good food to eat. Let us feast and regain our courage.'

Soon a fire had been lit on the beach and the venison was roasting over it. Wine was brought from the ship in painted jars and skins, and Odysseus and his men spread out their cloaks upon the sand and sat down to eat and drink. All that day they feasted and rejoiced, and that night they slept peacefully and free from grief.

In the morning early, Odysseus called his companions together and told them of the smoke he had seen rising above the treetops beyond the hill. 'We must go', he said, 'and see who lives in the wood. Perhaps we may meet with some hospitable folk who will give us food and drink and beds to sleep upon at night, until we feel ourselves able to set sail once more for Ithaca.'

Most of his men were fearful of what the wood might hide, for they remembered the Laestrygonians and the terrible Cyclops; but Odysseus was insistent, and dividing his followers into two bands of twenty-two men each, he put one group under the leadership of Eurylochus, whose courage he trusted, and remained himself in charge of the other. Then with black and white pebbles from the beach in a helmet, they drew lots to decide who should stay by the ship, and who should undertake the journey to the wood. And it fell to the lot of Eurylochus and his party to go, while Odysseus remained on the shore.

With grief and foreboding the comrades took leave of each other, and Eurylochus and his two-and-twenty followers climbed the hill from the beach and descended to the wood on the other side in the direction Odysseus had pointed out to them. Then they too saw the smoke rising against the blue sky from among the trees, as he had described; and unwillingly they entered the wood.

After a time they came upon a clearing where stood a large house of polished stone: wide rooms on three sides about a courtyard, with a flat roof above and a handsome entrance porch.

'It is a fine house,' they said, 'it might well be the home of kindly folk.' And they left the shelter of the trees and crossed the clearing towards the house.

But half-way across the open space they paused in horror, for from round about the building there leapt towards them a pack of shaggy wolves with several great tawny lions in their midst, and in a moment Eurylochus and his companions were surrounded by the beasts.

'Surely we shall perish here', they thought, 'and never see again our good ship or Odysseus, our king.'

But to their astonishment the wolves fawned upon them

like eager dogs, jumping up to greet them and howling a welcome with wagging tails; while the lions purred like cats and rubbed huge yellow-maned heads against their shoulders. But friendly as the animals seemed to be, they were yet wolves and lions, and the men were afraid.

'Let us seek safety in the house,' shouted Eurylochus; and without further thought than to escape from the wild beasts surrounding them, the men ran to the shelter of the doorway. The lions and wolves did not follow them there, and as the twenty-three comrades stood huddled together, they could hear, from within the house, the sound of a woman singing. Her voice was young and beautiful, and her sweet song brought courage to their frightened hearts.

Then Polites, one of Odysseus' bravest captains, spoke: 'Whoever she is who sings within the house, her voice would not disgrace one of the immortal goddesses. No woman with a voice like that could have an evil heart. Let us call to her and ask her hospitality.'

To this suggestion they were all agreed save Eurylochus, who strove to persuade them against the risk of entering an unknown house without finding out more about her who dwelt in it than that she could sing sweetly. But no one heeded him; it was as though the song had robbed them of their wits, and they called out loudly to whoever was inside the house; and instantly the singing ceased and the great doors opened.

A lovely woman in a bright robe stood upon the threshold. Her hair was divided and curled into seven locks and braided with purple ribbons; and her red lips parted in a smile of welcome. 'Come in, strangers,' she said. 'This is Circe's home. Come in and enjoy the hospitality of

Circe.' And she stood aside to let them pass, and led by
Polites, the men entered her house eagerly, all but Eurylochus, and the doors closed behind them. But Eurylochus
was afraid and hid behind a fig-tree that grew beside the
porch.

Circe led her guests into the great hall of her house,
furnished with chairs and couches of costly woods and
precious metals, and she bade them sit while she brought
them food and wine. They sat on the comfortable chairs
and lay on the couches covered with the many-coloured
cloths woven by Circe herself on her great loom, and con-
gratulated each other on their wise decision to call to the
fair singer for admittance to her home. But they did not
know that Circe was an enchantress whose delight it was to
turn men into animals—the wolves and lions that prowled
around the clearing had once been men—and that they
themselves were to be her next victims.

She brought them barley cakes with honey, and red wine
in silver cups, and bade them eat and drink, and smiled at
them. But with the wine she had mixed an evil drug which
caused them to forget the land where they had been born
and once lived happily. And when they had eaten and
drunk, she rose and took her magic wand and struck with
it each man in turn, and one after another, they were
changed into swine.

Then Circe drove them out into the courtyard and
penned them in the sty, two-and-twenty swine but with
yet their own human minds to deplore their plight, and
their own human hearts to sorrow at their fate. She flung
among them handfuls of acorn and beech nuts, the favourite
food of pigs; and for all their human minds they scrambled

for them, grunting and trampling on each other in their eagerness. And Circe laughed.

Hidden beside the porch, Eurylochus listened, and when he could no longer hear the murmur of voices from within, his fears increased; and after there had been silence in the house for a great while, he fled across the clearing, through the woods, and back to where Odysseus waited on the shore. There he related all that had happened since he and his companions had set off; how they had reached the house in the wood and how the animals had greeted them, and how the others had all entered the house and he had seen no more of them.

Odysseus buckled on his sword. 'Lead me back to the spot where stands this house,' he said, 'and I will discover, if I can, what has become of our friends.'

But Eurylochus fell upon his knees in fearful dismay and pleaded, 'Do not ask me to go back with you to that terrible place, for I am sure that our comrades have perished; as you yourself will also perish if you go to seek for them. Let us instead set sail from this unlucky island while there are still some of us left alive.'

But Odysseus answered firmly, 'I cannot desert my men while they may yet be living. Stay here by the ship, Eurylochus, and eat and drink to keep up your courage and strength, and I will go alone.' And he turned and went over the hill and down into the wood, while Eurylochus and the other men sat on the beach beside their ship and mourned him as one already lost, for they never thought to see him again.

Odysseus hurried through the wood, wondering what terrors his quest would bring to him; and among the trees there came to him Hermes, the swift messenger of the immortal gods, in the guise of a lovely youth.

'Greetings, unfortunate Odysseus,' he said. 'Have you come to free your comrades from the enchantments of the sorceress Circe? I fear that, unaided, you will fail, for her magic is powerful, and your men are turned to grunting swine and penned up in her sty. There you will surely join them if you lack my help. But I will give you a strong charm against her witchcraft and tell you what you must do. She will speak kindly to you and ask you to enter her house, and after she has given you food and drink into which she has put her evil drugs, she will strike you with her magic wand, that you may take the shape of a beast. But with my charm to help you, her spells will have no power over you. And when she touches you with her wand you must rise and draw your sword and make as though you meant to kill her. She will plead with you for her life and ask you to remain with her and offer you friendship and hospitality. Do not refuse her offers, but threaten her until she swears she means no evil to you, for otherwise she will surely do you harm when you lie helpless and asleep within her house.' And Hermes bent and plucked up from the ground a little plant with a twisted black root and flowers as white as milk. 'This plant is moly,' he said, 'a very potent charm against all evil.' And he gave it to Odysseus, and in the next instant he was gone.

Wondering, Odysseus went on towards the house, and standing in the porch he heard Circe within, singing as she moved to and fro before her great loom, weaving the bright-patterned cloth. He called to her and at once the singing ceased and the doors opened and Circe stood there, smiling. 'You are welcome, stranger,' she said. 'This is Circe's home. Come in and enjoy the hospitality of Circe.' And she stood aside and Odysseus entered the house, and she closed the doors behind him.

Filled with apprehension he followed her, and she bade him sit upon a chair of rare wood inlaid with silver and placed a footstool at his feet. She gave him wine mixed with her evil drugs in a golden cup; and when he had drunk she struck him with her wand. 'Go now and join your comrades in the sty,' she ordered.

But as Hermes had said, the little plant moly was a powerful charm, and Circe's spells had no effect on Odysseus. Instead, as he had been bidden, he leapt to his feet and drew his sword and rushed upon the enchantress.

She gave a great cry and fell at his feet, begging him to spare her life. 'What manner of man are you,' she asked in amazement, 'that my magic has no power over you? Surely you can be no other than the wise Odysseus, famed for his cunning and skill, whom Hermes once prophesied should come one day to my house. If you are indeed Odysseus, then I wish you no harm. Sheathe your sword and stay here with me in trust and friendship, an honoured guest, for as long as you will.'

But Odysseus replied, 'There can be no trust between us, Circe, until you have sworn an oath to plan no evil deeds against me. And how can I give friendship to one who has tricked my men and laid a wicked enchantment on them, and would without a doubt do the same to me as soon as there was an opportunity?'

So Circe swore a solemn oath that she meant no harm to Odysseus, and he put aside his sword.

And Circe called the four maidens who served her and bade them minister to Odysseus as befitted such a noble guest. One of them heated water in a brazen cauldron that he might bathe himself, and took from him his travel-stained garments and gave him instead a new tunic of finest linen and a warm cloak. Another spread the chairs with purple-dyed cloth and laid rugs upon the floor; and the third brought little silver tables to set beside the chairs; while the fourth mixed sweet wine in a silver bowl.

Odysseus sat in the chair of silver-inlaid wood and the four serving-maids brought him wine and bread and choice meats on golden dishes; but he was sad at heart for his comrades, penned in the sty, and he could not eat or drink.

And when Circe saw that he would touch neither food nor wine, she thought that he yet mistrusted her, and she came and stood beside him and asked, 'Why will you not eat of my food and drink my crimson wine, Odysseus? Is it because you suspect me of some treachery? You do me wrong, for have I not sworn an oath to harm you not?'

Odysseus sighed and answered her, 'Can a man eat who grieves for his friends, turned to swine and herded in a sty? If you truly wish me well and would see me enjoy your food and wine, release my dear comrades from your enchantment.'

And Circe went from the hall with her wand, taking with her a little jar of magic ointment. She opened the doors of the sty and the unhappy swine rushed forth into the courtyard, and Circe went among them and anointed each one of them with the ointment, and in an instant he became a man as he had been before. One after another they ran to Odysseus and greeted him with tears of joy;

and their mingled laughter and weeping filled the hall, so that even Circe was moved by the relief and happiness of her former victims.

Then Circe spoke to Odysseus, saying, 'Go now and call your other men from the beach, where they wait beside the ship, that they may also eat and drink with us.'

So Odysseus went himself to the shore, for he thought that his men might be hard to convince of Circe's well-wishing after the fears they had had of her. As indeed they were.

They saw him approach and gathered round with wondering welcome, for they had thought never to see him again. When he told them of all that had passed and how with the help of Hermes he had prevailed and overcome the powers of the enchantress, they rejoiced. But when he told them that Circe awaited them with food and wine and the hospitality of her home, they were afraid.

But in the end Odysseus persuaded them, and at last they believed that there was no longer anything to fear from the wiles of the sorceress, and they began to drag the ship up on to the beach and stow away the tackle in a nearby cave. All save Eurylochus, who, because he had once been to Circe's house, dared not go again, and sought to warn his comrades against trusting Odysseus' reassuring words.

'My friends,' he said, 'if you rely upon Odysseus who is rash and adventurous and go to the house of Circe, you will not return. Rather will she change you into swine or lions or shaggy wolves to guard her home. Do you not remember how six of our companions, who went with him into the Cyclops' cave, paid for his rashness with their lives?'

But Odysseus' men trusted him. Besides, they were weary and longed for the comforts of a house after their labours on the sea, and they replied, 'Good Odysseus, we will go with you to Circe's home. But if it pleases you, let us leave Eurylochus to guard the ship, since he is afraid to come with us.'

And with that they followed Odysseus over the hill and into the wood. And Eurylochus went after them, for he had no wish to earn his king's displeasure.

# III

## *The Land of Hades*

FOR a year Odysseus and his comrades remained in Circe's house, feasting and enjoying the comforts of idleness; but when a full twelve months were passed, the men grew restless, and besought Odysseus to remember Ithaca, their home.

'For still we long to see our wives and families and the shores of our own country,' they reminded him. 'Let us not stay here for ever, pleasant though it is to pass the days in luxury and ease.'

So Odysseus went to Circe and told her of what his men had said, and asked her favour for his voyage and her counsel as to how best to act that they might return in safety to their homes. 'For,' he said, 'we have had ill luck with our voyaging since we sailed from Troy, and we need guidance.'

'My favour for your voyage shall I give you willingly,' she said. 'But even I cannot tell you what the future holds for you. For that you must go to the land of Hades, the god who rules the spirits of all the dead, and ask counsel from Teiresias, the blind prophet. While he yet lived, Teiresias was the greatest seer in all the world, and still in death he has no equal.'

In astonishment and horror Odysseus cried out, 'But how shall I, a living man, reach Hades' land? No man has ever yet sailed his ship into the realms of the god of the dead.'

'You need have no fear, Odysseus, for you will be guided on the way. Put out to sea with your destination boldly in your mind, and the north wind will bear you over the water to the River of Oceanus in the land of the Cimmerians. There must you beach your ship and walk inland to where two of Hades' rivers, Periphlegethon and Cocytus, meet and flow on into Acheron, a third and greater river. There, at that place, sacrifice a ram and a black ewe to the memory of all the dead, and call upon the spirit of Teiresias. Then wait, and shortly he will come to you and tell you all you seek to know.'

At dawn the next day, Odysseus roused his men and told them that the time had come for them to sail once more, and great indeed was their joy when they heard his words. But their rejoicing was turned to grief when they learnt that it was not to Ithaca, but to the land of Hades, that they were to voyage first. But for all their misgivings, they stirred themselves to make ready for the journey with a will; though ill fortune came to one of the company, Elpenor, the youngest of them all, a simple youth and none too skilled at fighting. For he had climbed up on to the flat roof of Circe's house to sleep, the night being warm; and in the morning, hearing his comrades' shouts as they prepared to go down to the shore, he rose up hastily, forgetting where he was, and ran to go to them; and he fell from the roof and his neck was broken.

Down on the beach, Odysseus' men dragged the ship out from the cave where they had hidden her, twelve months before. They went over her timbers carefully, to see that none had decayed; and swept off the deck the sand that had collected there, having been blown into the cave by the winds from the sea. They tested the ropes of plaited ox-hide that went to make the rigging, to be sure that they would still hold against a storm; and they brushed cobwebs off the sail.

With ropes fastened to her blue-painted bow, they drew the ship down to the water's edge, and there they stepped the mast, securing it with the forestays and the backstays. Then, with a final push into the sea, they clambered on board, and falling to their oars, rowed her out into the deeper water. There, hauling on the halyard, they hoisted the yard; and then unfurled the sail, trimming it to the wind. And it was even as Circe had said, and a fresh breeze from the north filled the square white sail, and the ship sped over the sea without guidance from the helmsman.

And so Odysseus and his men came to the River of Oceanus at the ends of the earth in the country of the Cimmerians, who dwelt all their days in mist and fog, never seeing the golden sunlight or the silver rays of the moon.

A little way up the river they beached the ship and went inland through the groves of Persephone, among the tall

straight poplars with their ever-rustling leaves, and the
mournful drooping willows, until they reached the spot
Circe had told Odysseus of. Here, with a swirling of dark
waters, Periphlegethon, the river that flashed like fire, and
Cocytus, the river of wailing, mingled their streams and
flowed on into melancholy Acheron.

In this place Odysseus paused; and helped by Eurylochus
and another of his men, he dug a pit the width of a single
pace across both ways. Into this pit he poured out an offering to the dead of milk and honey, wine, water, and white
barley flour; and sacrificed a ram and a black ewe, which
Circe had given him; and called upon Teiresias.

At once the spirits of the dead appeared, and foremost
of their company came the spirit of Elpenor, who had
fallen from the roof of Circe's house at dawn. He had not
yet been buried, for his comrades had been in such haste
to embark from Aeaea that they had not spared the time
to build his funeral pyre, meaning to do so later, on their
return to the island.

He now came forward, looking as he had ever done in
life, young, and a little puzzled, and eagerly he made towards Odysseus.

Seeing him, Odysseus was filled with grief, and asked
him sadly, saying, 'Elpenor, my friend, how have you
come here, all among the darkness, in this place of gloom?
Truly, you have reached here more quickly, travelling on
foot, than the rest of us, in our swift ship.'

Elpenor gave a great sigh, and answered, 'King Odysseus, my good and noble leader, an ill fate overtook me,
for when I came to climb down from Circe's roof, in my
eagerness to join my dear comrades, I forgot to go to the

ladder, and I fell. With speed my spirit left my body and I came hence, even to the land of Hades, god of all the dead; and here, now, shall I ever remain. But you, King Odysseus, and all my other companions with you, will depart from this place and return to Aeaea. There, I beg of you, remember me, and do not sail for Ithaca leaving me unlamented and unburied. Build a barrow for me on the shore of the sea, and set upon it my oar with which I rowed in our ship, that men may not forget me utterly. I ask you this in the name of all those whom you love and left behind in Ithaca. In the name of good Lord Laertes, your father, and in the name of your fair queen, Penelope, and for the sake of your little son, to whom you will one day return. In their name do this for me, Odysseus, and do not forsake me.'

With tears Odysseus replied to him, 'I promise you, Elpenor, my unlucky friend, that we shall not forget you. All this shall we do for you, even as you say.'

Then, satisfied by the promise, the spirit of Elpenor drifted away, and from the midst of the great throng of spirits, stepped forth the spirit of Teiresias, the prophet, bearing a golden staff.

'You seek knowledge from me of your return to Ithaca, Odysseus?' he asked. 'Indeed, your return shall be long deferred, for you angered Poseidon, great lord of the seas, when you blinded his son, Polyphemus the Cyclops. Yet if you have a care, you will once again see your own land, in spite of Poseidon's wrath. But take heed if on your voyage home you should chance to light upon the island of Thrinacia and see there the herds and flocks of Helios, who rules the rising and the setting of the sun. Do not harm them, or your men will all be lost, and you yourself, if you should have the good fortune to escape, will only reach your home after many perils, alone and in the ship of another man; while in your own house you will find strife, and strangers despoiling your possessions. But in the end, Odysseus, whatever your misfortunes, it is fated that you will be avenged on all your enemies, and your old age shall be spent in peace and comfort in your home, with your own people all about you.'

With this the spirit of the prophet vanished, and the other spirits crowded round. Amongst them Odysseus recognized many whom he had known in the days of their life on earth; men who had fought beside him at Troy, and died there, and others whom he had known when young; and with them the spirit of his mother, Anticleia, whom he had thought still lived.

He called to her, 'Dear mother, tell me, how came you here?'

'My son,' she replied, 'I pined, and died of a broken heart, because you were so long away from home.'

'And my father, Laertes, has he too come to Hades' land?'

'Your princely father lives, my child, but in a wretched state, unfitted to his rank. He has gone from your house to his farm in the country, where in rags and patches he toils all day in the fields, like a common bondman, ever grieving for you and longing for your return. At night, in the winter, he sleeps in the ashes by the hearth, along with the slaves; and in the summer, he rests on a bed of fallen leaves, down by his vineyard. And always he sorrows for you.'

And Odysseus wept and said, 'My poor unhappy father,'

and he made to take his mother in his arms and kiss her, but her misty spirit flittered through his hands as though she had been a dream that is forgotten on awaking, or an insubstantial shadow, lost because a cloud has hidden the sun. Three times he tried, and three times she was not there. 'Dear mother,' he cried, 'may I not touch you?'

'Indeed no, my son,' she said, 'for I dwell now in Hades' land, while you still belong to the world of sunlight and the living. Farewell, dear child.' And so she went, and her voice died away.

When his mother had gone from him, Odysseus spoke with the spirits of many others; great ladies of the past, and his former comrades of the war with Troy, who pressed round eagerly, glad to speak with him again.

Among them was Agamemnon, mighty leader of all the Greeks at Troy, who on his return to his palace in the broad lands of Argos had been treacherously slain by his cousin Aegisthus, in vengeance for an old family quarrel.

'Unfortunate Agamemnon,' said Odysseus when he had heard the story, 'what an ill-starred home-coming there was for you.'

'But one day for you, Odysseus,' replied the spirit of great King Agamemnon, 'will there be a happy reunion with your wife and family. For among your loved ones, as I remember them, there are none who would strike you down by stealth.'

There came also to Odysseus the spirit of golden-haired Achilles, with his dear friend Patroclus by his side. They had both been slain at Troy in all the glory of their youth. And after them came Antilochus, who had been old King Nestor's son.

'Odysseus,' asked Achilles, as the other spirits gave way to him, 'why have you, still living, come among us here?'

'I came to ask counsel of Teiresias, for my voyage home to Ithaca has been ill fated since the day I sailed from Troy. Truly, I am a most unlucky man, and I could envy you, Achilles. You were a great prince while you yet lived, and even here, in Hades' land, you are still honoured and respected.'

But Achilles sighed. 'No, my friend,' he said, 'I would rather be on earth, alive, the slave of some poor wretched man, and live in drudgery and want, than rule here, king of all the dead. But what of my son, Odysseus? He was only a child when last I saw him; but when he grew older, did he fight with you at Troy?'

'Neoptolemus, your son, is very young, Achilles, but he is wise beyond his years, and he has inherited his father's valour. Indeed, when he came to Troy, there was none who would press forward in the fight so fast as he, or rush so eagerly to battle. For all his lack of age, he was among the bravest of us there. This will show you what manner of youth he is. In the tenth year of the siege, when it seemed to us as though we never should take Troy by storm, we decided to achieve our ends by stealth. We fashioned a huge horse of wood, cunningly carved, and running on wheels, but all hollow within. This horse we left upon the plain before the city; and then, with a great show of men and arms and ships, we set sail, so that the Trojans might think the siege had been abandoned. Then, in the darkness, one ship sailed back, and in it was the pick of all the Grecian army. We crept across the plain to the wooden horse and climbed inside; and in the morning the Trojans came, and thinking it an offering to the gods which we had left behind, they dragged it towards the city, and opened to it the gates that had been closed to us for nigh on ten years. Prisoned within the wooden walls we tarried until nightfall, when we might steal forth and fall upon the Trojans. All through that day of weary waiting many stout hearts faltered, and there were among us some who wished they had not been chosen for the task of taking Troy. But not your son, Achilles. In the dim light of our prison young Neoptolemus delayed impatiently, his sword clasped firmly in his hand. And to me, to whom the charge had been given to say the word when we should break from our hiding-place, he would ever whisper eagerly, "It must be dusk, Odysseus, let us go forth," and, "We have been here a lifetime, how much longer must we wait?" Indeed, Achilles, your son knows not fear.'

There came a smile to the lips of Achilles' spirit and his eyes grew bright, and without another word he turned and went with Patroclus, walking lightly and joyously away, across the dim fields of Hades' land, scattered with the amber-striped pale stars of the little asphodel.

And many were the questions asked of Odysseus by the other spirits who drew near; until at last he returned to his ship and he and his companions rowed down the River of Oceanus to the sea, and sailed once more for Aeaea.

There, on the shore of Circe's isle, they built a pyre of logs, strong oak and beech and resin-scented pine, and on it they laid the body of Elpenor, with his armour and his sword, and Odysseus fired the pile with a flaming torch. They stood by, sorrowing, until the fire died down, and then they heaped earth upon the spot where it had been, and placed his oar upon the mound as a memorial of their dead comrade, even as he had asked, so that he should not be forgotten.

They stayed one more night upon Aeaea. In the evening Circe came, followed by her serving-maids, bearing food and wine. Odysseus and his men sat upon the shore and ate and drank, telling Circe all that they had seen. And when night fell, they lay down to rest, but Circe led Odysseus aside and spoke with him.

'From Teiresias you have heard of perils that will beset you if you do not leave unharmed the cattle of the sun,' she said, 'but there are other dangers you may meet in sailing from these shores. Close by, upon a little isle, dwell the Sirens. They keep watch from the island, and sing to sailors rowing by. And of all the songs in the world, none is more beautiful than theirs, and whoever hears it forgets all else and would go to the Sirens on their isle. But all around them lie the bones of the men who have perished because of the spell cast by their singing. For on the island of the Sirens many men have languished, listening, till they died from want of food. Take care that you and your comrades do not hear the Sirens' song.

'Beyond this, two ways will lie open to you. One leads you by the Roaming Rocks, a high cliff against which the waves hurl themselves with so great a force that not even a bird might fly past, and no ship could make the journey. The other course lies along a narrow strait between two rocks, one tall and cloud-capped, the other low, with a great fig-tree growing upon it. Half-way up the tall rock there is a cave, and in this cave dwells Scylla, whose voice is as the yapping of a dog. She has twelve legs and six hideous heads on the ends of six long necks, and with each head she seizes one sailor from any ship that passes by. Beneath the other rock lurks Charybdis. Three times each day she sucks down the salt water into a foaming whirlpool, and three times each day she spouts it up, a seething fountain which engulfs all within its reach. If you would save your ship, Odysseus, sail close to Scylla's rock. It is better that six men should be lost than your whole company. And after that you will reach Thrinacia, where are herded the cattle of Helios, and against bringing hurt to these Teiresias warned you. To his sage words I add my entreaties. Sail clear of Thrinacia, Odysseus, if you and your companions wish to see your homes.'

Odysseus heeded well her words, and when she ceased, it was already dawn, and the golden sun was rising up above the water.

## IV

## *Scylla and Charybdis and the Cattle of the Sun*

THAT very day they set out once more on the long voyage home; and the enchantress Circe, who in the end had proved so good a friend to them, stood on the sand and watched the ship out of sight, speeded on its way by a fresh breeze which she herself had called up.

Once at sea, Odysseus thought fit to warn his men about the Sirens whose isle they soon would pass. But because he ever wished to know all that there was to know, he bade his comrades, when they neared the isle, bind him with strong ropes to the mast and resist all pleading to untie him; so that he might hear the song the Sirens sang. He took a round ball of beeswax, and cutting off pieces with his sword, he kneaded them with his fingers; until, warmed by the sunshine and his hands, the wax grew soft. Then with it he stopped the ears of all his men, so that they might hear nothing. Three of them then tied him to the mast with strong ropes, tightly knotted. A short distance on, the wind died down, and the men had to take to their oars; and thus they approached the Sirens' isle.

The two Sirens perched upon their little islet, which was like a flowery meadow whereon grew purple irises, many-hued anemones, and the little yellow crocus. But round the margin of the island, where the sea washed the shore, was a wide wreath of bones, whitened by the sun. The Sirens had the bodies of great feathered birds; wide wings and feet with claws; but their heads were as the heads of women, beautiful and kindly smiling, with long, flowing hair. And their voices were the sweetest sound in all the world.

'Come, brave Odysseus, noblest of the Greeks,' they sang, 'come to us and listen to our song. All men who go by our island pause to listen to our lay, and it gives them strength and courage and wisdom for all time. Only a madman or a fool would not stay for our singing, for we know and can sing of everything that has happened since the world began.'

When Odysseus heard their voices he forgot all else, and knew only that he must stay and listen to their song. And he signed to his men with nods and frowns to loose him from his bonds, and struggled to free himself; yet they took no notice of his signs, for he had bidden them heed him not. But when his struggles grew too violent, Eurylochus feared that the ropes might break, and jumping up, he went to Odysseus and tightened the bonds.

And when at last the ship had passed the Sirens and their singing could no longer be heard, Odysseus' men took the wax from their ears and unbound him.

But before he had time to answer their questions as to what song the Sirens sang and how sweet their voices were, a great noise was heard as of a mighty fountain, and Odysseus knew that they were near Charybdis. At once his men ceased rowing and stared before them in terror at the two rocks on either side of the narrow strait, one high and misty and the other low with a fig-tree growing on it.

Odysseus went among them with words of encouragement and comfort. 'My friends, we have been in many perils together, but we have lived through them all. And indeed, this new danger cannot be worse than the Cyclops in his cave; and yet I brought you out alive from that monster's den. Be guided by me now and we may be saved. Row as you have never rowed before, and look not aside from your oars.' Then to the helmsman he spoke, 'Steer clear of the churning and thundering around the lower of the rocks, and keep close in beside the tall cliff.' But he did not tell them of Scylla in her cave half-way up the rock, lest fear should take the strength from their arms and make them feeble.

In the hope that he might lop off one of Scylla's heads, Odysseus put on his helmet and took up his shield and sword and stood waiting on the deck, watching carefully the surface of the taller rock. It was indeed a high cliff, with its summit hidden in the mist, and its sides as smooth and polished as a silver mirror. But though he strained his eyes with looking, Odysseus could catch no sight of Scylla, nor hear her yapping like a little dog.

Opposite, no farther than a man could shoot an arrow, stood the low flat rock beneath which Charybdis dwelt. Upon it the great fig-tree stretched out its branches, thick with glossy leaves and green, unripe fruit. While below, when Charybdis sucked down the water, could be seen the very bottom of the sea; and when she spouted it forth again, it was like a great pot boiling over on a flaming fire, with spray and steam and swirling waters and a mighty hissing.

The nearer the ship came, the more awful grew the sound; and as they rowed into the narrow strait, Odysseus turned to see the foaming whirlpool and relaxed his watch for Scylla. Instantly she leant out from her cave half-way up the smooth rock and pounced upon a rower with each of her six heads. At their cries Odysseus turned, his sword ready, but it was even then too late and he could not reach the monster as she dangled the unhappy men above the ship. Her six hideous heads had each three rows of teeth, and struggle as they might, her poor victims could not escape; and she devoured them at the opening of her cave, while they yet called for help.

With all their might Odysseus' men rowed on, till at last they were safely past the rocks and out into the open sea.

But though they had won through the perils of Scylla and Charybdis with no more than the loss of six men, there lay before them that far greater danger of which both Teiresias and Circe had warned Odysseus: the cattle of the sun-god on the island of Thrinacia.

They sighted the island towards evening, and the thought of land was welcome indeed to the tired men. The first man to see it raised a shout, and all eyes looked eagerly to where he pointed. 'We are fortunate at last, and tonight we shall eat and sleep on land once more, away from the endless rolling of the sea.'

But even before they reached the island they heard the lowing of cattle and the bleating of sheep; and as they came nearer they could plainly see the herds and flocks grazing on the grassy meadows, fine beasts of mighty size and noble appearance, fit for the ownership of an immortal god, their sleek white hides and woolly fleeces gilded by the setting sun.

'It is the island of Thrinacia,' said Odysseus, 'and those beasts are the cattle and sheep of Helios, who is the sun. Both Teiresias the prophet and Circe the enchantress warned me with strict and earnest words that we should take care to harm not the herds of the sun if we would ever see our homes again. To avert the danger, let us not set foot upon the island. Row on, good men, and let us bear a small discomfort to avoid a greater grief.'

But they protested at his words, and called to him how tired they were, how weary of the sea; and reminded him that for hours they had been rowing, while he, their leader, had been idle, watching the blue water. He answered them without anger, for he knew they spoke the truth; but for all his compassion he would not let them land, but once more bade them row on; if need be, all through the night.

Then Eurylochus spoke bitterly. 'Because you are stronger than we are, Odysseus, and because your heart is iron, you will not grant us rest and the sweet relief of sleep upon a shore. Instead you order us to row on into the darkness, and who knows that we shall not be rowing on into a tempest which will wreck our ship and drown

us every one, and all because you ordered it. Just for tonight let us cook our supper on the shore and sleep upon
the sand, and in the morning we will sail with the first
light of day.'

The men all called out in agreement. 'Yes, Odysseus, let
us rest tonight. We will sail at dawn and no harm can come
of it.'

So Odysseus sighed and gave way to their entreaties.
But before they set foot upon the land, he made them swear
an oath to keep from the sacred sheep and cattle on the isle,
and be content with the provisions with which Circe had
stocked their ship.

They moored the ship in a little harbour near a spring,
and built fires upon the shore to cook their food, and un-
sealed a jar of rich crimson wine, made from the grapes
of Aeaea. And when they had eaten and drunk, they lay
down upon the sand and slept, wrapped in their warm
cloaks.

But in the night a tempest rose and the wind blew wildly
from the south, and in the morning it had not dropped and
they could not sail. They dragged the ship up on to the
beach and hid her in a cave; and once more Odysseus
warned his men against harming the cattle which grazed
peacefully in the pasture-lands so short a distance from the
shore, and he gave orders that of the food which remained
to them, no man was to have more than his fair daily share.

So long as there was food left they never questioned the
wisdom of his warning; for there were none of them that
doubted that it would be unwise to meddle with the property of an immortal god. But the south wind blew bois-
terously for a month, and long before the thirty days were

over, the food was gone; and there was no wild game upon the island.

They drank cold water from the spring to calm their hunger; they dug up to eat, from deep below the sand, the bulbs of the sweet-scented white sea-lilies which grew above the water's edge; and searched among the rocks for crabs. With hooks of bent wire they fished, wading out from the shore; but rarely caught a fish of any size. They tore limpets from the rocks, and endlessly they turned over stones upon the beach, seeking for the little sea-creatures underneath. And once in a while a well-aimed stone would kill a sea-bird, and it would fall upon the shore. And ever in the ears of the starving men was the lowing of sleek cattle and the bleating of fat sheep; and ever before their eyes were the glossy white oxen and the snowy-fleeced sheep of Helios the sun-god.

When it was the twentieth day since they had landed on Thrinacia, while Odysseus, weakened by starvation, slept in a place that was sheltered from the ceaseless wind, Eurylochus spoke to his companions. 'Whatever way death comes to us, it comes unwelcomed, but I, at least, would prefer not to die of hunger. What say you, friends, why do we not drive off a few of the fattest of those cows and kill them while Odysseus sleeps? If the gods are angry with us afterwards, and wreck our ship, then no doubt we shall be drowned. But is it not better to die quickly in the sea, than slowly to starve with so much good meat grazing on every side?'

And because the men were hungry, and saw no other way to save their lives, they agreed with Eurylochus, and at once they went and drove off three or four of the finest of the cattle and killed and flayed them on the beach. They built a huge fire, and cutting up the meat, turned it on spits before the blaze; and never had they waited so longingly for a meal to cook.

Odysseus awoke to smell the roasting meat, and instantly he knew what had been done. With horror in his heart he ran back to the shore, and bitterly he blamed his men for their rash disobedience. But it was too late for help, and no one could undo the deed. The sacred cattle had been killed and cooked, and such a crime it was certain Helios would never overlook.

'The immortal gods will avenge this sacrilege,' said Odysseus, 'there will be no escape for us.'

And truly, in that moment the anger of the gods was shown in wondrous signs. A lowing as of cattle came from the meat upon the spits, and the flayed hides moved upon the sands. But for all these portents Odysseus' men could not hold back from the meat, but fell upon it and ate eagerly.

For six days longer they remained on Thrinacia, and on the seventh day the wind dropped and veered, and at once they dragged the ship down to the water's edge, and unfurling the sail, put out to sea, leaving behind them the island where they had spent so many bitter days, and the herds which were soon to bring disaster on them.

When the island was out of sight, and no other land had appeared on the horizon, a black cloud moved across the sun and a heavy shadow lay over the sea and a wild wind came howling from the west. The wind broke the forestays of the mast, so that the mast fell into the ship, killing the helmsman as it fell. A flash of lightning struck the ship asunder, and Odysseus' men were hurled into the waves; and not one of them was saved.

But Odysseus clung on to the wrecked ship until the sea battered her apart, breaking away the sides and tearing off the mast by the keel. Then lashing the keel and the mast together with the ox-hide backstay, Odysseus held to them, driven over the waves by the rushing wind.

After a time the west wind died down, and the south wind arose, blowing Odysseus back across the sea towards the straits where dwelt Scylla and Charybdis.

At dawn, he saw that he was close by the vortex of Charybdis, and try as he might with all his strength, he could not keep the mast and keel from being sucked down by the hidden monster.

As they vanished into the whirlpool, Odysseus jumped clear and clutched hold of the trunk of the fig-tree growing from the rock. He held on to it with hands and legs, unable to climb up into the branches for they hung too high above his head, and unable to gain a firmer foothold for the rock was too low down. There he clung, like a bat upon a wall, until Charybdis spouted forth the mast and keel. Then he let himself drop back into the water, and clambering once more upon these precious spars, rowed with his hands in frantic haste, away from the dread rock where Charybdis lurked, before she should gulp down another draught of sea.

And after that, for nine days Odysseus clung to the mast and keel, borne here and there across the sea, and on the tenth day he was washed ashore on the island of Ogygia.

# V

## *Calypso*

ON the island of Ogygia lived the nymph Calypso, immortal and ever young, with unchanging beauty. She dwelt in a wide grotto set within a grove of trees; dark cypresses, alders, and the rustling poplar, which made a shelter for the cavern from the rough winds of the sea.

Before the entrance to her home grew many flowers; white, pink, and mauve anemones, the ivory spears of crocuses which opened to the sun, resin-scented rock-roses; and under the shade of the tall trees, little violets and bright blue squills. From four clear springs flowed water, cool and pure as crystal; while around each fountain flourished those plants which love damp soil, the sweet-scented, fragile, dark purple iris and the fragrant flowering rush. The grove was the home of many birds, swift hawks and harsh-voiced crows, and the owl which calls by night. Around the entrance to the grotto, its leaves fringing the opening, climbed a huge vine, where, all seasons alike, hung heavy bunches of ripe purple grapes.

Within, the cave itself was richly furnished and divided into rooms. The rocky walls were hung with patterned cloths, and green reeds and sweet herbs were strewn upon the floor. The chairs and tables were of cunningly carved wood; and set in a place where it caught the greatest light stood Calypso's loom, with a golden shuttle, whereon she wove the everlasting cloth which would not perish with the years.

The nymph Calypso, walking on the shore, found Odysseus lying on the sand, half-drowned, starving, and exhausted. She took him to her grotto and brought him back to life and health by virtue of her magic drugs. And as the days passed and he grew strong again, she came to love him, and offered him immortality and everlasting youth if he would only stay with her upon her island. But Odysseus was homesick for Ithaca, and he grieved for his wife and little son, and longed to see them both again; so with courtesy he refused her gifts. But for all that, Calypso would not let him leave her, and kept him with her on Ogygia for seven years.

In spite of the company of an immortal nymph and the ease and comfort of his life in the grotto, and in spite of the fair island and its many delights, Odysseus pined and mourned continually, sitting on the shore and looking ever out to sea, remembering that beyond the blue waters, somewhere, lay his home.

From the cloud-crowned heights of Mount Olympus, home of the immortal gods, the wise goddess Athene looked down upon the sufferings of Odysseus and pitied him. He was a man whose life she had watched with approval, for his wiles and his resourcefulness had given her much pleasure.

Blue-eyed and sternly beautiful, white-robed and with a helmet of everlasting gold, she stood up in the council of the immortal gods and spoke. 'Father Zeus and all you other ever-living gods, what profit shall a man have who lives in virtue, righteousness, and justice, ruling his people kindly and with ever an eye to good, if we, who ordain all things, take no care to reward him for his ways? Truly, it would be more to a man's advantage to oppress and steal, and to kill all those whom he rules over, if we, the immortal gods, send misfortunes to the good and bad alike. There was a king in Ithaca, Odysseus was he named, no prince ever ruled more kindly, and his people loved him with all their hearts. With many other leaders of the Greeks he left his home and family and sailed to fight at Troy. When the city was taken he set out for Ithaca once more, but ill fortune sailed with him. His ships were lost, his men were drowned, and he himself, after many perils passed, found safety on an island where the nymph Calypso dwelt. There for seven years he languished, longing for his home, a prisoner to her love for him. No ship had he in which to sail away, no skill to fight against the powers of the immortal nymph, no strength to break free from her toils.

Father Zeus and all you other ever-living gods, you all do know Odysseus, his virtue, his brave deeds, his courage. Judge you then he has deserved the misfortunes you have heaped on him?'

From his high throne, Zeus, father of gods and men, answered her, 'My daughter, we have not forgotten wise Odysseus, his virtue, his brave deeds, his courage. Nor do we think him to deserve the misfortunes you have told us of. Indeed, those misfortunes did not come from us, but from our brother, Poseidon, lord of all the seas. For he was angered when Odysseus blinded his son, Polyphemus the Cyclops, and since that day has he pursued Odysseus with his wrath, and brought to nothing all his struggles to see his home once more. It is from Poseidon, and from him alone, that all Odysseus' troubles come.'

Quickly Athene spoke again. 'Father Zeus, now let it be your will to free Odysseus from his durance on the island of Ogygia. If it is pleasing to you, send Hermes, our messenger, to bid the nymph Calypso release her prisoner.'

Zeus smiled a little. 'So let it be, my daughter.' And he called to Hermes the messenger to come to him, and said, 'Go, Hermes, and carry to Calypso our command, that she release Odysseus from her toils, so that he may once more see his home. But since it is fated that he shall return to Ithaca alone, after much suffering and by his own labours, then for him to leave Ogygia shall there be no ship, but only a raft built by his own hands. Go, my son, and tell this to Calypso.'

At once Hermes bound on his winged sandals, the gift of Zeus himself, which could carry him over the land and sea more swiftly than the wind; and taking his wand, with

the lightest touch of which he could give to mortals sleep
or waking at his will, he stepped down from Olympus,
home of the immortal gods, and sped across the sea to the
island of Ogygia, skimming over the waves like a bird.

On the island, Odysseus sat upon the shore and sighed,
looking out to sea, and Calypso was alone within her
grotto, weaving. She wore a silvery robe that gleamed like
moonlight, with a golden girdle round her waist; and over
her bright hair, a veil as fine as gossamer. She moved before
her loom, weaving the everlasting cloth from many-
coloured magic threads, and under her nimble fingers the
golden shuttle sped to and fro, faster than the eye could
watch. And as she worked, she sang.

Hermes called to her from the entrance to the cavern,
where he stood beneath the trailing vine. 'Greetings, fair
Calypso.'

She turned and saw him there, and at once she knew him
for the immortal messenger. For though they may deceive
a mortal man, the gods and divine beings cannot hide themselves from one another, and whatever shape they choose
to take, at once they recognize each other. She dropped her
golden shuttle. 'Greetings, swift Hermes, you are welcome
to my home.'

She led him in and set two chairs beside the blazing fire
of scented cedar logs which filled the grotto with its
fragrance. She placed between them a table with ambrosia
on a golden dish and nectar in two crystal cups; and together they sat and ate ambrosia, food of the gods alone,
and drank the rosy nectar which might pass only immortal lips.

And when they had eaten and drunk, she asked him,

'Tell me, Hermes, why have you come here today, across the wide stretch of barren sea that separates our homes? It is not often that I, living on this lonely island, entertain a guest from Mount Olympus. I must confess, I am curious to learn the reason for your visit.'

Hermes laughed. 'It is, as you have said, fair Calypso, a wide stretch of sea that separates our homes, and not willingly would one fly across that endless, tedious waste of blue. But it was Zeus who sent me, else should I not be here, despite the pleasure that it gives me to speak with you again.'

'And what message has Father Zeus for me?'

'He says that here upon your island there is a man, unhappiest of all the Greeks who fought at Troy, Odysseus, king of Ithaca. Here in your company he pines, and longs to see his home. It is the will of Father Zeus that you now release this man with speed, that he may return to Ithaca.'

For a long time Calypso did not speak, and then her voice was bitter. 'You are cruel and jealous, you gods who live far off upon Olympus. You envy me my happiness and would take it from me. I found Odysseus dying on the beach, washed upon my island shores by the heartless waves. I brought him to my grotto, I tended him and fed him, and with my healing drugs I gave him back his life. As we immortals may grant to whom we please the power to live for ever, so would I have given to Odysseus everlasting youth and eternal happiness here with me. But he would not take the gifts I offered in affection, for he still frets for a rocky island where once he had a home, and dreams of a woman who, I doubt not, for all she is a mortal, was fair enough, some seventeen years ago. But I had hope that one day he would forget his kingdom, that one day I might blot out utterly from his mind all remembrance of his wife. And I had no doubt but that in the end I should prevail, and we two should dwell here in happiness for ever. And now with your words you have torn away my hope.'

'The words, divine Calypso, came from Zeus, whom all gods and mortals must obey.'

'I had no thought but to obey. Odysseus may leave me when he will. It is the command of Zeus.' Calypso rose. 'But Zeus must see him safely back to Ithaca. I keep no ships upon the island for sending shipwrecked sailors home. It is enough that I let him go.'

'Be not too angered at the will of Zeus,' said Hermes gently, 'and give Odysseus what good counsel you can as to how he may reach home. For I know you would not have him perish on the ever-hungry sea.'

After a while Calypso smiled. 'I will give him all the good counsel that I can, for he is very dear to me,' she said quietly. 'Farewell, Hermes.'

Calypso went to Odysseus where he sat upon the shore, crouched on a rock with his head hidden in his hands. She touched his shoulder and spoke to him. 'Look up, Odysseus, and cease your sorrowing, for the seven years you have found so long and weary will soon be ended, and with my blessing and a fair wind to speed you, you will be sailing for your home.'

Odysseus looked at her. 'I have no ship,' he said. 'How can I sail to my own home, or to anywhere else in the world?'

'I will give you an axe,' she said, 'that with it you may cut wood and build yourself a raft, firm and stout to resist the waves, with a tall mast and a sail. And I will give you clothes to keep you warm, and food and wine for the voyage, and call up the wind to carry you swiftly home.'

But staring at the sand Odysseus thought well upon her words, for they brought no comfort to his heart, but only deep unease.

'Why are you silent?' she asked him. 'I had thought you would be glad to know that you were to see your home once more.'

He turned his head to her and spoke out his mind. 'Not even all the well-built ships that sail upon the sea reach safely home to port. How then shall a little raft, manned by me alone, survive the violence of the wind and the fury of the waves? No, immortal lady, I will not trust myself to the merciless sea and the sweeping tempests of the sky in a raft of my own making, though you induce me, for I fear you persuade me to my hurt.'

Calypso took his hands in hers and smiled at him. 'Odysseus,' she said, 'when will you learn that I love you well, and would protect you from all harm?'

'When you have sworn an oath that in this thing you mean no ill to me.'

'You are ever cautious and ever prudent, Odysseus. To please you I will swear an oath as you desire, an oath that would bind even an immortal god, and then perchance you will be satisfied.'

And when she had sworn he trusted her words, and considered with more favour the building of a raft, on which to sail for Ithaca.

Together they returned to the grotto and ate and drank their evening meal. As they sat beside the fragrant, smouldering cedar logs, Odysseus thought about the raft for his journey home, and in his mind he planned its making, rejecting one idea and approving another. As he leant forward, looking into the fire and seeing it not, his eyes were bright and on his face there was a look of eagerness which Calypso had not seen there before.

She laughed a little. 'Are you so impatient to be gone from me, Odysseus? Are you so wearied of my love for you that even in my company you sit silent, dreaming of your wife? Is she so fair, Odysseus? Surely no mortal woman could be more beautiful than I.'

Odysseus looked at her and shook his head. 'Do not be angry with my words,' he said quietly. 'Though I know well no mortal woman could compare with you in beauty, nor is it fitting that she should, yet to me my wife Penelope is fair enough. And that enough is more than all the immortality and ageless youth you offer me.'

'The choice is yours,' she said. 'But if you could guess the perils that wait for you before your journey will be ended, you might choose to remain here with me and take my gifts. And because I am no mortal, talking idly in the dark, and because to me it is given to read the future when I wish, my words are not the foolish babbling of a weak, fond woman trying to persuade you against your will.'

'Divine Calypso, I know you speak the truth, and for my good. But though I knew that I should almost surely perish on the sea, even so could I not hold back from this voyage, but would take still the chance that you offer me to see once more my home and family.'

And to his words she gave no reply, marvelling in silence at the strange ways of mortal men.

The next morning Calypso gave Odysseus a sharp axe of bronze and an auger for drilling holes, and he set off for the farthest shore of the little island, where the trees grew tall and straight. Here beneath the pines bloomed yellow crocuses and dark wine-red anemones, and from the branches the thrushes sang. Odysseus' heart was light as he went among the trees, choosing out those most fitted to his needs.

When he had chosen twenty trees, he set to work to fell them. That done, he lopped off all the branches and fashioned fifteen of the trunks into smooth poles of equal length. Drilling each pole at each end with the auger, he fastened them firmly together with wooden pegs, forming a level platform as wide as the hull of a merchant's ship.

From the five tree trunks that remained, he put by two straight firs, one for the mast and the other, slightly shorter, for the yard. The other three he split and hewed into planks which he laid athwartships across the platform to form the deck. Then he set up stanchions along each side, pegging the bulwarks to them; so making a strong wall against the waves, and finishing with a specially stout plank along the top to form the gunwale. As a final protection he enclosed each of the four sides with a wickerwork of plaited withies.

Across the bow of his raft he set up a thwart with an opening above a mast-step. And when he had made the mast smooth and round and drilled a hole from one side of it to the other, through which to reeve the halyard, he lowered it through the opening in the thwart and wedged it firmly into the step. Then at the stern he mounted an oar for steering.

Calypso brought him sailcloth, woven by her own hands; and while she watched him, he cut it skilfully, sewed it to the bolt rope and bent it to the yard. Lastly he braided strong ropes from thongs and pliant osiers; shrouds to stay the mast, a halyard for hoisting the yard, braces for trimming it to the wind, and sheets to hold the clews of the sail.

The raft was finished, and, with logs for launching ways, he brought her to the water's edge. Then at last his work was done, and it had taken him but four days, so eagerly had he laboured.

Odysseus spent one final night in Calypso's grotto, and in the morning he took to the raft the skins of wine and water she had given him, a leathern bag of food, enough to last him many days, and warm raiment to protect him from the cold.

She came down to the shore with him, and watched him stow away her gifts. 'Sail always with the Great Bear on your left,' she told him, 'and you will at length reach the land of Phaeacia.'

'I will remember,' he said. 'Immortal lady, my thanks are but a poor offering to you, but they are all I have to give. Take them and wish me well.'

'Thank me not, Odysseus, for were it not the will of Father Zeus, whom all gods and mortals must obey, my heart would be lighter at this moment, and,' she smiled, 'yours, I think, more heavy. Now go, for I wish you well, but I would not have you see an immortal grieve.'

Then bidding her farewell, he unfurled his sail, and blown on his way by the warm breeze she called up for him, he set off across the wide sea.

For seventeen days he sailed with a gentle wind and a clear sky, ever with the Great Bear on his left, and on the eighteenth day he sighted land. Overjoyed, he steered his raft towards the misty outline of the distant cliffs.

Yet his joy lasted but a little time, for Poseidon, god of the seas, saw him as he sailed, and remembering his implacable vengeance, he called the clouds together and stirred up the sea, drove forth the winds over the water, and hastened the night. The four winds flung themselves upon the sea and lifted up a mighty wave and bore it down upon the raft.

Odysseus saw it coming and clung to the steering oar. 'This', he thought, 'will surely be the end of my voyaging for ever. Better would it have been had I died before the walls of Troy, as did so many of the Greeks. There at least should I not have lacked friends to mourn me, and comrades to carry home the tidings of my death. But now shall I perish far from the sight of men, and no word of my ending shall ever reach to Ithaca.'

The great wave struck the raft, snatching the steering-oar from Odysseus' grasp, and sweeping him into the dark sea, snapping the mast in two and carrying away the yard. Weighed down by the heavy clothes Calypso had given him to protect him from cold winds, Odysseus struggled to climb back on to the raft. Once on her, he flung himself down upon the deck-planks, holding fast to one of her sides, while the winds chased her to and fro across the ocean, as though they played a game.

He would assuredly have been destroyed had not Ino, the sea-nymph, seen him, and because she herself had once been a mortal, she pitied him. In her life on earth she had been a queen, and fleeing from death had leapt into the sea, and the gods had given her everlasting life and magic powers. Remembering now her long-past misfortunes, she came to help Odysseus, flashing up through the wild sea and standing beside him on the raft, with her limbs like pale ivory in the darkness and the wind whipping through her long, wet hair.

Her voice was like the murmur that is heard inside a shell, yet he heard it clearly above the storm. 'Unhappy Odysseus, to have aroused the anger of Poseidon, ruler of the seas. But do not despair, for indeed he shall not slay you and your life is not yet done. Do but what I bid you and you will be saved. Strip off your clothes that you may swim the better, and leaving your raft to be blown by the winds, make for the coast that lies before you. I will give you my veil, for it holds a strong enchantment, and he who wears it cannot drown. But when you have reached the shore, then, with your eyes turned away toward the land, cast it back into the sea. Here, take the veil, wind it about your waist, and plunge into the waves.'

He took the filmy scarf she handed him, and when he looked again, she had gone, as silently and swiftly as a bird of the sea, and he was alone in the darkness. And if it had not been for the veil in his hands, he would have thought she never had been there.

It was not Odysseus' way to trust easily the words of others, and he thought carefully of Ino's advice. 'What if it should be', he said to himself, 'that one of the immortal gods has set a trap for me? Perchance the divine nymph was sent by Poseidon to tempt me to leave the raft, the only protection left to me from the all-engulfing sea. No,

I will rather remain here until my raft is torn asunder by the waves, then will it be time enough to swim.'

But even while he was thinking thus, a great wave curved over the raft and crashed down upon it, breaking the boards apart and scattering wood across the sea. Washed into the water, Odysseus clung to a plank, and clambering up to sit astride it, he flung off the garments Calypso had given him, and wound Ino's magic veil around his waist, knotting it securely. Then he dived into the water and swam in the direction of the coast.

For two days and two nights he was in the sea, sometimes striving against the waves, and sometimes drifting with them; but on the dawn of the third day the wind dropped and the sea grew calm, and Odysseus saw that he was close in to the shore. Eagerly he swam on, his weary body winning strength from the welcome sight to make one final effort.

But as he came nearer to the coast, he heard the sea thundering on the reefs, and knew that here were no gently sloping beaches where a tired swimmer might walk ashore; but only sharp rocks and craggy cliffs, and the surf battering against them.

'What now shall I do?' he wondered. 'Weary as I am, I yet dare go no farther in, for I should be torn to pieces on the pitiless rocks.'

At that moment he was seized by a huge breaker which carried him forwards towards the shore, and he would indeed have been killed upon the reef had he not grasped hold of a rock as he was swept along. There he clung while the wave rushed past him, but as it flowed backward again, he was torn from the rock and washed out to sea. With all his might he battled against the incoming waves until he reached the calm water beyond the breakers, and, keeping an eye ever towards the shore for the sight of a shelving beach where he might land, he swam farther along the coast.

Just when it seemed to him as though he could surely go no longer, but must choose between drowning in the deep sea or being dashed to pieces on the crags in a last attempt to land, he caught sight of the mouth of a river, where it flowed into the ocean.

Joyfully he swam to it, and a little way upstream, where the sand and stones sloped gently to the river's edge, he came ashore. On the ground he lay, weak and exhausted, with no longer the strength to move. But when he was a little recovered, the first thing that he did was to unwind from his body the magic veil, and with eyes averted, he dropped it into the river, and the stream bore it out to sea and across the waves to Ino.

Then Odysseus thought, 'Weary as I am, I cannot lie here, for when darkness falls and the chill night comes, then shall I likely die of cold, so weak am I after my torments in the sea.'

And he stumbled a little way farther up the river's bank, to where there was a small wood beside the stream, with a fair meadow beyond, running down to the water's edge. Here in this thicket he found two bushes growing near together, an olive and a wild olive, their branches close entwined to form a shelter from the wind, and their grey-green leaves thickly spread against the rain and sun. Under these bushes, on a heap of dried leaves, Odysseus lay down, covering himself with the dead, rustling foliage, and in this soft, warm bed he fell asleep.

# VI

## *Nausicaa*

IN the night before the morning when Odysseus reached
Phaeacia, swimming up the river's mouth to safety, in
the palace of Alcinous, king of that land, his young
daughter, Nausicaa, had a dream.

Nausicaa was a lovely maiden with a happy smile, and
not long since, she had been no more than a child. But now
she had reached an age at which a maiden begins to think
of marriage, and King Alcinous was watching carefully the
young Phaeacian noblemen, that he might choose a husband wisely for his daughter.

In her dream Nausicaa saw a friend of hers, a maiden her
own age, who said to her, 'Nausicaa, why do you lie abed
so lazily? Soon the day will come when you will be
wedded to a husband of your father's choice; not much

278

longer will you remain unmarried. Few things are more fitting for a young bride than that she should have a bounteous store of fair, clean garments to carry with her, folded in chests of carved or painted wood, to her husband's house. And what of the maidens who will follow you, singing the marriage songs? And your brothers who will dance and rejoice in the palace on your wedding-day? Is it meet they should not have fine clothes to wear? Come, Nausicaa, you are a princess and the daughter of a king, only the best in all things is good enough for you. It is a shame that there should be so many fine garments lying crumpled and unwashed about the house. Gather them together and take them to the river that they may be clean and smoothly folded for your marriage-day.'

When Nausicaa awoke in the morning, she remembered her dream, and thought the advice she had been given was good. So she went to her father and said to him, 'Dear father, may I take a wagon down to the river today with all our clothes that are lying in the store-rooms waiting to be washed? For you are the king and it is right that you should have a plentiful supply of fresh, clean clothes to wear at banquets and in the assembly place. And besides, I have five brothers, they are always wanting new, gay attire to wear for dancing.'

But because she was shy to speak to him of her own marriage, she said no word of that; yet King Alcinous understood and was glad that his daughter should take thought to have all things arranged fittingly for her wedding-day, when it should come; and he replied, 'You may have a wagon or anything else you want, my child. I will bid the servants make it ready for you, with two of the best mules to draw it, so that you may set out for the river at once.'

So while Nausicaa and her serving-maids gathered together the garments, the mules were yoked to the wagon; and by the time they carried out the bundles of clothes, white, with gay embroidery or woven patterns, or purple-dyed, or blue, the wagon was waiting before the porch. The clothes were piled into the cart and Nausicaa's mother, Arete the queen, saw that she had a basket of food and a jar of wine to take with her. Then Nausicaa climbed into the wagon and took up the reins and the mules trotted off through the streets of the city and into the country beyond at a good pace; but not too fast, for the serving-maids were walking behind the cart, chattering gaily.

On they went, past fields where the first green shoots of the corn showed above the earth; past hedges with straggling little almond trees whose blossoms, once white and rose and fresh, had faded to a greyish-pink among their opening leaf-buds as the year advanced.

When they reached the river close by the sea, they tumbled the clothes out on to the grass, and unyoking the mules from the wagon, tethered them where they might graze. Then Nausicaa and her maids tucked up their tunics to their knees and flinging the garments in the water, one by one, they trod them in the shallow basins by the river's edge, where the water flowed clear and pure above the flat stones. When all the clothes were washed, they wrung them out, then shook them and smoothed away the creases and laid them on the clean pebbles of the sea-shore to dry in the hot sun.

Then Nausicaa and her handmaidens took off their tunics,

and pinning up their hair carefully on the tops of their heads, they themselves went into the stream to bathe. Cooled and refreshed, they dried themselves upon the river bank, and putting on their tunics once again, they let down and combed their hair. The sun had by this time reached the highest point in its journey through the sky, so they chose a shady spot under a willow-tree, and unpacking the basket of food and opening the jar of wine, they sat down to eat their meal among the sweet-scented, many-flowered narcissi growing on the bank. They ate and drank and talked, and then for a time they sat quietly, idly plucking stems of the gold-cupped white narcissi to adorn themselves, while they waited for the clothes to dry.

At length one of the serving-maids said to Nausicaa, 'Mistress, may we not play a game? For the sun is less high now, and it will not be so hot.'

Nausicaa jumped up. 'Come,' she said, 'let us play. Did one of you think to bring a ball?'

The maid who had spoken ran to fetch her ball from the wagon; and when they had chosen out by lot one of their number, the others stood around her in a ring and tossed the ball over her head from one to another. The maiden in the centre tried to catch the ball as it passed her, and when she was successful she changed places with the thrower. While they played they sang, and Nausicaa, whose voice was the sweetest there, led them in the song.

For many minutes they enjoyed their game, until, the tallest of the handmaidens being in the centre, Nausicaa, trying to throw the ball too high for her to catch, sent it soaring up beyond the reach of the maid for whom it had been intended, and it fell into the river with a splash.

'Oh, my ball!' cried one of the maidens, running to the bank. 'Oh, mistress, you have thrown it into the river.'

The other maids ran after her, crying out and calling to each other. 'We shall never get it back, it is much too far out in the water. The river is deep in the middle, shall one of us swim out and get it back?'

Their excited cries awoke Odysseus, asleep under the olive-trees a short distance off, and he crept to the edge of the thicket to see what manner of people they were whose voices had disturbed him. When he saw the group of maidens clustered by the river he felt great relief. 'They look gentle and kindly', he thought, 'and doubtless will take pity on a poor shipwrecked wanderer. Naked and battered by the waves, I am no fit sight for strangers, but food and clothes I must have, and I shall throw myself on the mercy of these maidens.' So he came forth from among the trees and went towards them.

One of the serving-maids saw him and screamed. The others looked where she pointed and with cries fled in all directions. All save Nausicaa. And because she was a princess, and the daughter of a king, though no whit less afraid than they, she did not run away; but instead she stood there, between the river and Odysseus, in her white robe, with her heart beating very fast and her eyes open very wide, and a spray of narcissus in her hair.

Coming towards her, Odysseus wondered whether he should go to kneel at her feet, or whether she would be offended if he approached so close; and then he saw that she was very young and not a little afraid. So standing where he was he spoke to her with carefully chosen words; saying, though he knew well she was a mortal maiden,

'Noble lady, I know not whether you are one of the immortal goddesses, or some fair nymph whose home is by this river, for indeed you seem to me to be much like a goddess. But if you are a mortal maiden, then happy indeed are your parents to have so gracious a daughter, and fortunate are they who call you sister, yet most blessed of all will be he who will one day be your husband. But goddess, nymph, or mortal maiden, I here implore your pity for an unhappy wretch, cast upon your shore after twenty days of tossing on the sea. Who lives in this country I know not, but on your mercy I throw myself, pleading for some ragged piece of cloth that may serve me for a garment, and for word of how I may soonest reach a town.'

Nausicaa smiled a little, and felt much less afraid, now that she found the stranger was in distress and to be pitied. 'This is the land of Phaeacia,' she replied, 'whose king is Alcinous. I am his daughter, and I can promise you that the Phaeacians will treat you kindly, for they are friendly people.' And she called to her serving-maids, bidding them come back and leave their hiding-places, and scolding them for flying from a helpless wanderer. 'Come, see if there is food and wine left that he may eat, and I myself will pick out for him a tunic and a cloak from among the drying clothes.'

And while Odysseus bathed in the river, washing off the salt sea brine from his body, the maids spread out for him the bread and wine and little barley cakes left over from their meal; and Nausicaa chose for him a warm woollen cloak and a tunic of white linen with a woven border in a design of purple grapes, made by her mother, Queen Arete.

As he sat and ate the food, Nausicaa and her handmaidens folded the dry garments and packed them in the
wagon, whispering together with many glances towards
him. 'Indeed,' said Nausicaa, 'now that he is bathed and
clothed the stranger seems to me to be a goodly man. Perhaps he may remain among us and make Phaeacia his
home. Truly, when the day comes when I must marry, I
wish that such a man as he might be my husband.'

When the clothes were laid away, Nausicaa bade her
maids harness the mules to the cart, and going to Odysseus
said, 'Stranger, we are now returning to my father's house,
for the sun will soon be setting. If you will come with us,
I will direct you to the city. While we are on the track that
runs through the fields, until we reach the road that leads
into the town, follow the wagon with my maids; but
outside the city walls there stands a poplar grove, here
would I ask you to wait a little space alone, before entering
the city and asking for my father's house.' She blushed a
little and went on, 'For if I, their princess, were seen in the
streets in the company of a stranger, people might talk of
it, and gossip, and say that I think myself too fine to wander
in the country with my own fellow townsmen, but am
ready enough to bid a stranger pass the time with me.'

'You are wise, princess,' Odysseus said with courtesy,
'and I commend your prudence. I will do as you bid me,
and wait in the grove until such time as I think you will
have reached your father's house.'

'You will find my home easily,' said Nausicaa. 'Ask anyone in the city where lies the palace of King Alcinous, and
he will point it out to you. Even a child could tell you
where it stands. Pass straight through the courtyard into

the great hall and go at once to my mother, Arete, the queen, who usually sits spinning by the hearth. For my father respects her words and judgement, and if she gives you her protection, all will be well for you.'

With that Nausicaa climbed into the cart and urged the mules homewards; while Odysseus with the serving-maids walked behind along the roadway.

At sunset, outside the city walls, as she had said, they came to a grove of poplar trees. Here Nausicaa left Odysseus, going on with her maids alone. He waited in the pleasant grove until he judged she should be home, and then he walked on up to the city walls and passed through the tall gates.

The city had been built on an incurving stretch of coast-line, so that it had a sheltered harbour lying on either side, with many ships drawn up to the quay, their rigging black against the gold and yellow sunset. Because the Phaeacians were a sea-loving people, they had built their assembly place close by the harbour; stone benches in a semicircle, and a fine stretch of sandy ground before, for games or dancing.

Odysseus was directed to the palace by a little girl, and found it a lofty building surrounded by wide gardens and a hedged-in orchard with orderly rows of apples, pears, pomegranates, figs, and olives. Close by there was a vine-yard, and beds of herbs for cooking, spices and aromatic plants for flavouring the dishes. In these grounds there were two springs, one which flowed through the gardens and the other which ran to a fountain at the great gates of the palace, where the townspeople came to fill their pitchers.

Odysseus crossed the courtyard and stood on the threshold of the palace, marvelling at all he saw. The doors were golden, with door-posts of silver, and the threshold itself was of bronze. On either side of the door stood a dog fashioned of silver, the fierce-looking guardians of the palace. Odysseus passed through the door and crossed the pillared vestibule to the door of the great hall. Inside the hall was even more magnificence. The walls were bronze with a frieze of blue, and all along them ran seats with bright-coloured woven covers and soft cushions, and raised above the seats, on pedestals, stood golden statues, lovely youths holding torches which flared to light the feasting in the hall.

Odysseus saw King Alcinous sitting on his high throne among his friends and counsellors, and close beside the fire, not too far off from the king, he saw a stately grey-haired woman spinning. 'That will be the queen, whom the princess bade me ask for help,' he thought. And going forward boldly he knelt before her.

'Greetings, Queen Arete, and long life and happiness to you. I ask your pity for a stranger, far from his home, and beg that with your help he may once again see his own land, across the wide sea.' And Odysseus sat down in the hearth among the ashes and waited to see what the Phaeacians would do.

For a time they were all silent in surprise, and then an elder of the council, a much-respected nobleman, spoke. 'It is not fitting, King Alcinous, that a stranger should sit among the ashes in your hall, while we are feasting here.'

The king looked towards the queen, and when she smiled

in agreement, he rose, and going to Odysseus held out his
hand to him. 'You are welcome, stranger,' he said, 'come
and sit and eat with us.' And he led Odysseus to a seat next
to his throne, where his favourite son, Laodamas, was wont
to sit, and the young man rose with a smile and gave
Odysseus his chair.

The servants brought him food and drink, and he feasted
with his kind hosts well into the night; and when at last
the other guests rose to go, King Alcinous said, 'My
friends, we have among us today a stranger, and very
welcome he is to our fair city. In the morning let us all
meet at the assembly place, and there devise some means of
entertainment for him, before we send him home across
the sea, that in the years to come, when he is happy
in his own land, he may remember Phaeacia with kindness.'

To this they all assented, and one by one they bade the
king and his family good night and went. Then, too, the
king's five sons all went to their rest, and Alcinous, Queen
Arete, and Odysseus were left alone in the great hall, while
the servants moved quietly about, clearing away the tables
and the dishes.

Alcinous drew two chairs up by the fire, close to where
his wife was sitting, and the three of them sat together
silently, each thinking his own thoughts.

Arete was the first to speak. She had been waiting until
the guests were gone to ask her question, for from the
moment he had knelt at her feet, she had recognized the
tunic Odysseus was wearing, for she had woven it herself.
'Stranger,' she said, 'who are you, and where is your home?
Did you not say that you came from across the sea?

Tell me, from whom did you receive this tunic that you wear?'

'Most gracious queen, after seven years' captivity on the island of Ogygia, where dwells the nymph Calypso, I put out to sea on a raft which I myself had made. Upon this raft for seventeen days I sailed. But on the eighteenth day a wild storm broke, my raft was wrecked, and I myself, after two days and nights tossed upon the waves, was cast upon your shores, close by a river. Here, as I slept, I was awakened by the sound of voices. It was your daughter and her handmaidens. From her I begged a garment to clothe myself, and she gave me this cloak and tunic from among those which she had drying on the shore. And when I asked her to direct me to the city, she brought me with her as far as the fair grove which lies beyond your city walls. And there she left me to come on alone and make my way to your palace, where she promised me I should find a welcome.'

'She spoke truly,' said Arete. 'You are indeed most welcome, stranger.'

But Alcinous said, 'I must beg you to forgive her. She is very young, and young maidens are often foolish. She should not have left you at the grove, she should have brought you home with her and told me how she found you, and thus you would have been spared coming alone into a strange house to ask a favour.'

Odysseus spoke quickly. 'You must not blame her, King Alcinous, she did all she might for me, and indeed she bade me come with her to the palace to speak with you. But I would not, and waited rather in the grove, that I might come after, alone. For I had no way of knowing what manner of man you were, and sometimes we men are jealous when we see a stranger thrusting himself into our families and wheedling his way into the good graces or our womenfolk.'

This kindly lie Alcinous at once believed, and he was pleased to think both that the stranger was a man of such good sense, and that his young daughter had not shown herself so forgetful of the duties of hospitality as to leave a stranger in misfortune to find his way to her home alone. He laughed. 'As I hope you will have seen by now, I am not a man like that. I believe that tempers are best kept, and that all things and all men deserve to be judged on their own merits, and not by any common standard. And I well believe that you are of like mind, such a man as I would willingly see my daughter wedded to, should you desire to remain in this country, an honoured member of my family, with a goodly house and such possessions as I would gladly give you.'

For a moment Odysseus hesitated, wondering what best to say that would not make a refusal of such a kindly offer seem ungracious. But Alcinous noticed the hesitation and went on at once, 'Or if you should prefer to return to your own land, then willingly shall I have made ready for you one of our fine ships, with as many of our young men as may row her most swiftly to your home. For we here in Phaeacia love the sea, and there is no other land whose people are so skilled at managing a tall ship as are our men, who learn to know the sea from the time they are but children.'

Odysseus thanked him, his heart full with gratitude, that at last he saw near the end of his wandering. 'May you be rewarded for your kindness, good Alcinous,' he said.

That night, for the first time since he had left Ogygia on his raft, Odysseus slept in a comfortable bed with a woollen coverlet and purple-dyed blankets, in the vestibule beyond the great hall, where it was the custom for all guests to sleep.

# VII

## *King Alcinous and the Phaeacians*

IN the morning the Phaeacians gathered in the assembly place, beside the harbour, and to them came King Alcinous, with Odysseus at his side. He told his people once again about the stranger who had reached their shores, and of his promise to send him safely home. 'Go,' he said, 'pick out two-and-fifty of our finest sailors and let them make ready the swiftest ship we have, so that our unknown guest may with all speed be carried to his home.'

Quickly they obeyed him; and then, at the command of King Alcinous, all the noblemen of the city came together at the palace for a banquet in honour of Odysseus. There was food and wine in plenty, and talking and much laughter, and when the feasting was over, Alcinous bade the minstrel sing. 'Come, Demodocus, and sing for us some tale of old heroic deeds, for without your sweet voice no festivity would be complete.'

And someone led forth Demodocus and placed a stool for him in their midst, and put in his hands his lyre; for Demodocus was blind, though he had the sweetest voice in all Phaeacia. When he had plucked a few chords, Demodocus began to sing, and in the hall everyone else fell silent. He sang of the quarrel Odysseus and Achilles had once had when the Greeks were besieging Troy, and of the joy of the great king, Agamemnon, who led the Grecian host, when he saw the heroes wrangling. For it had been foretold to him that it would be a good omen for the Greeks if two of their best warriors should fall to quarrelling with each other.

The Phaeacians heard the minstrel's song with pleasure; but to Odysseus it brought only sorrow. For he remembered the old quarrel and the days at Troy, his comrades who had died there, and brave young Achilles with his long yellow hair and his quick temper, whose spirit he had seen in Hades' land when he went there to ask counsel of Teiresias; and he held his cloak before his face, that his tears might not be seen.

But Alcinous observed his grief and wondered at it, and instantly he rose. 'My friends and counsellors,' he said, 'we have feasted long and pleased our hearts with music, now let us return to the place of assembly and there display to the stranger our skill in wrestling, boxing, and running, that when he is once more in his own home he may speak of us to his friends and tell them how we excel in all manner of games.'

While King Alcinous, with Odysseus and the other older

noblemen, sat upon the stone seats in the assembly place, the young men of Phaeacia gathered on the stretch of sandy ground before them, eager to display their skill. And among them were three of the king's five sons, Halius, Clytoneus, and his favourite, Laodamas.

First came the foot-race, and at the word of command, the young men sped back and forth across the course until the full distance of the race was reached in a cloud of sand, and Clytoneus was proclaimed the winner.

The wrestling contests came next, and when lots had been drawn to pair off the opponents, the lithe antagonists twisted and struggled, and tripped and threw each other on the ground; and if a wrestler fell three times, his rival gained the victory. It was soon plain to see that a certain handsome young nobleman, Euryalus, excelled all the others, throwing first his own adversary, and then, one after the other, the victors from the other pairs.

After the wrestling was done, a space was marked out for the leaping, a long jump over a level stretch of ground. Here each youth held a metal weight, and after running a few paces to the mark, jumped, swinging his arms well forward with the weights, and where he touched the ground a peg was set.

Next the young men tried their skill at throwing the discus. They stood in spaces marked out by lines in the sand, holding the heavy metal plates high above their heads and swinging their arms down and forwards to throw the discus with all their strength as far as it would go.

The last contest of all was boxing. With thongs of ox-hide bound about their hands, the young men fought in pairs until one fell, and to Alcinous' great delight,

Laodamas was easily the victor here, swiftly striking down all his opponents.

While he was receiving the congratulations of his friends on his success, it came to the mind of Laodamas to say to them, 'Why do we not ask the stranger if he would care to join in any of our games? He is not so young as we, but he looks a fine strong man, he might be glad to try his strength.'

'That is well thought of, Laodamas,' said Euryalus, the handsome youth who had been winner in the wrestling, 'go now and challenge him.'

So Laodamas went to Odysseus and spoke to him with courtesy. 'Stranger, I know not if there is any among the contests at which you may excel, nor indeed whether you have a mind to games at all, but any one of us would welcome a trial with you, should you care for it. I know that you are eager to reach your home, but such a brief delay could make but little difference.'

Good-humouredly and with a smile, Odysseus answered him, 'I fear you must wish to laugh at me, Laodamas, that you offer me this challenge. I have been through too many misfortunes in the past years to have a mind to contests now. My only thought and care at this time is for my home and that I may return to it.'

Laodamas was about to speak again in polite acceptance of Odysseus' words, but Euryalus, who had followed him and was standing near, had caught Odysseus' answer and now spoke with scorn. 'Indeed, stranger, it was but a foolish thing to challenge you, for you do not look to me like a man well skilled in contests and men's games. You seem rather to be a merchant, one who travels from port to port

with his merchandise, hurrying his sailors across the sea,
lest a good bargain may be lost.'

Odysseus instantly grew angry. 'Young man,' he said,
'one should not judge by appearances alone. To but few
men are all the gifts given. One may be a poor, inferior
creature, yet when he speaks there is in his words all the
wisdom in the world, and his speaking may move whole
assemblies and persuade them to his way of thinking.
While another may be as beautiful as the immortal
gods, yet his speech may show naught but folly and an
empty head. So, I think, it is with you. You are very handsome, no one could deny it, yet you have but little wits.
I would tell you that when I was younger I was accounted
among the best in contests of all kinds, but after all that
I have suffered I have no heart for games. Yet in spite of
that will I prove my words, for your discourtesy has made
me angry.'

And with that Odysseus jumped up, not even throwing
aside his cloak, and going to where a discus lay that no one
had cast, for it was larger and heavier than the rest, he
snatched it up; and hampered as he was by his mantle, he
flung it from him along the course, and it fell far beyond
the pegs that marked the other throws.

There was a great murmur of admiration among the
watchers, and Odysseus, no longer so angry, smiled. 'Come
now, you young men,' he called, 'and beat that if you can.
Or if you would prefer, make test of me with wrestling
or with boxing, even with running if you will, and I can
promise you that I will acquit myself with credit. For I am
well skilled in all manner of contests; yes, and in all fighting too, for I can shoot an arrow and cast a spear farther

than most men. Indeed, it is only in the foot-race that I fear I might not be the winner, for I am no longer quite so young as once I was, and speed goes hand in hand with youth. Come, all you young Phaeacians, I am waiting for you.'

But there was no one there who answered his challenge, for they believed his boasts, having had a little proof of them in his throwing of the discus.

And at length Alcinous spoke, 'It does not surprise me, stranger, that you should have been angered at the ungracious words that Euryalus spoke to you. But come, forget them, and sit by me and I will show you something to remember when you are home again, something you may praise to your family and friends. For though we Phaeacians may not be the greatest boxers or wrestlers in the world, there are two things in which we excel all others, in seamanship and dancing. Of our skill in the former you will soon have proof, when in a Phaeacian ship you sail to your home, so come now and watch our dancing, and I promise you it will be a sight that you will remember with admiration all your days.'

Willingly, Odysseus took his place beside the king, while the young men and boys gathered on the level ground before them and took their places for the dance. Blind Demodocus was led to a chair in the centre of the dancing-floor, and there he sat, feeling carefully the seven strings of his lyre and tuning them to see that they were tightly strung. When the dancers were ready, someone touched him on the shoulder and spoke to him, and with a happy smile he began to play.

The tune was light and joyous, well suited to the dancers' mood and to their swiftly moving feet, and while he

played, Demodocus sang a gay tale about the immortal
gods; how Ares, fierce god of war and battles, loved gentle
Aphrodite, goddess of love and beauty.

Odysseus watched, marvelling at the grace and skill of
the young dancers, for never had he seen dancing so accomplished and so faultless. It was indeed a sight he would
remember all his days, and when the dance was over he
made haste to tell Alcinous so.

King Alcinous was delighted by his guest's enjoyment.
'But you have not yet seen all,' he said. And he called out
Laodamas and Halius, his sons, and bade them dance the
ball-dance for Odysseus. 'For of all our dancers there are
none like them,' he said to him proudly.

The two young men took their places, surrounded by
the other youths who clapped in rhythm to their dance.
From one to another Halius and Laodamas passed a purple
ball, twisting their bodies this way and that; bending backwards for a throw or leaping upwards for a catch and never
missing. Their feet seemed to flash and twinkle in the very
air, and they themselves to be no more things of the earth
than the ball which they never once dropped to the ground
in all the length of their dance; passing it from one to the
other, while the clapping hands marked the rhythm of
their measured movements, ever more loudly and ever
more fast. Until at last, in one wild burst of sound and
motion, the dance came to an end.

Odysseus turned to Alcinous. 'Indeed,' he said, 'never in
my life have I seen a sight so graceful and so pleasing.
Truly, not only in all Phaeacia, but in all the world, have
your two sons no equal in the dance.'

Gladdened by Odysseus' heartfelt praise, King Alcinous

rose and spoke to the Phaeacians. 'My friends and counsellors,' he said, 'the stranger has been pleased to praise our dancing and speak gracious words of it. The time will soon be here when he must leave us, to return to his own land. When he departs from our shores, let it be with gifts from all of us, that in his home he may ever have works made by our craftsmen to remind him of Phaeacia.'

To this they all agreed, and straightway every noble there sent to his home that he might make a present to Odysseus. And Euryalus, repenting of his discourtesy, was the first to bring his gift, a bronze sword of fine workmanship, with a hilt of silver, and a scabbard of carved ivory.

'Stranger,' he said, 'I beg of you to take this sword in proof that you have forgiven my unmannerly and disrespectful words. May you forget them, and when you look upon it, remember only the well-wishes of the giver.'

Odysseus smiled and took the sword. 'All that has passed between us before this moment, Euryalus, is forgotten, and I remember of the giver of this goodly sword, only that he was a young nobleman of Phaeacia, handsome above all others, and well skilled at games.' And he slung the sword about his shoulder by its strap of patterned leather.

And one by one the nobles of Phaeacia brought him gifts; cups of polished gold and silver, mixing bowls of bronze, jars of wine, fine woven tunics and embroidered cloths, belts of silver links, golden brooches and brazen pins to fasten garments, three-legged cauldrons, and many other gifts beside. All these things King Alcinous' servants carried to the palace where they were packed in carved and painted wooden chests; and to their number Alcinous and Arete added many gifts of their own.

Alcinous called the Phaeacians to one final feast in honour of his guest, and they gathered together in the great hall, a festive crowd.

As he passed to the hall for the banquet, Odysseus saw Nausicaa watching him from the shadows beside one of the pillars of the door. He stood by her for a moment and she looked away from him, and then looked back again, and with a little smile she spoke. 'Think of me sometimes when you are in your home, for of all the Phaeacians it was I who helped you first.'

With gentleness and with sincerity Odysseus answered her, 'If it is granted me to see once more my home, then shall I ever remember you when I am there, and to me shall you be as one of the immortal goddesses, and I shall offer you my prayers all the days of my life. For it was you who returned that life to me.' And he went from her into the bright torch-light and gay laughter of the hall.

All welcomed him with kindness, and once again his chair was placed next to that of King Alcinous himself, and for him were reserved the best portions of all the dishes, such as are offered to the most honoured guests.

And a thought came to Odysseus, how he would like to hear the blind minstrel sing once more of Troy and the valorous deeds of the Greeks, although the memory of them brought so much pain to him. So, cutting a thick slice from the portion of roast pork that had just been set before him, he handed it on a silver platter to a serving-man, bidding him take it with his greetings to Demodocus. 'Tell him,' said Odysseus, 'that above all men I honour the makers of songs, for it is they who celebrate in poetry and music the deeds of men that might otherwise be forgotten utterly.'

And when the feasting was over, Odysseus sent again to the minstrel and begged him, for his sake, to sing once more of the Greeks who fought at Troy. 'This time,' he said, 'I would ask that you might relate, if you know the tale, how the wooden horse was taken into Troy, and how the city fell.'

Demodocus at once sounded his lyre, and when the hall was hushed, in his sweet voice he began the story. He told of how the wooden horse was fashioned, and of how the Greeks set fire to their own camp and sailed away in pretended raising of the siege. He told of how the Trojans came and dragged the horse into their city, and there debated what to do with it. 'For a full day,' he sang, 'from the rising to the setting of the sun, they argued whether it were best to break open the great wooden beast lest there should come danger to them from within; or whether to drag it forth from the city again and cast it from the cliffs into the sea below; or whether to accept the horse as a sign of victory to them, and let it stand in the assembly place, as an offering to the gods. And at sunset, it was this final counsel that prevailed, and the Trojans departed to their homes; and in the midst of the city, unguarded, stood the wooden horse. And then,' went on Demodocus, 'as soon as it was dark and the city lay in sleep, from the side of the hollow horse, stole forth the Grecian warriors and slipped silently through the streets. They fell upon the Trojans, bearing death with them, and though they were outnumbered, the victory was theirs. Many were the brave deeds of the Greeks that night and great was their courage, but the valour and the deeds of none surpassed those of Odysseus, king of Ithaca, the most subtle of all men. For Odysseus

went with Menelaus, king of Sparta, for whose sake, that
he might regain his wife, stolen by a Trojan prince, the
war was fought, to the house of Deiphobus, son of the king
of Troy, where lodged lovely Helen, Menelaus' wife.
There they fought with Deiphobus, and Odysseus, well-
nigh slain against enormous odds, in the end won victory
and honour, for he was a mighty warrior and peerless
among the Greeks.'

So sang Demodocus, and remembering, Odysseus wept;
and Alcinous saw his tears and bade the minstrel sing no
more. 'For', he said, 'your song has grieved our guest, and
that must not be. Come, fill up the cups with wine and let
us drink and be merry, for that is the fittest way to honour
any guest.' Then turning to Odysseus, he said, 'Stranger,
soon you will be gone from us, and our wishes for your
safe homecoming and our gifts will go with you. Before
you leave our city, if it is pleasing to you, will you not
tell us your name and your homeland? For indeed, this last
you will have to tell to our sailors who will row you there.
It seems to me most likely from your sorrow at the minstrel's words, that you were one of those who fought at
Troy. Why does the name of that fair and hapless city
bring so much grief to you? Did you lose a kinsman there?
Or perchance a brother? Or perhaps it was your own dear
friend? For a kind and understanding friend can be nearer
even than a brother.'

'Indeed, good King Alcinous,' Odysseus replied, 'it is, as
you say, meetest at a banquet to drink the good wine and
laugh. Grief has no place at a feast, and I have had grief
enough in my day. Yet you ask me to relate my woes to
you. So let it be. You are my host, it would be churlish to

refuse, for a better host it would be hard to find. You ask my name. I am Odysseus, king of Ithaca, even that same Odysseus of whom your clear-voiced minstrel sang but now. Ithaca is only a small island, yet it is my home and very dear to me. It is a rugged land, with narrow ways and no broad roads, and its pasture-land is best fitted for the sturdy sure-footed goats. But yet it breeds fine men, brave and bold, and I long once more to see it, because, my friends, it is my home.'

Then, one by one, Odysseus related all his adventures. He told of the Lotus-eaters and the Cyclops, Polyphemus; and of the cruel Laestrygonian giants; and he told of Circe on her isle. He spoke of how he sailed into Hades' land; and of how he heard the Sirens sing and braved dread Scylla and Charybdis. And with grief he told of the slaying of the cattle of the sun, and the loss of his dear companions.

'And then, my friends,' he said, 'for seven years I was held in captivity on the island of Ogygia, where the nymph Calypso dwells. From thence I came on a raft across the tempestuous sea, and so landed on your kindly shores. And this, I pray, may be the end of all my wanderings.'

They heard him with amazement, and in silence sat watching him when he had finished, marvelling that they saw before their eyes a man who had lived through so many perils.

But Odysseus had talked far into the night, and Alcinous bade his noblemen and counsellors go home. 'Tomorrow,' he said, 'let all of you come here to speed the great Odysseus on his way. And though we have shown our friendship for him with gifts already, let each of us bring him a further present in the morning.'

To this they all willingly assented, and then went to their own homes, talking with wonder about Odysseus as they went.

Early in the morning their gifts were borne to the palace; great bowls with feet, silver cups and cauldrons, and many other treasures. When they had been carefully packed away in chests, they were carried to the harbour where the ship was waiting that was to carry Odysseus home; and King Alcinous himself watched them stowed away beneath the benches where the rowers sat.

Then after Odysseus had given his thanks to all, and waited once more on Queen Arete, he bade his kind host farewell, and went on board the ship. There the young men who were to row him home spread a rug and blankets for him on the deck, that he might sleep in comfort all through the tedious voyage. And while they rowed smoothly and swiftly through the blue water, with all the skill of a true seafaring folk, Odysseus slept.

He slept all that day and all through the night, and when on the following dawn, they sighted Ithaca, he still slumbered on. Being unwilling to waken him, they lifted him gently to the shore, still wrapped in the warm blankets, and left him on the sandy beach, his gifts all piled around him. Then quietly they put out to sea again.

But Poseidon, mighty god of all the oceans, had seen them take Odysseus safely to his own land at last, and he grew angry. And when the Phaeacian ship was within sight of home, he lifted up his hand through the water, and laying it upon the keel, turned her into a black rock, so that ever after people might wonder at it.

# PART TWO

# Telemachus seeks Tidings of his Father

# VIII

## *Athene in Ithaca*

AT about the time Odysseus was sailing from Ogygia on the raft that he had made, Athene, wisest of all the immortal goddesses, left the cloudy heights of Mount Olympus and went to the island of Ithaca. There, in the likeness of a traveller of middle years, she walked towards Odysseus' house.

The house was built of great blocks of grey stone, and, as was only fitting for the home of a king, was the finest in all Ithaca, with a wide courtyard surrounded by a high wall wherein stood two large wooden gates. Inside the courtyard, up against the wall, leant stalls for housing the beasts brought in from the farms, and kennels for the hounds; and near to them a flock of geese stepped solemnly, picking up corn and barley from the ground, or drinking, with uptilted heads, water from a trough. There, too, stacked against the wall were piles of wood and logs for fires; while towards the centre of the court, covered over with a roof of thatch to protect it from the dust, stood the well.

The house had a porch with four tall pillars, wide enough for several men to sit at ease beneath its pleasant shade and talk. Beyond the polished wooden doors of the house and leading into the great hall lay the vestibule, where guests and strangers slept. Down the great hall itself ran two rows of pillars to support the roof, and the wide hearth was in the very centre. Half-way along one side wall of the hall was a door opening into a covered passage-way which led to the store-room; while at the farthest end of the great room, opposite the entrance, was another door, this one leading to all the other rooms of the house and to the stairs which went up to the apartments of Penelope the queen.

Athene reached the house at the time when the evening meal was being prepared, and she stood on the threshold of the gates at the entrance to the courtyard waiting till she should be noticed.

Sitting in the porch there were a number of young men. They were playing draughts, throwing dice, or idly chatting to pass the time away until supper should be ready. Leaning against one of the pillars, with his arms folded, watching and listening to them with disapproval, stood a youth of some nineteen years of age, Telemachus, Odysseus' son. Slim and handsome and very like his father in appearance, this was the son whom Odysseus had left at home, a tiny babe, when he sailed for Troy.

Looking up for a moment, Telemachus saw, standing at the gates, a man whom he had never seen before; of middle age, with a face roughened by the winds and the sun, his cloak wrapped round him, he stood leaning on his spear.

'It is a shame that a stranger should stand outside the gates,' thought Telemachus. 'So long as there is any food left with which to welcome travellers, this house shall offer hospitality as though its master were at home.' And he ran across the courtyard to Athene, waiting at the gates.

'Greetings, stranger,' said Telemachus, 'you are welcome. Will you not come into the house and eat with me and rest?' And he led Athene across the courtyard, past the young men in the porch, and through the vestibule and on into the hall, taking her spear from her and standing it against a pillar, along with others belonging to his father.

The servants were making ready the supper, setting out chairs and tables, strewing fresh rushes on the floor, and mixing in heavy silver bowls the rich wine they poured from jars of painted earthenware.

Telemachus called to one of them to bring food and drink at once for him and for his guest, and placed two chairs and a table in a quiet corner of the great room. 'It will be full of noise in the hall when the others come in to eat,' he said, 'and perhaps an older man such as you are might prefer to avoid the company of boisterous young men.'

'You are thoughtful,' said Athene as she sat, 'and I thank you.'

Telemachus sat down beside her, and together they ate and drank; Athene noting with approval the courtesy of Odysseus' son; while Telemachus thought how later he might question the stranger to see if he could give him any news of his lost father.

Soon the evening meal was ready, and summoned by Medon, the herald of Odysseus, the young men came in from the porch and took their places in the hall, laughing and talking, and they were quickly joined by others who came up from the town. The whole company of them, more than a hundred in all, ate and drank and called to one another across the room, shouting out the latest news from the town and telling how they had spent the day, not even keeping silence when Phemius, the minstrel, sang.

Telemachus watched them angrily from where he sat with the stranger; until, no longer able to forbear from speaking of them, he complained, 'One might think it was their own food they were eating so greedily, and their own wine they were quaffing. How I long that the lord of this house might come home one day soon and drive them forth, every one.' He recovered himself and smiled. 'But I am being ungracious to a guest, you must forgive me, stranger. Will you not tell me your name and from whence you come?'

'My name is Mentes,' Athene answered, 'and I am a leader among the Taphians. My travels having brought me near to Ithaca, I thought that I might see whether my old friend Odysseus still lived and prospered. I know this is his house, and from your likeness to him, I think that you must be his son. Tell me, am I not right in this?'

'You are indeed,' replied Telemachus. 'You see in me the son of that most unlucky man. For of all the Greeks who sailed to fight at Troy, he is the only one who neither lived to reach his home, nor died, honoured by his comrades, on the battlefield. It is now close on ten years since Troy fell, and yet my father has not come home, and I and my mother have no word of him, whether he still lives or whether he has died in some far-off land.'

'Indeed, good youth, I do pity you, and I do pity the noble Odysseus. But remembering the man and his courage and his resourcefulness, I have no doubt that, if he lives, at the last he will come safely home. But what means this feasting in Odysseus' house? This jubilation in the absence of the master? Is this a wedding these young men are celebrating, or some other important occasion of rejoicing? Have you yourself called them together for a banquet?' asked Athene, knowing full well the answer.

'It is no wedding they are celebrating, though they wish it were,' said Telemachus with bitterness. 'And they are no guests of mine, being here uninvited, eating my father's meat and drinking his good wine and making free with his possessions as though the house were theirs. No, I have not called them together, and though I would, I cannot send them hence; for I am only young, and unused to commanding men older than myself, having until but lately been considered no more than a child. And they will not listen to courteous suggestions that they should go back to their own homes until my mother has made up her mind. For you must know they are my mother's suitors, all the unmarried young noblemen of Ithaca and the lords from the islands around. From Dulichium, from Same, and from the forests of Zacynthus have they come to gather here in my father's house. For though we have heard no word of his death, they have chosen to consider that he never will come home and that my mother is a widow, to be courted by another husband. For she is still young, and not without much beauty, and she is renowned throughout all Ithaca and the islands for her virtues and her prudence, and many a man would be proud to have her for his wife. But my mother, like myself, still hopes that one day Odysseus may return; and so she remains in his house, waiting and hoping, and will not give an answer to her wooers. And they say that since she will not decide among them, they will come here every day to make certain that they are not absent when she at last comes to a decision. Besides, they find it cheap and pleasant, to live on my father's food, ordering his servants as they will, and passing their days in idleness in the house of a king. And because I am young they will not hear me when I speak of it, but only laugh and tell me I should be glad to have a mother so beautiful and so accomplished that many men desire to marry her.'

'It is indeed a sorry tale you tell,' said Athene, 'and you have my sympathy, young man. I am ashamed to think that in these islands, and above all, in Ithaca itself, the home of my good Odysseus, there are so many men who could act so shamelessly. But take courage, my friend, for I am certain that your father will return, and when he does, it will be an unhappy day for these young men who feast so joyously tonight.'

'I thank you for your consoling words,' replied Telemachus, sighing, 'but waiting is not easy, and what if, after all, my father should never return?'

'I am an older man than you, and I have seen more of life,' Athene said, laying a kindly hand upon his arm. 'If you will not resent advice from a stranger, let me give some good advice to you. Show yourself a true son of Odysseus, as I remember him to be. Do not wait for his return, but try to drive away these rogues yourself.

Tomorrow, go to the place of assembly in the town and call together all the elders and counsellors, the noblemen and the lords, and put your case to them. Tell them openly and plainly how the suitors are wasting your father's goods and making free with his possessions. Then, when you see that there are those among the staider and wiser men of Ithaca who would support you, ask these suitors of your mother to begone to their own homes, there to wait her answer as well-behaved wooers should.'

Telemachus' eyes grew bright and he clenched his fists. 'Noble Mentes,' he said, 'I will do as you bid me. Perchance they will listen to me if I speak to them before the assembled men of Ithaca.'

'And after—hear me further—'went on Athene, 'fit out a small ship of some twenty oars and sail to Pylos, in the south, and there ask good Nestor, that wise old king, if he has news of your father. For Nestor fought at Troy with Odysseus, and so did Nestor's son, and it may well be that he has heard word of your father since he set forth from that city. And then go on from Pylos to Sparta, it is but two days' journey in a fast chariot, and there seek news from King Menelaus, and from Queen Helen, for whose sake the war was fought. They also may have words of comfort for you.'

'I will do even as you tell me, good stranger,' said Telemachus with eagerness. 'It well may be some gain will come of it.'

'And if it does not,' said Athene, 'if perhaps you should hear that your father is dead, then you will at least have learnt the worst there is to know. And if you should hear no news of him at all, why then, no harm will have come of it, and you will but have tried to solve your troubles, and you can wait perhaps another year in the patient hope that Odysseus may return. But if in twelve months he is not here, then you can consider him as dead, and urge your mother to take another husband and go to another home, leaving you in possession of your inheritance.'

Thus Athene spoke, for she wished to try Telemachus, whether he was a son worthy of his father, the wily Odysseus, schemer of many plots.

Telemachus, his young face flushed with enthusiasm, and his eyes shining, jumped to his feet so eagerly that one or two of the suitors marked his movements, though they could not hear his words, and wondered at him. 'Your counsel is good, and I will do even as you say,' he said. 'Stranger, I thank you with all my heart.'

Athene rose. 'It is well,' she said, 'and may your misfortunes soon be at an end and your noble father see once more his home. But now it grows late, the sun is setting, and I must be on my way. Farewell, brave son of Odysseus, good luck in all your ventures be with you.'

'Noble Mentes, will you not tarry here awhile? It is a father's advice and help such as you have this evening given me that I have lacked so long. I would be both pleased and honoured if you would remain as my guest for a few days.'

Athene smiled and shook her head. 'I thank you, Telemachus, but I would be gone tonight.'

'Stay at least until I have had time to find you a worthy gift to take with you,' pleaded Telemachus. 'No ordinary guest should leave a house without a present from his host. How much more should the giver of such serviceable counsel as yours receive a fitting gift at his departure?'

'No, Telemachus, seek not to keep me longer here, for I must be gone. Farewell, and remember all that I have said to you.' And in an instant Athene had vanished and Telemachus stood alone beside the chairs that they had used.

Marvelling, he thought, 'That was indeed one of the immortal gods, no mortal man could vanish thus. I have been honoured by a visitor from Mount Olympus, surely that betokens good fortune to the house?'

Phemius, the young minstrel, was once again singing, and lest it should be questioned that he sat alone, Telemachus moved closer to the suitors and took a chair among them to listen to the song.

Phemius sang of the return of the Greeks from Troy, and his voice rang so sweetly throughout the hall, that even the noisy suitors were silenced, and heard him with admiration. One of the servants had left open the door which led to the other rooms of the house and to the women's quarters, so the sound of the minstrel's singing reached up the stairs to Penelope the queen, where she sat spinning sadly among her serving-maids. She heard his words plainly, of how the Greeks, victorious and triumphant, set sail from the fallen city, their ships well packed with spoils; and her eyes filled with bright tears as she remembered Odysseus, who had sailed, but not yet come home.

She rose and laid aside her distaff, and beckoning two of the maidens to attend her, she came down the stairs and entered the hall. She stood awhile upon the threshold of the door with tears on her cheeks; until at last she could bear her thoughts no longer, and her clear voice called to Phemius across the hall, and bade him cease his singing.

'Phemius, you know many songs, on many different

themes. Sing one of them, if these young men must have music while they feast. But tell no more the tale of the Greeks' return from Troy, for one good man I know of, who left that unhappy city, did not come back to his home and his unfortunate wife; even my own dear husband, Odysseus.'

The song failed upon the minstrel's lips and his lyre fell silent, while the wooers gazed with surprise and admiration at Penelope where she stood by the door, and she drew a fold of her coloured veil across her face.

Telemachus saw in her arrival and her words a chance to impress the suitors with his new-born resolution to assert himself. 'Dear mother,' he said gently, 'let Phemius sing of what he will. Of all the noble warriors who fought at Troy, there were many who did not return, for they had found graves in Trojan earth. Odysseus was not alone ill fated. And it is not the fault of Phemius but the will of the immortal gods that these things came to pass, so do not blame him that he sings of them. It is now almost twenty years since my father sailed for Troy and left me, a tiny babe, in your arms. Today I am no longer a child. Good mother, I beg you, go back to your spinning, and leave me to order my father's house.'

Penelope was amazed to hear him speak thus, and pleased at his words, both because she was proud that her son should have shown himself to be no more a child and should have spoken with authority, and because she hoped that if he displayed a determined spirit, the suitors might be inclined to respect a little more her absent husband's property. So without another word, she turned away and left the hall, followed by her serving-maids, smiling a little

to herself as she went, and thinking, 'May Telemachus prove himself as good a man as his dear father, for this house has been too long without a master.'

But it was with annoyance that the suitors heard Telemachus speak, and they glanced at each other, with eyebrows raised and shoulders shrugging, and here and there a whispered word of mockery. But they said nothing out aloud, for each feared that Penelope might hear him and be angered, and his suit would thus not prosper.

When his mother had left the room, Telemachus turned to his uninvited guests. 'For tonight,' he said, 'let us feast and listen to the singing, since tomorrow I mean to call together the townspeople at the assembly place, as is my right as the son of your king. There will I ask you before all the gathered citizens to return once more to your own homes, or to find your meals in some other house. For I am weary of the waste and gluttony that for ever goes on in this hall. If you are men of decent feeling, you will respect my wishes and depart, but if, even after I have demanded it before the people, you refuse to listen to my words, then may some evil fate befall you, and may you perish, every one, even though it be within my house.'

There was not one among the suitors who was not astonished to hear him speak so to them. For before that day he had been mild in speech and meek in manners when in their company; and they had grown used to considering him as a child whose wishes might be ignored and whose words left unheeded.

For a moment no one answered him, for they all knew that what he demanded was only just and right, though they had no intention of submitting. And then Antinous, the son of Eupeithes, a nobleman of Ithaca, who was the most insistent and the most arrogant of all the wooers, spoke with ugly scorn. 'Why, Telemachus, if you are, as you say, no longer a child, then I fear you have grown up into a shameless boaster and one who delights to pick a quarrel. And I can only hope, for the sake of all my peaceful fellow citizens, that you may never rule in Ithaca as our king.'

'Indeed, Antinous,' Telemachus retorted, 'I could think of many a worse fate than to be king here in Ithaca. Kings and their houses and their goods are held in honour and treated with respect, and I could be glad of a little more deference and consideration.' He paused a moment and then added bitterly, 'Though of late it has seemed to me that however deserving he may be of them, even the best of kings loses that honour and respect which are his due, unless he is present to enforce the paying of them.' He went on, emboldened by the visit of a goddess, his voice raised in defiance of them for the first time since they had come to his father's house, 'But who shall be king in Ithaca, once it is proved Odysseus lives no more, is not for me or for you to decide. Yet whoever is king of the island, I intend to be master in this house.'

Antinous glowered at him in anger, but Eurymachus, a suitor no whit less disagreeable than Antinous, but with a smoother tongue, said pleasantly, calming the uneasy moment, 'You are not mistaken, Telemachus. It is not for any of us here to decide who shall succeed your honoured father. But as for you, who would deny to you the right to be lord in your own house? The rights of each man, that is something we would willingly see upheld, and now that you are of an age to manage your own matters, we would gladly see you paid your due respect.' Then, because Eurymachus suspected that Telemachus' sudden change of manner towards his mother's suitors might in some way be owing to the visit of a stranger to the house that day, he asked, easily, and as though the answer mattered very little to him, 'But to talk of happier things than the sad loss of your father, tell us, Telemachus, who was the stranger who supped with you? He seemed a man of some distinction, and he disappeared so suddenly—one moment here, and the next time I looked, vanished utterly—that I had no chance to have speech with him. Did he perchance have any news of Odysseus?'

For a moment Telemachus was silent, then because he was his father's son, he answered subtly, 'Indeed, Eurymachus, I begin to fear my father never will come home. Unlike my dear mother, I am fast losing all hope of seeing him again. The stranger was no more than an old friend of his, one Mentes, from Taphos.'

'From Taphos?' said Eurymachus, 'Would that I had spoken to him.'

But Antinous threw aside the golden cup which he had just drained, so that it rolled, ringing, on the floor. 'We have had enough talking of old fools from Taphos. Come, let us dance.' He rose. 'Strike up your lyre, Phemius, and give us a gay tune.'

The minstrel played for them, and thrusting aside the chairs and tables, the suitors danced. Telemachus watched them for a little space with hatred in his heart, and then he turned and left the hall through the door at the far end, calling as he went to Eurycleia, his old nurse, who had been nurse also to Odysseus, when he too had been a child. 'Bring me a light, Eurycleia, I am sickened with the sight of those shameless rogues. I can be with them no longer. Light me a lamp in my own room.'

He lay awake upon his bed for hours, thinking over all that Athene had said to him, and resolving in his mind the words that he should speak before the assembly on the morrow.

But the suitors danced and drank until far into the night, then one by one they drifted from the house; the Ithacans to their own homes, and the other island princes to their lodgings in the town.

# IX

## *The Assembly*

AS soon as it was morning, Telemachus sent forth heralds from Odysseus' house to call together all the noblemen and leaders of Ithaca for an assembly. It was the first conclave of the townspeople of that island that had been called since Odysseus, their king, had sailed for Troy, and they were much surprised at the summons. Wondering, they gathered in the place of assembly in the centre of the town, old men and young men; and because Odysseus had been gone for twenty years, a few among them were young enough for this to be their first public assemblage.

Some came eagerly and asking questions of all their friends as to why they had been called together. 'It is the first time for twenty years,' they said. 'What of importance can have occurred?'

Some paced slowly and with dignity and replied to all questioners with a solemn shake of their heads, as though they knew full well why the summons had gone forth, but considered the matter too grave for light discussion before the meeting. 'After the assembly, my friend, after the assembly will I tell you. These things should first be debated publicly,' they would answer.

Yet others came reluctantly and with annoyance, grumbling as they came, 'We have had no assembly for almost twenty years, why should we have been called together on today of all days. I was going to walk early from the town to my farm in the hills to see how things went there. I am certain that my steward has been cheating me,' or, 'My wife's brother lies sick upon the island of Zacynthus, I should have sailed this morning to see how he fares.'

And so they came together, taking their places on the stone seats in the early morning sunshine; and among them were all those of Penelope's wooers whose home was Ithaca, and they alone of all the citizens knew why the assembly had been called and by whom. But they were silent, answering no questions and offering to speak to no one save among themselves.

When the appointed time had come, and the townspeople were all gathered, Telemachus left his home and walked to the assembly place. In a gleaming white tunic and wearing a purple cloak with a yellow striped border and a yellow fringe, his long curls bound up by a garland of ribbon, his sword slung about his shoulders and a spear in his hands, with his two favourite hounds at his heels, he looked a youth whom Odysseus might well have been proud to call his son, had he been there to see him. He was excited and a little afraid, but none of this he showed, as with apparent calm he took his place, greeting gravely and with courtesy all who were present.

And the older men there, who had known Odysseus as a youth, whispered to each other, 'He has grown up into a fine young man, so very like his father was, at the same age,' and, 'I wish our king were here today to see his handsome son.'

For a while they sat expectantly, now that their numbers were complete; then an old nobleman, very bent and frail, rose to his feet, and too feeble to leave his place for the speaker's stand in the centre of the assembly, spoke from where he stood, in a thin, cracked voice. 'My friends and fellow countrymen of Ithaca,' he said, 'this is the first assembly that has been called since our good king Odysseus sailed away to fight at Troy. Who among us here has called it, and why? Has he some news of importance to impart to us? Is it that he perhaps has heard that the king is coming home at last, or—may the gods forbid it—that he is dead? Whoever he is that has called us here, and whatever his news may be, let him show himself and declare his purpose.'

Telemachus instantly rose up, and leaving his spear propped against the seat, a hound crouched on either side of it, he stood out in the centre of the assembly place, and turning first to the old man who had spoken, he said, 'Noble lord, it was I, Telemachus, son of Odysseus, your king, who called this meeting of the men of Ithaca today. I have, alas, no news of Odysseus' return, nor, indeed, any public matters to report to you, my fellow citizens. My reason for calling this assembly here today is to speak to you on something that touches me alone.' He turned and looked around the gathering. 'My friends, and lords of Ithaca, hear my grievance and give me your support. Two great troubles have come upon me. The first is fate, and fate we cannot strive against. My father Odysseus, as you all do know, has not yet returned from Troy, though that city fell nigh on ten years ago and the war was ended. But in all that time have I had no word of him, whether he be alive or dead, and I have no means of telling if he will ever see his home again. This should surely be grief enough for any man, and as I have said, it is fate and there is no remedy in our hands for that. But my other grievance can and should be removed. My friends, ever since it seemed as though there were a chance that Odysseus might never again come home, my mother, the good Queen Penelope, has been harassed by scores of suitors. There is, it seems, not one young man in Ithaca or in our neighbouring isles who does not wish to marry her. But they are not content to wait upon her and bring her gifts at seemly intervals, handing them with fair words to her housekeeper, and lingering within her walls only long enough to drink a cup of wine and make a courteous greeting. No, these young men come in tens and scores, uninvited and without presents, and every day in my father's house they sit and eat and drink his food and wine, order his servants as though they were their own, call to his minstrel to sing to them, and in all things comport themselves as though they were at home. My mother is embarrassed by their presence, and I, her son, am slighted by them and treated as of no account in my own father's house; while Laertes, my grandfather, driven away by grief for the loss of his son, and by the insolence of these suitors, lives in misery on his farm across the hills. These daily ravages upon our stores and food are lessening my father's wealth; cattle are slaughtered to feed these men, wine-jars broken open to satisfy their never-ending thirst, his servants corrupted to neglect their duties, waiting day after day upon these wooers. This is no fitting way to behave towards the wife, or perchance the widow, of a king, and towards his only son, and I ask my mother's suitors, here, before all the assembled men of Ithaca, that they will cease to frequent my father's house, and conduct themselves as any self-respecting wooers should.' He stopped, and carried away by his unhappiness, he could not restrain his tears, so that there were many there who pitied him.

But Antinous jumped to his feet from where he sat beside his father, the Lord Eupeithes, his face dark with fury, his brows drawn together in a frown, and he shouted to Telemachus, 'You are a liar who would blacken the good name of your mother's suitors for your own ends. For I tell you, Telemachus, it is not our fault that we are kept idly loitering in your house. It is, and has always been, the fault of your scheming mother.'

Eurymachus, who sat on the other side of him, laid a restraining hand upon his wrist, but Antinous shook it off angrily without a glance, and went on, 'It is she who has kept us waiting for an answer, it is she who is delaying her choice of a husband, and that not openly or honestly. For years she has cheated us, cunningly and with fair words. Three years ago, when first we gathered at your house and pressed her for an answer to our wooing, she excused herself from making any choice with the plea that she was occupied with her spinning and her weaving. She said that she was making a shroud for old Laertes, King Odysseus' father; that when the time came for him to die, as all mortals must, he might have a winding-sheet fit for one of his high rank.

'"He is an old man," she said to us, "and I must not delay the work. When it is over, then will I name my choice of a husband from among you all."

'Would any man of honour not have respected her request? We suitors all agreed to wait until the work was finished, and for three years we waited while she spun and wove. All the mornings she spun the fine white wool, and all the afternoons she spent in weaving the yarn that she had spun; and then at night, when we had left the house and all the servants slept, she would rise up from her bed and unravel all that she had woven in the day. And so the months passed, month after month, and she worked industriously. Month after month she worked, but the skeins of wool piled up in her apartments and there was no shroud for Lord Laertes. One of her waiting-women told us of the queen's deception, how she played us false; and one night two or three of us returned to the house by darkness and surprised her at her task of unravelling her work. Her trick has been found out at last, and she must now complete the winding-sheet for her husband's father, but her craft has delayed us for three years. And yet, Telemachus, you dare to say that we suitors are at fault.' He paused for breath, and then went on more calmly, 'I say to you, Telemachus, and to all you other men of Ithaca, that never will we suitors leave Odysseus' house until Queen Penelope has made her choice among us. So long as she keeps us waiting, we shall remain in her home.' He looked round the assembly, 'Am I not right in that, and are we not all agreed, you fellow wooers of the queen?'

And at once, all those other suitors who were present, called out that they were in accord with what he said.

Antinous smiled with satisfaction at their agreement. 'So you see, young Telemachus, your only hope of being quit of us, is to persuade your mother to come to a decision, and marry once again.'

'She is my mother,' said Telemachus, 'and was the wife of a king. It is not fitting that I should try to persuade her in this matter, or hasten her to make a choice against her will. She loved my father dearly, and would not think it seemly to hurry to another's house, without even being sure that he is dead.'

Antinous made an impatient gesture and sat down and whispered to Eurymachus, and they both glanced up contemptuously at Telemachus.

Telemachus grew angry, and, as a young man will, he spoke without considering his words. 'I demand that all you insolent men shall leave my father's house this very day. For I swear that otherwise I shall pray to all the immortal gods that they send down a ghastly vengeance on you and destroy you utterly, every one of you.'

There was silence in the assembly at his bold words, though a few of the suitors murmured among themselves. Then one or two of them laughed aloud, mockingly, and whispered to each other, 'The little puppy is showing his teeth at last.' But there were several among the older men, who hearing him, nodded their approval.

At that moment two eagles soared up from the wooded heights of Mount Neriton, lying inland on the island, and wing outstretched to wing, they flew towards the town; two mighty birds, in perfect accord. But directly above the place of assembly they fell to fighting in the air, tearing at each other with hooked talons and curving beaks, scattering feathers to the wind and screeching angrily the while.

The men of Ithaca watched them in amazement, wondering what such an omen might foreshadow, for it was not every day that a similar sight was seen. Finally, the two eagles, still battling above the island, flew away eastwards, and their cries faded on the air.

'It is a portent,' whispered the people to one another. 'What can it signify?' And they debated among themselves as to the meaning.

Then Halitherses, an old nobleman who had once been known for his skill in prophecy and the interpretation of omens, both good and ill, rose up and spoke. 'Hear me now, you men of Ithaca, for I think that I can tell to you the meaning of the sight which we have all just seen. The thought is upon me that soon Odysseus, our king, will be home. When he sailed to Troy I foresaw that he would not return until twenty years had passed, and it is nigh on twenty years since he left our midst. Soon will he be back, and when he comes, then will it be an unhappy day for those that waste his substance in his house. That, my friends, is how I explain the fighting of these eagles above our town. Heed my warning, all you suitors of the queen, lest in the days to come you shall regret it.'

A few of the suitors seemed perturbed, and Antinous glowered angrily and seemed about to reply; but it was Eurymachus who answered with a laugh. 'Go home, good Lord Halitherses, and tell fortunes to amuse your grandchildren, but do not expect grown men to believe your prophecies. Why, I warrant myself as good a seer as you over this matter, and I say it bodes no ill. Besides, there are many birds which one may see, flying in the sky, if one only looks for them, yet but rarely does their flying signify disaster, or indeed, anything at all. No, sad as it is for our friend Telemachus, it seems plain by now that King Odysseus is dead and never will return to Ithaca. It is but heartless and shameful to seek to raise up false hopes in the lad's mind of his father's return, no doubt in the expectation of a reward from him and the queen. And ill indeed would it be to urge him to violent conduct against his fellow countrymen.' Then, turning to Telemachus, he said pleasantly, 'Come, my friend, forget your quarrel with us, and go home and persuade your mother that she is a widow, and that it is only right that she should gladden the house of another husband. Then shall your home be free of all her wooers, for, as Antinous has warned you, we shall all remain within your walls until she has chosen one of us. For she is a most excellent lady, and there is none among us who would give up hope of winning her while she yet hesitated to make up her mind.'

Telemachus then bethought himself of Athene's further advice to him, and silencing his anger, he answered quietly, 'Eurymachus and all you other suitors, I have stated my case before you and before all Ithaca, and you have made me your reply. You know my wishes, and I know your intentions. Let us not speak further of them here. I now propose to fit out a ship that I may sail from here to Pylos, where wise old King Nestor rules, and to the palace of King Menelaus in Sparta, and in those places ask tidings of my father. For Nestor had a son who died at Troy, and Menelaus was at the sacking of the city, perchance they both might tell me news of their one-time comrade. If the news is good, and there is still hope of Odysseus' return, then shall I continue to wait for him in patience. But if it seems certain that he is truly dead, then shall I return to Ithaca and build him a memorial, fit for the great and goodly king he was, and urge my mother to take another husband and go at last to another home.'

With this, Telemachus went back to his place and sat down once more. His two hounds stood and wagged their tails to see him come, and then lay at his feet.

Upon that Mentor rose, who had been a firm friend of Odysseus. 'People of Ithaca,' he said, 'I am grieved to see how easily a good man is forgotten. Odysseus was a just and kindly king, one who always had our benefit at heart, yet today not one of us has spoken up for his young son, who has but so lately reached man's estate. I expect but little merit from his mother's wooers, for they are blinded by the virtues and the beauty of our fair queen. But it is you others, you older men, whose silence offends me, for, save for Lord Halitherses' timely warning, you have uttered no single word of condemnation, nor attempted to restrain these young men, though your numbers are greater by far than theirs.'

One of the wooers instantly jumped to his feet. 'For shame, Mentor,' he cried, 'why do you seek to stir up strife? Shall grown men quarrel over a few plates of meat and jars of wine? Besides, it is Odysseus' food we eat, not yours, and therefore not your concern at all. And should Odysseus come home as you seem to wish, well,' he smiled unpleasantly, 'we suitors far outnumber him, and maybe after all, his wife would not have so much joy of his home-coming as she hopes. As for Telemachus, no one will pre-vent him from going to Pylos and to Sparta if he wishes. Indeed, it will be a pleasure not to have him sulking in the house, resenting our good appetites, for a few days at least. And doubtless you, Mentor, with old Halitherses ambling at your side, will be glad to go and bid him farewell at the harbour and wish him a successful voyage.' He paused and looked around him with insolence, then added, 'Truly, men of Ithaca, I should imagine that by now we have all said what we had to say, so let us consider the assembly ended, and go back to our homes.'

At once all the suitors rose, and in a group left the assembly place and went to the house of Odysseus for the midday meal. And after them, the other townsfolk also rose, and with much talk about the events of the morning, made their way back to their own homes.

But Telemachus went alone to the sea-shore, and there, standing upon the golden sands, he prayed to immortal Athene, that she might help him to get ready a ship to sail to Pylos and might prosper his voyage; and that in the end she might send his father safely home.

And all of these prayers Athene heard, and answered in due course.

# X

## *King Nestor*

WHEN Telemachus returned home it was nearing evening, and he found the suitors awaiting
supper after having spent the afternoon at
javelin-throwing in the courtyard. He tried to slip through
them unobserved and go to his own quarters; but Antinous
saw him and hurried forward with a smile and took his
hand in a warm greeting.

'Why, here is Telemachus, our fiery orator. He is home
at last,' he laughed, and laid a hand upon Telemachus'
shoulder. 'Come, Telemachus, let us forget our wrangling
of this morning, and let us feast in friendship as before. See,
meat and drink are even now being set before us, come and
sup with us here, and tell us all how you have passed the
day since we parted in the place of assembly. But do not

think to leave us yet to go to Pylos to seek tidings of your father. Some day, I have no doubt, will the men of Ithaca provide a ship for you to sail in where you please, but till then, let us enjoy the pleasant things in life, all of us, here together.'

But Telemachus snatched his hand away and said, 'Antinous, it is no longer possible for me to bear your company with any show of pleasure. When I was a child I suffered your insolence in silence, as befits a child. But I am a boy no longer, and I will not stand by unmoved while you waste my property before my eyes. And I am going to Pylos and to Sparta, to see King Nestor and King Menelaus, as soon as it can be brought to pass, and no word from you or any other man shall prevent me. And if at Pylos and at Sparta I can find no news that will drive you from the house, scattering for shelter from the anger of your king like leaves before the wind; then, when I return, in Ithaca itself shall I seek for a means of ridding my house of all you hated suitors, and I shall not rest till I have found it.' And he turned from Antinous and went across the hall.

But the suitors who had heard his words laughed and mocked him. 'Indeed, Telemachus is going to murder us, every man, the brave youth that he is,' said one.

Said another, 'He is going to Pylos to ask old Nestor's help, or perhaps he goes to Menelaus to ask for a Spartan army with which to kill his fellow countrymen in Ithaca.'

'No,' said yet another, laughing, 'I think it far more likely that our dear Telemachus will travel even farther afield and buy a deadly poison, and drop it in our wine when he comes home, he loves us so.'

While with pretended seriousness, another young man

called out, 'Perhaps he has inherited his father's knack of losing himself at sea, and so may be lost between here and Pylos. That would indeed be a sorry day for us, for we should have the tedious task of sharing out his possessions among ourselves. His cattle to some, to some his slaves, and to others his land, while this fine house would go to him who weds the fair Penelope. What irksome labour it would be for us.'

At this they all burst out laughing, and Telemachus, ashamed and angry, went through the door at the side of the great hall and made his way along the passage to the store-room of Odysseus, calling as he went for Eurycleia who kept the key. The old nurse came hurrying from the women's quarters, and unlocked the strong door for him, and together they went inside.

Here, in this wide room, were ranged the treasures of Odysseus; gold and silver cups and platters, wrought silver dishes, chased golden bowls for mixing wine, and polished brazen ewers and cauldrons. In wooden chests lay dyed and woven cloths and embroidered garments smelling of sweet spices; filmy scarves and dainty veils, fit for the queens of Ithaca, and plaited girdles for a slender waist. In little caskets of carved ivory or curious woods lay brooches, rings, and bracelets, and pins of bone and metal for pinning up a woman's hair.

Here, too, were kept the close-sealed wine-jars, on shelves along the walls, placed carefully in order of their vintage. Around the plump black crocks ran wreaths of leaves or twining flowers in yellow, red, or white; or here and there would be a jar which had a band of fishes swimming on a wavy sea, or a handsome pattern of lines and dots painted boldly in rich red. While on one shelf were collected flasks, both large and small, of scented oil for perfuming and anointing.

To one side of this treasure-chamber lay the armoury. Heavy spears and light javelins in stands against the wall, and shields piled upon the floor, swords laid carefully in their scabbards, and polished armour, shining brightly. And on the wall, upon a peg, hung the great bow of Odysseus, which he had left behind him when he sailed to Troy.

But Telemachus had not come to look at all his father's wealth, his mind was too full of troubled thoughts to give any heed to the treasures gathered here. He turned to the old woman. 'Nurse, fill me twelve jars with wine, the best we have, save for that special vintage which I know you are keeping to celebrate the day my father shall come home —may it be soon. Twelve jars of wine, well covered, and barley flour in leather bags, and have them ready by tonight for me. But say no word of this to any one, not even to my mother, for I am going to sail south to Pylos, and from there shall I journey on to Sparta, to see if I can learn tidings of my father, and I would not that any man should hinder me from my intentions.'

But Eurycleia cried out and flung her arms about his neck. 'My child, whatever made you think of doing such a thing? To go alone, all the way to Sparta. To travel half across the world and perchance never to come home again. Or if you do, to find these wicked men who ravage our home have planned some dreadful deed against you so that they may take what is rightly yours and enjoy it quite unchecked, without you to say them nay. No, no, my little one, stay here with us. No matter how hard life may be for you, it is always better for a young man to stay in his own home than to voyage over the seas.'

'Hush, nurse, Sparta is not so very far away, and I shall come back again, and soon; for I think that one of the immortal gods is with me in this. And, nurse, if I should be successful in finding good news, think how those men would run for their homes when they heard that Odysseus was coming back.' So he spoke to comfort her; but in his heart he doubted, after all that had passed that day, whether the suitors would be so easily driven from the house, even by Odysseus, should he ever return.

Eurycleia dried her eyes and sniffed. 'It seems but only the other day you were a little boy, playing at my knee, and now here you are, saying that you are going to Sparta, where great King Menelaus rules. But it is no use an old woman's speaking, for you will no longer listen to my advice, though you were glad enough to take it once.'

Telemachus put his arm around her. 'Nurse, dear old nurse, I may not be taking your advice today, but I am trusting you instead. Of all the servants in the house, I have chosen you to help me. Not even my mother am I telling of my plans, and you must promise me that you will keep the truth from her until, say, twelve days shall be passed, for I do not want her to grieve and fret herself for me. Let her think that I have gone to my grandfather on his farm, or to Philoetius the cowman, to see how our cattle increase on the mainland.'

'She would think it strange that you went either to Philoetius or to Lord Laertes without bidding her goodbye,' said Eurycleia doubtfully.

'That is how you must help me, nurse, by telling her a likely story to set her mind at ease. Come, dear old Eurycleia, promise me that you will aid me in the first important endeavour of my life, and say nothing about it to anyone.'

So Eurycleia promised him to keep silence; and she set to work to draw off the jars of wine, and fill the bags with barley meal, so that they should be ready for him when he needed them.

But Telemachus returned to the great hall and joined the suitors at their supper, and to calm any suspicions that they might have had, he talked and laughed with them, so that they thought he had forgotten his earlier angry words. But when dusk fell, he slipped from the hall, and aided by Athene, went through the town. There a kindly citizen named Noemon lent him willingly a small ship, and Athene gathered together for him a company of adventurous youths of his own age, who, encouraged by his friend Peiraeus, readily undertook to sail with him to Pylos.

Then, when the suitors had left Odysseus' house and gone to their own homes to sleep, Telemachus led his shipmates back to the house. Quietly they entered the hall and gathered up the bags of flour and jars of wine from the place where good Eurycleia had left them, hidden behind a group of chairs, so that neither Penelope nor the other servants might see them, should any of them pass that way.

The youths returned quickly to the ship and stowed everything on board; then in the darkness they set sail for Pylos, and Athene herself gave them a fair breeze. All night long they sailed, and all the while Telemachus sat at the prow and watched through the dim light for a sight of land, so eager was he to reach his goal.

Soon after dawn they sighted the sandy coast of Pylos, and as they came closer in, they could see a great crowd of people gathered on the shore. For it was a holiday in honour of the great Poseidon, god of the seas, and all the townsfolk of Pylos had come together to offer sacrifice and do him homage. There were in all nine companies of them, with five hundred men in each; and each company was making its own sacrifices and offering up its particular prayers.

One company, consisting of the most noble men of Pylos, was led by the king, old Nestor himself, renowned throughout all Greece for his wisdom and discernment. He was now very old, but his understanding and true judgement were as they had always been, and he was yet respected far and wide. Though he had been old already when the Greeks had sailed for Troy, almost twenty years before, he had sailed with them, along with his eldest son, and the Grecian host had found his prudent counsel of the greatest service. But he had returned alone from Troy, for his son, Antilochus, had perished in the fighting, and his spirit had been among those Odysseus had seen in Hades' land.

As the young men from Ithaca rowed in to the shore a little way along the coast from where the people were gathered, the sacrifices had been done and the folk were building fires and spreading rugs upon the ground that they might sit and feast. Busily and gaily they unpacked baskets of food and broke open jars of wine, setting out the good things on the coloured cloths. They were all in festive holiday attire, garlanded and with their brightest garments, and made a cheerful sight to greet Telemachus as he stepped out on the beach.

But he was a little fearful of how he might approach the king before all this vast concourse, and stood hesitating by the little ship, for it was the very first time in all his nineteen years that he had gone to visit a man of such importance as wise King Nestor.

But one of Nestor's youngest sons, Peisistratus, who had long since spied the ship when she was but a white sail on the horizon, had kept a careful watch on her as she drew close in to the shore; and now, as soon as he saw Telemachus set foot upon the golden sand, he came forward to the water's edge to welcome him.

Telemachus looked up to see a youth of his own age coming towards him with a smile, and he recovered his spirits and smiled in return. Peisistratus held out his hand. 'You are welcome, stranger,' he said cordially, 'we men of Pylos are about to start the feasting, come and join us.' He led the way back to the group that he had left. 'My father is King Nestor,' he said. 'I will take you to him, for he is ever glad to receive a stranger.'

As Telemachus came among them, many of the men of Pylos greeted him with friendliness, and by the time he stood before the king, he was once again at ease. Nestor sat upon a heap of fleecy sheepskins talking with his sons.

'Here is the stranger who has just moored his ship a little way along the coast, father,' said Peisistratus.

Nestor looked up at Telemachus, and the eyes in his wrinkled face were very bright and keen. He smiled, 'Come and sit close beside me, young man, and eat and drink with

us. Afterwards we will talk together, and you shall tell me
who you are and from whence you come.'

They ate barley cakes and meat that had been roasted on
spits over the fire, and out of the golden cups from the
king's own house, which had been carried to the shore
wrapped in linen and laid in a wooden chest, they drank
wine to the long life and good health of Nestor and his
sons, and fair weather to prosper the voyaging of Telemachus.

When they had eaten and drunk, Nestor turned to Telemachus. 'Stranger,' he said, 'now that you have been
welcomed among us with food and wine, it is a fitting time
to ask you your name and your country. Do you voyage
to a destination, or is the sea your home?'

'Good Nestor, I am not a sea-robber, if that is what you
mean, for my home is in Ithaca. And I voyage to a destination which I have even now reached. For it is you, most
noble king, whom I have travelled over the sea to seek. My
name is Telemachus, and I am the only son of Odysseus,
king of Ithaca. But it is not on behalf of my father's people
that I have come to you, it is to ask your aid for my own
self. I have come to question you if you have heard news
of Odysseus since he sailed from Troy. You were in that
city with him when it fell, perchance you may have sailed
for home together, and then been parted on the way, or
perchance you may have heard from another's lips of some
mishap that has befallen him. For you must know that
though it is near to ten whole years since Troy was taken,
my father has not yet returned to Ithaca. Good Nestor, if
you know anything of him, tell me now, and tell me truly.
Do not seek to spare me if your news is bad, for I would

rather learn the worst there is to know, than live on longer in this uncertainty, ever wondering whether my father really will come home again or whether he is lost to me and to my mother for evermore.'

Nestor laid a hand on Telemachus' shoulder. 'Truly,' he said, 'I should have known you, for you are very like your father. May you as much resemble him in courage and resourcefulness as you do in looks.' He nodded his head thoughtfully, and smiled. 'Good Odysseus, well do I remember his cautious counsel and his cunning wiles, no man of all the Greeks was like him; never-despairing through all those dark days of war and composed in the time of victory. For those were unhappy years for us, as all years of war must be, when before Troy perished so many goodly leaders of the Greeks. On Trojan earth fell Achilles, beautiful and so young, and brave Patroclus, his friend. There, too, died Antilochus, my son. Indeed they were unhappy years, Telemachus. But of the number who were slain, your father was not one, for when the city was taken, he sailed for Ithaca with his twelve ships. More than that I cannot tell you, for when the time came for the Greeks to set sail for home, a quarrel arose between Agamemnon, our leader, and his brother Menelaus, king of Sparta. One was for doing one thing and the other was for doing another, and between their two opposing counsels the whole Greek host was divided. I was among those who agreed with Menelaus, and we set sail together, but your father turned back while out at sea, returned to land, and stayed to follow Agamemnon. Thus have I no tidings of Odysseus, whether he set sail again and perished on the sea, or whether he is even now wandering about the world, ever striving to reach his home. For in the years that have passed since I myself reached Pylos, I have heard from travellers news of one or other of the Greeks who fought at Troy, but there has been no word of Odysseus, your father.'

'Good Nestor,' said Telemachus, 'I thank you for what you have told me, little comfort though it brings me. For I fear that if my father comes not soon, he will find no home left to him, no possessions to call his own, and his land and his servants given to another.' And Telemachus told King Nestor of the suitors and how they wasted Odysseus' goods, and of their overbearing ways and their insolence to him.

Solemnly, old Nestor shook his head. 'It is indeed a grievous thing, that in the master's absence such things can come to pass within his house. I would for your sake, good Telemachus, that the day may not be far distant which sees Odysseus return to his home.'

'Though I long every minute for that to come to pass,' said Telemachus, 'yet of late have I grown afraid that day will never come, and that my father's bones are even now lying in an alien grave, or washed beneath the restless sea.' He sighed. 'But this is no fit way for a guest to talk who has been so kindly received, and on a day which should be a day of rejoicing and holiday for his hosts. Good King Nestor, let us talk of other things than of my troubles. Tell me instead tales of the other leaders of the Greeks, for you have known them all, and in your wisdom judged them all aright, and can tell me truly what manner of men they were.'

And so they sat, and Nestor talked all through the afternoon of Agamemnon, Menelaus, and the other mighty

men, while Telemachus listened eagerly to all he had to say. And the sun went down while Nestor talked, and he looked up at the sunset-colours of the sky. 'I have talked enough for one day,' he said, 'and you have listened very patiently, but before we rise and leave this place, there is one thing that I would tell you. Stay not long away from your home, my child, lest those suitors of your mother begin to plot fresh mischief. But before you return to Ithaca, I would urge you to go to Sparta and talk to Mene-laus. For he has but lately returned to his own home after many wanderings and much delay in foreign lands, and it may well be that he has tidings of your father. If you would travel to Sparta over land, and that is surely the best way, then shall I willingly lend you horses, and one of my sons shall be your guide.'

Telemachus thanked him; and after one last cup of wine had been poured and drunk, the men of Pylos rose to pack away their rugs and cups and platters in chests and baskets for carrying home. Telemachus would have gone to the ship to pass the night on board with the young men who had come with him, but Nestor would not permit this, saying, 'No guest shall ever be turned away from any house of mine while there are blankets and rugs to spare. And never shall the son of my good friend Odysseus say that Nestor left him to sleep upon a ship moored on the beach at Pylos.'

So Telemachus went with Nestor and his sons to their house, and after they had feasted they went to rest; and for Telemachus a bed was set in the guest-chamber in the vesti-bule, and young Peisistratus slept with him for company.

In the morning Nestor sacrificed to Athene a pure white

heifer, garlanded with flowers, and with gilded horns, that she might look with favour on the mission of Telemachus. And after the sacrifice they feasted, King Nestor and his family together with Telemachus and his young companions from Noemon's ship.

When the feasting was done, Nestor called to his sons to bring out his finest travelling chariot and yoke to it his fastest horses, for Telemachus to drive to Sparta with Peisistratus. Then, after they had said farewell, and Nestor and his elder sons had wished Telemachus god-speed, Peisistratus took up the reins and they set off at a good pace across the level land that led to Sparta.

To Telemachus the drive was strange and exciting, and he envied Peisistratus his skill in driving. For Ithaca had steep and rocky ways and narrow roads where driving was impossible, so there were but few horses on the island.

They drove all day, and spent the night half-way to Sparta in the house of a kindly host; and early in the morning they set off once more. By the afternoon they had reached the wide lands of Menelaus, driving through the valleys past his cornfields with the young green wheat, and the fields of sprouting barley where the little yellow-eyed red tulips grew; and at dusk they came in sight of the high roofs of his palace in hill-encircled Sparta.

# XI

## *Menelaus and Helen*

IN his splendid palace great King Menelaus was celebrating with a banquet the betrothal of his daughter,
Hermione, Queen Helen's only child, to young Neoptolemus, Achilles' son, whom Odysseus had seen acquit
himself so bravely in the wooden horse at Troy. For while
they fought side by side, Menelaus had promised Neoptolemus that one day he should marry his fair daughter;
and he was even now making good his word, and after
days of feasting and rejoicing, Hermione would be sent
from Sparta with an escort of many chariots to the land
of the Myrmidons where her bridegroom ruled and waited
for her to come to him.

With singing and with music and with the antics of two
acrobatic jugglers, King Menelaus entertained his guests.

The minstrel played upon his lyre and sang a song that was fitting for a betrothal feast, while to the music the acrobats danced in and out among the feasters, walking on their hands, leaping over each other's back, and whirling on hands and feet like wheels down the length of the great hall; and much applause and praise they got for their skilled performance.

While the banquet was in progress, Telemachus and Peisistratus arrived at the palace and were received by Menelaus' steward who left them waiting in the courtyard, while he went to ask his master what he desired should be done with the strangers. 'Shall I bring them here to you, or shall I send them on to find hospitality in another house, my lord?'

Menelaus smashed his clenched fist down upon the carved arm of his chair. 'Why, man, you are a fool even to think of asking me such a question,' he roared. 'Have I ever turned away a guest? Do I not always welcome all strangers in my house? Go at once and bring them in.' The steward turned and hurried off and Menelaus gave a good-humoured chuckle. 'The man is growing crazed in his wits,' he said. 'He knows he does not need to ask a thing like that.' He took a draught of wine. 'These strangers come at a timely moment, the more guests at a betrothal feast, the merrier for the feasters. Come, my friends, do not stint the wine.'

Menelaus was a big man with a loud voice and a jovial laugh and a sandy beard streaked with grey, and a kindly heart which even his rough manner could not hide. He greeted Telemachus and Peisistratus warmly and called to them, 'Sit down, young men, and eat and drink and make merry with us. And later you can tell me who you are and whence you come, for I can see at a single glance that you are nobly born. No peasant breeds such sons as you. Come, sit and eat, there is food and wine in plenty in this house.'

Telemachus gazed in admiration and wonder at the splendour of the great hall of Menelaus, for Menelaus was a rich and mighty king and his house well displayed his wealth. To Telemachus it seemed most wonderful that any mortal man should own such glory and magnificence. For in all his life he had seen nothing comparable and had never been so far from home, or indeed travelled farther from Ithaca than the islands which lay close by. And though Odysseus had been a prince much respected among the Greeks, Ithaca was only a small land, and a poor one when compared with the hills and vales of Sparta, and Odysseus' house seemed but simple beside the lofty palace of King Menelaus.

With astonishment Telemachus saw the walls inlaid with bronze and gold and silver, and set with amber and with ivory designs; and marvelled at the ornaments and furnishings. He leant across to Peisistratus and whispered, 'Look well, Peisistratus, at all this pomp around us. I have never seen the like before. Surely not even the immortal gods themselves have so much splendour on high Olympus.'

But Menelaus heard his words and said, 'Come, good youths, you must not compare my possessions with the gods', it is not seemly. For the home and riches of the gods are everlasting, while mine must surely perish and one day fall to dust.' Then he smiled and looked around the hall with satisfaction. 'But though my goods are in no way comparable to those of the immortal gods, yet am I counted

rich among men, and well may that be so, for I have
gathered much wealth from many corners of the world,
far-off lands and places where strange creatures dwell, and
many curious sights have I seen in all my travels. The
Egyptians with their rare, healing drugs; and the Ethio-
pians who are black; and, if you can believe it, in Libya
lambs which are born with horns, not once, but three times
a year, so that to the Libyans there is a never-failing supply
of woolly fleeces and fresh ewes' milk cheese. But if I were
to tell you one part of all that I have seen, I should talk
until the dawn.' He drank a cup of wine and sighed. 'Yet
all my riches do not avail to keep away the sorrow that
comes upon me when I remember the many friends of
mine who fought with me, and died at Troy. I would give
up my wealth willingly if it could bring them back from
among the dead, for they were fine men and good companions.' He paused a moment, then went on, 'But of all
those who are dead and gone, I think I mourn not any so
much as brave Odysseus of Ithaca, for I considered him the
best of all the Greeks. Yet do I not know today whether he
is alive or dead, for ten years after Troy has fallen he is still
not returned to his home. Truly, if I do grieve so much for
him, who was my friend, how much more must he be
lamented by his father, old Laertes, and by good Penelope,
his wife, and by Telemachus, his only son, who was but a
tiny child when his father sailed for Troy. Indeed, poor
souls, I do pity them.'

Telemachus' eyes filled with tears when he heard his
father talked of, and he turned away his head so that Menelaus might not see him weep. But Menelaus marked him,
and even as he wondered what there should have been in

his words to make a young man weep who was not old enough to have known Odysseus and to have been his friend, he saw the likeness of Telemachus to his father.

'That is Odysseus' son,' he thought to himself. 'It can be no other.' And he weighed in his mind whether to ask him outright if he were his old friend's son, or to wait until the youth spoke himself. 'It were perhaps best to wait,' he thought. 'I do not wish to grieve him more. He will tell me his name in his own good time.'

He was about to speak of other and more happy matters, when his wife, Queen Helen, accompanied by three of her maids, came into the great hall. The guests greeted her with courtesy, and quietly and graciously she answered them, taking her place near Menelaus, seemingly intent upon receiving from her serving-maids the spinning they had carried for her. Yet had her swift eyes seen the two strangers present, and marked the likeness of one of the youths to Odysseus, though she had but glanced at him for a single moment.

On their part, Telemachus and Peisistratus watched her with curiosity, for was she not Helen for whose sake the Greeks had fought at Troy, accounting their sufferings a privilege? Helen, said once to be the most beautiful woman in all the world; who, twenty years before, had slipped away from this very hall, and sailed to Troy with King Priam's son, leaving her husband, Menelaus. Yet because she was beautiful, and because these things are as the gods will them to be, no one blamed her for the sorrow she had caused.

The two young men watched her as she took up her golden distaff and moved her shapely hands among the violet wool, and though one of them had had a brother who had died at Troy, and the other mourned a father, whom, because of her, he might never see again, they knew that Helen was still blameless and still worth dying for; and that though twenty years had passed since that fatal day when she had left her home, she was still the loveliest woman in all the world.

Helen laid a hank of purple yarn in her silver work-basket which ran on little wheels, and as though she knew they had been watching her, looked up with a smile at Telemachus and Nestor's son, before turning to her husband. 'Do you know, Menelaus,' she asked in her sweet, low voice, 'who these strangers are? Have you asked their names?'

Menelaus replied, 'They have but now arrived within our walls, and I have not harassed them with questions, hoping that when they had feasted, they would feel inclined to talk and tell their names and country.'

Helen smiled again and went on, 'Never in my life have I seen so great a likeness to another man as in the resemblance of this youth to Odysseus. I am certain that this is no other than Telemachus, Odysseus' son, whom he left as a tiny babe when he sailed to Troy with you.'

Delighted that he too had guessed the same, Menelaus said, 'Truly, that is the very thought that had been also in my mind, that this is Odysseus' son. He has Odysseus' features, his very gestures and the movement of his eyes. I surely could not be mistaken.' And he looked inquiringly towards Telemachus, who suddenly felt very young and very shy in all the distinguished company, and very much afraid that his quest might prove unpleasing to his host.

But Peisistratus came to his aid and answered for him. 'You are right, King Menelaus, you and your noble queen, this is indeed Telemachus, the son of Odysseus and his wife Penelope, who has travelled from rocky Ithaca to speak with you. For a son is lonely when he has no father to advise him. My own father, Nestor, king of Pylos, has sent me with him to guide him on the way, since he is unfamiliar with the mainland.'

'Glad am I to welcome to my house the son of my dear friend Odysseus,' said Menelaus. 'But indeed, I should be gladder if I might see his father here with him tonight. While I fought at Troy I often thought, how when the war was over and Odysseus and I were returned to Greece, I should give him to rule over, one of the towns of Argos, near to my own Sparta. There he could have lived with his family and all his people, so that we might have often met, remaining firm friends until the day death parted us. But although I returned safely to my house, notwithstanding after much toil, fate has been hard to great Odysseus, and denied to him his joyous homecoming.'

At his words a deep sadness fell upon the gathering, and many wept; for dear ones they had lost, or for troubles of their own, or just for the unhappiness of man, who lives not only to rejoice, but to suffer also.

Then Peisistratus spoke, 'Noble Menelaus, it is right that we should mourn for those who have died before us, it is indeed the only gift we can offer to the dead, our poor unavailing tears. But this is a festive occasion, the betrothal of your fair daughter, Queen Helen's child, so let us not mar it with grief for things we cannot alter even by our weeping.'

'Old Nestor has ever been famed for his wisdom,' said

Menelaus, 'and it is plain to see that in this respect, at least, you, his son, resemble him. You are right, Peisistratus, let us have no more of grief. Come, fill up the cups with wine again and we will drink to happier days.'

Then spoke Helen, with all the quick perception that was hers, 'Dear husband, and all you noble guests of ours, why do we not tell tales to while away the time? For there is no way by which we mortals can so forget our ills, as in the telling and the hearing of stories of brave deeds and stirring times.'

Many were the voices raised in accord, and Menelaus said, 'That was well thought and well spoken, Helen. Let you be the first to tell a tale, for I know of no one more skilled than you in relating a good story.'

With her eyes now on the wool she spun, now swiftly passing over the company with a smile of charm and sweetness, in her low, clear voice Helen began, 'Since it is the noble King Odysseus whom we have foremost in our hearts tonight, the story that I shall tell you is of him. I cannot relate to you all the perils and the hardships he endured so bravely when he was fighting with his comrades, for I was not there, but I can tell you one tale about him which only I recall. You all have heard of his resourcefulness and cunning, how he was pre-eminent in subtle ways and means, and how an artful contrivance was to him the chiefest joy of life. Once, during the siege, seeking for some way of gaining knowledge of how things went within the Trojan walls, it came to his mind to disguise himself as a beggar, and in this humble dissemblance to wander through the city, watching carefully all that he could see. In dirty rags and hungering, his body bruised

and tired—even so well had he disguised himself—he came
to the city gates and was passed through. As a beggar he
asked for alms in the street, and thus continued for several
days, always noting things that might have been of value
to the Greeks. It was then that I saw and knew him, and
that in spite of the dirty rags and his thin ribs showing
through them. For of all in Troy, I alone had not only seen
him from the city walls at a distance in his armour on the
battlefield, but also close at hand as a guest in my husband's palace, here in Sparta, in the olden days. So I asked
him to my house under pretence of offering him my bounty,
and he came willingly, for he thought that I might know
the counsels of the Trojan king. I called him Odysseus, and
tried to trick him by every means I had into admitting that
he was the man I knew him to be. But all my skilful wiles
he countered with his own, and at last I saw that he had
won, and that I could never trap him into discovering himself. So I swore a great oath not to betray him to the
Trojans, and he laughed and said, "Truly, Helen, there is
no deceiving you, I am indeed Odysseus, as you well do
know."

'After that we talked long together. He told me of the
plans of the Grecian army and asked me many questions
about the Trojans, and every one of them I answered truth-
fully, for of all the women within the walls of Troy, my
heart alone was with the Greeks. For I was even then repenting of my rash folly, and longing to see once more my
home and Menelaus, my dear lord.'

'Why yes,' said Menelaus, when she had done, 'I well
remember the many wiles and ruses of Odysseus. I have
known and watched many warriors and many men of

thought and counsel, but never have I found combined in one man the qualities of both, save in Odysseus.' And he smiled happily as he recollected the many tricks of his old friend.

And Telemachus felt a glow of pride burning in his heart, and he thought, 'Even if it is never given to me to see him, at least my father will have lived for me in the good words and in the praise of other men.'

Menelaus chuckled. 'And what a fine thing it was he did when all we leaders of the Greeks lay hidden in the wooden horse,' he said. 'It was his wisdom and his craft that saved us then. It was when the hollow wooden horse, with all us warriors hid inside, had been dragged within the city walls by the men of Troy. There we waited in the stifling darkness until night should fall, ever wondering if at any moment the Trojans would regret their action in receiving in their midst the wooden horse, and begin to batter it to pieces, and find and slaughter us like helpless children, one by one, or to lay beneath it burning fire and char us all to ashes. It was then—do you remember, Helen?—you came to the assembly place with Prince Deiphobus, old King Priam's son, to look upon the horse. Three times you walked around it, sounding with your knuckles its hollow sides, and we waited in terror within, almost not daring to breathe, while we wondered if our secret had been guessed. As indeed it had; but the immortal gods were good to us and it was only you who suspected that there were men hidden inside the horse. And after that you called to us, the leaders of the Greeks; you called to us every one by name, crying out the name of each man in the voice of his beloved wife. So that in the darkness each of us in turn leapt to his feet and would have answered you, believing that it was indeed his wife who called upon him, but that Odysseus guessed the trap at once and bade us in a whisper give no reply. Not even, Helen, when you spoke to him himself, and he heard from beyond the wooden wall, a voice that was even as the voice of his own dear Queen Penelope, pleading with him tearfully to speak with her, did he for one second falter. And as one after another, the false voices called to us by name, he would not let us answer, and one by one we were at last persuaded by his wisdom. All but Anticlus, and he, the obstinate one, would not believe Odysseus, and whispered to him, "You are a fool, Odysseus, not to recognize your own wife's voice. I swear that if I heard my wife speak to me so, I should answer her."

'And when he heard what he thought to be the voice of his wife, he started up and made to call to her, and so would we all have been destroyed, but that Odysseus, quick and crafty as ever, laid his hand upon the mouth of Anticlus and held it there until once again there was silence from without. Thus did Odysseus save us all, the leaders of the Greeks.'

'That is a noble story,' said Peisistratus. 'A tale worthy to be remembered and told many times.'

'Yet did all my father's wisdom and his guile in no way help him to avoid whatever fate it was that overtook him,' said Telemachus sadly. 'All his craft and all his cunning have not saved him nor brought him home to Ithaca.' He sighed. 'And now, great Menelaus, I beg of you that you will keep me here talking no longer, but instead let me lie down and rest, for I have heard much today that has moved me greatly, and I would think over in quiet all that you have said to me of my father, before I close my eyes in peaceful sleep.'

Helen ordered the servants to set up two beds in the guest-chamber for the visitors and spread them with warm blankets; and Menelaus bade all his other guests good night and they went to their homes in the town of Sparta. Then with many wishes for their comfort and sweet sleep, Telemachus and Peisistratus were lighted to their beds.

But in spite of their weariness, and in spite of the many thoughts that sped round in Telemachus' mind and his wish for quiet rest, the two youths could not refrain from talking long of all the wonders they had seen in the palace of Menelaus; his golden walls, his ivory-inlaid chairs, his embroidered hangings, the graceful acrobats; and Queen Helen, the loveliest woman in the world, for whose sake a city had been burnt.

## XII

# The Old Man of the Sea

VERY early in the morning Menelaus went to Telemachus, and finding him alone, sat down beside him, and without any hesitation, spoke his thoughts. 'Why have you come here, Telemachus?' he asked. 'For I do not believe that you have journeyed all the way from Ithaca to Sparta just to look at me and Helen, and compliment us on our lordly house. I think you had another purpose in your mind. What is it, young man? Come, tell me.'

'Great Menelaus,' replied Telemachus, 'you are right indeed. My reason for coming here was to ask you if you had any tidings of my father. For I am sore beset at home by the suitors of my mother, since they lay waste our house and our possessions. If my father returns not soon,

we shall be ruined utterly.' And he told Menelaus of the
suitors' greed and insolence; and of how he had called the
people of Ithaca to an assembly, and how he had slipped
forth from his home by night to sail to Pylos and to Sparta
that he might seek for news of Odysseus. 'And now I beg
you,' he said, 'if ever you loved Odysseus and wished him
well—and if you spoke truly last night, you must indeed
have done so—tell me the truth about him. If you have
heard that he is dead, do not conceal the sorrow from me
with kindly intentions, or if you have learnt that he is lost
upon the wide sea or in some far-off land, then tell me all
you know, King Menelaus, hiding nothing from me. For
I am well-nigh desperate and I must know the truth,
whether I can still hope for my father's return or not.'

When he had ceased, Menelaus exclaimed indignantly,
'The shameless rogues, to plague a good man's wife so in
her husband's absence, and to devour his food and wine
like vultures. I warrant that were you older, but few of
them would dare to show their faces in Odysseus' house.
It is indeed a sorry thing when young men can act in such
a fashion, and I will not pity them, no, not I, when vengeance falls upon them. For a sad day will it be for them,
the day Odysseus comes home once more and drives them
forth with slaughter.'

'It will be a sad day for them, Menelaus, and a great day
of rejoicing for me and my unhappy mother. But when
that day will come, or whether I do merely hope for it in
vain, are the questions I have come to ask of you. Good
Menelaus, have you any tidings of my father?'

'Would that I could give you comforting news, but I
have none to offer you.' Menelaus shook his head. 'No,

none. Since we set sail from Troy, I with certain other leaders of the Greeks, and Odysseus to follow my brother Agamemnon whither he would lead him, I have heard but once of your good father, how he fared, and that was from Proteus, the Old Man of the Sea.'

'What news did Proteus give you?' asked Telemachus eagerly.

'But little, I fear, Telemachus, yet I will tell it to you. Sailing home from Troy my ships were becalmed on an island off the coast of Egypt. There we waited, day after day, for a wind to speed us back to Sparta. But for twenty days never a breeze blew heavier than a man could breathe. The supplies were finished and my men were in despair, and I do not know how it would have ended, had not the sea-nymph Eidothea looked up through the blue water and seen and pitied me. To me she came as I walked alone along the shore, rising up out of the sea, all wet, and with a crown of seaweed on her dripping hair. She spoke to me in a voice that was like the crying of a seagull as it flies inland on a windy day. "Stranger, why do you tarry here upon this isle?"

' "Because the sea is calm and flat, and there is no wind for me to sail by," I answered her. "I fear that in some way I must have displeased the gods, that they make no wind to blow to carry me over the water to my home. But," I went on, "if you, gracious goddess, whoever you may be, could give me your blessing and your help, then might my men be saved from starving and we might leave this island."

'She answered me in that same strange, melancholy voice, harshly musical, "I am Eidothea, daughter of Proteus, the Old Man of the Sea, who serves the god Poseidon and who knows all the oceans as you know the rooms of your own house. I cannot tell you wherein you have offended the immortal gods, or what you should do to leave this place, yet my father Proteus could tell you. But you must lie in wait for him and catch him and hold him fast before you ask your questions, or he will not stay to answer them. If you lay hold of him, he will be bound to answer any question that you put to him; when you will see again your home and in what manner; and, if you should wish to know, all that has happened in your house since you left it, long ago. But Proteus will not be easily caught, and being caught, not easily held, so you will need much strength and skill and other men to help you."

'This seemed to me to be but poor advice, that I should lay hold of an immortal being from the sea, who was hard to catch and harder still to hold, and who most probably dwelt in the blue depths of the water where no man might venture. So I said to her, "Tell me then, of your kindness, some way that I may take your father, some trap which I may prepare for him, and where he may be found. For alone, without your enchantments for my help, could I accomplish nothing of all you bid me."

'Instantly she answered, promising me her aid. "Every day," she said, "at the time when the sun is highest in the sky, the Old Man of the Sea rises up out of the blue water with his myriad seals, like a shepherd with his flock. And he lies down to sleep among them in the heat of the afternoon, all of them together, lying in slumber upon the sand. If you would capture my father, early in the morning you must hide yourself on the beach with three of your men and lie in wait until he comes with all his seals. First will he count each one, and then lie down to sleep, and at that moment you and your companions must rise up and take hold of him. In spite of all his struggles you must not let him go, and do not be deterred by the strange shapes he will take. For he will turn himself into all manner of beasts, and into fire and water, in his crafty efforts to escape. But you must remember, that whatever fearful shape he takes, you must not fail to hold him fast. For if you once let him go, he will be lost to you, and you will have no chance to speak with him again. But when at last you see him as himself once more, then may you release him, and he will answer all your questions truly." And with that the strange sea-nymph dived back into the water.

'I returned to my ships thinking over all that she had said to me, and in the morning I chose out three of my companions, good men all, whom I thought best fitted for the adventure, and together we went to the place where, the day before, I had seen Eidothea. We had not been there above a moment, when she came to us, up through the sea, bearing with her the skins of four seals. She led us to the spot where every day her father came to sleep, and there she showed us how to hollow out in the sand four hiding-places; and when we had lain down in them, she covered us with the skins. And I can tell you, Telemachus, that those skins smelt most unbearably of fish, but thoughtful Eidothea had brought with her ambrosia, such as the gods alone may eat, and a particle of this she placed beneath the nose of each one of us. And so sweet was the fragrance of the ambrosia to our mortal senses, that all the while we lay in wait for Proteus, we could smell nothing else.

'Then Eidothea left us to watch and wait alone, and

exactly at midday the seals came up out of the blue water and lay down upon the shore to bask in the hot sun. They lay all around us, thinking from the skins with which we were covered that we too were seals. And lastly came old Proteus himself. And if his daughter was strange to look upon, the Old Man of the Sea was a great deal stranger, of that I can assure you. First, as Eidothea had told me that he would, he counted all his seals, and never suspecting the trap that we had laid for him, he counted us among their number. Then he too lay down to sleep upon the sand.

'As soon as we judged that he was fast asleep, we crept quietly upon him and laid hold of him, all of us together, with a mighty shout. At once he awoke and struggled, and when he found that he could not free himself, then did he begin to take the shapes of other things, even as Eidothea had warned me. First he became a lion with a shaggy mane, roaring most terribly. Then he was a huge snake, hissing and writhing in our hands and ever striving to slip from our grasp. After that he turned himself into a spotted leopard which growled and bit and tore at our hands with long curved claws. And then he took the form of a great boar, fierce and snorting, with mighty tusks. After that, perhaps most difficult of all, he lost his shape and melted into water, which would have trickled through the sand and been lost, had we not all held a few drops of it in our cupped hands. Then suddenly he became a tall tree, with a broad trunk and wide leafy branches, growing higher every moment as though it would outreach our grasp.

'But in spite of all these bewildering changes, we held on to him, and at last he became wearied of the struggle, and taking once more his own shape, he said, "I doubt not but

that one of the immortals told you how I might be overcome, you bold men, or else should I have escaped easily
from you. But what is it that you would ask of me?"

'At once I spoke up and told him what I longed to know,
and he answered me, "The gods are angered with you, for
you forgot to make them fit offerings before setting sail for
home from Troy. And truly, until those offerings are made,
you will never see your own land. You must return to
Egypt first and there pay to the immortal gods those sacrifices you have neglected. Then only will you find a favourable wind to bear you quickly over the sea to Sparta."

'I can tell you, Telemachus, my heart was heavy to hear
his words, that I had to return to Egypt and meet with
more delays. But I thought that while I had before me the
Old Man of the Sea who knew the answers to all questions,
I should be foolish if I did not ask him further concerning
the matters which were dear to me. So I questioned him
about the other leaders of the Greeks, whether they had
reached their homes safely, or if any had perished on the
waves. And old Proteus told me truly about all that I asked,
for in every case except your father's, I heard later that all
these things had come to pass, just as he said. But of what
he said about Odysseus, I have yet no way of finding if it
were the truth.

'But this is what he said to me of your father. "Odysseus,
king of Ithaca, is alive and has not perished in the sea,
though all his ships and all his men are lost to him. He
alone of all the men of Ithaca who fought at Troy, still
lives, but in great sorrow. For the immortal nymph Calypso
keeps him in her toils, a prisoner on her island of Ogygia."

'After that I had no heart to ask him further, and he

dived down into the sea, and all his seals went with him, a mighty herd. And the next morning we rowed back to Egypt, and there offered sacrifice to the immortal gods, as he had said. And they were appeased and sent us a fair wind, and we sailed with all speed to Sparta. But that is indeed all that I have learnt of good Odysseus since he set out from Troy, that he is not dead, but the captive of a fair immortal nymph.'

Telemachus sighed deeply. 'There is comfort in that my father still lives,' he said, 'but his plight brings me to despair. My mother has ever told me, and I have heard, too, from many other lips, of my father's famed cunning and resourcefulness. But how can even the most wily of all men break free from the bonds of an immortal?'

Menelaus laid a hand upon his shoulder. 'You know that I wish my news had been more consoling, but, good youth, you must never give up hope, Odysseus may yet come home. Meanwhile, you are welcome in my house for as long as you care to stay. And when you wish to return to Ithaca, I will see that it is well laden with gifts that you go. Among other things that I should like to see you call your own, I have a mind to give you three of my finest horses, pure white, with flowing manes and tails, and a swift chariot, for I think that you have nothing comparable to them at home.'

'King Menelaus, replied Telemachus, 'I thank you with all my heart. And I am telling you the truth when I say to you that gladly would I spend whole months with you in Sparta, listening to your tales and hearing of my father's deeds. But the good comrades who sailed with me to Pylos will already be impatient for my return, and kind Noemon, who lent his ship to me, may soon have need of her, so I must not tarry many days. For your gifts I thank you, they will be truly welcome, but please, great Menelaus, give me no horses. For Ithaca is a rough and rocky land, with narrow roads and stony tracks and no wide paths suitable for driving on. That indeed is why at home we have no horses. Though I am grateful for your thoughtfulness,' he went on seriously, 'I would rather that you kept your horses, for here in Sparta the ways are broad and you have wide fields and pasture-lands, good ground for swift and noble steeds.'

Menelaus gave a mighty chuckle and clapped him on the shoulder. 'You shall go without your horses, I promise you,' he said. 'But I will see that old Nestor's chariot is well filled with other gifts for you to stow on board your borrowed ship. Gold cups and mixing-bowls and dishes and such like. Things that will be acceptable and useful even in little rugged Ithaca.'

And they looked at one another and both laughed together.

## XIII

### *Telemachus returns to Ithaca*

BUT at the very moment when Telemachus, in Menelaus' palace, was talking with his jovial host, in the house of Odysseus the suitors were competing with each other at throwing the javelin in the courtyard. And Antinous and Eurymachus stood out among the others for their skill, and showed themselves the wooers' acknowledged leaders in games as in all else.

While they amused themselves thus, up from the town to Odysseus' house, came friendly Noemon, who had lent Telemachus his ship. Telemachus had been gone from home longer than the kindly man had expected, and he was even now in need of his ship, for he wished to sail to Elis on the mainland, where he had a young mule he wanted to break in. He stood at the gates looking around

366

the courtyard and saw no sign of Telemachus, as indeed he had not thought to do, for he knew that had the youth returned, he would at once have come to him in the town and told him that his ship was back, for it was not like Telemachus to be careless and neglectful with a friend.

Catching sight of Antinous, Noemon went over to him, and greeting him, asked, 'Do you know, Antinous, when Telemachus will return from Pylos? He borrowed my ship for the journey, and now I need her to sail to the pastures of Elis, where I keep my mules.'

The suitors were astonished when they heard his question, for they had not thought Telemachus had gone to Pylos as he had vowed he would. 'It is true we have not seen him for several days,' they whispered to each other, 'but it seemed most likely that he was sulking in his room because we laughed at him, or that he had gone to visit his grandfather, old Lord Laertes, on his farm, or that he was with his swineherd or his cowman, counting over his pigs and cattle, to see how many we have eaten.'

Antinous frowned in anger, and with difficulty controlled his rage. 'I did not know our host had gone to Pylos,' he said as pleasantly as he could. 'Tell me all you know of this voyage of his, Noemon. Was he accompanied by slaves, or did he persuade some of the young men of Ithaca to go with him? And did you willingly lend him your ship, or did he, in the name of his father the king, take her from you against your wishes?'

'Why no, Antinous,' replied Noemon, 'I lent her to him willingly. What else could I have done? The good youth seemed so eager for a ship, pleading with tears in his eyes that I would lend him mine. He has taken with him about twenty companions, young lads like himself, all still boys enough to enjoy the sail to Pylos as though it were an adventure.'

Antinous' frown grew blacker and his fingers tightened on the javelin he held, but he said nothing, though in his heart there were evil thoughts.

'Since you can in no way help me by telling me when he will return,' Noemon went on, 'there is small good in my remaining here to interrupt your sport. I will go back to my home now and sail to Elis another day. I have no doubt but that Telemachus will come to me the very moment that he lands to tell me of the arrival of my ship. Farewell to you all, noble wooers of our queen. May you enjoy your games.' And with that he went, walking back towards the town.

But Antinous and Eurymachus called the other suitors around them, and Antinous spoke to them all. 'My friends,' he said, 'Telemachus has won in this matter of the journey to Pylos. If this is the beginning of his new attitude towards us, then we had best take warning from it.' He paused a moment, and then said with evil meaning, 'My friends, would it not be a good thing for us if Telemachus did not return to Ithaca, but instead were, like his father, lost at sea?'

Many voices agreed with him, and others murmured, 'It would indeed be a happy day for us, for he has become a tedious critic of all we do and we should be well without him. Besides, with husband and with only son both lost to her, the queen would be forced to make up her mind to marry once again.'

Antinous looked at his companions. 'Give me a ship, and

let twenty of you come with me, and Telemachus will not return to Ithaca,' he said shortly. 'I will lie in wait for him in the narrow strait that lies between Ithaca and the isle of Same.'

The suitors one and all agreed to his proposal, and, well satisfied, he set himself to pick out his twenty comrades for the slaying, urging every one of the suitors to speak no word of what they proposed when they were within the house lest report of it should reach Penelope.

But Medon, Odysseus' faithful herald, had been sitting behind a pillar in the porch while they were at their games, resting himself, for he was no longer quite so young as he once had been, and he overheard all their plotting. Quickly and quietly and unseen he now slipped into the house and hurried to Penelope.

With old Eurycleia, the queen was sorting yarn for weaving, laying it away in baskets in careful skeins. She looked up and saw Medon coming. 'Have my suitors sent you, Medon,' she asked bitterly, 'to demand more entertainment from this unhappy, despoiled house? Truly, that is all you seem to do these days, to run errands for the wooers and request more food and wine from me for them.'

'No, good queen, though with all my heart I wish that today I had to come to you only to ask more food and wine for these wicked men. But it is no longer meat and drink alone that will content them. I heard them but even now plotting against the life of our dear prince. For it seems Telemachus has sailed to Pylos to seek tidings of his father, our lost king, and false Antinous with twenty more of the suitors is going to take a ship and ambush him as he returns to Ithaca.'

Dark despair fell upon Penelope when she heard his words, and for a while she could find no thoughts to speak. So, with a heavy heart, Medon left her quietly. At last she said, 'Why did no one tell me sooner that my son was gone to Pylos? Perhaps had I known of his intentions I might have persuaded him to stay at home. But he is gone, because you would not tell me, you cruel, faithless women, and now he will be killed.'

'Blame not the others, mistress,' said Eurycleia, 'for they knew not of what Telemachus proposed to do. To me alone he told all and made me swear a great oath not to tell you he was gone until at least twelve days had passed.'

'So has he gone to his own death,' sobbed Penelope. 'Nurse, what shall we do? Poor helpless women as we are with no menfolk to aid us.' In her despair she remembered Odysseus' father. 'Let us send to old Laertes on his farm, he will perhaps devise some plan which may yet save Telemachus from death.'

But Eurycleia thought of Telemachus' words, when he had told her, 'I think that one of the immortal gods is with me in this.' And she took Penelope in her arms to comfort her, and said, 'No, dear mistress, do not trouble further that good old noble lord, Laertes. He has grief enough of his own, and besides, what could he do to help? No, rather dry your eyes and cease those tears, and pray to the gods that they may see our Telemachus safely home. For with the gods, and with them alone, are all things possible.'

Penelope took the nurse's good advice, and going to her room, prayed to Athene, till, from weariness and worrying, she fell asleep. And while she slept she dreamt that she spoke with her sister, Iphthime, whom she had not seen for many years, for she lived far away. And Iphthime said to her, 'Fear not for your son, Penelope, for great Athene guards him well, and he will come back in safety to his home.' And in her sleep the queen was comforted.

But Antinous went with twenty others towards the shore, and setting sail in a small ship belonging to one of their number, they moored her in the harbour of a tiny isle half-way across the strait that lay between the islands of Ithaca and Same, and from there they kept a look-out for the ship which bore Telemachus.

That very same night, Athene appeared to Telemachus where he lay in the guest-chamber of Menelaus' palace. 'Come, Telemachus,' she bade him, 'make all haste home to Ithaca, for it is unwise of you to leave so long un-watched those suitors in your house. Who knows what mischief they may not do in your absence? Indeed, even now, with Antinous as their leader, twenty of them with a ship lie in wait for you in the strait between Ithaca and Same, with death in their hearts for you should your ship pass that way. But with speed sail home from Pylos, row-ing day and night, and steer clear of the little isle that lies midway across the strait. When you reach Ithaca, go not at once to your father's house, but send instead your ship and your comrades to the town, and go yourself to the farm of Eumaeus the swineherd, who loves you well, and bid him take to your mother the message of your safe return.' With these words she vanished, and Telemachus jumped up, and going to the other bed, woke Peisistratus.

'Quickly, Peisistratus,' he exclaimed, 'we must leave this

place at once. The immortal Athene has just appeared to me to bid me hasten home.'

Peisistratus sat up in bed, rubbing his eyes. 'But, Telemachus,' he protested, 'it is yet dark. Not even that you have seen a goddess, will excuse our discourtesy in rousing Menelaus from his rest before the dawn to speed us on our way. What would he think of such inconsiderate guests?'

'But, Peisistratus, it is most urgent that I should go home.'

'Then you will have to go alone, and on foot,' replied Peisistratus firmly, 'for I cannot drive the horses in the dark, and you, remember, cannot drive a horse at all. So be patient for an hour or two.'

Telemachus saw the reasonableness of his friend's objections, and waited, though not patiently; and as early in the morning as he might without too much discourtesy, he went to Menelaus and asked that he might leave his house at once.

'I shall be sorry to see you go,' said Menelaus. 'But if you must, you must. Wait only until I have seen your gifts safely stowed in Nestor's chariot.' And he hurried off to choose fitting gifts for his two guests, and to order a meal to be prepared for them before they set off on their journey.

Among many other gifts from his treasure-house, Menelaus took a costly bowl of silver overlaid with gold, which had been given to him years before by the king of Sidon, who was famed for his wealth, and to Telemachus he said, 'This is indeed one of the most splendid of all my possessions, and gladly do I give it to you to take back to your home. Not only because you are the son of my dear friend

Odysseus, but for yourself alone, because you are a youth after my own heart.'

And Queen Helen chose out from her store of richly embroidered robes, packed away in chests of cedarwood, the finest and most lovely, worked in a many-coloured design of little flowers and olive leaves. So great indeed was the number of blossoms on it, that its wearer might well feel herself to be enwrapped in a fresh and fragrant meadow rather than in a garment. Taking it to Telemachus, Helen smiled at him and said, 'Give this robe to your mother to keep for you until the day you marry, and on that happy day may your young bride wear it, a gift from Helen, made by her own hands.'

When all the farewells had been said, Telemachus and Peisistratus took their places in the chariot and drove off at a fast pace across the lands of Sparta.

On the second day, when the town of Pylos came in sight, Telemachus said to Peisistratus, 'Good friend, if I ask a favour of you, will you do it for me?'

'Ask anything you want of me,' replied Peisistratus.

'Drive me down to my ship upon the shore at once, that I may embark today. Take me not first to your father, for that will cause me more delay. I do not wish to be discourteous to King Nestor, for I bear him a great respect, but the need is pressing that I should go home at once.'

Peisistratus sighed. 'My father will be angry with me if I do not bring you home with me. But, come, I will take you straightway to your ship, if that is your wish. For I would not have it said of me that I would not do a service for a friend.'

When they reached the shore, Telemachus found his

young companions waiting for him, and at once he bade them make ready to set sail.

'Go quickly, good Telemachus,' said Peisistratus. 'For if my father hears word that you are back in Pylos and about to leave for home, he will send for you with all speed, and there will be no refusing his invitation. I can assure you of that, for I know my father well.' With that he turned his horses' heads and drove the chariot towards the city and his father's palace.

'Make all the haste you can, my friends,' Telemachus urged the youths. 'We will not wait for a wind, but row to Ithaca.'

And led by Peiraeus, they ran to do his bidding, stowing away the tackle and Menelaus' costly gifts within the ship, and fitting the oars in their places.

Many of them were already on board, and Telemachus was on the point of giving the word to embark, when he saw a man coming towards him across the beach. The stranger had been walking quickly at first, but when he saw that the ship was about to put off to sea, he began to run, lest he should be too late to reach her. As soon as he was within hailing distance, he called to Telemachus and the other youths, 'Stay for me, good people, and I will be with you in a moment.' And at the command of Telemachus they waited for him while he ran over the sand.

When the man came up to them, recognizing Telemachus at once as the leader of the little group, he spoke to him, his breath coming in gasps, for he had been running fast. 'Good youth, are you leaving Pylos even now?'

'With all the speed that we may, stranger.'

'Whither are you bound?'

'To Ithaca, my home. My father is Odysseus, king of that island,' replied Telemachus, and then he added, 'Perhaps I should say Odysseus was my father, since he has not seen his home for twenty years, and I know not whether he still lives.'

The stranger said eagerly, 'Then I beg that you will take me with you. My name is Theoclymenus and my home was in Argos. But there, by mischance, did I slay a kinsman. His friends and brothers are searching for me and will kill me if they find me, and I believe that they have pursued me even to Pylos. If I can leave the mainland, and find sanctuary on one of the islands, it is most likely that they will not come after me, and I shall be safe. I pray you, let me sail to Ithaca with you.'

Telemachus hesitated and frowned a little, thinking, 'How can I offer hospitality to this stranger when in my father's house I have no authority? The suitors will insult him and maybe drive him forth. Because he is my guest and under my protection they will do this, since they have ever done all they can to slight me, and now are they eager even for my death. What safety can I offer to another man?'

Theoclymenus saw him frown and laid a hand upon his arm. 'I throw myself upon your mercy, good youth. Have pity on me.'

Telemachus looked at the stranger from Argos wondering what he should do, his young mind torn between two courses; on the one hand, to do nothing that would make more difficult and dangerous his own position in his father's house, and on the other, to help a man who was in peril of his life. He saw that Theoclymenus was young, not above thirty years, but his face was haggard and had grown old from weariness in no more than a few days, and there was fear in his eyes.

'Perhaps even so, at this very moment, my father pleads with some stranger in a far-off land, seeking safety from a foe,' said Telemachus to himself. 'What would I think of the man who could refuse him what he asks? Besides, were he in my place, here today, would he send away this man?' He looked again into the stranger's eyes and smiled and held out his hand. 'Come, Theoclymenus,' he said, 'but speedily, for I also am in haste to leave the shores of Pylos.'

They went on board together and the youths of Ithaca fell to rowing, and in a few moments, they were out at sea.

Theoclymenus sat by Telemachus in the stern of the ship and told him all his story. 'For generations,' he said, 'have my fathers been renowned throughout all Greece for their powers of prophecy. I also have this gift, which brought me honour and respect from men. But I quarrelled with a cousin at my home in Argos, and we fought together, and I killed him. His brothers are many and powerful in the land, and they and his friends have all sworn to slay me in revenge, so have I been forced to fly from my house, alone and friendless. I came to Pylos, thinking that so far from Argos, I might be safe from them, yet I found that even to Pylos did they follow me. But once I have left the mainland, I hope that they will weary of their search, and return to their lands in Argos.'

'I shall be glad indeed if I can help you,' said Telemachus, 'but the hospitality which I and my mother can offer you is not such as you would have received at my father's hands were he in his own house.' And as they sailed northwards, past the green fields of Elis, Telemachus told Theoclymenus about the suitors and the sorrow in his home. And all the time he was wondering whether he would reach that home alive, or whether the wooers would kill him, as they hoped.

But with Athene's help they sailed safely past the suitors' ambush, without a sight of Antinous' ship, steering clear of the little island midway in the strait, as she had bidden, and at dawn they reached the coast of Ithaca at a point distant from the town.

'Put me on shore here,' said Telemachus to Peiraeus, 'and go on with the ship to the harbour. There return her to good Noemon who lent her to me, then do you yourself guard the gifts that I have brought with me, until such time as I can take them to my house.'

'And what of me, my friend?' asked Theoclymenus. 'Shall I go to your house and there await you?'

Telemachus thought a moment. 'No,' he said, 'it were perhaps best that you did not go to my home until I am there myself.' Then turning to Peiraeus, he said, 'One more charge would I lay upon you, that you receive this stranger in your house until I return to the town and can myself be his host.'

Peiraeus smiled. 'Willingly,' he replied, 'shall I do as you ask, Telemachus. The stranger shall come with me.' And to Theoclymenus he said, 'You will be welcome among my family to such entertainment as we can offer, until the time when our prince can receive you in his own home.'

'I thank you all, you young men of Ithaca,' said Theoclymenus, 'I thank you with deep gratitude for your kindness and your hospitality.'

'The gods be with you all, stranger and friends, until
I see you once again,' said Telemachus. And with that he
set off to walk across the hills to the farm of Eumaeus,
Odysseus' swineherd, where he lived with his grunting
droves.

# PART THREE

# Odysseus in Ithaca

## XIV

## *Eumaeus the Swineherd*

MEANWHILE, on the shore of Ithaca, where the Phaeacian sailors had left him sleeping, Odysseus awoke, sat up and looked around. A light sea mist covered the rocky hills behind him and the water before him, obscuring all horizons, landward and seaward, and making unfamiliar all the country round about; so that Odysseus did not recognize his home.

He jumped to his feet. 'Truly I am an unhappy man,' he said to himself. 'I thought that I should have had my fill of dangers and of wandering, and yet here am I, cast away upon an unknown shore. Who would have believed those kindly seeming Phaeacians to be so base? Fool that I was to trust them and fall asleep upon their ship.'

But looking round him, Odysseus espied the gifts his

hosts had given him, all laid carefully upon the sand. He puzzled over them. 'If they had meant to steal my gifts they would not have left them here with me, yet if it was not shameful theft they had in mind, wherefore would they have deserted me in this strange land?' And with care he counted over the number of the gifts to see if there were any missing. For nigh on an hour he pondered, looking closely at each costly treasure, uncording the chests to count each cup and bowl or woven tunic that lay inside. But at length he found that as he remembered them to be, they were all there, and not a single gift was missing.

He was marvelling at this when he heard a merry whistling, and looked up to see a youth approaching him. The youth appeared from his garments to be a shepherd, but in reality it was Athene come to see how Odysseus had fared.

Odysseus was glad at the sight and called to her, 'Good shepherd, tell me, I pray you, what is this country? You are the first man I have seen upon it, and I trust that all your fellow countrymen are of as kindly an aspect as you, for I am utterly alone and friendless, and cast adrift in a strange land. Tell me, I beg of you, in what part of the world I may be.'

Athene answered him, 'In truth, stranger, this island may be small, but it is not mean nor barren, for all its size. Though it breeds no horses and has but little pasture-land, yet that pasture-land is rich, and the corn it grows in its little fields is among the finest man can find no matter where he seeks, and the wine pressed from the grapes that grow here is very sweet, and brings great joy to the drinker. Yes, stranger, I think that I speak truly when I say that even

in far-off unhappy Troy the name of Ithaca was not unknown.'

Odysseus was gladdened by her words, but as she was strange to him, and yet unproved, he would not let himself believe her and take her saying for truth; lest it might be once more his lot to be still far from his home, deceived and mocked at by a heartless stranger. So he hid his joy and hope and said, 'I have heard of Ithaca. In Crete, where I come from, men sometimes talked of Ithaca. I remember, now that I hear you speak the name. I have but even now sailed from my home in Crete, where I had the misfortune to kill a man who would have stolen from me these treasures you see here. When I found that he was dead I fled by night upon a ship with my possessions, meaning to go to Pylos, but the sailors cast me ashore while I was sleeping, together with all my goods.'

And Athene smiled at him and laughed a little, and changed her shape and became a lovely woman, tall and proud, in a glittering robe. 'You are ever my cunning Odysseus, my favourite among mortal men,' she said. 'Will you not leave your crafty ways even in your own Ithaca? I, among all the immortals, save only Father Zeus, am pre-eminent in wisdom and subtlety, as you among the mortals have no peer in craft and guile.' She smiled again. 'And yet you did not know me, Odysseus; I, Athene, who have been with you and guarded you through all your life. But for me you would not have reached your home, so angered with you was mighty Poseidon, lord of all the seas.'

'Great goddess,' said Odysseus, 'it is hard for a poor mortal to know you in the many guises that you take, but I thank you for all your years of aid. And now, I beseech you, deceive me not, but tell me truly, if this is really Ithaca. For with this mist that clouds the land, I cannot guess where I may be.'

Well pleased, Athene answered, 'Not even an immortal goddess is safe from the suspicions of your cautious mind, it seems. Yet that is why through all the years I have not deserted you. For you are such a man as I ever cherish, prudent, resourceful, and slow to be deceived. Yes, Odysseus, my friend, this is indeed Ithaca your home, and over the hills in your house, Penelope, your queen, awaits you. Look around you now, and see if you do not know your own dear island.'

And while she spoke the mist lifted from the hills and the sea, and as it rose, so were the last doubts and fears lifted from Odysseus' heart. He saw at once the old haunts that he knew so well, the places he had dreamed of with yearning for twenty years. He was standing on the beach of the little harbour of Phorcys, that was crowned by a great old olive-tree, near by the cavern that was called the Cave of the Naiads. And behind him, rising nobly over all, wrapped in a cloak of tall trees, stood Mount Neriton.

Odysseus knelt down and touched the sand and let it trickle through his fingers. He smiled up at Athene. 'It is indeed Ithaca,' he said, 'and I thank you for bringing me home at last.'

'You are home, my friend,' said Athene, 'but your troubles are not all ended. Come, let us first hide away the gifts the Phaeacians gave you, and then will I tell you what has come to pass in Ithaca while you have been away, and advise you what next to do.'

So Odysseus hid his treasures in the Cave of the Naiads,

until such time as he could fetch them to his house, and Athene set a great stone before the entrance to keep them safe. Then they sat down together, immortal goddess and mortal man, beneath the shade of the grey leaves of the huge olive-tree at the head of the harbour.

There Athene told Odysseus of the wooers, and the ruin they were causing in his house; and of how his faithful, loving wife, still hoping in her heart for his return, kept them waiting for an answer, day after day; and of how the wicked men were plotting to kill his son as he sailed home from Pylos.

'It is well for me,' said Odysseus when she had done, 'that I have you to protect me, else should I have gone at once to my home, perhaps only to be slain in my own hall by these villains. But tell me, goddess, what it were best that I should do, and be with me still. For if I knew that there were three hundred of these men, I would fight against them all and rout them, if you were by my side, inspiring me with your divine courage, as you ever did in the old days at Troy.'

'I have no doubt that you would, my brave Odysseus. You need have no fear, for I shall not desert you now. But let us not go openly into this matter, let us enter it with craft and subtlety, in a way such as you and I delight in. First shall I make you old and like a beggar, so that you may be unknown to those who might recognize you, and of no account in the sight of all, even in the eyes of your own wife and son. Then must you go to the farm of Eumaeus your swineherd, who has been your devoted servant all these years. Tell him not who you are, but ask him concerning all that has befallen in your house, and from him will you learn much. Meanwhile, I shall go to Sparta and warn Telemachus, who is even now in the palace or mighty Menelaus, of how the suitors seek to kill him as he returns from Pylos.'

'Let it be as you say, great goddess,' replied Odysseus, 'it is a scheme such as I ever love. But I would ask you one thing first. Why is it that you, to whom all things are possible, should have sent Telemachus upon this vain journey to Pylos and to Sparta, endangering his life at the hands of these men? Surely you could not wish that he too should face perils such as I have met with in my travels?'

'Do not be disturbed on his account, Odysseus, for I shall guard him well, and, indeed, at this very moment he sits feasting in the house of Menelaus, rejoicing in the kindness of his host and fair Queen Helen. I did but send him forth on this quest for tidings of your homecoming—though well I knew he would find none—that he might prove his manhood and live through an adventure, however small compared with yours, that would show him to be a son worthy of his father. And now I must away to Sparta.'

Athene rose and touched Odysseus on the brow, and instantly he grew aged, becoming, in as many seconds, thirty years older. The skin of his face shrivelled into wrinkles and his hair became sparse and grey, his arms and legs lost their firmness and his sharp blue eyes grew dim. Clothed in a ragged tunic through which his spare ribs showed, and an ancient leather jerkin, with a battered wallet such as travellers carry, and a staff in his hand, he was even such a beggar as might be seen, any day, crouching at the gate of a rich man's house, whining for alms.

'No one in Ithaca will recognize you now,' she said.

'Nobody will guess you to be Odysseus the king. Go to the swineherd's house and wait, and there will I come to you again. Until that time, farewell.' And instantly she vanished from his sight as though she had never been with him, for such are the ways of the immortal gods.

Odysseus at once set off along the track from the beach that would lead him through a nearby wood and over the hills to the swineherd's farm. In the wood the path was cool and shaded, and the birds sang in the trees; but as it wound up the hillside it was bare and rugged, and the sun shone down fiercely upon the grey rocks and the clumps of scented thyme. And every step of the way was familiar to Odysseus, and it seemed to him as though he could remember each tree and crag, and he rejoiced as he walked once more in his own Ithaca.

Eumaeus, the faithful swineherd, had built the farm to keep his master's swine after Odysseus had sailed for Troy, so to Odysseus the house itself was unknown. It was a small house of wood and stone, with a sheltering porch and a roof of logs overlaid with clay, and it stood in a wide yard surrounded by a strong wall of stones and a thick thorn hedge. In the yard, around the walls, were twelve large sties, and in each of them were fifty sows and their little grunting piglets.

Three of the four men who helped Eumaeus herd the swine had taken them to the edge of the wood to feed on roots and acorns, while the fourth had driven a fat pig into the town, that the suitors might have pork for their feasting. So when Odysseus approached the farm, Eumaeus was alone, sitting on a bench before his porch, fashioning himself a pair of sandals from a strong piece of leather.

Odysseus pushed open the gate and entered the courtyard, and immediately the four savage hounds which the
swineherd kept as watchdogs rushed upon him, barking
and growling; and he would most assuredly have been
hurt had he not had the good sense to remain quite still and
incite them no further. Eumaeus heard the barking, and
dropping his sandals on the ground, he ran to the gate,
calling off the dogs.

Odysseus laughed. 'It is plain to see,' he said, 'that your
dogs do not like strangers. But you must find in them a
most sure protection for your swine.'

'It was well for you, old man,' said Eumaeus with agita-
tion, 'that you did not attempt to run away, for if you had,
the dogs would surely have thought you were a thief and
torn you in pieces. And I have troubles enough on my
shoulders, with my good master wandering the gods alone
know where, and his house full of shameless gluttons, without a man being killed upon my doorstep by my own dogs.
But come, old stranger, you are very welcome to my
house, though the dogs may have made you doubt it. Come
in with me and rest and eat, and we will talk together.'

Odysseus thanked him and followed him into the little
house, and there Eumaeus bade the master whom he had not
recognized, so well had Athene altered his appearance, sit
down upon a couch of reeds and brushwood covered with
a goat-skin, which served him for a bed, while he threw
more sticks upon the fire burning on the hearth. Odysseus
was well pleased with this kindly welcome, and sitting
down and holding out his hands to the blaze, he said, 'May
fate reward you, good swineherd, for your friendliness, and
give you your heart's desire.'

'My heart's desire?' repeated Eumaeus. 'It is not likely I shall gain that.' He fetched his strip of leather from the porch and began to roll it up. 'I had a good master once,' he said. 'He was just and generous and kindly, and what more in a master could any slave want? But he went away to fight in a far-off land, and after twenty years he has still not yet come home. I have no doubt but that he has perished, struck down by the sword of a foe, or wrecked upon the ocean, and I shall never see him more. In the years of his absence have I served him faithfully, and his herds of swine have prospered and increased in numbers, in spite of the many slaughtered wastefully of late. Were my master but here to know it, he would reward me, I am certain. But he never comes, though I wait and hope. So there is nothing left for me but to live on, serving faithfully the memory of a good and kindly lord. But you will be hungry, old stranger, and I doubt not but that you have troubles of your own, so let us eat and drink, for good food and wine bring a measure of contentment to those who have a share of them.'

Eumaeus roasted a joint of pork over the fire and mixed sweet wine and water in a wooden bowl; and when the meal was ready he sat down beside Odysseus. 'This food, though good enough, is not such as is eaten in my master's house,' he said. 'The best and fattest of the swine are taken by the suitors of my master's wife. They spend their days and half their nights lording it in his house, guzzling his food and drinking all his wine. My master's son is very young yet, and my master's wife is but a woman, and there is no man to forbid these wooers. My lord was a rich man, with many flocks and herds and much fertile land, more than any twenty other men on this island might possess together. But even his riches are not measureless and his beasts are not without number, and the grain from his cornfields and the wine from his grapes will not endure for ever, if the waste of food and drink continues, that goes on daily in his house at the command of these insolent suitors.'

'Tell me, my friend, the name of this master of yours, for it may be that in my travels I have met with news of him.'

'Old man,' replied Eumaeus, 'every beggar and every wanderer that comes to Ithaca and would have hospitality, goes to my master's wife and to his young son with a tale of having met my lord, or having heard of his whereabouts, or having seen him once, or what you will. And most of the tales are lies, but they serve to earn the teller a good supper. No, Queen Penelope and young Telemachus have long since ceased to believe these stories. They are only distressed by them and grieve yet more for their lost king. For you must know that my lord was king of all Ithaca, noble Odysseus, Laertes' son. Even now I speak his name with reverence, for his care for me was great, and he is still my master, though I may never see him again.'

Odysseus drank his wine slowly. 'Odysseus, king of Ithaca,' he said. 'I know the name well, and I can promise you, one day and not so far distant, he will return to his home and take vengeance on all those who have treated with insolence his wife and his son, and wasted his wealth.'

'I do indeed wish that I could find it in my heart to believe you, old stranger. For I desire nothing more than that King Odysseus should return to his home, and that soon. But it must be that he has perished in the wars, or been drowned with all his men, for in twenty years we have heard no word of him. Yet do I grieve for him ceaselessly, and long for a homecoming that I dare not expect. And for his son Telemachus, a princely youth and handsome, do I also grieve, for he has sailed but lately to Pylos to seek tidings of his father, and I have heard a rumour that those wicked suitors have sent a ship to lie in wait for him on his return and kill him. If it be true or false I know not, though it is most likely true, for I would put no evil past them, even to the slaying of their host. May all the gods protect him, for there is naught that I and those who love him can do for him. But come, old stranger, tell me of yourself awhile, and let me think on other things than the sorrows of Odysseus' house.'

So they talked together until the sun went down the sky, and many were the entertaining and lying tales Odysseus told the swineherd about himself; both to give the good man amusement and to cheer him, and to make quite certain that he himself was not recognized.

Close on sunset Eumaeus prepared the supper for his four men and his guest; and just as the sun was sinking behind the hills, with a great squealing and grunting, those swine who slept within the pens were driven into the yard by the men and securely enclosed.

The six of them sat down to supper, and after they had eaten and drunk they stayed beside the fire and talked. While they talked the night wind rose and blew howling from the hills; a wet west wind, sending the clouds across the moon and the rain beating on the house walls.

'It will be a wet and chilly night,' said Eumaeus.

Odysseus reflected that in his beggar's guise he had no

warm cloak to wrap himself in when he lay down to sleep; and as a jest for his own diversion, he decided to test his swineherd's hospitality, and see whether or not he would offer a poor wanderer the comforts of a cloak for the night. He drank off the last of the wine from his wooden cup and smiled. 'My friends,' he said, 'I am not so young as all of you, and my head is not so strong. I fear that your good wine has confused my wits a little. But what matter if I am a little drunk? It shall make me bold to tell you a tale of the time when I fought at Troy. In those days I was no beggarman, wandering from town to town, suing for my bread from those more fortunate than I. No, I was a warrior of no mean might, and oft I fought alongside the great Odysseus himself. One evening we lay in ambush under the walls of the city. Odysseus and Menelaus, king of Sparta, were our leaders, and I was the third in command. We crouched below the walls in the dusk, all among the coarse reeds on the boggy ground, and while we waited, night came on, even such a night as this, cold and wet and windy, with sleet and the cold north wind. Alone of all the others I was without my cloak, for when we had set forth from the camp the evening had been mild. Now while the others lay and dozed, wrapped warmly in their cloaks, I shivered in my tunic and cursed my folly. At length I could bear the cold no longer, and leaning across to Odysseus, who was beside me, I shook his shoulder, whispering, "Odysseus, I shall be dead by morning, I am so cold. You wily one, tell me if there is aught that I can do to save my life."

'Odysseus whispered back to me, "Be silent now, for I have a plan that will win a cloak for you, but it must not be suspected by the others." With that he raised himself upon his elbow and spoke to our comrades. "My friends," he said, "I have just had a dream, it must surely have come from the immortal gods, in which it seemed to me that it would be a wise thing if one of us were to return to the ships and ask Agamemnon, our leader, if he will send us more men for the ambush, for we are but a small party and far from the camp."

'No sooner had he spoken than a young man rose, flung off his cloak, and ran swiftly back towards the shore.

' "There is your cloak," Odysseus whispered to me, "just as I promised you."

'And in it I slept comfortably until the dawn.' Odysseus paused, and Eumaeus and the others laughed.

'That is a good tale, stranger,' said the swineherd, 'and I see well the point of it. We are all poor here and have but one cloak apiece, yet is there one to spare which we keep aside lest in stormy weather one of us should be drenched to the skin in the rain. That shall you have tonight, and if our good Prince Telemachus should come safely home from Pylos, I can promise you that he will give you a warm cloak for yourself and a new tunic without rags and patches, for he is ever generous, as was his father.'

Eumaeus made a bed of reeds beside the fire and spread upon it rugs of sheepskin, and when Odysseus had laid himself down, he covered him with the spare cloak and wished him a good night.

The other men lay down upon their beds of brushwood, but Eumaeus cared not to leave the swine unguarded when the night was wild, so flinging around him his thick mantle, and taking up a spear, he went out from the house to where the boars were sleeping, beyond the courtyard gate, beneath a high rock which sheltered them from the wind and the rain, and there he spent the night. And Odysseus was glad to see the care his honest herdsman took of his master's swine.

## XV

### *Odysseus meets his Son*

TOWARDS morning the wind dropped, and the driven rain ceased, and for a short space the stars shone in the blue night-sky. But soon they faded at the approach of dawn and the green and saffron streaks of light low down in the east changed to pink and gold and spread across the sky; while the sun rose up above the sea, like a fiery ball coming from the water to proclaim the start of a fair, calm day.

At the first light of dawn Eumaeus returned to his house, and very early the four swineherds set out with the pigs, driving them forth from the yard grunting eagerly, and they themselves, wrapped in their cloaks, for the morning was still fresh, were carrying each a wallet filled with bread and meat, and a flask of wine.

Odysseus and Eumaeus were left alone, and Eumaeus set to work to prepare breakfast for himself and his guest. He raked away the ashes and blew upon the embers and flung sticks upon the smouldering wood, and soon there was a fine fire blazing. Then making a paste of barley flour and water with a little honey, he kneaded it into cakes and set them upon a hot stone in the midst of the fire.

After they had enjoyed their meal, Eumaeus fed the sows in their sties and busied himself about the tasks of the farm, while Odysseus helped him, fetching water and collecting faggots and sweeping the yard.

During the day they talked together, and Odysseus said, 'It is not right that I should longer be a burden to you. Tomorrow I shall walk down to the town and see if begging will gain me meals in the houses of the noblemen of Ithaca, for I must not stay here, eating the food and drinking the wine you and your men can so ill spare. Let the rich show their generosity for a change. Besides, I have a mind to go to the house of my old comrade Odysseus and see for myself how things stand there. Maybe the suitors will be glad to grant to an unfortunate wanderer some scraps of another man's food. Yet I would not expect their charity for nothing, and I shall be ready to do services for them, running errands, chopping wood, and waiting on them at table.'

But Eumaeus would not hear of it. 'So long as I have any food and drink to offer you,' he said, 'you shall not need to beg. My friend, you are welcome to stay up here in the farm as long as you please. And do not think that in the house of Odysseus you will get a welcome from the suitors of the queen. No, they would rather do you an injury, throwing you from the doors and cursing you, than give you a portion of the food they eat. And their servants are not staid, honest, aged men the like of yourself; they are sleek, insolent rogues, much resembling their masters in many ways. No, my old friend, wait up here with us, and when and if young Lord Telemachus comes home, he will give you food and clothing, I am sure of that.'

Later, Odysseus asked the swineherd for news of his parents, saying, 'In the days when I knew him, Odysseus often spoke of noble Laertes and gentle Anticleia, his much-loved father and mother. Tell me, good swineherd, what has befallen them?'

'Laertes still lives, though Lady Anticleia is dead, worn out by sorrowing for her lost son. Truly, it is a sad death to die, to pine away before one's time through grief for a beloved child. Lord Laertes, saddened by her loss and ever grieving for my master, and unable to bear longer the insolence of the suitors, left the house and went to live upon his farm across the hills from the town. There he passes his days in toiling in the fields, labouring in a way most un-fitting for the father of a king. Though indeed, no one could wonder that he cares not to live in my master's house, watching the wooers despoiling the estate and making merry in the home of his absent son. I myself go seldom to the house these days, preferring to send one of my men with the fatted hogs for the feasting, for I grow angry to look upon such waste. Though in the old days, while yet Lady Anticleia lived, I went often to wait on her, for she had been good and kind to me from the time I was a little child, caring for me as though I had been one of her own children, rather than a slave.'

The remembrance of his mother, whose spirit he had met in Hades' land, filled Odysseus' heart with sorrow; and to forget his woes and to hide his grief from Eumaeus, he said quickly, 'Yesterday I told you many tales of my life and misfortunes, do you now tell me of your own birth and parentage, and of how you became a slave, for I am sure that so goodly a man as you is no mean peasant, but rather the son of some free and noble lord.'

'You are right, old friend,' replied the swineherd, 'I was not born in slavery, and my father was a king. The story of my early years makes an unhappy tale, yet, because you ask, will I tell it to you. There is an island called Syrie, you may have heard of it. Few people dwell there, for all that it is rich in pasture-land where graze fine flocks and herds. And the cornfields on Syrie are like a golden sea at harvest time, and the vineyards bear fine purple grapes, so that never there comes famine or pestilence or poverty, but all the people live secure and safe, dying peacefully of old age. There are two cities on Syrie, and my father was king over them both, ruling well and wisely. To the island, once or twice a year, came the Phoenicians from the city of Sidon, with merchandise to sell; necklaces, bracelets, little jars of perfume, and great bales of cloth all piled up in their ship. Tall, handsome rogues they were, with striped head-dresses and golden rings, well able to drive a bargain by their wheedling ways, and with ever a lie on their lips. In my father's house there was a Phoenician woman, bought many years before from pirates. Comely she was, and skilled in all women's crafts, and often would I play by her side while she went about her work. One day as she was washing garments in the river close by its mouth, where it flowed into the sea, the traders from her country put in to the shore. One of them talked with her, asking her whence she came, for he guessed from her looks and stature that she was a woman of Phoenicia.

'"I am from Sidon," she replied, "and my father is a rich man there. But I was stolen from my home by pirates and sold to the king of this little island."

'And the man said to her, "If you would see your home once more, have patience until the day our trading here is finished and we set sail for Sidon, and we will take you back with us and see you safely to your father's house."

'To this the woman agreed gladly, bidding the merchant tell no one on Syrie of his promise. "If you should see me in my master's house, when you bring your wares there to sell, or if you should pass me in the street at any time, make as though we have never spoken together before, for I would not have anyone suspect what we have in mind." She told him further, "My master here is rich, and when your trading is done and you send me word that I am to come to you, I will bring with me much gold and silver from his store-room. Nay, more than that, he has a little son who loves me well and ever joys to be by my side, him will I bring with me, for he should fetch a good price in Sidon, more than gold and silver. And what others could do when they sold me to my master, the same can I do to his child."

'For some months, as was their wont, the Phoenicians remained on Syrie, selling and bartering and making great profit. When at length the time came for them to depart, one of their number came to my father's house with a necklace of amber beads linked with gold. Such a pretty thing it was that all my mother's women crowded round to see it while she held it in her hands, wondering whether the price was too high. But unseen by the others, the merchant signed to the Phoenician woman, and she nodded back in token that she had understood. When he had left the house with the price of the necklace in the leathern purse at his belt, she took my hand and bade me come with her to walk upon the shore. As we passed through the great hall of my father's house, she picked up three golden goblets from a table and hid them in her cloak. I asked her what she did, but she only told me to be silent and hurried me through the doors. We went past the city and down to the harbour where waited the Phoenician ship. She took me on board and the merchants set sail, and I never saw my home again. Many days later the ship touched at Ithaca, and the men went to the town to trade, taking me with them. They sold me for a slave to Lord Laertes, in whose house I found only kindness, and good Lady Anticleia cared well for me. So in the end, my misfortunes were not as heavy as they might have been.'

'Truly, Eumaeus, your fate could have been much harder, as you say,' said Odysseus. 'Indeed, your sorrows are no worse than mine, who am a wanderer and a beggar.'

Since he had found that the swineherd would not let him go to town, Odysseus was easily able to remain at the farm awaiting Athene's commands, and he passed the next day in a similar fashion to the first, helping Eumaeus and talking much.

It was at dawn on the following day that Telemachus reached Ithaca in safety, and in obedience to Athene's words, sent Noemon's ship on to the harbour and set out alone to walk to the swineherd's house.

As on the two previous mornings, when the other men had gone forth with the swine, Eumaeus made ready to cook the breakfast. Odysseus was sitting on a stool facing the open door, and through it he saw someone entering the yard. Immediately the dogs rushed forward, but in greeting, joyously wagging their tails, barking and leaping up at the newcomer; yet in quite a different fashion from the way in which they had barked and leapt at Odysseus, two days before.

Odysseus, who guessed at once who the young man must be who patted the shaggy heads of the dogs and called to them by name, said to Eumaeus, 'There is a friend of yours on his way to your house, someone whom your dogs know and like, for they are giving him a welcome quite unlike the one they gave me when I came here the other day.'

He had hardly spoken before Telemachus stood in the doorway, and the swineherd jumped up with a cry of joy, dropping from his hands the wooden bowl in which he had been mixing the wine, so that it was all spilt upon the floor.

'My dear young master,' he exclaimed, 'you have come safely home! Indeed, I feared that I should never see you more when I heard rumours of the suitors' plot. It is a happiness that I had not dared to hope for, to greet you once more in Ithaca. But come inside, my dear prince, and sit down, that I may enjoy your company, for it is not often in these days that you find time to come to the farm.'

Telemachus embraced the swineherd with affection. 'I am trusting, my dear good friend,' he said, 'that you will give me word of all that has befallen in my father's house since the day I sailed for Pylos. How fares my mother? Is she still steadfast in her sorrowing for my father, or has she at last made up her mind to take another husband?'

'If she had made her choice from among the suitors, news of it would have been brought to me even here. No, dear prince, she still waits and hopes with patience.'

As Telemachus entered the house, Odysseus rose and offered him his place, as was a fitting gesture from a beggar to a prince.

But Telemachus said with courtesy, 'Do not disturb yourself, stranger, I beg of you, let me find myself somewhere else to sit. It is not seemly that a younger man should take an elder's place.'

Odysseus was pleased to see that his son showed respect even to a ragged wanderer and displayed no arrogance, though he was the son of a king.

Eumaeus laid a sheepskin upon a pile of brushwood beside the fire for Telemachus. 'This stranger and I were about to breakfast,' he said, 'will you not share our meal with us?' And he set cold meat in wooden platters beside the three of them, and laid a basket of bread on the floor between his guests, and bade them eat, while he mixed more wine and water to replace that which he had spilt.

When the meal was over, with a kindly smile at Odysseus, Telemachus asked, 'Tell me, Eumaeus, whence comes the stranger? And is there aught that I can do for him?'

'He has told me the story of all his woes and wanderings,' replied Eumaeus, 'and a grievous tale it is. But now he is come to Ithaca, for once he knew King Odysseus in the days when they both fought at Troy, and would seek what help he can in the house of his old war-time comrade.'

Telemachus frowned a little in embarrassment. 'Stranger, I would gladly welcome you to my father's house, and so too would my good mother. But I have no authority in my own home, and she is but a woman. For in the house of Odysseus his wife's suitors order all things as they will, and I fear that if you come down to us they will offer you some insult ill fitted to your years when I am not by; or indeed, it may be in my very presence, for they care not for me either, counting me but a child. And they may well be dangerous now and seek to do me and my friends some hurt, since I escaped unharmed from their ambush in the strait.'

'It is surely pitiful when a man is thus oppressed in his own home,' said Odysseus. 'Would that your father might return and scatter all these evil men.'

'I thank you for that wish, good stranger, and echo it with all my heart. But see that you remain here in safety with Eumaeus for so long as it shall please you, and I will send you food and wine in plenty, and new clothes.' He turned to the swineherd. 'And now, Eumaeus, my good friend, I have a task for you. Will you go down to the town and bear word of my safe return to my mother? For I would not have her left longer in torturing doubt. Yet see that you tell no one else but her, for the sooner her wooers learn of my escape, the sooner they will think out another base deed against me. Meanwhile,' he smiled, 'if you can bear with another guest, I will stay on the farm with you for a day or two, while I think out what it is best for me to do.'

'Gladly will I have you here with me, dear prince,' said Eumaeus, 'for then I know at least that you are safe, when I have you before my eyes. And I will go at once and tell the queen, and her alone, that you are back in Ithaca. But should I not also go to Lord Laertes on his farm and tell him the welcome news? For I doubt not but that he too has heard the rumour of the suitors' plot and will be grieving for his grandson's plight.'

Telemachus thought a moment, then he replied, 'No, it is best that you come back here quickly with tidings of how things fare at home. Ask my mother to send a servant she can trust, good Eurycleia perhaps, with word of my return to my grandfather, that he may no longer grieve for me.'

So Eumaeus went to bear to Penelope the tidings of Telemachus' return, and Odysseus was left alone with his son. But before either of them had time to speak, Odysseus, from his seat opposite the door, saw Athene, once again in the likeness of a lovely woman in a shining robe, standing on the threshold. Telemachus saw her not, only Odysseus and the dogs were aware that she stood there. And the four hounds, recognizing her for a more than mortal being, neither barked nor growled, but slunk away with their tails between their legs, and crouched down by the house wall, whimpering. Telemachus heard their whining and turned to look out into the yard, but though he looked straight at Athene, he could not see her, for it was only to Odysseus that she had chosen to appear. She beckoned to him and he rose and went outside and followed her out of the sight of his son.

'The time has come, Odysseus,' said Athene, 'for you to

disclose yourself to your son, that together you may plot
the destruction of the suitors. Make your plans and go to
the town with speed, for I am eager to see those shameless
men reap their just reward. And remember, my friend, I
shall be with you, even though you may not see me
there.'

And she touched Odysseus, and once more he became
his true self, a strong straight man of two score years and
a little over. Again his dark hair hung in curls about his
shoulders and his eyes were bright and keen. Even his very
clothes were no longer the garments of an old beggarman,
for he wore a rich tunic of snowy white, and a short fringed
mantle of blue. And immediately upon the change, Athene
vanished.

Odysseus returned to the house, and when Telemachus
saw how he had been transformed, he was afraid. He
started to his feet, and in spite of himself he backed towards
the wall. 'Stranger,' he said fearfully, 'you are not as you
were but a few moments past. Indeed, you must be one of
the immortal gods. I pray you, be compassionate to me and
to my house, and I and my mother will offer you much
sacrifice.'

Odysseus smiled. 'Have no fear, Telemachus, I am not
a god. I am your own father, Odysseus, come home at last.'
And he made as though to embrace his son.

But Telemachus had inherited a measure of his father's
caution, and he would not believe him. 'No,' he said, 'you
are rather one of the immortals come to deceive me so that
I may have still more sorrow. For but now you were
ragged and old and like a beggar, and yet in so short a space
of time you have become like a mighty king. Only an

immortal could accomplish that. I implore you, do me no harm, for I have suffered much already.'

'My son,' replied Odysseus, 'why will you not believe that it is really I, your father? It has been with the aid of all-wise Athene that I have reached Ithaca after years of wandering. And she it is who made me to resemble the old beggar whom you saw until now, so that no one might recognize me as Odysseus. And though you saw her not, she appeared to me but a moment ago, and gave me back my own shape that you and I might know each other. Wondrous it is that such things can be, but to the immortal gods they are easy.'

Telemachus looked well at him and believed his words, and suddenly realizing that Odysseus had come home and all his hopes for that safe return were fulfilled and all his fears were ended, he flung himself in his father's arms and wept in sweet relief.

'How did you reach Ithaca, father? In what ship? Tell me everything.'

'The kindly men of Phaeacia brought me home and left me safely on the beach in the harbour of Phorcys with all the gifts that they had given me. The gifts have I stowed in the Cave of the Naiads until such time as we can fetch them. But all my adventures will I relate to you presently, for now we must decide together how best to destroy the suitors. Tell me how many there are, and whether they are warriors or weaklings, so that I may know if we two alone should have any chance against them.'

'Dear father,' protested Telemachus, 'I have heard from all who knew you that you were ever a mighty fighter, but this task that you would try is too hard even for you.

Two men alone could not fight against the suitors. Why, there are above a hundred of them altogether, and we should soon be slain. Twelve young noblemen there are from Ithaca, and the rest from the islands close by. Two and fifty from Dulichium with their six serving-men, four and twenty from Same, and from Zacynthus, twenty. No, father, we two should have no chance against so many.'

'Athene herself has promised me her help, my son. What say you to Athene as a comrade-in-arms?'

'If she will aid us,' said Telemachus thoughtfully, 'our cause may prosper, though we shall have a bitter fight.'

'Let us believe we shall gain a great victory,' said Odysseus, 'and lay our plans with confidence. Best would it be if you were to return home at dawn tomorrow. Go among the suitors as though you did not suspect them of having tried to kill you, be affable and friendly towards them. And I, in the likeness of a beggar, as I was before, will come to the house with Eumaeus. There shall I act as though I had come for alms, meantime watching carefully the wooers, that I may make my further plans. If what you and the swineherd say of them is true, then will they most likely insult me and mistreat me. But do not forget, to all others I am an old beggarman and not your father, and suffer these insolent men to treat me as they will, for we shall, in the end, take vengeance on them. For above all, no one else but you must know that I have come home, not even your mother.'

And so they talked together and laid their plans; but in the evening, Odysseus looked up and saw Athene at the door. She touched him and smiled and vanished, and once again he became old and ragged, so that he knew Eumaeus must be on his way home. And indeed, in a few moments the good swineherd appeared, and they greeted him eagerly and asked him his news.

'What tidings have you for us of the happenings in your master's house?' inquired Odysseus.

'And what of my mother, was she glad to hear that I am safe?' asked Telemachus.

'Indeed, my prince, she rejoiced much at the news.'

'And the suitors who sailed to kill me, have they returned yet to the town?'

'I did not stay long enough to discover that,' replied Eumaeus, 'I thought it better to return home at once. Yet it can make but little difference, for as I was going to the apartments of the queen with my message, a young man, who, it seems, had sailed with you, came also to the house to tell her you were back in Ithaca. But not content with telling her, he shouted out his tidings to all around as he went through the hall. Therefore the suitors are aware already that their plot has failed.'

Telemachus sighed, and then he brightened, remembering how his father had come home. 'We have had labours enough for one day,' he said, 'let us eat and drink and take our rest. Come, Eumaeus, and you, good stranger.' And Telemachus smiled at his father when the swineherd was not looking and Odysseus smiled back at him, in the way two people smile at one another when they share a secret, known only to the two of them.

## XVI

## *Penelope and her Suitors*

WHEN the suitors heard that Telemachus had
returned unharmed to Ithaca, they grew angry
and dejected; for they thought that not again
might they have such an opportunity to kill him, secretly
and far from his home, and in such a way that they themselves should not be blamed for his death.

'It is a great misfortune for us, that our plans have come
to naught,' said Eurymachus. 'But let us at once send forth
a ship to tell Antinous and our other friends that Telemachus has slipped through the ambush. Otherwise will
they wait on for him in the strait between Ithaca and Same,
wasting their time without profit.'

They set off for the town to find a ship, but on the way,
one of them, pointing out to sea, said, 'Surely that is the

ship good Antinous sailed off in, making her way to the
coast? He must have seen Telemachus escape him, and is
coming home.'

They went down to the harbour to meet Antinous and
his twenty comrades; and when the ship was moored they
all went together to the assembly place. They turned away
a few men who had gathered there to pass the time in idle
talk, saying that they had private matters to discuss; and
posted two of their number to keep a watch on any of the
other townsfolk who should come that way, lest they
should overhear them.

Antinous spoke first with harsh anger in his voice. 'Day
and night we kept watch for Telemachus,' he said, 'but yet
we missed him. One of the gods must have helped him, or
he never could have escaped our net. But though he has
evaded us this time, let us not waver in our design to kill
him, for until he is removed we shall not prosper in Odysseus' house, and the queen's determination to give us no
answer and make no choice of a husband will be, as now,
strengthened by his support. Do you not all agree with me?'

He paused, and there were murmurs of assent; but a
few of the wooers objected, saying, 'We are playing a
dangerous game, Antinous. Easy is it to say, "Let us kill
him," but he is a man and the son of a king, and not an
outcast or a wild animal to be hunted and slain for sport.
And things will go ill with all of us if we are found to have
murdered him.'

Several voices of those who had until then supported
Antinous were raised in agreement, and Antinous frowned
blackly, biting his lips. 'My friends,' he said, 'you are
foolish. Have you not thought that Telemachus may know

that we tried to take his life as he returned from Pylos? And if he knows, surely he will not rest until he has called together the men of Ithaca and denounced us to them? He will stir up the people against us, and those of you who come from the neighbouring islands will have to return home without a wife; while we who are townsmen of Ithaca will have to flee to another land until the trouble is forgotten. No, my friends, Telemachus must die, it is the only way for us to secure not only success in our wooing of the queen, but our own safety.'

They were afraid when they heard his words, for few of them had considered that Telemachus might tell the people of their treachery, for, in spite of the determination he had shown in his decision to sail for Pylos, they had grown into the way, through many years, of thinking him a child who put his faith in all others older than himself and was content always to be bidden what to do. 'You are right, Antinous,' they said, 'Telemachus must die, and that before he has time to call an assembly.'

Antinous smiled in satisfaction. 'We must fall upon him in some place far from the town,' he said. 'For suspicion must not come to rest on us, nor must we risk the townsfolk's witnessing his death. When he goes to overlook one of his farms, perhaps, or when he visits old Lord Laertes, we must lie in wait for him as he comes alone along the road, and slay him swiftly. We must watch for an opportunity and not let it slip, for as long as he remains in the house, he is safe. We cannot kill him there without the truth being known to every man. Are you all in agreement with me?'

Though most of the suitors spoke for him, there were still

a few who were silent, counting the plot too dangerous to themselves. These Antinous addressed, saying, 'There is no alternative to this, my friends, save only that we all depart for our own homes, abandoning our efforts to win the fair Penelope.'

'That we will never do,' they cried.

'Then must Telemachus die,' said Antinous.

'You are right,' they said. 'We are with you over this, good Antinous, every one of us.'

Antinous was pleased at the success of his persuasion. 'Let us all return now to Odysseus' house,' he said, 'and wait to see how Telemachus greets us when he comes. For from his manner we may haply guess if he intends to tell the people of our plot to kill him on his journey from Pylos, or indeed, whether he has learnt of it or not.'

Together they all walked back to the house and sat down in the great hall, talking and dicing and playing draughts, apparently with no other care in the world but to amuse themselves and pass away the time as pleasantly as possible. But the minds of many of them were filled with thoughts of ways and means of murder, and all of them were wondering if and when Telemachus would come back to the house.

By the time that the suitors had returned to her husband's house, Penelope's first joy and relief at the swineherd's news had grown calmer; and she, who all through the days of distraction and grief, while Telemachus was with Menelaus, had not dared to face them, now made up her mind to go down to the hall and confront the men who would have killed her son.

She called her maids and bade them bring out a splendid

robe, and they were glad and ran to do her bidding eagerly. For she had had no care for what she wore since Medon the herald had told her of the suitors' plot, but had sat, silent and disconsolate, her clothes awry and her hair dishevelled, speaking to no one, and ordering away with a gesture all who had tried to ask her what was amiss. So now they went willingly and fetched her three robes to choose from; two of them white with embroidered borders, and the other palest saffron yellow with a woven band of stiff, formal flowers in red, and a scarlet fringe. She chose the yellow robe and put it on, fastening it at each shoulder with a golden brooch which she took from a little silver casket. Her handmaidens then combed her hair into seven long curls, held in place by ribbons around her head; three tresses down her back, one upon each shoulder, and two on her breast. Then over all her head and round about her white throat she flung a crimson veil, so fine that through it her bright hair could be seen.

When all had been done, she told three of her maids to come with her, and descended the stairs from her apartments, passing through the women's quarters on her way to the hall. In the doorway she paused, looking in on the company of the wooers, and disdain and contempt for them filled her heart.

One of the suitors saw her and rose, crying out, 'It is the queen!' And instantly the eyes of all were turned towards the door at the far end of the hall which led to the other rooms of the house.

'Greetings, fair Queen Penelope,' they called to her. 'It is not often lately that you have honoured us with your presence.'

But her eyes searched the hall for Antinous, their acknowledged leader, and she looked hard at him. 'Have you
no shame, Antinous,' she said with scorn, 'that you still
dare to show your face in my husband's house after the evil
you sought to do his son? I have heard it said of you that
you are the flower of all the young men of Ithaca, wise in
counsel and fair in speech.' She laughed bitterly. 'In the
three long years and more that you have been daily in this
house, my son and I have learnt to know differently. The
flower of the young nobility of Ithaca! Thus may men be
mistaken who only see you as you walk abroad in the pride
of your wealth and birth. But I who have seen you
throughout these years, eating another man's food and
drinking his wine, all uninvited; I who have seen into the
black caverns of your evil heart, cannot be deceived by any
outward show.'

She paused, and Antinous and all the other suitors were
silent, not knowing any reply to make her. Angrily she
went on, her voice ringing through the hall, 'How could
you try to kill Telemachus, Antinous? You out of all the
others. Have you forgotten how, when you were yet a
child, your father Eupeithes joined once with the Taphian
pirates and went a-plundering? The anger of all the men
of Ithaca was against him, and in his sore distress he fled
for help to Odysseus his king. Yes, Antinous, he came to
the father of Telemachus, and Odysseus defended him
against the crowd, and with his wise and sober counsel
won his people to hold their hands and seek no more to do
violence to Eupeithes and his house.' Her voice grew softer,
'Oh, Antinous, have a thought for past favours, devour
no more my husband's goods, have no evil intentions

against his son, and desist from your hated wooing of Odysseus' wife; and bid your fellow suitors do the like.'

For a time all were quiet in the hall, and they watched her without speaking any word, while they all debated in their minds what it were best to say. Antinous frowned at the table before him, and tossed angrily from one hand to another the dice he had been playing with when Penelope had entered; but he could think of nothing that he might say to her.

It was Eurymachus, who, recovering his composure first, answered her with his customary soft words. 'Gracious queen, and fairest of all the noble ladies on Ithaca and the neighbouring isles, be not distressed by all these things, for they are but the imaginations of your troubled mind, which, by too much grieving for your lord, has been made ready ever to accept fresh sorrows but never to admit more joyous happenings. Or perhaps they are but the rumours whispered in your ears by those, who, through their spite and jealousy, would discredit us with you. For we suitors of the loveliest lady in the land would never seek to harm her son, no more indeed than we would seek to injure her, and what than that could be farther from our thoughts?'

'Your tongue is glib, Eurymachus,' said Penelope, 'it was ever so.'

'No, dearest queen, you do me wrong. Indeed, you wrong us all, I beg you to believe me. We wish no evil to Telemachus, for is he not the beloved son of the woman we most wish to please?' He turned from one to another of his companions, 'My friends, tell me, is that not so?'

And with one accord they called out eagerly, 'It is the truth, Eurymachus.'

Eurymachus smiled at Penelope. 'You see, fair queen, how wrong you were to distrust us, you have our words in proof of it. Will you not now believe me?'

But Penelope gave him no answer, for she knew that he was lying.

When she did not reply, Eurymachus went on, 'Let it comfort your mind and make you of good cheer to know that there lives no man—no, nor shall he ever live—who shall do Telemachus the slightest hurt, while I yet breathe. I swear to you, Queen Penelope, that were any man so rash and so evilly disposed as to seek to harm your son, very quickly would his blood be flowing on the ground, and his base life be leaving him, thanks to my good spear. For of all men in Ithaca, young Telemachus is the dearest to me, both for himself alone and for his fair mother's sake. Believe me, I implore you, good Penelope, for I speak the truth.'

Again she did not answer him, and Eurymachus sought to persuade her further with his flattering tongue. 'And even if it were not reason enough, that I should cherish him for his own sake and for his mother's, could I forget his father, good Odysseus? For he was always kind to me when I was a little child, and often would I come to this very hall, running eagerly to see him, in the old days before he wedded you and brought you to his house. And always did he welcome me with friendliness, talking to me as one talks to a child one loves, and asking me about my boyish games and pleasures. In the feasting he would set me upon his knee and give me meat and bread from off his plate, and let me sip wine out of the king's own cup. Oh, fair Queen Penelope, if not for the sake of anyone else, then for the sake of the memory of good Odysseus, would I hold dear his son. For Odysseus was a fine man whom I loved well, and the greatest pity it is, that Ithaca will never see him home again.'

At the mention of her husband, Penelope's eyes filled with tears, and fearing she could no longer contain her grief, she turned and went from the hall, going up once more to her apartments with her handmaidens. There upon her couch she lay and wept, remembering Odysseus.

But Eurymachus sat down, and turning to Antinous who sprawled beside him, said, 'It is with all speed that Telemachus must die, for while he lives no one of us has a chance to win the queen. The wretched youth has poisoned her against us.'

Early the next morning Telemachus told the swineherd that he was returning to the town to his mother. 'For,' he said, 'I fear that she will not be satisfied until she has seen for herself that I am safe and well.'

'Dear prince,' said Eumaeus, 'you will take good care for your life, I beg, and trust none of the suitors.'

'I shall be cautious, never fear, Eumaeus, but now I must be gone. Do you come after me later in the day, bringing with you the stranger. For he and I talked together yesterday when you were with my mother, and it seems that he will not be content until he has tried his fortune in the town and seen for himself the home of Odysseus, whom he knew. So come to the house, both of you, and I shall be waiting there.'

He bade Eumaeus farewell with affection, and said to Odysseus, 'Stranger, I shall expect to see you later.' But unseen by the swineherd he clasped his father's hand and smiled at him, whispering, 'Good luck be with you.' Then he was gone, walking quickly down the hill-side.

When he came to the house of Odysseus it was still early and the suitors had not yet arrived. The first person he saw when he entered the hall was old Eurycleia. She was spreading fleecy rugs and woven cloths over the chairs to make all comfortable for the wooers when they should arrive, muttering to herself as she worked, and grumbling that she should have to toil for wicked men when her good master was far from home.

'Greetings, nurse,' called Telemachus from the great doorway, and with a cry of joy she dropped the coverlets she held and went to him.

'My dear child, I had thought never to see you again, and when the swineherd brought your message yesterday, it was almost more joy than my old bones could bear,' she said, kissing him; and then could speak no more, for she was weeping for happiness.

One of Penelope's handmaidens came into the hall and saw him there, and called out to the other maids, 'Prince Telemachus is back,' and instantly they came running and gathered round him, greeting him and asking questions. Penelope heard the bustle and excitement and came down herself to find out what had befallen.

Telemachus saw her standing in the doorway at the far end of the hall, and leaving the women, he ran down the room to her and took her in his arms. 'Dear mother,' he said, 'were you very troubled for me?'

'My son,' she said, and her tears flowed fast, 'I was afraid that I should never see you again. You are all that I have left to me since your father sailed for Troy. For twenty years you have been my only comfort. If those cruel men had killed you, I think that I should have died from grief.'

Telemachus kissed her and laughed. 'But dry your eyes now, mother, for I am home, and safely. This is no time for weeping.'

Penelope smiled at him. 'In truth, I have been so afraid, and now am so overjoyed, I know not whether I should laugh or cry. But you must tell me, what news was there of your father in Pylos?'

Seeing the anxious longing in her eyes, Telemachus had not the heart to see her further wounded, and he was afraid that if he spoke longer to her, he might betray his father's secret and perhaps spoil all their plans. So quickly he said, 'I beg you to excuse me now, dear mother, but I must go to the assembly place to speak with our old friends and father's, good Mentor and the others, and tell them I am home. For though they knew not of the suitors' plot, rumour of some danger to me may have disturbed them. Besides, there is a stranger, one Theoclymenus, who seeks refuge here in Ithaca from his enemies. He sailed with us from Pylos, and I gave him in charge of Peiraeus until such time as I could bring him here. I must go now and fetch him, that we may make him welcome in our house. When I return I will tell you all that passed at Pylos and in Sparta. Meanwhile, dearest mother, go to your room and pray to all the gods that they may be with us, for I believe that soon will come a day of reckoning for your suitors.'

He left her wondering at his words, but hardly daring to hope that they meant more than just that he, as she did, still waited patiently and with devoted confidence for Odysseus to come home.

As Telemachus passed through the courtyard on his way to the town, he met certain of the suitors coming through the gates. They crowded round him with fair words, and questions as to the success of his mission to King Nestor; but with no more than a brief greeting he hurried past them, whistling to him his two favourite hounds who had come into the courtyard on hearing his voice. Patting the dogs, and running with them as if in play, he was able to avoid the more persistent of the suitors who were eager to learn where he was going, and he went on alone towards the town.

'He is going to the place of assembly,' said one of them. 'Let us follow him lest he speak against us in our absence.' And some of them hurried after him.

But once at the assembly place, Telemachus again avoided them, and sought out among those present the old friends of his father, good Mentor who had stood up to speak for him when he had accused the wooers before he sailed to Pylos, and old Halitherses, who had known his father as a boy, and several others.

They greeted him warmly and asked him many questions concerning all that had befallen him on his journey; and he sat down beside them and answered willingly, telling them of King Nestor and Menelaus and Helen. And all the while the suitors watched him carefully to see if he should at any time stand up before the men of Ithaca and denounce them for their crimes. But Telemachus had other plans, and talked only of his travels.

After an hour or so there came to him Peiraeus, with Theoclymenus by his side. 'Greetings, Telemachus,' Peiraeus said. 'The gifts you left with me are safely in my home, would you that I should send them to your father's house?'

'Peiraeus, my friend, replied Telemachus, 'all things are not well between me and my mother's wooers. Should any evil come to me from them, it would be my wish that you, who proved yourself so good a comrade on the voyage to Pylos, should have for yourself those gifts that King Menelaus gave me, rather than that the suitors should divide the treasures among themselves with never a friend of mine there to forbid them. So keep the gifts for me until I may call my father's house my home again, and not the gathering-place of all my enemies.' Then turning to Theoclymenus, he said, 'But if you have a mind to come with me, good friend, my mother and I will make you very welcome. Unless,' he smiled, 'you would prefer not to meet her wooers. For they are not men one would chose to meet, I can assure you.'

But Theoclymenus laughed and replied, 'I am ready to meet even your mother's wicked suitors, so long as I am safe from my own enemies. And I think, Telemachus, that those men who waste your possessions in your father's house will not do it unchecked much longer. That is my belief, and as I told you, I have some skill in prophecy.'

So Telemachus went back to Odysseus' house once more, and Theoclymenus went with him. And there Eurycleia set food and wine for them upon a table in a quiet corner of the hall, while Penelope brought her spinning and sat close by, to hear all her son's adventures.

He told her everything that had passed between him and Nestor, and of King Menelaus' splendid palace, and of beautiful Queen Helen; keeping till the last the tidings of

Odysseus that Menelaus had had from the Old Man of the Sea. 'At least he was alive when Menelaus heard those words, and it is likely he is living yet, and, dearest mother, soon he may be home, if the gods are good to us,' he said, thinking while he spoke of how before long Odysseus would be entering the hall with the good swineherd, Eumaeus.

But Penelope wiped away a tear, and her spinning lay idle on her lap. She shook her head. 'How shall he break free from the snare of an immortal nymph?' she said. 'He never will come home.'

'With the help of the gods all things are possible, and I know that there is an immortal god with us, aiding us, even this very day,' said Telemachus, longing to ease her grief by telling her the truth.

Theoclymenus leant forward, 'Good queen,' he said, 'believe me when I tell you that all things will come to pass favourably for you and for your family. Even now is your husband Odysseus on his way home, and soon he will be standing in this very hall. I cannot tell you how I know this, but only that I am sure of it, and my soothsaying has ever been proved true in the past.'

Telemachus looked at his guest with admiration, marvelling at the man's foreknowledge of what was, as yet, a secret known only to him and to his father.

'May what you speak be true, good Theoclymenus,' said Penelope, 'so shall you ever be honoured by me and mine.'

But at that moment Medon the herald went into the courtyard where the suitors were disporting themselves with games and contests of skill, and called them in to their midday meal, and Penelope retired to her own rooms.

# XVII

## *Odysseus goes Home*

IN the afternoon Odysseus and the swineherd set out
for the town. As they made their way down the hill-
path and were nearing the outskirts of the city, at a spot
where there was a spring from which many of the townsfolk fetched their water, they fell in with Melanthius, who
kept Odysseus' goats on a farm beyond the hills. With the
help of two of his herdsmen he was driving a flock of goats
to Odysseus' house that the suitors might have plentiful
meat for their feasting. And glad he was to do it, for the
suitors were men to his liking, extravagant, reckless, and
impudent. He served them well, and looked forward to
the day when one of them should be married to his mistress
and he might gain a higher position in the household.

423

Melanthius had stopped to chat with some women who were drawing water, and when he saw the swineherd approach with a ragged old beggarman, he came forward, and looking Odysseus up and down with a contemptuous air, said, 'Indeed, our friend Eumaeus keeps fitting company, one cringing whiner with another. Have you really the impertinence, Eumaeus, to bring another beggar to the house to eat good food meant for his betters, and trouble with his demands for alms the noble suitors? You would do better to give him to me, to sweep my yard and fetch fodder for the kids and help in many ways. I should soon find work for him to do, I promise you. But then I have no doubt he does not wish to earn his keep, preferring to wander from town to town and house to house, with some unlikely story of his misfortunes, relying on the kindness of others. I know that manner of man, and we want none in our house. If he shows his ugly face there, I hope the noble suitors will give him all he deserves and fling him out into the road again speedily.'

And with that he aimed a kick at Odysseus, who, however, stood firm, wondering whether he should strike down the insolent wretch with his staff, or whether he should hold his peace and wait for his revenge until his more important task of destroying the wooers was accomplished.

'For shame, Melanthius, to strike an old man,' cried Eumaeus. 'Your ways have grown insufferable since the suitors took to favouring you. Would that the immortal gods might hear my prayers and send our master, King Odysseus, home. In his days no needy wanderer was turned from the door, and in his days no servant would have dared to speak as you have done.'

'Just hear how the swineherd snaps. He is like a snarling dog,' jeered Melanthius. 'You can cease your praying, Eumaeus, you fool, for you only waste your time, the master never will come back, he is lying dead, somewhere far away from Ithaca. And my only wish is that Prince Telemachus were lying beside his father. A happy day would it be for us should that prim youth die suddenly.' And with that he called to his men to hurry up the goats, and strode away after them shouting at the beasts.

But Odysseus and Eumaeus followed slowly and without speech. Eumaeus in embarrassment because he could think of no words to say that might soothe his guest's feelings, hurt by the goatherd's discourtesy, and considering himself to be in a certain measure responsible for what had occurred, for he and Melanthius were old enemies, and railed most times they met. While Odysseus was silent because he was at last approaching his home again, after nearly twenty years; but not in the way he had dreamed of, as a king, proud and happy, clad in clean and shining raiment, escorted by his people, to see his wife and son waiting for him at the gates with smiling faces; but as a tattered old beggar, bent and aged, leaning on a staff and wearing dirty rags, led only by a swineherd, while his wife did not even know that he was coming, and his son might not acknowledge him.

Close by the gates Odysseus paused and was the first to break the silence. 'My friend,' he said, 'had I been asked, I should have said this to be the house of Odysseus. Am I right?'

'It is indeed my master's house,' replied Eumaeus. 'You have guessed well.'

'It seemed to me to be the house of a king,' said Odysseus. 'See how high and strong the walls are, and how great the gates. The courtyard, too, is spacious, and the house itself is large and lofty, even that little I can see of it from here, beyond the half-open gates.'

'It is a wide and stately house, well fitted to be the home of a mighty and noble man such as my master was. But now is it filled with the evil thoughts and unseemly revelry of those who have no right to sit beneath its roof,' said Eumaeus. He paused for a moment, lost in bitter reflection, then went on, 'Good stranger, we must now decide whether we shall go together into the great hall, or whether you would prefer that I should go in before you, that you may follow me to try your fortune with the wooers, if they will give you food or not. Or perchance you would go first, alone, and have me come after you? For if any sees you standing for long at the gates, he may drive you away with stones and harsh words.'

Odysseus smiled. 'Full used am I to harsh words and blows, no beggar may evade them. So go you in first, good swineherd, and I will follow you.'

'Let it be as you wish, stranger,' said Eumaeus, and made to pass into the courtyard.

At the gates there lay an old hound, dozing in the sunshine. He had once been a fine animal, full of strength and speed, but now he was old and neglected. In the very year that Odysseus had left home to go to Troy, he had bred and trained him, naming him Argus. He had shown promise of being the finest hound that his master had ever had, but Odysseus had not seen the fulfilment of that promise, for he had left Argus barely more than a puppy when he had sailed from Ithaca. But in spite of all the years that had passed since then, Odysseus thought that he knew the hound, and he spoke to Eumaeus, 'It is a strange thing to see a fine hound such as this lying neglected at the gate. He is old now, but he looks as though he must once have been swift and unerring in the chase.'

Argus heard and recognized his master's voice, and opened his eyes, pricking up his ears. He moved his head a little and wagged his tail. The eyes of Odysseus filled with tears, and he turned away his face from the swineherd.

'He was indeed a fine animal,' said Eumaeus, 'and my master trained him himself. He was once the fleetest of foot and the keenest on the scent of all the hounds in Ithaca. But now that he is past his hunting days the servants never care for him, though my good master would not have forgotten him in his old age. Truly, servants grow neglectful in the master's absence, and in King Odysseus' house nothing is as it should be.'

Argus tried to rise and go to Odysseus, but he was too old and feeble, and the effort was too much for him; and he dropped his head and died.

'I will go on into the house,' said Eumaeus, 'come after me as quickly as you may.' And he went across the court-yard and under the porch.

Odysseus stepped over to Argus and bent to pat him, but he saw that the old hound was dead. He brushed away his tears, and then smiled a little, gratefully, as he reflected that, after all, he had not come quite unwelcomed to his home. Then he crossed the courtyard to the porch, and entered once more, after twenty years, his own house, an aged, tattered beggar bent over a stick.

In the great hall the suitors had gathered together for their evening meal and their talking and laughter echoed to the roof. Odysseus sat down upon the threshold and waited, looking around him carefully at those assembled there. He saw Eumaeus carrying forward a stool to place it near Telemachus who leant across to speak to him. He noticed, too, Melanthius, the goatherd, sitting close to Eurymachus, drinking and laughing with him. For Eurymachus was the one of all the suitors whom Melanthius believed most likely to win the queen, and therefore he ever sought out his company, with an eye to future benefits.

Odysseus had not been waiting long before Telemachus caught sight of him. Quickly he gave Eumaeus a loaf of bread and a platter of meat and bade him take them to his father. 'The stranger has come,' he said. 'Go, give him food, and tell him, if he wishes more, to beg it of the wooers. For shame and an empty purse are but ill-matched companions, and modesty takes a poor man nowhere.' So he spoke that his father might have a chance to see for himself what manner of men the wooers were.

The swineherd brought the food over to Odysseus at once, and told him what Telemachus had said.

'May the gods bless the good prince,' said Odysseus; and Eumaeus returned to his seat.

Odysseus ate the bread and meat, and when it was all eaten, he rose and went among the suitors to see if they would spare him more. He began with the man on the left of the room, working his way round the semicircle of feasters which ended with Antinous on the very right. He held out his hand before each man and muttered a word or two of appeal, in the very way a real beggar would have done. Most of them gave him something, a scrap of meat or a piece of bread, and a few of them asked among each other where he had come from, for they had not seen him in the house before.

'I can tell you where he comes from,' called out Melanthius, who had heard the question, 'and who brought him here, for I saw the swineherd leading him to the town. But who he is I have no idea.'

Antinous caught his words and frowned, for he cared not for Eumaeus, because the swineherd loved his master whose possessions Antinous coveted. 'Swineherd,' he shouted across the hall, 'we have enough beggars in Ithaca already, why did you bring us another to molest us at our feasts? Are you so eager to waste your master's food?' He sneered, 'You are ever speaking in his praise, and whining that he comes not home, so that I should have thought you would have shown more care for his goods.'

'Lord Antinous,' replied Eumaeus, 'you may come of a noble family, but your words are base. No one could turn away from his door an unfortunate wanderer whose very livelihood depended on charity. It is a duty of all more fortunate men to help such needy folk. But you, Lord Antinous, have always been harsh, not only to beggars, but to all the slaves of my dear master, and to me above all others. Yet can I bear it, so long as our gracious Queen Penelope and the young prince are kind.'

Telemachus interrupted him. 'No, Eumaeus,' he said, 'do not give angry words to Antinous, or let him provoke you by his gibes. For it is ever his pleasure to stir up strife and quarrelling with an ill-intentioned speech.' He turned to Antinous and said with irony, 'I thank you, Antinous, for your fatherly care for my goods, in that you will not let me waste a few crumbs on a beggar. But I do not grudge it to him, rather would I see you give liberally of that which is not your own to give. Come, Antinous, help yourself to my father's food, bestow it, and earn the thanks of a beggar. Or do you prefer to keep for yourself all that you take from this house?'

'You are again at your boasting, young Telemachus,' said Antinous with fury. 'I had hoped that we should have been spared more of it, but it seems we are unlucky. As for your old beggarman, I can tell you that if all my comrades were to give him what I should like to offer, the rogue would keep from this house for three months or more.' And as he spoke he picked up the footstool from beneath his feet, and with it threatened Odysseus.

The other suitors laughed, but for all that they seemed not to heed his words, for they gave Odysseus food in answer to his pleading, down to the very one who sat to the right of Antinous.

And then Odysseus stood before Antinous himself and said, 'Lord, you seem to me to be the noblest of all present, in pride and bearing like a king. Do then give me a gift as your companions have done, and let it be a greater gift than theirs, even as you are the greater man. And in return I shall speak your praises in every land where I may wander. For know that I, too, was once a rich man, with great possessions of my own; and so long as I had enough, would I give to all who asked. But I came to misfortune and am now even as you see me today, a poor and homeless wanderer dependent on the kindness of good men like yourself.'

'Spare us the tale of your misfortunes,' said Antinous, 'and begone. Or else you will regret the gift I give you.' And he turned away contemptuously and called for more wine.

Odysseus looked at him. 'It seems I was mistaken in my judgement,' he said, 'and you are not the man you appear to be from your outward show. I wonder,' he went on with a mocking smile, 'since you are so miserly with other people's goods, what would you give of your own possessions to a beggar in your own house? Not a single grain of salt, I fear.'

Jumping to his feet Antinous seized the footstool and flung it at Odysseus, saying, 'Now begone, you shameless wretch that dare to speak so to me. You heeded not my warning to go in peace, so now shall you be driven forth.'

But Odysseus stood firm beneath the blow and gave no answer, though his heart was filled with wrath. Instead he went back to the door and sat down once more upon the threshold.

And a few among the wooers said to Antinous, 'Was it not rash, Antinous, to strike the stranger? What if he should prove to be one of the immortal gods come down to earth to see how we mortals live? For, remember, we know nothing of whence he comes, save only that the swineherd brought him here.'

But Antinous only scowled at them and drank his wine and cared not for their words. And Telemachus clenched his fists and swore to be avenged for the cowardly blow given to his father.

One of the servants, going through the door at the end of the hall to fetch more food, met a handmaid of Penelope going about her tasks, and told her of how Antinous had struck a harmless beggar who had been brought to the house by Eumaeus. The woman later told Penelope, who grew angry, crying out, 'So may the arrogant Antinous himself one day be struck down.'

'May the gods hear your prayer, mistress,' said the old nurse, Eurycleia, fervently.

'In truth,' said Penelope, 'out of my suitors he is the most hateful of all. What a pass things have come to if in Odysseus' house his own wife and son cannot shield from insult and violence a poor beggar.' She called to one of her serving-maids, saying, 'Go now and bid Eumaeus the swineherd come and speak with me, for I would ask him of the stranger.'

When Eumaeus had come to her, Penelope questioned him concerning Odysseus, who he was and whence he had come. And when the swineherd had answered her, she said, 'Tell him, good Eumaeus, that I would speak with him, for from your account of him he seems an honest and a much-travelled man, and perchance he could give me news of my husband.'

'Indeed, mistress,' replied the swineherd, 'he is a fine talker. Three days I had him with me in my house, and yet all his tales were not told, nor do I think they ever would be, though one had him at one's side for three months, or even years, for there seems to be no end to his adventures. And of my master he often spoke, saying that he had fought with him at Troy.'

'Go quickly, Eumaeus,' said Penelope eagerly, 'go quickly and bring him to me.'

So the swineherd returned to the hall and gave

Penelope's message to Odysseus. But Odysseus answered, 'I am afraid of the anger of the suitors, if they see that the queen is kind to me. Therefore beg her to wait until they have gone to their homes tonight, and then let her ask me what she will about her husband, and I shall gladly answer her.'

When Penelope heard from Eumaeus this reply, she said, 'Truly, that stranger is a wise man, and in a little space of time has he seen clearly how things stand in our house. I will go down to the hall myself tonight when the suitors are gone, and speak with him.'

Eumaeus then went to Telemachus to bid him good night. 'I must return to my swine,' he said. 'But take good care of yourself, my prince,' he added in a whisper, 'for you are among your enemies, they stand thick on every side.'

'Good night, Eumaeus,' replied Telemachus. 'Come early in the morning, and see how we have fared.'

And with a kindly word of farewell to Odysseus as he passed him in the doorway, the swineherd returned to his farm, glad to be away from the suitors once again, but disturbed for his young master's safety.

Soon after this the suitors fell to merry-making with song and dance, and Phemius the minstrel played long for them; while Odysseus sat upon the threshold and watched all that went on, warily.

Now there was in Ithaca a rogue named Irus, a fat, greedy man, whose trade it was to go from house to house seeking food and drink and entertainment, posing as a man whom fortune had misused, though the truth was that he had ever preferred a life of idleness and would not have had it otherwise. He would sometimes run errands when he was bidden, but mostly when there was any work to be done, Irus was not there. He was well known to the suitors who found his company amusing, and was even favoured by Antinous, who otherwise seldom encouraged beggars.

This Irus now came to Odysseus' house, and finding Odysseus by the door, he made to fling him out from his own home. 'Away, old man,' he said, 'that place is mine. Go speedily, before I have to chase you out. I am sure the noble suitors will be glad to see no more of you.'

'My friend,' said Odysseus, 'I grudge you nothing that the queen's suitors may give to you, and I would not take anything that was yours by right. But this house is large, and the threshold is wide enough for the two of us. Come, be peaceable and let us agree, for though I am an old man I am still good for a fight, and I shall defend myself if you provoke me with your fists.'

Irus laughed scornfully. 'How could you fight with a younger man? Your boasts are idle. Get you gone, or else stand up that I may show the noble suitors how I can protect my rights.'

Antinous heard his words and laughed. He leapt to his feet, his face flushed and his legs a little unsteady from the wine that he had drunk. 'My friends,' he said, 'one of the immortal gods has sent us a rare entertainment. Irus and the stranger are quarrelling together. Let us set them on to fight and see which of them is the better man, fat Irus or the old ragged fool.'

Gleefully they all agreed; and Telemachus hated them more than he had ever hated them before.

Antinous moved over to the hearth, and with a hand that still held a wine-cup, pointed to the fire. 'Here at the fire, my friends, we have some fine black puddings cooking for our supper. I say that we should give to the winner of this contest his choice among them tonight. And more than that, I say that we should give him the freedom of our table, that he may always feast with us, and we shall allow no other beggars in the house.'

His words were met with cheers and laughter. 'It will be a mighty jest,' the other suitors said.

Odysseus rose. 'Noble lords,' he said, 'I will undertake to fight only if you will promise me that no one of you, eager to see his favourite Irus win, will strike me down. Let me have only Irus matched against me, I beg of you, for I am an old man.'

To this they all agreed and gave their word, and Telemachus cried out, 'Stranger, if you should be the victor in this combat, I swear to you that if any man here dare fall upon you, he shall find me fighting at your side.'

The suitors crowded round to see the sport, and Odysseus put aside his old leather jerkin and tucked up his ragged tunic round his thighs.

'He has a fine pair of legs, for all that he is an old man,' said the wooers to one another. 'And his shoulders are broad enough, under those rags of his.' And straightway there were many among them who said, 'In spite of his age, I have a fancy that the stranger will soon lay Irus on the floor.'

And Irus heard them and was afraid, for he was no fighter, and had only dared to flout Odysseus thinking him to be a weak old man and spiritless; and he tried to slip away unseen from the hall. But he was prevented, and with force he was led back and ranged opposite Odysseus.

Odysseus and Irus put up their hands and circled round each other for a few moments, urged on by the suitors, who called out, some for Irus and some for the stranger. Encouraged by the men who called his name, Irus struck the first blow and caught Odysseus on the shoulder. At once Odysseus replied with a mighty stroke upon the side of Irus' head, and the fat rogue fell down to the ground and lay there groaning.

The wooers rocked with laughter and drank more wine in celebration of the victory, while Odysseus dragged Irus by the foot out of the hall and across to the courtyard gates. There he left him, propped against the wall, and returned to the suitors. They greeted him with cheers and laughter, and bade him sit and eat with them. Antinous handed him the largest of the black puddings, and the others brought him bread and drink, and pledged him with many draughts of wine. 'Better fortune to you, stranger, in the days to come.'

# XVIII

## Odysseus speaks with his Wife

WHILE the suitors made merry in his house, with Odysseus in their midst, his thoughts full of irony at the strange situation, it came to the mind of Penelope to go down to the great hall and show herself once more to her wooers and bid her son spend less time in their company. Adorned and fair she left her rooms and descended the stairs with two of her maidens. They opened for her the door at the far end of the hall, and she passed through and stood close by the threshold with a maid on either side. When the suitors saw her they ceased their clamour and drinking, and stared at her; and never had she seemed to them more lovely.

And Odysseus looked up and saw her standing there, in

a robe of many-pleated white linen, with a purple veil over her hair.

'Telemachus,' she said, 'when you were a child your deeds were ever governed by the knowledge of what it is right to do. But of late it seems that you have changed. Perhaps it is because of the company you keep.' She glanced around at the suitors with contempt, and went on, 'It was not well done to let a stranger be insulted and mistreated in our house, and I am indeed ashamed that such a thing should have come to pass.'

Odysseus watched her as she stood there speaking, and thought how in twenty years she had not really changed. 'She is older,' he said to himself, 'how could she be otherwise? For now she is a woman, and I left her a young bride. Yet she is still the same Penelope.' And seeing her there, he knew at last, that in spite of his disguise and the suitors and the dangers he was about to face, he was truly home. And his heart felt great content.

Telemachus answered her quietly. 'Dear mother, I do not wonder at your anger in this matter. In my heart I know what it is right and what it is wrong to do, even as I did when I was but a child. Yet I am not master in my own father's house, and all things here are not ordered as I could wish.' He went over to her, adding in a low voice, 'The servants may have told you how they set Irus and the stranger on to fight with one another. But the combat fell not out as they expected, for the stranger showed himself to be by far the better man, and Irus sits, witless, beyond the gates. Oh, mother, how I wish that all your suitors were ranged alongside him, and our home were ours once more.'

While Telemachus yet spoke to her, Eurymachus called out, 'Fair Queen Penelope, you are more beautiful tonight than ever I remember you. If all the men of Greece might see you now, then tomorrow would you have many more suitors than we are, and the house would not be large enough to hold us all.'

Gravely Penelope answered him, 'Eurymachus, the immortal gods took all the joy and comeliness from me on the day my husband sailed for Troy. If he might but return to me again, then indeed might I seem fair. For the happy have always a beauty of their own, even though their countenance may be ill favoured. Hard it is for a woman to lose her beloved husband and be forced to choose another lord and leave her home. But harder it is when her wooers are such as you and your companions, who are ever in that home of hers, eating and drinking and wasting her son's inheritance. Shame on you all, this is no way to win a wife.'

Antinous spoke up, 'Sweet Penelope, I shall not move from this place until you have chosen the best out of us all to be your husband, and all my comrades are agreed with me in this. And here I drink to you in pledge of my word.' And he drained another cupful of red wine.

But Penelope drew the folds of her purple veil across her face and turned away from them and left the room, followed by her women. And the suitors called for lights, for evening was come on.

Three braziers set with torches were lighted at the fire and placed about the hall, and a few of the serving-maids stood beside them to see that they did not go out or weaken, keeping them fed with faggots; laughing meanwhile with

the suitors, calling to them and answering jest with jest;
until Odysseus grew annoyed to see them spend their time
thus.

'You idle wenches,' he said, 'go back to your mistress,
that she may find you work to do, and I will tend the
lights for you.'

The maids laughed at his words, and with a toss of her
head, one of them answered him pertly, 'Foolish old man,
why do you come here to plague us all? Go, find shelter
for the night in some peasant's hovel, under a roof more
fitted to your rags.'

Angry to think that a servant in his house should speak
so to one she believed to be a homeless wanderer, Odysseus
said, 'You shameless creature, to speak such words to an
old man. Beware lest I tell Prince Telemachus of your impertinence. Now go as I bade you, and leave me to mind
the lights.'

Afraid at his threat, the serving-maids ran from the hall,
and Odysseus was left to keep the burning braziers re-
plenished with dry wood.

Then Eurymachus taunted Odysseus, saying, 'Old man,
shall I find you work upon my farm that you may earn an
honest living, gathering stones to build walls between my
fields or planting out young saplings? Or are you rather
one of those who prefer to live in idleness on the gifts that
others give you?'

Odysseus answered him, 'Indeed, Eurymachus, I wish
that you and I, each with a sharp scythe in his hands, could
be matched against each other from dawn to dusk in the
season of haymaking; or that we were each in a good-sized
field with a plough and two strong oxen to draw it. I

warrant that my hay would be sooner reaped than yours,
and that I could plough a straighter furrow. You would
not scorn me, could you see me at work. Or better yet,
were you to watch me in the press of battle, with my
armour on and my good sword in my hand, putting my
foes to flight, you would not jeer at me for long. But you
have grown insolent, Eurymachus, and think yourself a
mighty man. because you spend your days among those
who are even weaker and of less account than you.'

Eurymachus grew angry and forgot his usual smooth-
speaking ways. 'The wine you have drunk has gone to
your head,' he said, 'or perhaps your defeat of Irus has
made you proud, for else you would not dare to speak so
to me.' And as Antinous had done, he picked up a footstool
and flung it at Odysseus. But Odysseus stepped aside, and
the stool struck a servant who was carrying a bowl of wine,
and with a clatter of metal all the wine was spilt upon the
floor. And instantly the suitors were making an outcry and
complaining, and there was an uproar in the hall.

Telemachus rose, and shouting to make himself heard
above the clamour, he said, 'Surely you have all of you
drunk too much of my father's good wine, that you disturb
my house with your rioting. Go now to your own homes
and sleep, leaving me in peace.'

They were all amazed at his words, that he should have
dared to speak so boldly to them, but they said to one
another, 'Perhaps it is best that we go, sleep will be welcome to us, and tomorrow we can feast again.' And when
they had each taken a last cupful of wine, they went from
the hall to their own homes, peaceably enough.

Now, it was the custom to keep certain weapons in the

hall for when they might be wanted; long spears and javelins propped beside the pillars, so that they were ready for hunting or javelin-throwing contests such as the suitors were wont to hold in the courtyard. There were, also, upon the wall, swords and shields hanging, in case they should be needed by someone going on a journey, that the traveller might protect himself from robbers.

Odysseus considered these weapons, how the suitors could snatch them up and arm themselves when he and Telemachus fell upon them; and though two well-armed men might prevail against a hundred who had, with which to defend themselves, only the swords they wore, those two would have but little chance against a hundred men with spears and javelins to throw, and shields to hold before their bodies.

So as soon as the last of the suitors had departed, and Odysseus was alone in the hall with his son, he said, 'These weapons must we put by in the armoury where lie the other arms, or the suitors will use them to our hurt. And if any should observe and ask questions of you as to why this thing has been done, say that you have laid them away because they needed polishing, having become grimy with the smoke from the fire; or that you feared that in the evenings, when they have drunk much wine, some of the suitors might fall to quarrelling, and it were best that no weapons should be by. Leave only for yourself and for me, two swords, two spears and a shield for each, and place them where you may reach them easily when they are needed. Come now, and let us hide the rest away.'

So Telemachus sent for Eurycleia and asked her for the key of the store-room which she kept, and together he and his father laid by the weapons in the armoury, alongside the others that were there. And many journeys did they make to and from the great hall through the door half-way down the side wall, along the passage to the high chamber where the treasure of Odysseus lay, their arms full of swords and shields or bunches of long spears, observed of none at their task.

When only the two swords and spears and shields that Odysseus and Telemachus would need for themselves remained in the hall, Odysseus said to his son, 'Go now and sleep while I wait here, for your mother has sent word that she would speak with me.'

So Telemachus bade his father good night and went alone to his own room; his mind so full, pondering the happenings of the day, and wondering what might befall on the morrow, that he feared he could not rest; but nevertheless, in spite of all, he soon fell into a sound sleep.

Then came the servants to clear away the cups and dishes and the tables which the suitors had used for their feast, and to make all tidy and orderly in the hall. Then, too, Penelope came down from her apartments with her maids, who set for her beside the fire her own chair of wood inlaid with a pattern worked in silver and ivory

One of the servants who was favoured by the wooers, seeing Odysseus still waiting in the hall, spoke discourteously to him, saying, 'Old stranger, is it not time that you were gone from the house? Surely you have had your fill of food and wine? There is no more for you, so begone, before you are driven forth.'

Angrily Odysseus answered, 'It is more seemly to be patient and kindly to those less fortunate than oneself.

Some day you too may meet with ill luck and find yourself a wretched outcast, with no kind mistress or young master to give you protection.'

Penelope, too, heard the unkind words, and she rebuked the servant, saying, 'Be silent now, and suffer the stranger to remain in peace. You are not so insolent with my suitors who come here unbidden, as you are with my son's invited guests. What an ill thing it is when the servants think to rule in the house. But beware, impertinent one, lest even yet your master should come home.' And Penelope called Odysseus over to her, and her maids set a chair for him, beside the fire, close to hers.

'Tell me, stranger, what is your name and where is your home?'

'Good queen,' replied Odysseus, 'my story is an unhappy one, ask me no more to relate it, for the remembrance of all that has befallen me lies heavily on my sad heart, and I would not speak of it. Ask me of anything else that you will, and I shall answer truly. But ask me not to tell you of my sufferings, for I could not speak of them without tears, and it is not seemly that a guest should weep and wail in another's house. I know that you will be understanding in this, good queen, for the fame of your virtues has travelled far, even beyond the shores of Ithaca.'

'No, stranger,' Penelope said sadly, 'that is not so, for all my virtues of beauty and of character died when my dear husband sailed to Troy. Since then I have been but the shadow of a woman, a poor pale creature groping through life, ever grieving and ever fearful, as a woman must be who has lost the husband she loved and has no lord to protect her.' She sighed. 'And now am I beset by suitors who would wed me and take me from my home. For three years have I kept them waiting for an answer, while I ever hoped Odysseus might return. I have tricked them and deceived them, trying to gain time, but at last the day has come when I can no longer delay my choice. My son is now a man and should rule in his own house, but so long as my wooers remain in his halls, defying his authority and eating his food, he never will be master in his home. And since here they have sworn to remain until I take from among their number a new lord, then must I now make my decision. But any husband that I take will be without a doubt far inferior to my dear Odysseus, and that is a hard fate for any woman to face.'

'Your husband was in truth an excellent man,' said Odysseus. 'I remember how once he came to my house on his way to Troy. I was in better fortune then and could offer him entertainment with a willing heart. Twelve days did he and his men remain in my home, and many were the hours in which Odysseus and I talked together. Truly, he was a goodly man.'

Penelope wept at his lying tale, for she thought he spoke the truth and she was sad to think that this stranger had seen and talked to Odysseus after he had gone from her, perhaps for ever. But though she believed the story, she had been deceived by other tales before, and so cautiously she tested him. 'Tell me, good stranger, that I may be sure you speak the truth, what my Odysseus looked like when he came to your house. What garments was he wearing?'

'Gracious queen, it is many years since I saw him, and it is not easy to remember such things. But I will tell you all that my memory can recall for me. He wore a soft, close-fitting tunic, woven of some shining thread, and over it a purple cloak, fastened upon the shoulder with a golden brooch fashioned in the likeness of a hound bringing down a deer. A curious brooch it was, and therefore can I see it now with my mind's eye.'

Thus did Odysseus describe the clothes that he had worn when he had left his home to sail to Troy; and Penelope remembered them and her tears flowed fast.

'Now, indeed, stranger, am I certain that you speak the truth and I will trust you in all things. For it was I who gave him the garments that you saw him wear. The cloak I had woven for him myself, and the brooch I chose out from my jewel-casket, for it was a favourite one of mine.' She paused a moment, then went on with a deep sigh, 'How sad it is to talk of one whom we shall never see again. Good stranger, you must pardon my distress.'

'Gracious queen, it is most fitting that a wife should grieve for a husband who is dead, but I would bid you cease your weeping, for Odysseus is alive. I swear to you that very soon he will be home again, and you and your son may rejoice at his return. Believe me, noble lady, for I speak the truth.'

Penelope shook her head. 'I wish that I might believe you, stranger,' she said sadly, 'but I am afraid that Odysseus never will come back, he has been gone too long, and I must now accept my fate and make my choice from among my suitors. But it grows late, let me not keep you longer from your rest with the recital of my sorrows.' And she called to her maidens to prepare him a bed in the vestibule, as befitted an honoured guest, and sent for old Eurycleia and bade her bring a basin of water to wash the stranger's feet; and the old woman came hurrying with a brazen bowl, a towel of white linen, and two ewers with water, both hot and cold.

And even as she came towards him Odysseus remembered the scar upon his leg where once he had been wounded by a boar, while out hunting when he was but a youth, and he knew that his old nurse would recognize it if she saw it; so he turned away towards the shadows, hoping that in the dim light her old eyes would not notice anything.

Eurycleia laid the basin at his feet, and looking at him closely, said, 'Never in all my life have I heard a voice so like my dear master's as yours. You are many years older than he would have been had he lived to return to his house, but if I closed my eyes to listen to you speak, I should think he had come back.'

Odysseus answered her quickly, 'Indeed, good woman, many others than you have marked the likeness and said the same to me.'

The old nurse knelt before him and poured water into the basin and took hold of his foot, and at once she saw the scar. With a cry she started back and the bowl tipped over and all the water was spilt upon the floor.

'You are my dear Lord Odysseus,' gasped Eurycleia, and she looked towards Penelope to tell her the glad news.

But swiftly Odysseus grasped her by the shoulder, 'Hush, nurse, would you see me slain by the suitors? Keep silent, I charge you. For I must first destroy those wicked men before I can enjoy my homecoming.'

'You may depend on me, dear lord,' replied the old woman. You must surely remember how of old I was ever to be trusted. I will keep silence and help you in any way an aged woman can.'

He smiled at her, and trembling, she rose and went to fetch more water, for every drop had been spilt. But Penelope had noticed nothing of all that had passed, for she had been staring into the fire, wondering how best to order her future.

When Odysseus came to her to bid her good night, she asked him, saying, 'One thing further would I beg of you, good stranger, that you might interpret for me a dream which I had the other night. Twenty grey geese have I in the courtyard, and often do I go myself to give them grain, for they come to me when I call them and they are a pretty sight to see when they eat together from the trough In my dream I saw the geese here, in this very hall, pecking up their corn, but a great eagle flew down from the hills and fell upon them and killed them, all the twenty, and they lay dead upon the floor. Then the eagle rose up into the sky and flew higher and higher, and the sun shone brightly upon his wings. But in my dream I wept, for my geese were slain. Yet even as I wept, the eagle came back again and alighted on the house-roof and spoke to me.

'"Weep not, Penelope," he said, "for I am your husband Odysseus, and the geese were your wooers. And when I come again to you, it shall be as a man, and as a man shall I slay the suitors, every one. For this is no dream, but reality."

'Upon that I awoke and it was dawn, and when I went to the courtyard, there were my geese, feeding on their grain, just as they had ever done. Tell me, stranger, if you can, what means this dream.'

'Surely, good queen, there can be no other meaning to it than the very one which seems most apparent, that Odysseus himself will soon be home and wreak great vengeance on your suitors.'

Penelope sighed. 'I wish I dared believe you, but truly dreams are curious things, often meaning just the contrary of what they appear to signify. But now no longer can I put off the day when I must decide my fate and leave this house which has been my home for twenty years, however loath I may be to go. Stranger, tell me if you think this well that I have thought to do. In the happy days when he lived in this his home, my husband, who was skilled in all manner of games and contests, had a favourite sport. He would set up here in the hall a row of axes crossed, and through the gaps made by the handles and the heads, he would shoot arrows, never missing; a truly clever feat. I have it in my mind to bring out my husband's bow and set up once more those axes, and bid the suitors shoot through them when they have strung the great bow. And the man who can accomplish this test of skill, him will I marry and to his home will I go, for of all the wooers he will be nearest to my husband. What think you of my plan, stranger?'

Odysseus smiled. 'It is a clever scheme that you have thought of, Queen Penelope, and I counsel you to tell your wooers of this contest soon, and to put them to the trial. But I am certain that Odysseus will be home before any among the suitors has even strung the bow, and most certainly before any one of them has shot an arrow through the axes, for it sounds a hard exploit indeed.'

Penelope rose. 'I thank you, stranger, for your kindly

words and the advice and comfort you have given me. Now do I bid you good night and pleasant rest.' She beckoned to her maids and turned and went from the hall, followed by all the women; and Odysseus was left alone.

He went to the bed which had been prepared for him in the vestibule, but he lay long awake, pondering the deeds of the morrow and planning the slaying of the suitors, before at last he fell asleep.

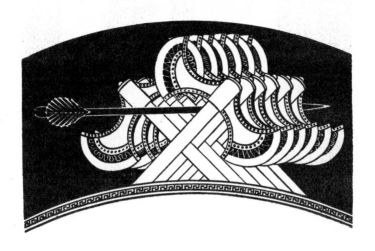

# XIX

## *The Great Bow*

THE next day was a holiday in honour of the god Apollo, patron of art and learning, and the servants in Odysseus' house were stirring early to make all things ready for an even more splendid day of feasting for the suitors than was usual.

Eurycleia bustled round the hall seeing that no one was idle, but that all were working hard in preparation for the banquet. Twelve women were set to grind the corn and barley into flour, that fresh loaves might be baked; while others polished the seats and tables in the great hall and washed the wine-bowls and the drinking-cups and the gold and silver platters; and others spread with clean draperies and fleecy rugs the chairs and stools, and strewed fresh rushes on the floor. Yet others were kept busy going to and from the well, drawing pails of water, that there might be as much as was needed when the suitors came. In the court-yard the men chopped wood for the fires; and everywhere there was work and activity.

Odysseus stood in the porch and watched all that was going on, thinking to himself, 'All this is being done for the wooers of my wife, that they may enjoy the feast-day at my cost. But with Athene's help, not much longer will they live to waste more of my substance.'

Soon Eumaeus came, having set out at dawn from the farm with three fat swine. Leaving his beasts in the court-yard he went straight to Odysseus and greeted him warmly, saying, 'Good morning to you, my friend. Tell me, how fared you at the hands of the suitors after I was gone last evening? Did their evil conduct mend?'

'They were as arrogant and as insolent as men could be,' replied Odysseus. 'Truly, they are wicked, and I only pray that the gods may bring them soon to a day of reckoning.'

As they were talking together, Melanthius the goatherd drove a flock of goats through the gate. He saw Odysseus and Eumaeus at once, and going to them said, 'So your friend is still with us, swineherd, and you are wasting your time listening to him babbling about his better days, when he had a house and servants of his own.' He laughed mock-ingly, and turned to Odysseus. 'You old liar, why do you not go to another house and trouble some other men, and leave the noble suitors in peace? Sooner or later I can see that I shall have to drive you away from here, and I warn you that when I take a hand in this matter, it will be long before you dare to come here again.' And with that he left them, going on into the house.

At this moment there arrived in the courtyard Philoetius, the chief of Odysseus' cowherds, who kept his cattle on the mainland where Odysseus owned some pasture-land and a farm. Philoetius had an ox and some fat goats for the suitors' feast, having brought them over to Ithaca on the ferry. He came straight to the swineherd who was an old friend of his, waving his staff in greeting. Seeing Odysseus, he smiled at him, and offering his hand, said, 'I have not seen you here before, welcome to our master's house, old stranger. I wish the good king were here himself to give you entertainment, for he was a man who would never turn away a poor wanderer. But in his absence it is his servants who must honour a guest, since the unrighteous men who despoil his house spare no word of welcome for one who has naught to offer them, and the young master and our good mistress, the queen, can have no heart, these days, for anything but grieving, may the gods protect them both.'

'Truly, may the immortal gods protect them,' echoed Eumaeus.

'When I look at you, stranger,' went on the cowherd, 'I feel a great fear that, even like you, our good king may be wandering through the world, begging his bread from unfriendly men. But even that, I suppose, would be better than that he should be dead, never to return. For while he lives there must always be hope in his heart that one day he will see Ithaca again. He was a good master to me, and he believed in my worth, for I was only a youth when he put me in charge of all his cattle on the mainland. He said that he knew that I would work for him so long as I had breath and that I could ever be trusted. And indeed, though he is far away and cannot see his words come true, I have never betrayed his trust, nor ever shall, but always will I serve him faithfully. Sometimes I long to leave this place and flee away, for I cannot bear to see the suitors of the queen wasting all my master's goods and eating the cattle that I have reared for him, increasing their number manyfold in twenty years. But for his sake, for good King Odysseus' sake, I will remain here, however hard my lot may be.'

Odysseus saw at once that here was a man who would fight for him if need be, and remembered with satisfaction the day when he had set him over his herds because he had foreseen his worth, though he had been but a lad. He said, 'Good herdsman, I can promise you that Odysseus will soon be home. He is not dead, and I tell you that before you leave the island to return to your farm, he will be here to take vengeance on the suitors.'

'If that should truly come to pass,' said Philoetius eagerly, 'then will King Odysseus see how I can fight for him. I ask no more than to strike a blow for him and for his family against these insolent thieves who have entered his home to rob it while he is far away.'

Meanwhile, the suitors were gathering at Odysseus' house, coming through the great gates in laughing, chattering groups, and crossing the courtyard to the hall where the midday meal was almost ready. Odysseus and Eumaeus and the cowherd went into the hall together, and Telemachus came forward at once and placed a chair for his father beside the big door, whispering to him, 'It is best that you sit again by the doorway, father, lest later any of them should try to escape.'

While Odysseus whispered back, 'That was well thought of, my son. It is the very place I would have chosen.'

Aloud, Telemachus said, 'You may sit there, stranger, and eat and drink your fill, and you may rely on me to protect you from any insults that may be offered to you in my own house by the men who choose to gather here.' And turning to the suitors as they were sitting down to their meal, he said, 'All you wooers of my mother, I bid you respect my guest and my house and keep from quarrelling and violence while you are in it.'

The suitors were surprised at the unaccustomed authority in Telemachus' voice and they looked at one another and shrugged their shoulders, murmuring. But of them all, only Antinous spoke out. With a sneer he addressed his companions loudly. 'I suppose we must bear with this insulting attitude of our good queen's son, or earn her displeasure.' In a lower voice he added, 'It is a pity that our plans went awry, or we should for ever have been spared the sound of that carping voice.'

Most of the suitors ignored Odysseus, where he sat beside the door, but a certain Ctesippus, a noble of great wealth, who came from the neighbouring island of Same, and was ever a man who loved to be considered quick to make a jest and to give to his companions a witty word to laugh at, now sought to amuse the other wooers at Odysseus' expense. 'My friends,' he called out, 'the ragged stranger has already been given a good meal, as is, of course, only right and seemly. But watch, for now I am going to give him an extra portion, such as is fit for the most honoured guest of all, one whose presence graces the house even of a king.' And with that he picked up a large bone from the dish before him, and flung it at Odysseus. But Odysseus moved his head quickly, and the bone struck the wall beside him.

Telemachus jumped up at once. 'If you had had the misfortune to aim better and hit your mark, Ctesippus, it would have gone ill with you, for I should have thrust my spear through your heart, and it would have been a burial and not a wedding that your parents would have celebrated for you. Listen, all you suitors of my mother,' he went on. 'I am not a child and I will not bear with this brawling and this misconduct in my house. I have yet found no way to drive you forth, so unwillingly must I bear with your presence and your feasting off my father's food and wine, but I will not stand by and see my guests insulted and provoked. If only when you have caused my death, will you be satisfied, then it is almost a better thing that you should murder me, than that I should have to see your cowardly attacks on an old man who has sought my hospitality.'

For a while they were silent, pondering his words, then one of them said, 'You have spoken well, Telemachus, and I assure you that there shall be no more mistreatment of the stranger or your slaves. But now, Telemachus, let me ask a favour of you in return. So long as you and your gracious mother could still hope that one day King Odysseus would come home, no one could blame the two of you for resenting our presence. But as he has not returned though ten years have passed since he set sail from Troy, there is surely now no hope for him, and your mother would do well to resign herself to accept the truth and choose another husband. Go, urge your mother to make up her mind and all your troubles will be over.'

'Never,' said Telemachus, 'never shall I seek to persuade my mother against her will. That have I sworn to you often before, and I swear it again now. My mother's choice shall be free and she shall make it when she wishes.'

But the only answer that the suitors gave him was to laugh as though he had been jesting. Then one after another they mocked him, saying, 'Poor Telemachus, how hard he tries to play the man and rule his household,' and, 'What a dutiful son, to have such a care for his mother's happiness.' And again, 'But think, my friends, of what this house will be like when good Penelope is married and gone. It will be filled with all the old beggars from the land of Greece, sitting at the door and eating good food, while Telemachus presides over their entertainment, a willing, careful host.' And they laughed until they held their sides, and drank ever more good wine.

But suddenly Theoclymenus the seer stood up in their midst. His face was pale and he cried out in a strange voice, 'You fools that laugh at your own destruction. I can see blood upon the floor, and the bodies of the slain; and the spirits of dead men thronging in the porch. Take heed, you suitors of the queen, before it is too late.'

But they met his words with laughter and jeering, and Eurymachus said, 'Truly, the stranger that has come from over the sea must be out of his mind. Make haste, some of you, and hurry him forth to find a welcome elsewhere, since he finds this fine house so dismal.'

'I need no one of you to help me on my way,' said Theoclymenus. 'I have two feet which will carry me from here speedily enough, for I see a terrible doom about to come on you, and not one of you shall escape it.' And flinging his cloak about him, fearfully he hastened from the house, and running down the roadway to the town, he returned to the home of Peiraeus.

And in their mirth the suitors mocked Telemachus further, 'Truly, poor youth, how unfortunate you are in your choice of guests. First is it that greedy old man who does naught but eat and drink, and now it is a mad prophet, seeing visions. Poor Telemachus, you have our sympathy. But never despair, for in time, when you are older, you will have learnt how better to pick your friends.'

It was then that it came to the mind of Penelope to try her wooers with Odysseus' bow, even as she had told her husband, thinking him to be a stranger, the night before. So calling to her Eurycleia, who kept the key of the store-room, with her and two other maids she came down from her apartments and passed through the hall to the door in the wide wall to fetch Odysseus' bow from the armoury.

Penelope herself reached up to the peg where hung the great bow, and lifted it down. It was a massive weapon fashioned of wood upon which strips of horn had been laid along the inside, while on the outer edge it was protected by a casing of strong ox-hide. It was covered with a leather sheath to protect it from the dust and damp, and as soon as Penelope had taken it out from the sheath, and seen once more the bow that her husband had so often handled, she sat down upon a stool, holding it in her arms and weeping piteously.

But after a time she rose and dried her tears, and speaking to her women, bade one of them fetch her the quiver full of arrows which lay upon a shelf, and told the other to carry the twelve double-headed axes that Odysseus had used for his sport. Then, herself bearing the bow and the quiver, she returned along the passage-way to the hall, and passing through the side door, she stood in the midst of the suitors by a pillar, and spoke to them.

'Hear me, my suitors,' she said, and they all kept silent to listen to her. 'For long enough have you feasted here with no one to prevent you, giving as the reason for your conduct your desire to win me for a wife. Therefore I have at last decided that the time has come for me to save for my son what still remains to him of his inheritance after you have wasted his possessions for more than three long years. Here in my hands I hold the bow of my dear husband Odysseus, with which he was wont to make great sport. A favourite feat of his was to shoot arrows through the space between twelve axes set up in two rows, a task not easy to accomplish. My suitors, I challenge you to prove yourselves as good men as my dear lord Odysseus, by stringing his bow and shooting through the axes, even as he so often did. Yet it is no easy feat, so there will be many who will fail to achieve it. But the man who proves himself the ablest at it, and therefore most like my lord, him will I marry and to his home will I go, quitting the house of Odysseus for ever, though my heart will ache to leave it, and for it shall I ever pine, seeing it and weeping for it even in my dreams. But come, my suitors, take up the challenge, for here before you stands the prize.' And turning to Eumaeus she bade him carry the bow and arrows to the wooers. But in her heart she hoped that all of them might fail in the trial, so that she might stay a little longer in Odysseus' house.

Like his mistress, the good swineherd wept when he

touched the bow, remembering his master and the good old days; and Antinous marked the tears and cried out with scorn, 'Look how the slave wails for his master. Cease your tears, you fool. Would you distress your mistress more? Come, give us the bow and let us try our skill with it. But I think it will not be an easy feat even to string it, such a mighty weapon it is. I remember once, in this very hall, when I was but a child, seeing Odysseus shoot through the axes, and I marvelled at his achievement.' So spoke Antinous, not belittling the difficulty of the test the suitors had been set, for he wished thus to excuse his failure should he be unable to string the bow, and to magnify his prowess should he be successful, as he secretly hoped he might.

Telemachus, his heart beating very fast, for he saw that the moment was approaching when he and his father would stand alone against their enemies, rose, and called out with a gaiety he did not feel, 'Come, lords of our land and the neighbouring isles, you are offered the hand of the fairest lady in all Ithaca. Do not hold back from the test. Let me set up the axes for you, so you may all take your turn in shooting, and may it be the best man among her suitors who wins my dear mother.'

So he set up the axes and fixed them firmly in two rows, an axe leaning alternately to the left and to the right, so that their handles crossed and the sides that were innermost of their two-headed blades were overlapping. It was through the small space between the upper part of the hafts, where they crossed, and the lower edge of the blades, that the arrow had to pass.

When the axes were arranged to his satisfaction, Telemachus said, 'Eumaeus, give me the bow, I have a mind to try myself, to see whether I am as good a man as my honoured father was. My friends the suitors will not grudge me the delay.'

He took the bow, and with all his strength tried to bend it so that it might be strung. But the tough wood and horn proved too much for him; and after the fourth attempt he laid the bow down, sighing, 'It seems that I am still too young to try such a feat, or perhaps it is that I am a poor weakling who will never equal my father in skill and strength. But it is as the gods will it, so come, my friends, take your turns and show what you can do, for you are older and better men than I.'

Antinous at once took charge, suggesting that they should, one after another, try to string the bow and shoot a single arrow through the axes, starting with the man who sat to the left of the company, and working round to the right. To this the other suitors agreed, and instantly the man who was on the extreme left strode from his place and came forward to try his luck. But though he put forth all his might, he could not string the bow.

'My friends,' he said to his companions, 'never will this bow yield to my hands, so let the next man take his turn. But I foresee that it will bring great grief to many of us here, before the day is over. Many of us there shall be who will have to woo another lady, for Penelope will never be ours.' He put down the bow and returned to his place.

Antinous was angered by his words, for he feared that the bow might be even harder to string than he had expected, and he was afraid of his own failure. 'You speak nonsense,' he said, 'and all because you have too little strength to string the bow yourself. Why should it bring

great grief to us? You were ever a weakling, and there was
no hope of your success. But only watch the rest of us. I
warrant there will be many of us to do the deed.' He called
to the goatherd, 'Come, Melanthius, fetch a brazier and
some wax, that we may grease the bow to make it more
pliable, and thus shall we succeed in stringing it.'

So they greased the bow with the melted wax, and one
by one they tried to string it, but one by one they failed.
And while they were still trying to bend the bow, Eumaeus
and the cowherd went from the house and walked in the
yard, talking together of their lost master, and debating on
the wooers' chances to win the queen.

Odysseus, who had seen them go, slipped out after them,
and calling them to him, said in a low voice, 'My friends,
if Odysseus were to come home now, quite suddenly, and
the suitors were to take up arms against him in his own
house, for whom would you fight, for him or for them?
Or would you save yourselves from both, and run away?'

'Not I,' said Philoetius. 'I would find a weapon, any one
would do, and stand beside my master until I was struck
down.'

'And I too,' said Eumaeus. 'I would fight for my good
master's rights, and if it pleased the immortal gods that I
should die, why then I should have met a good death,
fighting for our king.'

Well pleased by their words, Odysseus made himself
known to them, saying, 'Good herdsmen of mine, I am
Odysseus, returned to his home. Soon shall I give you a
chance to prove your words, and I think you will not fail
me, for you are loyal men both. If you should doubt me,
know me by this scar upon my leg—you both have seen

it before—where I was gored by a boar's sharp tusk one day when I was hunting. You are the elder, Eumaeus, you will remember the day.'

Great was the joy with which the two faithful servants welcomed their master home, and high was their hope of seeing things in his house ordered well once more.

'We must not tarry longer here in the courtyard,' warned Odysseus, 'for our absence may be noticed and the suitors grow suspicious. Let us return to the hall, but not together. I shall go in first, and after me, singly, you must come, and this is what you must do. Eumaeus, I am going to ask the suitors to let me try my skill with the bow. If they should refuse me, you must yet bring it to me; and then, once it is safely in my hands, go quickly and tell old Eurycleia to lock and keep fast the door at the end of the hall which leads to the women's quarters, for I want none of them to enter the hall until our task is over. And you, Philoetius, are to fasten and bolt the great gates of the courtyard, so that no one can go out or come in.'

With that Odysseus returned to the hall and sat down on his stool by the door. He was soon followed by Eumaeus; and after he had closed the gates, Philoetius too came in.

It was by now the turn of Eurymachus to string the bow, all the other suitors save Antinous and himself having failed, and only the two of them remained to try. But like all those before him, Eurymachus failed too. 'What puny men this proves us,' he said bitterly, 'that we cannot do a thing which Odysseus often did. We shall be forever dishonoured in that we fell short.' And he handed the bow to Antinous.

Now, Antinous was afraid that where his companions had not succeeded he, too, would fail, so he said, 'Today

is a festival in honour of immortal Apollo, and no fit day
for contests of this sort. Let us put off this trial till tomorrow, when we can all try our strength once again.
Leave the axes where they are to await us in the morning,
and let us be merry now, and drink. Come, Medon, send
the cupbearers about their tasks.'

Odysseus then spoke up. 'My noble lords,' he said, 'now
that you have deferred this contest till tomorrow, I have a
favour I would ask of you. I was once, when I was younger,
no mean bowman, and I would like, for the sake of the
time when I was youthful and active, to see whether my
misfortunes have taken all my strength and weakened these
arms that once were strong. Good Lord Antinous, and you,
noble Eurymachus, grant me your permission to try to
string the bow.'

They were angered at his request, for although it seemed
to them most unlikely that an old man should succeed
where a hundred young men had failed, they wanted to
take no risks of being proved less skilled than a wandering
beggarman; and Antinous called out furiously, 'Are you
still here to molest us? Because we let you share our food
and listen to our talking, do you think we shall allow you
to take part in all our deeds? You have drunk too much
wine and grown impertinent. Be silent, or else leave the
house.'

But indignantly Penelope spoke up. 'Shame on you,
Antinous, to be so discourteous to a stranger. He is the
guest of myself and my son, therefore it is for us and not
for you, to deny him what he wishes, if we would. But I
say that he should take his turn with the rest of you, if he
wants to. And should he string the bow, surely you have

no fear that he would set himself up as a suitor and com-
pete with you for my hand? Is it that of which you are
afraid, Antinous and the rest of you?'

It was Eurymachus who answered her. 'Gracious queen,'
he said, 'it is not that we fear that this old stranger might
try to win you for his wife, it is that, should he string the
bow after we have failed, all Ithaca will say of us that we
are feeble and weakly and unworthy of our noble names,
and so should we be disgraced.'

Penelope's eyes flashed angrily. 'No one who lives on
another man's goods, shamelessly preying on his substance,
can be disgraced any further than he is by his own actions,
Eurymachus. Let the stranger do as he wishes. I promise
that if he should succeed and string my husband's great
bow, I will give him fine new clothes to travel in, and
a sharp sword and a javelin to protect him on his wanderings.'

It was then that Telemachus saw that soon the battle
would begin, and he thought, 'I must send my mother
away to safety, for there are sights no woman should look
upon.' So he said to her, 'Good mother, the bow belonged
to my father, and since that is so, there is no one more
fitted than I to decide who shall touch it and who shall not.
It is my right to give it to whom I please, that he may try
to string it or that he may take it for a gift, just as I allow.
So, dearest mother, leave this matter to my authority and
go to your own rooms and attend to your spinning and
weaving, for the handling of bows is the care of men, not
women.'

Wondering at his words, Penelope rose, and beckoning
her maids and Eurycleia to follow her, she left the hall. As

the old woman went, Telemachus whispered to her, 'Give me the key of the store-room, nurse, I may have need of it tonight,' and she took it from her girdle and gave it to him without a word.

As soon as the women had gone, Eumaeus took the bow and the quiver and made to carry them to Odysseus, and the suitors all cried out to forbid him, and for a moment he faltered. But Telemachus called to him in encouragement, and he went forward boldly and placed the great bow in his master's hands. Then quickly he went to the door of the women's quarters through which Penelope had just passed, and calling back the old nurse, bade her lock it and keep it locked until they should summon her to open it. Eurycleia understood at once what was about to happen, and with fear in her heart for her beloved master, she closed the door with trembling hands and made it fast. Eumaeus himself then locked the side-door leading to the store-room, and at the same time Philoetius went from the hall, and as an extra precaution, fastened the doors of the house which opened into the courtyard. Then both he and the swineherd stood near their master on the threshold of the great hall.

Meanwhile, Odysseus was looking carefully at his bow, turning it this way and that to see if in ten years it had decayed at all. But he was satisfied with what he saw. The suitors watched him and jeered, 'He thinks himself an accomplished bowman. See how he looks at it. Perchance he is a dealer in bows, or perchance he hopes to be one on the knowledge he acquires tonight.'

Calmly, without rising from the stool where he was sitting, Odysseus bent the bow and strung it, and with his

thumb he sounded the string, so that it hummed clear throughout the hall, and the suitors were amazed. He took one arrow from the quiver and fitted it to the bow, and still sitting, he took aim, and the arrow sped through the axes and lodged at the far end of the hall in the wood of the door that led to the women's quarters and the rest of the house.

Odysseus smiled, and called out to his son, 'Telemachus, the stranger to whom you showed favour and kindness has not shamed you. It seems the years have not destroyed my strength and skill. But now is the time for more feasting. Come, let the banquet begin.' And he signed to Telemachus who took up his sword and his spear and went to his father's side, before the door of the great hall.

# XX

## *The Battle with the Suitors*

ODYSSEUS rose, and taking up the quiver full of arrows, stood on the wide threshold of the door, and looked down the hall upon the suitors. 'The old man is indeed skilled and can shoot straight,' they said to one another. 'But come, let us drink and forget that our marksmanship has been put to shame by a tattered old beggar.'

'Well spoken, my fellow wooers,' said Antinous. 'Good wine was ever the best friend of man.' And he stretched forth his hand to take his cup.

Odysseus fitted a second arrow to his bow. 'I have scored one victory,' he called, 'and now is the time to aim for another mark. No one has yet hit it, but by the help of the immortal gods, my arrow shall fly home.' And with that he took careful aim at Antinous.

The young man had at that moment raised his golden cup, holding it by its two handles, and his head was tilted back to drink from it. The arrow passed right through his outstretched neck. The cup fell from his grasp and clattered to the floor, spilling the red wine; and clutching at his throat, Antinous fell dead beside it, his blood mingling with the wine upon the ground.

Instantly every suitor leapt to his feet and a great cry was raised. They all turned upon Odysseus in furious anger. 'You miserable beggarman, you have killed the peerless Antinous, the first of all the noblemen of Ithaca. You shall never leave the island alive, for with your life shall you pay for your carelessness and folly.' Thus they spoke, believing that it was by a mischance that Antinous had been killed.

But Odysseus cried out to them, 'You shameless, evil men, who have dared to woo my wife, and devour my food and use my house as though it were your own, you never thought that one day I should return and take my revenge. But, late though it may be, I have come home, and this shall be your last day upon this earth.'

'It is King Odysseus,' they said fearfully and with amazement among themselves, and some of them looked around the room for the arms that they were used to seeing there, the swords and shields upon the walls, and the spears and javelins in the stands beside the pillars. But nowhere was there a single weapon with which they might defend themselves, save only the swords which some of them wore, and the twelve axes through which Odysseus had shot his first arrow. And others looked round wildly, not for arms, but for escape; but when those who were nearest tried the two doors leading from the hall, one to the women's quarters and the other to the store-room, they found that they were locked. And Odysseus with his bow and quiver full of arrows stood before the big door leading to the vestibule.

Of all the suitors only Eurymachus found the courage to speak out. 'If you are indeed Odysseus,' he said, 'then you have reason enough to be angry at the things that have been done in your house while you were absent. But the man who was alone to blame for all these things lies dead already. Antinous, whom you have killed, it was who urged us to follow him and lay waste your property, for though the rest of us were here to woo the fair Penelope, he cared not for her. His only thought was to take your place, and be king here, in Ithaca. That is the truth, good Odysseus, the fault was his and he lies dead, so spare, I beg you, us others who remain, and we will in full restore your goods, making repayment of what we have deprived you.'

Odysseus looked at him with scorn. 'You wretched coward,' he said, 'even at the moment of your death you still speak glibly and utter lies. But it shall not save your life. No, nor the lives of any of you here, for with no other recompense shall I be satisfied, but only with your blood.'

When they heard this they knew that there was no hope for them, and trembled; but Eurymachus rallied them together. 'My friends,' he called, 'we are many and he is but one, and though he has a quiver full of arrows and his bow, we have our swords. Let us draw them and rush upon him before he has time to shoot us all.' And with that he took his sword in his hand, and giving a shout, ran at Odysseus down the hall. But long before he reached him, Odysseus had sent an arrow flying, and it struck him through the heart, and his shout faded on his lips as he sank to the floor.

A third suitor fell to a spear thrown by Telemachus, who was now left only with his sword. He whispered to Odysseus, 'I have the key of the store-room. I took it from Eurycleia. I will go and fetch us more arms, for I have no spear and the two herdsmen have no weapons, and soon your arrows will all be shot.'

'Go quickly, my son,' said Odysseus, 'while I still have arrows left, for I can hold them off so long as the arrows last.'

Taking the key of the side door from Eumaeus, Telemachus slipped down the wall of the hall, unnoticed by the suitors who were wildly trying to rush upon Odysseus, or to defend themselves from his rain of arrows by holding tables and chairs before them as if they had been shields. He reached the door and unlocked it, and leaving the hall, ran down the passage-way to the store-room. There he gathered together eight strong spears, four shields, and four helmets each crested with the flowing hair cut from a horse's tail. Burdened with these, he did not lock either door behind him, and stealing back into the hall he gave a spear and a shield and a helmet apiece to Eumaeus and Philoetius, and armed himself as well, putting up his long curls and twisting them around his head under the brazen helmet.

So long as there were arrows left in the quiver, Odysseus sent them flying down the hall, and one suitor fell to every shaft. But at last the arrows were all spent, so laying aside the bow, he put on the helmet Telemachus had brought for him, and took up two spears.

Melanthius the goatherd whispered to the suitors, 'Lords, I believe the weapons of Odysseus are kept in the store-room. We have tried the door to the passage which leads to it and found it locked. But if I could break down the door, perhaps I might find a way into the treasure chamber and bring you arms.' With that he went unobserved to the door in the side-wall, and to his surprise, found it was unlocked, for Telemachus had forgotten to fasten it. He hurried through and discovered that the door of the great store-room was also open, and went inside. Bringing out with him twelve shields and spears, he returned to the wooers, who seized upon them eagerly.

When Odysseus saw that some of the suitors had shields, he wondered at it, for he was sure that he and Telemachus had left none but two in the hall when they had cleared it of arms the evening before. And then a spear came hurtling by and lodged in the door beside him. 'Someone has been to the armoury,' he said, 'and brought out weapons for them. But surely the door is locked?'

Instantly Telemachus remembered. 'The fault is mine, father,' he said. 'I forgot to lock either of the doors.' He turned to Eumaeus. 'Go, good Eumaeus, take the keys and fasten well both doors, before they can fetch more arms.'

As he hurried away, the swineherd saw Melanthius slip through the door again, and beckoned to Philoetius to come with him; and they went together after the goatherd. They found him in the armoury, choosing out more weapons, and fell upon him and bound him with a rope they took from round a wooden chest. Then after carefully locking both the doors behind them, they returned to Odysseus' side.

Together the four of them faced the many wooers who sought to make a last effort, crying out, 'Let us all aim together at Odysseus, for with him dead, the other three will have no heart to fight on, and we may escape.'

Six among them threw each a spear, but their throws were wild, and Odysseus received not a single scratch. Then he and Telemachus and the two herdsmen flung their spears among the suitors, and to each spear there fell a man. The rest of the suitors fled to the farthest end of the hall, while Odysseus and the three others rushed forward with shouts of triumph and caught up their spears again. Once more they threw, and once more their aim was good and four men died. And among them, to the great joy of Philoetius, was Ctesippus, the man who had cast a bone at his master, killed by the cowherd's own spear.

And now panic came upon the suitors and they dropped their weapons and fled, rushing distractedly at the walls and two locked doors in their attempts to escape destruction.

'Come,' called Odysseus, 'let us fall upon them and cut them down,' and followed by Telemachus and the herdsmen, he ran along the hall, and with his sword struck down man after man, pausing for no appeals for mercy.

Holding his lyre, the minstrel Phemius stood against the wall, wondering if he had a chance to escape by the great door which was now left unguarded, and fly from thence into the courtyard. But he saw Odysseus bearing down upon him, his sword in his hand, and flinging aside his lyre, he ran forward and fell at his feet.

'Grant me mercy, King Odysseus,' he pleaded, 'for my voice is very sweet. No one in all Ithaca can sing as I. You will one day regret it if you kill me now, for all men love good singing, and a poet's life should be sacred for the sake of his art.'

'You sang for the suitors,' said Odysseus. 'I heard you myself.'

'And what if I sang for them? A singer cannot be silent so long as there are men to hear him sing. And if those men be evil, it does the song no harm, nor yet the singer, that he pleases them. And to a poet, more than the worth of those who hear them, is the value of his songs.'

The minstrel's long hair grasped in his left hand and his sword at his throat, Odysseus hesitated, looking down upon the young man's face and wondering whether to spare his life or not. But Telemachus saw him and called out to him, 'Do not kill Phemius, father, for his singing gives great joy. And spare Medon, too, for he is innocent of ill doing, and only served the suitors when they demanded it. And more, it was he who warned mother that the suitors were plotting against my life.' He looked around. 'But I fear he may be killed already, for I see him not. It grieves me that he should have died, for he often played with me and told me tales when I was a child.'

But Medon had hidden himself beneath a rug behind a great chair, where he lay crouched; and when he heard Telemachus' words, he came forth from his hiding-place and ran to him, imploring him, 'Do not let your father kill me, for I have ever wished well to you and to the queen.'

Odysseus smiled at him. 'Then go quickly to the courtyard and wait there until I have finished all I have to do in here.' His left hand unclenched and released Phemius' hair. 'And the minstrel may go with you,' he said.

Phemius delayed only long enough to snatch up his lyre

before following Medon out of the hall to the great house-door, where with trembling hands they unfastened the latch and fled into the courtyard.

One by one Odysseus hunted down the suitors, until none remained alive; then he spoke to Telemachus, saying, 'Go, my son, and call Eurycleia.'

Telemachus knocked on the door at the far end of the hall and shouted to the old nurse until she came and unlocked it to him, then he led her to Odysseus. When she saw her master standing amid his slain enemies, she raised a cry of victory, but Odysseus silenced her. 'It is not seemly to rejoice over the dead,' he said. 'Restrain your triumph and let your joy be silent. But I would have you tell me which of all my servants have been faithful to me, and which of them have served too well the suitors.'

'There are but twelve of all your slaves, and Melanthius the goatherd,' she replied, 'who have grown out of hand and disobedient, preferring to follow the demands of the suitors than to obey the queen.'

'Send the twelve to me,' ordered Odysseus.

When the disloyal servants came, he set them to carry the slain suitors from the hall and lay them outside the house, and to sweep and clean the hall and put the furniture to rights. Then, their last task done, he sent them into the courtyard, and there the two herdsmen killed them. And with them died Melanthius the goatherd.

Then Odysseus called to Eurycleia to bring brimstone and fire to purify the hall, and to bid Penelope and her women come down to him. But she protested, 'You will surely not meet your wife dressed still in those rags? Let me bring you clothes more fitting to your rank, dear child.'

Odysseus laughed at her. 'Hurry, good nurse, and do as I tell you, there will be time enough for fine garments later.'

So she went off to fetch sulphur and a brazier, murmuring and complaining to herself about the wilfulness of men, and how they never would grow up.

When the serving-women heard that Odysseus was home, they flocked into the hall to greet him, with tears of joy. And of all the older women, there was not one he did not recognize, calling them all by their names.

But Eurycleia went to Penelope's room and found her asleep upon her couch. 'Wake up, dear mistress, wake up,' she called eagerly. 'Our Odysseus has come home and all the suitors are dead.'

Penelope sat up and rubbed her eyes. 'The troubles in this house have crazed you. You have lost your wits, nurse, or else this is a dream.'

'It is no dream,' said the old woman. 'Odysseus is downstairs and he has slain the suitors. The stranger whom they mocked at, he is our king. To be sure, he looks many years older than one might have expected, but perils and dangers and misfortunes age a man like nothing else. I knew my master's voice as soon as I heard it, and then I saw the scar upon his leg where he was wounded by a boar. Get up, mistress, and come and greet your husband.'

Penelope jumped from her bed happily and kissed Eurycleia. Then she grew solemn again. 'Oh nurse,' she said, 'your tidings are too good, and I dare not believe them. Surely it is one of the immortal gods in the shape of the old stranger who has done this thing, and not my dear husband. For it is certain by this time that he must have perished far away.'

'How wary you are, my child,' laughed the old nurse. 'Come with me and I will show you Odysseus.'

So, her mind filled with a great turmoil of joy and hope and fear, Penelope went down to the hall. There she saw Odysseus sitting by one of the pillars near the fire. She hesitated in the doorway, wondering whether she should go to him and call him husband and embrace him, or whether she should question him further to find if it were really he. She watched him for a few moments undecided, and then she thought that surely her Odysseus could not have grown so old in only twenty years, and that the stranger must be someone else. She went slowly to a chair on the other side of the fire, and stared at him, trying to recognize him; believing at one moment that she knew his features, and then at the next thinking herself to be mistaken because he was too old.

Telemachus stood close by, surprised at his mother's strange behaviour. 'Dearest mother,' he said, 'you have hoped and prayed for twenty years that father would come home. Now he is here, you sit like a statue and have no word to say to him. Would any other wife act thus?'

'Indeed, Telemachus,' she replied, 'I do not know what to think or say or do. The suddenness of everything that has happened here today has robbed me of all action. But if the stranger really is Odysseus, I shall know him when I have questioned him.'

Many another man would have been dismayed by this cold reception, but not Odysseus. He was delighted at his wife's prudence and caution, feeling it to be almost worthy of himself. 'Go, Telemachus, and leave your mother and myself to talk together. I shall surely prove to her that I

really have come home. But first let me please old Eurycleia and bathe, and dress myself as befits a king. That perhaps will help our good queen to know me.'

He went with Telemachus, leaving Penelope sitting
beside the fire, still wondering and hoping. Flinging off
his rags he took a bath in a huge cauldron of warm water,
and as he stepped forth from the water, Athene gave him
back again his own appearance. In a new tunic of white
linen with a golden belt, and a purple cloak embroidered
with a border of green, he returned once more to the hall.
And Penelope looked up and saw him come, his own self,
as he would have been after only twenty years from home.
No longer the old stranger with his thin white hair and his
wrinkled cheeks, but Odysseus, with his long dark hair and
his bright eyes and the smile that she loved so well. But her
joy was so great that she still dared not believe in it, and
stayed quite quietly, watching him.

He sat beside her and laughed a little. 'How strange you
are,' he said gently. 'After all these years I come home, and
you are silent. I had thought that all women talked too
much, but it seems that I am wrong.' Teasing her, he
turned to Eurycleia, 'Come, nurse, I am tired, find me a
room and make me up a bed. My wife has nothing to say
to me, so I may as well go to sleep.'

Quickly Penelope looked round and spoke to the nurse.
'That is well thought of,' she said. 'If he is really my husband, he must sleep in the bed which he himself made.
Move it out of my bedroom, Eurycleia, and make it up
comfortably for him with warm rugs and blankets.'

'Indeed,' said Odysseus sharply, 'what has been happen-
ing to my bed? For I built that bed myself, taking as the

headpost an olive-tree that grew beside the house, lopping off the branches and trimming the trunk, and fastening the frame with its webbing of leather straight to the post. Then around my bed I built the room, as a bedchamber for myself and my bride. No one could move my bed without cutting down the headpost that was once a tree.'

When she heard him speak thus, Penelope knew that he was indeed Odysseus, for he had not failed in the test that she had set him, but had known the secret of the fashioning of his bed. No longer she feared to trust her joy, and jumping up she ran to him and kissed him. 'Do not be angry, dear Odysseus, that I doubted you at first. Too many lies have been told to me, and too much ill doing have I seen in all these years to dare to rely on any man. But now at last I know that it is truly you.'

Happy and joyful in their reunion, they retired to rest, and long into the night Odysseus talked and told Penelope of all his adventures, and many were the questions that she asked him of all that he had seen. And when she had heard the story of the Cicones and the Lotus-eaters and Aeolus; and shuddered at the cruelty of Polyphemus and the Laestrygonians; when she had listened eagerly to the tale of Circe and the Sirens and Scylla and Charybdis; and shed a tear at the dread fate that had come upon his men when they had slain the cattle of the sun; when she had heard of Calypso and the raft and the kind Phaeacians; and after she had questioned him on each of them, they both fell asleep, and slept until the dawn.

# XXI

## *Laertes*

IN the morning Odysseus set out with Telemachus for his father's farm, that old Laertes might learn the good news. They walked across the hills to the wide, low farmhouse, set about with fields and orchards of apples, figs, and pears. Olive-trees too, were there in abundance, and a fine vineyard, and gardens with vegetables and herbs.

When they arrived, Telemachus went into the house, and Odysseus found Laertes working among the vines. He wore an old tunic with patches, leathern leggings and gloves and a tattered goatskin cap; and he looked more like an old slave than the father of a king.

Odysseus, who ever loved to speak unrecognized with people who were familiar to him and see what they would say, greeted his father as a stranger, saying, 'Who are you, old man, that your gardens are so well cared for, while you yourself are so ill clad? Are you a slave whose master neglects him? Truly, your industry deserves better treatment than this. But somehow I think that you are not a slave, for there is yet a nobility about you, in spite of your clothes, and you look to me like a great man who has fallen on evil times.'

Old Laertes looked up with a sigh. 'Stranger,' he said, 'for you must be a stranger or you would not need to ask all this, you have come to Ithaca at an unhappy time. A fine welcome would my son Odysseus have given you, and royally would he have entertained you, as was his way, had he been home. But, alas, I fear he must be dead. Yet tell me, stranger, who you are and whence you come.'

'I come from Alybas,' replied Odysseus, wondering what his father would say in reply, 'and there I once met Odysseus, your son.'

At his words the old man wept, and quickly Odysseus sought to spare him further grief. 'Dear father,' he said, 'I am your son. I have come home at last, and all the suitors are slain in my house.'

But the old man shook his head. 'Too many griefs have come upon me,' he said sadly. 'Such great joy could not be true. If you are indeed my son, then prove it to me.'

Odysseus thought a moment, then he said, 'See this scar upon my leg, where once a boar gored me. You will remember it. But if that is not enough, then will I tell you something else. One day when I was a boy I walked with you in the orchard here and asked you to give to me all the trees I liked best, and you said they should be mine.

Thirteen pear-trees were they, ten apples, and forty figs.
And as well you gave to me fifty rows of vines. Do you
remember that?'

At this old Laertes flung his arms around Odysseus' neck
and embraced his son whom he had thought never to see
again. And for a while their joy was too great for them to
think of other things. Then Laertes said, 'But tell me, my
son, did you say that you had slain the suitors?'

'Every one of them, father.'

'Then, my son, all the noblemen of Ithaca and the lords
from the neighbouring isles will be against us. What will
you do to save yourself?'

'I am their king,' said Odysseus, 'and the suitors were
evil men. In the end all must be well for us. But let us go
to the house now, and eat and discuss our plans, how we
shall act should the townspeople rise in anger.'

At the farm a feast had been prepared on the orders of
Telemachus, to celebrate the return of Odysseus, who was
joyously welcomed by the servants as they came in from
the fields. And together, with great gladness, they sat down
to enjoy the good food spread out before them. And
Laertes put away his rags and wore once again clothes
worthy of his rank. 'I wish I had been with you yesterday,
my son,' he said wistfully, when they told him of the battle
in the hall. 'Then would you have all seen that I am not so
old that I cannot strike a blow for the right.'

In the assembly place the men of Ithaca gathered to discuss the return of their king and the slaying of the suitors
in Odysseus' house. The first to speak was Eupeithes, the
father of Antinous, he who had once joined the Taphian

pirates and been condemned by his countrymen for his deeds. 'This is indeed a grievous crime,' he said, 'and it must be avenged. Odysseus is our enemy, and he must die.'

But Medon the herald stood up and said, 'I was in the house of Odysseus myself when the wooers were slain, and I swear that there must have been a god with him, else could not four men alone have slain more than a hundred.'

Old Lord Halitherses now spoke. 'Good men of Ithaca,' he said, 'all this that has happened was the suitors' fault. Had they been less wild in their ways and listened more to reason, then would they be alive today. It is not Odysseus who is to blame for their deaths, but they themselves. This do I truly believe.'

One half of the townsmen agreed with his words, but the others sided with Eupeithes. They ran to their homes and gathered up their weapons, and with him at their head, set off for Laertes' farm, where they had heard Odysseus to be.

Odysseus and his family saw them in the distance, coming over the hills, and armed themselves to meet them, making ready to fight if need should be.

But from far-off Mount Olympus, great Zeus, father of gods and men, looked down on little Ithaca and called to Athene, saying, 'Now should you be satisfied, my daughter, now Odysseus is safely home and his enemies are slain. But it is not our will that there should be more bloodshed in Ithaca, so go yourself and see that all is settled peaceably, and Odysseus restored to his power as a king.'

Willingly Athene left Olympus to obey him, and going to where Odysseus, with his father and his son and their faithful servants, waited, armed and ready, for Eupeithes and his friends, she filled with strength and courage old Laertes, and he grasped his spear firmly and poised it; and when the attackers came within a throwing distance, he flung the spear and killed Eupeithes. And there were very few to regret the father of Antinous, for he had ever been disliked in Ithaca.

Then Zeus sent a flash of lightning, and Athene called in a mighty voice that all fighting was to cease; and instantly, in terror, Eupeithes' followers fled.

And no one again questioned Odysseus' right to avenge himself upon the wicked suitors, and from that time he was once more paid every honour as king of Ithaca. And all his days he dwelt in peace with his dear wife, Penelope, happy and prosperous and well beloved, in his own home, as Teiresias had prophesied he should.